DATE DUE

OCT 20 80			
DEC 22 1994			

The Book of European Light Opera

SELECTED BOOKS BY DAVID EWEN

Complete Book of the American Musical Theater
The World of Jerome Kern
Richard Rodgers
A Journey to Greatness: The Life and Music of George Gershwin
The Story of America's Musical Theater
The Encyclopedia of the Opera
The Encyclopedia of Concert Music
A Panorama of American Popular Music
Milton Cross' Encyclopedia of Great Composers and Their Music
    (with Milton Cross)
The Complete Book of 20th Century Music
Music for the Millions
Dictators of the Baton
Music Comes to America
The New Book of Modern Composers
The World of Great Composers

BIOGRAPHIES FOR YOUNG PEOPLE

The Story of George Gershwin
The Story of Irving Berlin
The Story of Jerome Kern
Haydn: A Good Life
Tales from the Vienna Woods: The Story of Johann Strauss
The Story of Arturo Toscanini
Leonard Bernstein

THE BOOK OF

EUROPEAN
LIGHT OPERA

BY DAVID EWEN

A GUIDE TO 167 EUROPEAN COMIC OPERAS,

LIGHT OPERAS, OPERETTAS, OPÉRA-COMIQUES,

OPÉRA-BOUFFES, AND OPERA BUFFAS FROM *THE*

BEGGAR'S OPERA (1728) AND *LA SERVA PADRONA*

(1733) TO IVOR NOVELLO'S *KING'S RHAPSODY*

(1949)—BY 81 COMPOSERS—WITH PLOT,

PRODUCTION HISTORY, MUSICAL HIGHLIGHTS,

CRITICAL EVALUATIONS, AND OTHER

RELEVANT INFORMATION.

GREENWOOD PRESS, PUBLISHERS
WESTPORT, CONNECTICUT

Library of Congress Cataloging in Publication Data

Ewen, David, 1907-
    The book of European light opera ...

    "A guide to 167 European comic operas, light operas,
operettas, opéra-comiques, opéra-bouffes, and opera.
buffas from The beggars's opera (1728) and La serva
padrona (1733) to Ivor Novello's King's rhapsody (1949),
by 81 composers, with plot, production history, musical
highlights, critical evaluations, and other relevant
information."
    Reprint of the 1962 ed. published by Holt, Rinehart
and Winston, New York.
    Discography: p.
    Includes index.
    1. Operas--Stories, plots, etc.   I. Title.
II. Title: European light opera.
[MT95.E9 1977]   782.1'3   77-1795
ISBN 0-8371-9520-9

Originally published in 1962 by Holt, Rinehart and Winston,
New York

Reprinted with the permission of Holt, Rinehart and Winston
CBS Educational Publishing, A Division of CBS Inc.

Reprinted in 1977 by Greenwood Press, Inc.

Library of Congress catalog card number 77-1795

ISBN 0-8371-9520-9

Printed in the United States of America

PREFACE

The world of the European light opera is the world of the Viennese operetta, the French opéra-comique and opéra-bouffe, the English comic and romantic opera, and the Italian opera buffa. It is a world of laughter and enchantment, of romance and glamour that has delighted the hearts of young and old of all continents. Who does not know and love *The Merry Widow, Die Fledermaus, The Chocolate Soldier, Orphée aux enfers, Countess Maritza, The White Horse Inn, The Mikado*—to single out only a handful of riches from a veritable cornucopia? Who does not react with pulsing heartbeat to the lilting strains of "The Merry Widow Waltz," the "Florodora Sextet," "I'll See You Again," or "Thine Is My Heart Alone," and many other similarly unforgettable musical gems?

It is this wonderful world of stage make-believe in all its infinite variety that is revealed in this volume.

Nobody has yet set the exact boundaries for "light opera" which separate it, on the one hand, from the world of musical comedies, revues, and musical plays and, on the other, from grand opera. For the purposes of this volume, light opera is considered to embrace not only operettas, comic operas, opéra-comiques, opéra-bouffes, and opera buffas, but also many romantic and serious operas so ingratiating in manner and so readily assimilable by audiences at first hearing that, while they cannot be strictly classed as "light," nevertheless they will deserve to be included within this category. I allude to works such as *Martha* or *Hansel and Gretel* or *Gianni Schicchi* or *The Bohemian Girl*. Still other stage works are somewhat beyond the limited artistic scope and dimension of the average operetta or opéra-bouffe. Nevertheless, I felt strongly that of these masterworks many have so much charm and wit and popular appeal that their inclusion in this volume would bring to it a welcome comprehensiveness. In the last group I consider such works as Ravel's *L'Heure espagnole* and Stravinsky's *Renard* and *Mavra,* for example.

However, certain limits, however flexible, simply had to be set. Therefore, I have included those creations of the lighter European musical theater that have durability, whose principal songs have given or give promise of survival, which are occasionally revived, or have become familiar through various recordings. Stage works of a more ephemeral quality—however successful the productions may have been in their time—have not been included. Thus the book omits all of those popular European productions that lie beyond "light opera": musical comedies, revues, musical plays, and other of the more popular forms of musical-stage entertainment. Omitted, too, are those masterworks of the comic-operatic theater that are too demanding in their aesthetic and musical appeal to be considered "light." Much as I may be partial to such works, I deemed them completely out of bounds for this book. I refer to Mozart's *Don Giovanni,* Wagner's *Die Meistersinger,* Verdi's *Falstaff,* and Richard Strauss's *Der Rosenkavalier.*

Although, basically, light opera consists of those popular stage works produced in Europe's equivalent of Broadway, many of the works discussed in this volume were born in the opera house. The European opera house has always been a gathering place for entire families seeking stage entertainment. Consequently, many outstanding light operas were born there. I refer to the incomparable opera buffas of Pergolesi, Rossini, Donizetti, Galuppi, and their eminent contemporaries and successors. By any definition, however arbitrary, the opera buffa—even if at best it rises above the plateau of entertainment to the peaks of great opera—is light opera.

Since this is a reference book which (it is hoped) readers will read in search of basic information about European light operas, I felt impelled to discuss many works which may be little-known to Americans, material which is hard to come by but which, once found, is likely to arouse the curiosity and interest of well-informed music and theater lovers. Some of the works have had pioneer importance; others are the delightful creations of such world-famous serious composers such as Mozart, Gluck, Berlioz, Gounod, among others; still others are the lesser and little-known, but nonetheless rewarding, creations of such light-opera masters as Lehár, Rossini, Donizetti, or Gilbert and Sullivan.

This volume presents, alphabetically by title, what I consider to be the cream of the crop of Europe's light operas. For each work discussed, there will be found a summary of plot, a commentary on musical highlights, its production history, some analytical comment, and such other relevant information that seems interesting or illuminating. Appendix One lists the works chronologically, from *The Beggar's Opera* in 1728 and *La Serva padrona* in 1733 to Novello's *The King's Rhapsody* in 1949. Appendix Two lists the foremost achievements of the European light-opera stage by some eighty composers—alphabetically from Paul Abraham the composer of *Victoria und ihr Husar* to Karl Michael Ziehrer creator of *Die Landstreicher*. Appendix Three consists of "Selected Recordings," listed alphabetically by title.

A word or two of explanation is in order regarding what at first glance might appear to the reader to be an inconsistent use of titles throughout the book. Some appear in their original language, others in an English translation. It has been done because I felt that the book would be more functional for an English-speaking audience if the names most familiar to it were used, whether foreign or English. Titles like *The Chocolate Soldier* and *The Merry Widow* are more familiar to us than *Der tapfere Soldat* or *Die lustige Witwe*. By the same token, I am quite sure that *La Belle Hélène* is a title used more often by us than *Beautiful Helen;* *La gazza ladra* than *The Thieving Magpie; Das Dreimaederlhaus* than *The House of Three Girls*. There should, however, be little confusion. The listing at the head of each light opera contains both the foreign and the English titles, with cross-references to guide the reader to the title under which each work is discussed. Lesser-known titles of adaptation revisions are listed in the index.

–D.E.

Little Neck, New York

FOREWORD

The first English comic opera and the first Italian opera buffa appeared within five years of each other. Both represented a reaction against the clichés and ritual of formal serious Italian opera.

In England, the reaction was against the operas of George Frideric Handel, then so popular in London; and the vehicle of the reaction was the ballad opera, *The Beggar's Opera*, in 1728, text by John Gay, music assembled by Pepusch. If Handel liked to build his operas around the formidably austere and imposing characters of history and mythology, Gay ridiculed this practice by penetrating the lowest strata of English society—petty thieves, harlots, corrupt little officials. If Handel's music was the last word in classic majesty, Pepusch went to the opposite extreme by adapting to Gay's text some of the most popular tunes of the day. The sensational success of *The Beggar's Opera* threw Handel—and the kind of opera of which he was a spokesman—into the shade. But this is of only incidental importance. What concerns us much more vitally is the fact that with *The Beggar's Opera*, the ballad opera came into vogue and the English comic opera was born. As a lively commentary on the social and political mores of the times, with a text filled with all kinds of humorous and satirical overtones, with realistic characters of the everyday (if somewhat sordid) world, and with music that was simple, direct, and unpretentious in style and structure and of immense mass appeal, *The Beggar's Opera* became the foundation stone upon which all later English comic opera would rest, and whose apex, of course, was the masterly work of Gilbert and Sullivan.

Pergolesi's *La Serva padrona*, in 1733, with which opera buffa came into existence, also rebelled against the use of the stuffy historical and mythological characters and texts of Italian operas, as well as the pretentiousness of Italian composers, scenic designers, and stage directors. Opera buffa differed from its more sedate brother, the opera seria, in several important respects. It had a comic, and not a tragic, plot; its characters were simple, everyday people who became involved in homey, farcical situations. Love intrigues, the despair of cuckolds, the contrivances of deceiving wives, scheming servants, mistaken identities, and absurd disguises were all the warp and woof of almost every opera buffa plot. That plot was invariably sent merrily spinning by a deus ex machina in the form of some wily conniver, usually portrayed by a basso buffo. Musically, the opera buffa sidestepped the elaborately ornamented arias of serious Italian opera written to show off the vocal gifts of principal singers, and the big ensemble numbers calling for a large choral body, by offering simple, melodious tunes of folk-song ingenuousness; merry tunes, often with swift, staccato passages; patter songs. Where serious opera often presented dialogue in accompanied recitative (recitativo accompagnato)—a comparatively developed kind of declamation with an orchestral accompaniment that is at times quite elaborate—opera buffa had recourse to a "dry" recitative (recitativo secco)—dialogue accompanied by music with little or no melodic interest but which simply emphasizes the normal accentuation of the words by a few fundamental chords on the harpsichord or piano.

Most of the traits identifying opera buffa for almost two centuries can be found in Pergolesi's pioneer work, which still affords delight to present-day audiences. Pergolesi evolved the form of the opera buffa out of the Intermezzo. This was a brief comic scene set to music, a diversion which became so popular in Italy in the sixteenth and seventeenth centuries that a special theater was opened in Naples in 1709 for such presentations. Very often, too, producers of serious opera in Naples would introduce a note of light entertainment into the evening's proceedings by interpolating an Intermezzo between two acts of an opera seria. With these Intermezzos, Pergolesi served his apprenticeship as a composer of comic operas; with *La Serva padrona*, he achieved full maturity and a place of permanent significance in operatic history.

The immense popularity of Pergolesi's opera buffa in and out of Italy (detailed elsewhere in this volume) established this form of stage entertainment as a favored medium for composers everywhere. In Italy, a new school of musicians arose to emulate Pergolesi in writing comic operas. The most significant of these composers were Domenico Cimarosa with *Il Matrimonio segreto;* Baldassare Galuppi, with *Il Filosofo di campagna;* Giovanni Paisiello, with *The Barber of Seville* (more than thirty years before Rossini wrote his celebrated opera buffa on a similar text); Niccolò Piccinni with *La buona figliuola*. These were the steps leading to the summit: Gioacchino Rossini, composer of many opera buffas—of which *The Barber of Seville* is still the yardstick by which all such works are measured—and Gaetano Donizetti, the creator of *Don Pasquale* and *L'Elisir d'amore*. The form of the opera buffa was even carried into the twentieth century: by Giacomo Puccini with *Gianni Schicchi;* Ermanno Wolf-Ferrari with *The Secret of Suzanne;* Igor Stravinsky with *Mavra;* and Gian Carlo Menotti, the Italian-born American, with his very first opera and first triumph, *Amelia Goes to the Ball*.

The impact of *La Serva padrona* was felt outside of Italy, too, and with far-reaching consequences. In 1752, a traveling Italian opera company performed Pergolesi's little masterpiece in Paris, with the result that a schism was created between French musicians who considered the work representative of a true operatic art and those still faithful to the more serious and formal Italian opera or to the sedate and classical French operas of Jean-Philippe Rameau. Jean Jacques Rousseau, the philosopher, who stood among those favoring *La Serva padrona*, wrote a work of his own (music as well as text) in a similarly light, jocular vein—*Le Devin du village*—in unashamed and undisguised imitation. Other Frenchmen, like Pierre Alexandre Monsigny and André Grétry, also felt impelled to write comic operas in the style of *La Serva padrona*.

But by 1752, a new form of light musical theater was already slowly evolving in France. It was into this mold that the successors of Monsigny and Grétry were to pour their creative gifts. The form was the opéra-comique. Despite its name, it is not essentially "comic opera"—although a work may occasionally boast an amusing text—but opera which may have a serious or even somber libretto. It differs from the more serious type of French opera mainly in the fact that it has spoken dialogue instead of recitatives; also in that the music is generally of a lighter, more buoyant, and more tuneful character and thus easily assimilable by audiences at first hearing.

If *The Beggar's Opera* and *La Serva padrona* were created as opposition to formal serious opera and its set methods, opéra-comique came into being as a rival for the existing Académie de Musique, which had a monopoly in Paris for the performances of operas. As a subterfuge, a new light form of opera was evolved—musical plays with spoken dialogue—which could not properly be classed as operas and thus were not in the domain governed by the Académie de Musique. This new form of entertainment was first given yearly at the two large fairs of Paris, then formally introduced at the Foire St. Germain in 1715; it was on the latter occasion that the term "opéra-comique" was used for the first time. Originally, opéra-comique did utilize comic and satirical texts—some were even parodies of the staid operas given by the Académie. But, in time, the opéra-comique form became flexible enough to embrace even highly serious subjects. Opéra-comique achieved final crystallization through the efforts of a triumvirate of composers who helped make it a French cultural institution—François Boieldieu, Adolph Adam, and Daniel François Ésprit Auber. They, in turn, were succeeded by such outstanding personalities of the opéra-comique as Louis Joseph Ferdinand Hérold, Charles Lecocq, and Robert Planquette.

Much closer to the spirit and style of the Italian opera buffa is the opéra-bouffe, a light, trivial, and often highly satirical kind of French musical production that was a logical outgrowth of the opéra-comique. The term "opéra-bouffe" was derived from the theaters, known as "bouffes," where these sprightly entertainments were given. This genre found its first master in Hervé, composer of *Mam'zelle Nitouche,* and achieved its greatest popularity, and its highest peak of artistic fulfillment, with Jacques Offenbach.

In the German-speaking world, the Italian opera buffa was a particularly favored form of stage entertainment. Indeed, it was for Vienna that Cimarosa wrote his *Il Matrimonio segreto,* and somewhat later, it was also in Vienna that Rossini and his comic operas proved all the rage. Several of the German and Austrian masters created charming little works in the recognizable opera buffa style, among them were Gluck, Haydn, Mozart, and Dittersdorf.

German comic opera, as opposed to opera buffa, developed out of the Singspiel. The latter, the creation of Johann Adam Hiller in the mid-eighteenth-century, was a popular form of stage entertainment using songs and dialogue. It differed from the French comic theater (which actually had influenced Hiller) in that the songs were often in the style of popular German tunes of folk songs. The Singspiel continued to be popular in Germany and Austria for many years. The boy Mozart wrote several delightful Singspiels; the adult Mozart carried the form to such an advanced stage of artistic development with *The Abduction from the Seraglio* and *The Magic Flute,* that these works are Singspiels no longer but monumental German comic operas.

German comic opera flourished in the nineteenth century in the hands of composers like Otto Nicolai, whose masterwork was *The Merry Wives of Windsor;* Albert Lortzing, with whom some of the stylistic attitudes of German romantic opera were first carried over into the more popular musical theater; and, most of all, Franz von Suppé.

It is with Suppé that we finally make the step from German comic opera into German operetta, although it is more usual to describe Suppé's works like *Boccaccio* and *Die schoene Galathea* as comic operas rather than operettas. Strongly affected by Offenbach, and having made a conscious effort to transform the opéra-bouffe into a Germanic form of stage entertainment, Suppé managed to create scores in which the lilting, caressing warmth of lyricism and over-all Gemuetlichkeit are essentially Germanic rather than French.

It did not take long for the operetta to find its crowning genius. It found him in Johann Strauss II, the waltz king of Vienna, whose greatest operettas are *Die Fledermaus* and *The Gypsy Baron.* It is with Strauss that operetta as we came to know it thereafter achieves its recognizable physiognomy and personal attributes. The operetta became a make-believe world filled with glamour, romance, and sentiment, usually with a storybook setting and characters. The basic musical element of the operetta is the waltz—a big waltz as the axis on which the entire plot pivots. Strauss began the golden age of German and Austrian operettas, an age that soon produced Franz Lehár (*The Merry Widow* and *The Count of Luxembourg*); Oscar Straus (*The Chocolate Soldier* and *Ein Walzertraum*); Emmerich Kálmán (*Countess Maritza*); Leo Fall (*The Dollar Princess*); Ralph Benatzky (*The White Horse Inn*); and many others.

The operetta, the comic opera, the opera buffa, the opéra-comique, the opéra-bouffe—this is the voice of a world now dead. A new age, which started unfolding with the end of World War I, has created new stage forms in Europe, just as it has in the United States. But it is the inescapable charm and grace of the Old World, for which present-day audiences will probably never lose their nostalgia, with which the present volume is concerned. The last dying echoes of the old-fashioned European musical theater have sounded in Noël Coward's *Bitter Sweet* and *Conversation Piece,* Fritz Kreisler's *Sissy,* Robert Stolz's *Zwei Herzen in Dreivierteltakt,* and Ivor Novello's *King's Rhapsody* and *Perchance to Dream.* Nobody today writes operettas, or any of the other favored light forms that brought such delight to so many for so long a time. For us now are only the memories of enchanted evenings in the European theater. It is these memories that this book tries to fix in permanent form.

CONTENTS

The Book of European Light Opera

(The) Abduction from the Seraglio [*Die Entfuehrung aus dem Serail*] by Wolfgang Amadeus Mozart.

> Comic opera in three acts with libretto by Gottlieb Stephanie, based on a play by Christoph Friedrich Bretzner. First performance: Burgtheater, Vienna, July 16, 1782. First American performances: Brooklyn, New York, February 16, 1860 (in Italian, under the title *Belmonte e Constanze*); German Opera House, New York, October 10, 1862 (in German).

This work has the dual distinction of being the first important opera in the German language and the first German comic opera still being performed. Actually, *The Abduction from the Seraglio* is a Singspiel—the German variety of musical comedy in which a comic, and often trite, text in the vernacular is combined with popular tunes. Mozart wrote his first Singspiel when he was eleven (see *Bastien and Bastienne*). But before he wrote *The Abduction from the Seraglio*, the Singspiel was just popular entertainment for the masses, with no lasting artistic value whatsoever. It was entirely due to Mozart's remarkable musical invention that the Singspiel first became a vehicle for a significant comic art.

Having left his native Salzburg for good, Mozart settled in Vienna in 1781. Soon after his arrival, the Emperor commissioned him to write an opera for the Burgtheater. That opera was *The Abduction from the Seraglio*. But before it reached performance, court cabals and intrigues joined against Mozart and his opera. Antonio Salieri, one of the most powerful musicians in Vienna, recognized a dangerous rival in Mozart, and used the power of his prestige to prevent the production of the work. Salieri found important allies. Delays, embarrassments, and procrastinations followed, until Emperor Joseph II himself interceded and ordered that Mozart's opera be given. Despite the efforts of organized opposition in the theater to discredit the work, *The Abduction from the Seraglio* was an outstanding success. The applause was so insistent that many of the numbers had to be repeated. "The populace is quite crazy about this opera," Mozart wrote. "It does me good to hear such applause. . . . The people will hear nothing else, and the theater is constantly filled to the doors." Between its première and February 4, 1788, *The Abduction from the Seraglio* was performed thirty-four times.

Both the setting and many of the characters are Turkish. In the seventeenth and eighteenth centuries (after the siege by the Turks in 1687), Vienna was seized by a fascination for all things Turkish. One could buy Turkish candies in the Viennese sweetshops; Turkish coffee was widely drunk. Street merchants dressed as Turks and peddled exotic wares. At masked balls, people masqueraded in Turkish attire. Turkish musical instruments were introduced to Viennese military music. Composers in Vienna often wrote music in a supposedly Turkish style. (Notable examples include Beethoven's "Turkish March" from *The Ruins of Athens* and the *"Marcia alla turca"* movement from Mozart's Piano Sonata in A-flat major.) Operas based on Turkish subjects were extremely popular. At first, Turks appeared only as unpleasant characters, but later, they assumed benign or even noble roles.

There was good reason, then, why Mozart should have been delighted to write music for a Turkish story with a Turkish setting—a text previously used for another opera by a different composer—and there was equally valid reason why the Viennese public should have gone wild over Mozart's opera.

The Turkish element first becomes pronounced in the lively little overture through the use of percussion instruments, in the frequent alternations between loud and soft passages, and in the sudden key changes— all elements which the Viennese public identified with Turkish music. The main melody—a saucy little tune heard in the strings without preliminaries—has, however, nothing Turkish about it; it is in Mozart's own identifiably gay and ebullient style.

In sixteenth-century Turkey, Constanza and Blonda are captives of

Selim, the Pasha, having been kidnapped by pirates and sold to the Turkish ruler. Constanza's beloved, Belmonte, a Spanish nobleman, has come to Turkey to rescue her. He is ecstatic at the thought of seeing her again (*"Hier soll' ich dich denn sehen"*). Belmonte makes a futile attempt to enlist the co-operation of Osmin, the fat Turkish overseer of the women, who expresses his cynicism about females in *"Wer ein Liebchen hat gefunden."* When the Pasha comes upon the scene in the company of his captives, Belmonte goes into hiding, jubilant that he is about to catch a glimpse of his beloved Constanza (*"Konstanze! dich wiederzusehen"*). From his hiding place, he hears Constanza tell the enraged Pasha that she can never belong to him, since she is in love with another man (*"Ach, ich liebte, war so gluecklich"*).

Later on, within the palace garden, Blonda is trying to elude Osmin's amorous advances, while Constanza is lamenting her tragic fate (*"Welchen Kummer herrscht in meiner Seele"*). She would rather face torture than submit to the Pasha (*"Matern aller Arten"*). When Blonda learns that Belmonte has devised a play to effect their escape—by the simple expedient of getting the guards drunk—she is overjoyed (*"Welche Wonne, welche Lust"*). Subsequently, Constanza and Belmonte are finally able to exchange tender words of love (*"Wenn der Freude Thraenen fliessen"*). Upon his arrival to effect the escape, Belmonte serenades Constanza (*"Ich baue ganz auf deine Staerke"*). Then the two flee, but all are caught and brought to judgment before the Pasha. At first, the ruler severely reprimands Constanza for trying to get away. But his good nature soon comes to the surface. He not only forgives the women but also allows them their freedom. Everyone now raises a hymn of praise to the Pasha for his magnanimity (*"Nie werd' ich deine Huld verkennen"*).

Despite the trite plot, stock characters, and manufactured situations, the text inspired a remarkable score from Mozart. Karl Maria von Weber once went so far as to maintain that although Mozart might have written greater operas after *The Abduction from the Seraglio*, he never again captured the spirit of youth and effervescence found in this inimitable comic opera. Aria after aria testifies to Mozart's wonderful lyricism. The comedy is no less pronounced and fresh—for instance, the drinking song of the second act or Osmin's amusing ditties.

Again and again, Mozart introduces into his writing elements of harmony, melody, and instrumentation suggesting Turkish music: passages in the minor mode; melodies with Oriental intervals; instruments like the triangle and cymbals, which Vienna associated with the Turks. "This is not to mean," says Paul Nettl, "that Mozart deliberately composed oriental-sounding phrases, but during the composition of the opera he lived in such a kind of oriental state of imagination that the fairy-tale coloring of the East impregnated his score."

One of the unusual features in *The Abduction from the Seraglio* is that Selim, the Pasha, is not assigned a singing role, but only a speaking part. In their book, *The Opera*, Herbert Weinstock and Wallace Brockway explain that this does not arise from "a well-considered intention to produce a specific effect; it is more likely that either he [Mozart] did not have peculiarly Pasha-like music on tap or he could not find a singer for music he thought suitable for a Turkish Pasha."

Abu Hassan by Karl Maria von Weber.

> Comic opera in one act with text by Franz Karl Hiemer, based on a tale in *The Arabian Nights*. First performance: Munich, Germany, June 4, 1811. First American performances: Park Theater, New York, November 5, 1827 (in English); New York, September 8, 1877 (in German).

Although Weber became famous as the founder of the German romantic school in opera with *Der Freischuetz*, he had dabbled with comic opera earlier in his career. *Abu Hassan* is one of the best of these lighter inventions. Its score originally embraced an overture and eight vocal numbers, but in 1812 Weber added a duet, and in 1823 an air. Its première performance in Munich was not fated to proceed smoothly. Lucy Poate Stebbins and Richard Poate Stebbins have written in *Enchanted Wanderer*: "The overture had been applauded; the duet, 'Lovely Woman, Glorious Wine,' was in progress when there was heard the cry of 'Fire!' The curtain fell and the theater emptied. The alarm was false, but it was some time before the performance could be resumed. Then all went well. Five numbers were encored, and Weber could call his little opera a success."

The slight story is built around the character of Abu Hassan, a beggar rascal. He, and his wife Fatima, are heavily in debt and are hard pressed to pay off their many creditors. In despair, Abu Hassan contrives a scheme whereby he can put his hands on some money. He dispatches Fatima to the Sultana, her employer, to bring the tidings that he, Abu Hassan, is dead; thus she can receive the payment due all widows. Then Abu Hassan hurries to the Sultan, his own employer, with the news that Fatima is dead, in order that he might become the recipient of similar compensation. The Sultan and Sultana, however, become so aggrieved over the sudden death of their respective employees that they decide to visit Abu Hassan's house to attend the funeral. There, the Sultan is deeply moved at the sight of the "corpses," to a point where he offers a prize of a thousand gold pieces to anyone able to tell him which of the two had been the first to die. Abu Hassan and Fatima now suddenly come to life, and beg the Sultan to forgive them. The Sultan proves magnanimous. He not only forgives the culprits but he even endows them with the thousand gold pieces so that they can completely liquidate all their debts.

The gay overture is still sometimes heard at concerts, and has been recorded. A vivacious subject is first given quietly, but soon allowed to develop into a sonorous episode. A second theme, as sprightly as the first, is followed by a stately passage. These ideas are then freely worked out, after which the initial gay tune is recalled, followed by a more sedate subject. The overture concludes with a brilliant coda.

Weber must have found more than passing amusement in setting to music the opening chorus of the creditors—*"Geld, Geld, Geld!"*—for at that time he himself had had more than a casual acquaintance with pressing debts. In any event, this gay little episode forthwith establishes a mood of mockery that prevails throughout the little opera. Two arias by Fatima have particular melodic interest: *"Wird Philomena trauern"* and *"Hier liest welch' martervolles Los."* Also of particular appeal are Abu Hassan's lengthy song, *"Ich gebe Gastereien,"* and the duet of Abu Hassan and Fatima, *"Thraenen, Thraenen, sollst du nicht vergiessen."*

In his discussion of *Abu Hassan*, Philip Spitta has written: "The fun in German comic opera has always been somewhat boisterous; for more refined comedy we must generally go to the French, but *Abu Hassan* is almost the only German work which produces a hearty laugh and at the same time charms by its grace and refinement and by the distinction of its musical expression. . . . Various little instances of want of finish appear in the music, but defects of this kind may well be overlooked for the sake of the invention, so spontaneous and spirited, and the downright hearty fun of the whole, mingled as it is with rare and touching tenderness."

Abu Hassan was revived in New York on March 23, 1934, when it was presented in a new English version by A. Houghton.

Alt Wien [*Old Vienna*] by Joseph Lanner.

> Operetta in three acts with text by G. Kadelburg and J. Wilhelm, and music adapted by Emil Stern from Lanner's compositions. First performance: Vienna, December 23, 1912.

Joseph Lanner was Vienna's first waltz king, the distinguished predecessor of the two Johann Strausses, father and son. Unlike the younger Johann Strauss, Lanner never wrote an operetta. But out of the wealth of his lovable melodies, waltzes, marches, and other kinds of dance tunes, from such light-music classics as *Die Schoenbrunner, Romantiker,* and *Abendsterne* waltzes, Emil Stern developed a melodious score for a text set in mid-nineteenth-century Vienna. Highlights of that score are a sentimental song by Lini, *"Schwalberl, mein alles, mein Schatz,"* and a lilting march tune, *"Aufg'schaut ihr Leute, lasst uns vorbei."*

Lini—barmaid and waitress in a Vienna suburb—is in love with the soldier Franz. But she must leave the home of the wine-tavern keeper, whom she has so long regarded as her father, to go to live with Count Leopold, who has put forth a claim that she is his daughter. Within the luxurious setting of the Count's palace, Lini moves unhappily, for she longs for old friends and places. Some of her former comrades—and with them her foster-father and her sweetheart—invade Count Leopold's palace, hoping to help celebrate Lini's birthday. They are denied access. Indeed, the Count even sends Lini into seclusion at his Bohemian castle. En route, Lini manages to escape, and drops off at a little inn where her foster-father is now being employed as bandleader. Although she appears disguised as a gingerbread vendor, Lini betrays her true identity to her foster-father and her sweetheart by singing to them her favorite song, *"Schwalberl, mein alles."* Just as the Count is about to spirit her away again, new information arrives at the inn revealing she is not the Count's daughter after all. Thus, at long last, she is able to return to her former carefree life with her foster-father and resume her romance with Franz.

A new version of *Alt Wien,* adapted by Alexander Steinbrecher, was successfully introduced in Vienna in 1944.

(L') Amore Medico [*Doctor Cupid*] by Ermanno Wolf-Ferrari.

> Opera buffa in two acts with libretto by Enrico Golisciani, based on Molière's comedy *L'Amour médecin.* First performance: Dresden Royal

Opera, Dresden, Germany, December 4, 1913 (in German, under the title *Der Liebhaber als Arzt*). First American performance: Metropolitan Opera, New York, March 25, 1914 (in Italian).

Wolf-Ferrari carried the age-old traditions of Italian opera buffa into the twentieth century with several extremely popular and valuable works. *L'Amore medico*—although a lesser achievement than his masterpiece in this genre, *The Secret of Suzanne*, has much to recommend it in the way of effervescence, vivacity, and frivolity. It employs such basic devices of opera buffa as a mock marriage; characters parading about in disguises; a deus ex machina who resolves all the problems and difficulties through his wiles. But *L'Amore medico* also departs from the formal opera buffa style. There is no spoken dialogue; the work is set to music throughout and has no detachable arias or ensemble numbers, as such.

In Paris, during the reign of Louis XIV, Lucinda is in love with the young cavalier Clitandro. The path of true love is obstructed by Arnolfo, Lucinda's father, who wants to keep his daughter near him permanently. When Lucinda falls sick with unrequited love, her father summons a physician. Lucinda's maid knows full well that her mistress is suffering from a broken heart. She, therefore, arranges for Clitandro to come to the house disguised as a doctor. After his examination, the "physician" prescribes a mock marriage, with himself as the bridegroom. But the mock marriage turns out to be the real thing, and thus Lucinda and Clitandro are finally married.

Wolf-Ferrari's gift for sparkling tunes—and a personal style that skillfully combines a classic, almost Mozartean, manner with modern orchestral and harmonic devices—is most effective. Of particular interest is Lucinda's opening number, *"Voi ci diffuse nell'aria,"* Arnolfo's buffa air, *"Io mi compro un bastimento,"* and a highly melodious orchestral intermezzo.

When *L'Amore medico* was given its American première at the Metropolitan Opera it was heard in Italian for the first time, the language in which the opera is given most often today. (The world première in Munich had been in a German translation.) Lucrezia Bori appeared as Lucinda, Italo Cristalli as Clitandro, and Toscanini was the conductor. At that time, W. H. Henderson described the work as "an opera buffa of real beauty, of airy and playful humor, of ingenious workmanship." Nevertheless, it did not remain in the Metropolitan Opera repertory, and has not been given there since 1914.

(The) Apothecary [*Lo Speziale* or *Der Apotheker*] by Joseph Haydn.

> Comic opera in three acts with text by Carlo Goldoni. First performance: Esterház, Austria, autumn of 1768. First American performance (probable): Neighborhood Playhouse, New York, March 16, 1926 (in English).

Haydn wrote this comic opera while employed as Prince Esterházy's Kapellmeister at Esterház. Sempronio is an apothecary eager to marry his ward, Grilletta. But she is in love with young Mengono. The latter enters the employ of the apothecary as a clerk in order to be near the girl he loves. Meanwhile, Grilletta is also being sought by the frivolous Volpino (a male part assumed by a mezzo-soprano). When the latter enters the shop, he forthwith recognizes Mengono as his rival. During Sempronio's absences, Grilletta and Mengono manage to use their time to good advantage by flirting and kissing. One day, Sempronio catches them and instantly decides that he must waste no more time in marrying Grilletta himself. To effect the marriage, Sempronio summons a notary. In turn, both Mengono and Volpino arrive disguised as notaries. Each draws up a marriage contract; each skillfully inserts his own name in place of Sempronio's. When Sempronio discovers the trick, he angrily sends away both "notaries." Now it is Volpino's turn to appear in a new disguise, this time as a Turk; his ruse is that he represents the Pasha and has come to purchase Sempronio's stock of medicines at a fancy price. Indeed, before long the Pasha himself makes an appearance—and the Pasha is no one else but Mengono. When Volpino gains access to Sempronio's medicines, he smashes the bottles, creates bedlam, and threatens the old apothecary's life with a dagger. Mengono saves the old man's life, but only after Sempronio promises he will do nothing further to prevent the marriage of Grilletta and Mengono.

Four arias boast Haydn's characteristic light touch of wit and graceful style of lyricism: that of Mengono, *"Sitzt einem hier im Kopf das Weh'"*; that of Grilletta, *"Wie Schleier se'e ichs nieder schweben"*; and those of Volpino, *"Wo Liebes Goetten lachten"* and *"Es kam ein Pascha aus Tuerkenland."*

In his biography of Haydn, Karl Geiringer describes *The Apothecary* as a "true musical comedy." He goes on to analyze Haydn's music as follows: "The conceit of narrow-minded Sempronio, whose knowledge is based mainly on newspaper reports, is beautifully described in the first aria. Mengono's aria in A major paints the sufferings of indigestion and the soothing effects of rhubarb with a daring realism that makes the piece hardly suitable for a refined audience. Very different is the attitude of the young man in the trio at the end of the first act. Here Grilletta and Mengono whisper tender words of love while the old man meditates on war in the Far East (a conflict that seemed fantastic and improbable in Haydn's time), but as soon as the apothecary leaves the room the flame of suppressed passion starts to blaze. The bold impudence of Volpino is well expressed in his aria in E major of the second act. . . . In the finale (of the second act) Sempronio dictates to the two suitors, disguised as notaries, his marriage contract with Grilletta. While pretending to repeat the words, they really burlesque them, changing every sentence to their own purposes. A tender melody of the oboe accompanies the main part of the scene. Repeated changes of tempo and the introduction of roguish, but also affectionate mirth, makes this piece one of the most effective numbers of ensemble music in the pre-Mozart opera buffa."

When *The Apothecary* was performed in New York in 1926—in what, in all probability, was the American première—it was heard in an English translation by Ann MacDonald, while the music was adapted by Howard Barlow. In the fall of 1959, *The Apothecary* was revived in a concert version in New York by the Little Orchestra Society under Thomas Scherman. A later revival in New York, by the Actors' Group, on May 8, 1961, utilized an edition by G. Henle in which important sections of the opera, long considered lost, were restored. The performance boasted a new English version by Naomi Ornest and Kurt Saffir and it may truthfully be said to have been the first one in America of the *complete* opera.

"Now that it has been restored," said Ross Parmenter in the *New York Times* in 1961, "it should have a long, new life. . . . It is worth doing. . . . When true humor and beauty go hand in hand, there is almost no pleasure on earth that can match it. This little work often has that combination, and for at least one stretch it has the combination in a sustained degree that is rare in musical annals. One refers to the beautiful quartet that ends the second act."

The first recording of *The Apothecary* was released by Epic in 1960, in a performance at Salzburg, Austria.

(The) Arcadians by Lionel Monckton and Howard Talbot.

Operetta in three acts with text by Mark Ambient and A. M. Thompson, and lyrics by Arthur Wimperis. First performance: Shaftesbury Theater, London, April 28, 1909. First American performance: Liberty Theater, New York, January 17, 1910.

With an initial run of over eight hundred performances in London, *The Arcadians* was one of the most successful English operettas of the 1910's. "A more exquisite or amusing entertainment," wrote B. W. Findon in *Play Pictorial*, "has not been since the days when genuine comic opera was in vogue."

The action takes place in Arcadia, a land remote from the follies and indiscretions of the so-called civilized world. The inhabitants of Arcadia are shocked to learn from one of their girls, Sombra, that there exists a country like England where people tell lies. As it happens, an Englishman, James Smith, drops into their midst from an airplane by parachute. In short order, he becomes an Arcadian, assuming the name of Simplicitas. As an Arcadian, and in the company of lovely Chrysea, he makes a pilgrimage to England. Dressed in Arcadian attire, they land at a fashionable race track near London, where they arouse considerable curiosity. When one of the jockies is unable to control an intractable horse, Simplicitas takes over and rides the animal to victory. Later on, Simplicitas is fêted at the Arcadian Restaurant in London—so-named in his honor. During the festivities, he succumbs to the temptation of telling a lie. Because of this indiscretion, he is transformed from an Arcadian back to a Londoner.

The jockey's topical song, "My Motto Is, Be Merry, Be Bright," is one of the more amusing tunes in the score, while one of the most lyrical is Sombra's air, "Arcady Is Ever Young." Two other melodies were popular in the early 1900's: "Erin's a Spot Famous for Greenery," and "When I Wander In My Garden."

When *The Arcadians* was successfully introduced in New York, Frank Moulan was starred as Smith-Simplicitas. Ethel Cadman appeared as Sombra, Percival Knight as the jockey, and Julia Sanderson in a minor role.

Arlecchino or **Die Fenster** [*Harlequin* or *The Windows*] by Ferruccio Busoni.

Comic opera in one act with text by the composer. First performance: Zurich, Switzerland, May 11, 1917. First American performance: New York, October 11, 1951 (concert version).

One would hardly expect a vivacious little comic opera from the pen of a savant, philosopher, and trenchant musical intellectual and theorist like Ferruccio Busoni. But if this were madness on Busoni's part there was method in it. Busoni's Italian compatriots always considered him something of an outsider because he spent a good deal of his time in Germany and allied himself intimately with German musical culture and traditions. *Arlecchino* was Busoni's attempt to ingratiate himself with his fellow Italians by writing the kind of opera buffa his countrymen liked so well. *Arlecchino* is in the spirit of Rossini, with echoes and quotations from Mozart and Donizetti. In structure and method it is pure opera buffa, even though Busoni could not always free himself from German influences in his harmony.

The setting is eighteenth-century Bergamo. Five bars of music bring on Harlequin (a speaking part), who explains: "'Tis not for children, not for gods, this play; for understanding people 'tis designed." Then comes the play—its four sections entitled, respectively, "Harlequin as Rogue," "Harlequin as Soldier," "Harlequin as Husband," and "Harlequin as Conqueror."

Matteo, a tailor, is reading Dante, while within his household Harlequin is making love to Matteo's wife. When Harlequin makes his escape by jumping out of the bedroom window, he terrifies Matteo by spreading the false rumor that the country is being invaded by barbarians. Harlequin now manages to lock up the poor tailor in his shop; from the window, the victim shouts at a nearby doctor and abbé about the invasion. They laugh at the news, and suggest mockingly that they will pass on these "important tidings" to the Burgomaster. Harlequin now appears, dressed as a recruiting officer. He is at the head of some decrepit looking soldiers, and has come to free the tailor from his confinement and to conscript him into the ragged army. Meanwhile, Columbine—Harlequin's wife—accuses him of having been unfaithful to her. He brushes her off, then enters a tavern for some refreshment. Spurned, Columbine finds consolation in the attentions of Leandro—to the chagrin of Harlequin, who beats him with a wooden sword. When the doctor and abbé leave the tavern in a somewhat inebriated state, they find the prostrate Leandro and think him dead. But Columbine reassures them, and Leandro is revived. All drive off in a donkey cart. These developments provide Harlequin with an opportunity to elope with Matteo's wife. Returning home, Matteo, fully confident now that there is no invasion whatsoever, can return to reading Dante with peace of mind.

After the curtain has fallen, all characters reappear in pairs: Leandro and Columbine; the doctor and the abbé; the carter and his donkey; two silent soldiers; and Harlequin with Matteo's wife. Harlequin tries to point up the moral of the tale but soon desists, deciding to leave such matters entirely to the critics and the audience. The curtain now rises for a last time to reveal Matteo still reading Dante, and waiting for his wife to come home.

The sardonic levity of the text is admirably carried over into Busoni's music: in the mock heroics of the little soldier's march of the second part (where Donizetti's *The Daughter of the Regiment* is quoted), to the strains of which Harlequin made his appearance with his shabby soldiers; in Leandro's serenade to Columbine, a parody of all similar serenades; and in the satirical love duet of Harlequin and Columbine which follows.

(The) Armorer by Albert Lortzing. *See (Der) Waffenschmied.*

Aufstieg und Fall der Stadt Mahagonny by Kurt Weill. *See (The) Rise and Fall of the City of Mahagonny.*

Barbe-Bleue [*Bluebeard*] by Jacques Offenbach.

> Opéra-bouffe in three acts with text by Henri Meilhac and Ludovic Halévy. First performance: Théâtre des Variétés, Paris, February 5, 1866. First American performances: New York, July 13, 1868 (in French); New York, February 15, 1870 (in German); New York, October 30, 1886 (in Yiddish).

The attempt of Offenbach and his librettists to burlesque the grim Bluebeard legend—and to make a mockery of this tale of horror—caused considerable misgiving among the cast selected for the première performance. Offenbach had to use all the wile and the persuasive arguments at his command to induce Hortense Schneider to play Boulotte, and to prevent Dupuis (cast as Bluebeard) from deserting the play during rehearsal. Nevertheless, Parisians loved *Barbe-bleue*. They were delighted at its satirical thrusts at court life; highly sympathetic to the democratic overtones of a text in which a simple peasant girl (Boulotte) assumes an unconventional, and at times even a defiant, attitude toward royalty.

Bluebeard, having murdered five wives, calls upon his peasants to choose a Rose Queen for him. Their choice falls upon Boulotte, a peasant girl. After Bluebeard has crowned her, he takes her as his sixth wife. Subsequently, Bluebeard falls in love with Princess Fleurette, daughter of King Bobeche, and he decides to do away with Boulotte. She is poisoned by an alchemist and is consigned to the same cave where her murdered predecessors had supposedly been buried. But all these women, instead of being poisoned, had actually been given sugared water, and they are not really dead. Their "resurrection" proves most embarrassing to Bluebeard, who finds himself suddenly blessed with an overabundance of wives. This unhappy situation leads Fleurette to lose all interest in him and to marry Prince Saphir.

Offenbach's music accompanying the "resurrection" of the wives within the cave is one of the composer's happiest and wittiest inventions. The most popular song in the score is an air of Count Oscar, *"C'est un métier difficile,"* which was a rage in Paris in 1866. The following are some of the other delectable musical moments: Boulotte's ballad, *"Nous possédons l'art merveilleux"*; the duet of Boulotte and Bluebeard, *"Pierre, un beau jour parvint"*; Bluebeard's legend, *"Ma première femme est morte"*; the Princess' song with chorus, *"C'est mon berger"*; and Bluebeard's lament, *"Madame! Ah! Madame, plaignez mon torment."*

The American première of *Barbe-bleue* introduced to the New York stage the "pert and saucy" French soubrette, Marie Aimée.

(The) Barber of Bagdad [*Der Barbier von Bagdad*] by Peter Cornelius.

Comic opera in two acts with text by the composer, based on an episode from *A Thousand and One Nights*. First performance: Weimar, Germany, December 15, 1858. First American performance: Metropolitan Opera, New York, January 3, 1890.

The Barber of Bagdad is a classic in the repertory of German comic operas. Its première played an important role in the personal history of

Franz Liszt. Liszt was musical director in Weimar when, in 1852, young Cornelius came to the city and promptly became Liszt's disciple, and an ardent propagandist for Liszt and Wagner and their "art of the future." In his attempt to apply to the comic theater some of the aesthetic principles and techniques propounded by Wagner, Cornelius wrote *The Barber of Bagdad.* Liszt conducted the world première. So great was the opposition to the new opera that only a single performance was given. It was principally this hostile reaction to Cornelius' opera that led Liszt to resign his post in Weimar.

The Barber of Bagdad never again was played in Cornelius' lifetime. It was revived in Hanover in 1877 (about three years after Cornelius' death), when once again it encountered an unsympathetic audience. And there was only mild approval when Felix Mottl conducted a performance in Karlsruhe on February 1, 1884 (in his own revised and reorchestrated version). But success finally came on October 15, 1885, with a revival in Munich. From this point forward, it went on to enjoy "a high reputation as one of the most elegant and refined comic operas ever composed by a German," in the words of A. Maczewsky.

When *The Barber of Bagdad* was introduced in the United States— at the Metropolitan Opera in 1890—W. J. Henderson said: "The score is full of the most characteristic and fluent melody, admirably written and distributed among the various voices and instruments." The first performance in London took place at the Savoy Theater on December 9, 1891, when the opera was heard in an English translation sung by the pupils of the Royal College of Music. Not until 1906 did Cornelius' comic opera reach the stage of Covent Garden.

In Bagdad, in ancient times, Nureddin is ill because of his unrequited love for the Cadi's daughter, Margiana. When Nureddin receives word that Margiana will receive him, his health is magically restored. He summons his barber, Abul Hassan, to make him properly presentable. Like barbers everywhere, Abul is garrulous; he does not hesitate to prophesy for Nureddin a dire fate. The young man remains deaf to these warnings. Abul now insists upon accompanying Nureddin to the Cadi's palace, but Nureddin has his servants waylay the barber while he himself makes a hurried exit.

In the palace, Margiana and Nureddin have a tender meeting. Outside, the barber has managed to extricate himself from Nureddin's servants and is waiting impatiently for developments. When Abul hears the anguished voice of a slave receiving punishment within the palace, he is sure that Nureddin is the victim, that his young friend is being murdered.

In danger of being discovered within the palace Nureddin is hidden inside a treasure chest by Margiana—and just as the Cadi makes his entrance. When the barber rushes into the palace to save Nureddin, he accuses the Cadi of having murdered the young man and having concealed the body in the treasure chest; for his part, the Cadi suspects the barber of trying to steal his treasures. At long last the chest is opened. Nureddin is found inside, almost suffocated, and is revived. The Cadi now orders that the treasure be turned over to Margiana as a dowry for her impending marriage to Nureddin.

The popular overture is heard most often in Mottl's revised version. It begins with a strong subject for the brass, representing the barber, and continues with several snatches of melody from the opera itself: the barber's song, *"Bin Akademiker,"* Nureddin's appeal to Margiana, *"Komm deine Blumen zu begiessen,"* the first-act duet of Nureddin and Bostana (Margiana's attendant), and the chorus of Nureddin's servants from the first-act finale. "All these themes," says Ernest Newman, "are worked up in the liveliest fashion, and the overture ends with the brass vociferating the simple little phrase which, in the opera, Nureddin says to Bostana, 'Don't forget the barber!' Cornelius no doubt intended the reminder of this at the end of the overture as a gentle admonition to the public not to forget his own *Barber*."

Two musical highlights, in which affecting lyricism and innocent merriment are delightfully married, are the first-act aria of Abul Hassan and the second-act duet of Nureddin and Margiana. In the first, *"Bin Akademiker,"* the barber gives a breathless, even whirlwind, account of his many talents as a barber, doctor, chemist, mathematician, and so forth; the second, a love duet, is the radiant melody, *"O holdes Bild."*

These are other gems in the iridescent score: Nureddin's song, *"Ach das Leid hab' ich getragen";* the effective orchestral tone poem, in the spirit of a religious meditation, which precedes the rise of the second-act curtain; the fluttering trio, *"Er kommt er kommt, o Wonne meiner Brust,"* with which the second act opens; and the exultant tribute to the ruler of Bagdad with which the opera ends, *"Salaam aleikum!"*

(The) Barber of Seville or The Vain Precaution [*Il Barbiere di Siviglia or La Precauzione inutile*] by Giovanni Paisiello.

Opera buffa in four acts with text by Giuseppe Petrosellini, based on *Le Barbier de Séville* by Beaumarchais. First performance: Hermitage,

St. Petersburg, Russia, September 26, 1782. First American performances: Philadelphia, 1794 (in English); New Orleans, July 12, 1810
(in French).

Paisiello's *Barber of Seville* preceded the more famous one by Rossini
by over a quarter of a century. In its day, Paisiello's opera was so extraordinarily popular that many opera lovers were aroused against Rossini for daring to compose a work on a text similar to the one used by
their favorite. It is not difficult to see why Paisiello's opera buffa was so
well liked. It is lyrical; it is witty; it is effervescent; and it is thoroughly
effective theater. Had Rossini never written a crowning masterwork on
the same subject, Paisiello's *Barber of Seville* might well have retained
its appeal up to the present time. As it is—even though eclipsed by Rossini's opus—Paisiello's opera is a notable achievement in the early history of opera buffa. "Its musical material," wrote Howard Taubman in
the *New York Times*, "is genial and is handled with grace. The ensemble
numbers have delicacy and wit. There are any number of felicitous bits
of characterization by means of music."

Paisiello's *Barber of Seville* was introduced in London on June 11,
1789, where it duplicated its earlier Russian and Italian successes. It
became the first opera ever performed in Mexico in the Italian language
when it was given there on December 4, 1806. Between the years of 1868
and 1918—after having been thrown completely in the shade by Rossini's *Barber of Seville*—Paisiello's opera was occasionally revived in
Italy. In 1939, it enjoyed a highly successful and eventful revival at La
Scala in Milan. In 1959–60, it was given at the Komische Oper in East
Berlin, and in 1960 it received its first complete recording.

Since the story of Paisiello's *Barber of Seville* is virtually the same as
Rossini's (see next entry), it need not be outlined here. In *High Fidelity*,
Conrad L. Osborne points up some of the differences between the operas
of Paisiello and Rossini: "Giuseppe Petrosellini's libretto hews much
more closely to Beaumarchais than does Cesare Sterbini's text for Rossini. Figaro's first entrance provides an excellent case in point. Rossini, of
course, uses the occasion for one of the greatest of all bravura arias,
'Largo al factotum [*della città*].' Paisiello and Petrosellini, on the other
hand, place a paper and pencil in Figaro's hand, and in his opening aria,
'Diamo alla noja il bando,' have him improvise a song—exactly as Figaro
does on his first appearance in the play. Beaumarchais' delightful scene
for Bartolo and his two impossible servants, to give another example,
does not turn up in Rossini at all, except in the vestigial character

Ambrogio; in the Paisiello version, it becomes an uproarious trio, with one servant (the dullard Brightboy) yawning almost uninterruptedly, the second (the senile Youthful) sneezing continuously, and Bartolo maintaining an incessant scolding patter. . . . The pleasing little serenade sung by Paisiello's Almaviva sounds a bit prosaic after the melting beauties of [Rossini's] '*Ecco ridente* [*in cielo*]' and '*Se il mio nome* [*saper*],' and the '*Calunnia*' aria of Paisiello's Basilio, evocative as it is of slander's storm, is not the malevolent *tour de force* that Rossini gave to his Basilio. Nevertheless, if the listener will accept Paisiello's music on its own terms he will find the score full of charm and wit. The melodies fall very easily on the ear, and as in Mozart, the working of them contains countless unexpected little turns that keep the theatrical pot bubbling. Everything is done with the simplest of materials, but done with precision and dramatic shrewdness."

Howard Taubman also notes some of the differences between Paisiello and Rossini, particularly in the famous singing-lesson scene in which Almaviva, disguised as a singing teacher, is confronted by Basilio. "Paisiello's quintet as he gets the embarrassing Basilio out of the way is light-footed and diverting. It has balance and grace, and the small orchestra in the pit supports the singer with chuckling airiness. This is an extended concert number that has logic and dramatic point. It is easy to see how it won the hearts of 18th and early 19th century patrons. It is also easy to see how Rossini's immense gusto overwhelmed a public accustomed to a politer form of expression."

(The) **Barber of Seville** [*Il Barbiere di Siviglia*] by Gioacchino Rossini.

> Opera buffa in two acts with text by Cesare Sterbini, based on *Le Barbier de Séville* and *Le Mariage de Figaro* by Beaumarchais. First performance: Teatro Argentino, Rome, February 20, 1816, under the title *Almaviva*. First American performances: Park Theater, New York, May 3, 1819 (in English); New York, November 29, 1825 (in Italian); New York, October 19, 1831 (in French); New York, December 4, 1863 (in German).

This masterwork is the yardstick by which all subsequent opera buffas were measured. Strange to report, in view of its now worldwide popularity, Rossini's *Barber of Seville* had a turbulent birth. The world première in Rome was a fiasco. This was due mainly to the fact that many Roman opera lovers deeply resented having Rossini set a subject previously used so effectively by Paisiello. Rossini himself apparently had some qualms, even though it was a common practice at the time for several different composers to use the same text. He wrote Paisiello inquiring if there was any objection to his setting *The Barber of Seville* to music and was told that Paisiello was perfectly agreeable. Nevertheless, to make sure there would be no confusion between his opera and Paisiello's, Rossini originally called his own work *Almaviva*. (He did not use the title of *The Barber of Seville* until August 19, 1816, when the opera was given at the Teatro Contavalli in Bologna. From then on the title of *Almaviva* was permanently discarded.)

Paisiello's admirers—possibly spearheaded by the composer himself —saw to it that Rossini's opera underwent a stormy première in Rome. A carefully organized claque disturbed the performance with shouts, catcalls, whistles, and laughter. And a poorly prepared production—plus some unfortunate mishaps—played right into the hands of Rossini's enemies. At one point, Don Basilio fell through a trapdoor; at another, a stray cat wandered across the stage. A string of Almaviva's guitar snapped while he was singing an affecting aria. The guffaws in the audience increased in volume and intensity until, in the second act, it was virtually impossible to hear the music. Rossini, who was conducting the performance, was hissed. When the opera ended, Rossini fled from the theater and sought refuge in the privacy of his home.

The second night, things went better. The performance improved; there were no untoward accidents on the stage; and, most important of all, Paisiello's followers were not present to create confusion. Rossini had made several changes in the score, including the interpolation of the beautiful serenade, *"Ecco ridente in cielo."* The third performance was a triumph. Unfortunately, the season in Rome ended soon after, and the opera did not have an opportunity to solidify its success that season. But five years later, when Rossini's *Barber of Seville* went on tour throughout Italy, it found admirers everywhere.

Outside Italy, Rossini's *Barber of Seville* also met a cool reception initially. In Germany, many thought Rossini's treatment too heavy-handed and too confused, in comparison with Paisiello's delightful version. In England, several critics considered its musical content too slight for serious consideration and prophesied a brief life. In France, the general complaint was that the opera was too noisy and lacking in effective melodies. But, in time, Rossini's opera buffa conquered Europe decisively. Some of Europe's most eminent musicians expressed their unqualified enthusiasm. "It will be played as long as Italian opera exists," Beethoven told Rossini in 1822. Berlioz, Brahms, and Wagner were some of the other distinguished composers who fell in love with the opera, "Oh, Rossini, Rossini!," exclaimed Wagner during a performance of *The Barber of Seville*. "How I love him! But, for goodness sake, do not tell my Wagnerians. They will never forgive me."

The opera is truly a miracle—especially when we recall that Rossini finished his entire score in about two weeks. "Every situation," writes Francis Toye, "almost every idea, seems to have suggested to him one musical train of thought after another, nearly all equally felicitous." The lyricism is consistently radiant; the comedy, effervescent; the orchestration and ensemble writing, brilliant. The score is rich in variety, each number a gem of its kind. Toye was perfectly right when he maintained, "no comic opera can show anything better."

Sterbini's libretto is one of the best Rossini ever set. In Seville, in the seventeenth century, Count Almaviva is in love with Rosina. She is being jealously watched by her guardian, Dr. Bartolo, who would like to marry her for her money. Almaviva, passing himself off as a poor student named Lindoro, serenades her (*"Ecco ridente in cielo"*), then expresses his love in a touching avowal (*"Se il mio nome saper"*). When Figaro, the jovial barber, appears, he introduces himself with a patter song (one of the most famous buffa arias in the entire opera repertory) in which he describes his many occupations and activities (*"Largo al factotum della città*). Almaviva consults him on the best way to gain access to the well-sheltered Rosina. Figaro advises him to disguise himself as a drunken soldier and demand a roof over his head. Inside the household, Rosina is reading a love letter from "Lindoro" (*"Una voce poco fa"*); and Don Basilio, a music teacher, his suspicions aroused by Almaviva's being seen so often in the neighborhood, vows to destroy him through the power of slander (*"La Calunnia"*). Finally, Almaviva, disguised as a drunken soldier, makes his entrance. Establishing contact with Rosina, he reveals to her that, in reality, he is "Lindoro," and exchanges love missives with her. Bartolo senses that the drunken soldier is a fraud, and orders his arrest. To forestall this, the Count is compelled to reveal his true identity. The next time Almaviva tries to gain admission into Rosina's home, he appears as a music teacher, come to substitute for Don Basilio who had suddenly become indisposed. He greets Rosina and Bartolo unctuously (*"Pace e gioia sia con voi"*). Once again Bartolo's suspicions are aroused; he insists upon staying in the room throughout the lesson. But Rosina and Almaviva slyly introduce into their lesson the plans for an elopement. When the real music teacher appears, Figaro bribes him to simulate illness. All the while Bartolo's suspicions mount until, finally, he decides to take action. He engages a notary to draw up a marriage contract between himself and Rosina. But the notary is bribed to insert into the contract the names of Rosina and Almaviva. Although furious at first to discover the deception, Bartolo's wounded feelings are completely placated when he learns that he will be allowed to keep Rosina's wealth for himself.

The *Barber of Seville* starts off with its best foot forward—a gay and dashing little overture that is a masterpiece. It is so much in the spirit of the play that follows that it is a shock to discover that it was not written for this opera at all; that Rossini had used it previously for several other operas, tragic as well as comic. It opens with a slow introduction in which a melody for violins is prominent. Four chords provide a transition to the main section. A saucy tune for strings and piccolo is heard, followed by a second theme, for oboe and clarinet—reiterated by the horn—which retains the spirit of gaiety introduced by the first theme. A characteristic Rossini crescendo leads to the development of both tunes, and the overture concludes with a vivacious coda.

The fact that its famous overture was not written for this opera is only one of several curiosities about Rossini's *Barber of Seville*. Bartolo's second-act aria, "*Manca un foglio,*" was not written by Rossini at all, but by another composer, Romani by name; it has often been used through the years as a substitute for Rossini's less singable aria, "*A un dottor della mia sorte.*" Nor do we hear Rossini's own music in the Lesson Scene; Rossini's score for this section was lost soon after the opera's première. Since that time, prima donnas have made it a practice to interpolate into this scene any one of several songs or arias by other composers; some of the favorites have been Payne's "Home, Sweet Home," Alabiev's "The Nightingale" and Arditi's "*Il Bacio.*"

The *Barber of Seville* was the first opera sung in the Italian language in New York, when the opera was revived on November 29, 1825. (At the United States première, in 1819, the opera was heard in an English translation.) The first performance of Rossini's *Barber of Seville* at the Metropolitan Opera took place on November 23, 1883, during that company's initial season.

The role of Rosina was originally written for a mezzo-soprano, but the part proved too inviting to be resisted by sopranos. Since 1826, when Henriette Sontag was acclaimed for her performance as Rosina, it has been the custom to assign the role to sopranos; but on several occasions Rossini's original intentions have been adhered to.

(Der) Barbier von Bagdad by Peter Cornelius. *See (The) Barber of Bagdad.*

(Il) Barbiere di Siviglia by Giovanni Paisiello, or by Gioacchino Rossini. *See The Barber of Seville* by respective composers.

(The) Bartered Bride [*Prodaná Nevěsta* or *Die Verkaufte Braut*] by Bedřich Smetana.

> Comic opera in three acts with text by Karel Sabina. First performance: National Theater, Prague, May 30, 1866. First American performances: Chicago, August 20, 1893 (in Bohemian); Metropolitan Opera, New York, February 19, 1909 (in German); Metropolitan Opera, New York, May 15, 1936 (in English).

The Bartered Bride is the cornerstone of Bohemian nationalist music. The opera is rich and colorful with Bohemian dances, folk melodies and rhythms; and backgrounds, and characters taken from Bohemia's countryside. Yet so universal is its comedy, sentimentality, and atmosphere that, for all its authentic Bohemianism, it has captured the heart of the entire world. Indeed, this is the only comic opera from Eastern Europe to maintain a permanent place in the repertory.

Smetana wrote his masterwork out of pique: He had a point to prove to his severest critics. When the nationalist movement infected Bohemia in the early 1860's, a national theater was opened in Prague. This provided a stimulus for the emergence of native drama and opera. For this new theater, Smetana wrote his first opera, in 1863—*The Brandenburgers in Bohemia,* based on an episode from Bohemian history. *The Brandenburgers in Bohemia* was a moderate success with audiences, but not with the critics. Some found the music too derivative of Wagner, others felt that Smetana's touch was too heavy-handed to be enjoyable. Aroused by such condemnation, Smetana decided to write a "trifle . . . not from ambition, but from defiance." He asked Karel Sabina for a light libretto, and then proceeded to write music which "according to my-then notion not even Offenbach could equal."

But *The Bartered Bride* had to undergo a considerable amount of surgery before its health and survival were assured. In its first version (1866) it was a musical comedy: a spoken play with interpolated popular songs and dances. When plans were afoot by the Paris Opéra-Comique to include *The Bartered Bride* in its repertory (plans that never materialized), Smetana revised his score by adding a male chorus and some additional vocal numbers. Later the same year, he added also some folk dances, the furiant and the now highly popular polka. This revised version was seen for the first time in Prague on January 29, 1869. Still other revisions followed. The most significant replaced spoken text with recitatives, thus changing the character of the work from a musical comedy to an opera. This form, introduced in Prague on September 25, 1870 with Smetana conducting, was a complete triumph. From then on, *The Bartered Bride* became one of the best loved operas in Prague: between 1870 and the outbreak of World War II, it was performed there over fourteen hundred times.

A performance at the Vienna Royal Opera in 1892, with Gustav Mahler conducting, was also highly acclaimed. On February 19, 1909, *The Bartered Bride* had its first performance in the United States, at the Metropolitan Opera. Gustav Mahler was the conductor, and the cast included Emmy Destinn and Albert Reiss. "That it pleased last night's audience is beyond all question," reported W. J. Henderson. "The applause broke in upon scene after scene, and the comedy won the tribute of cheerful smiles and not infrequent laughter. The question whether there can be any sustained popularity for an opera of [this] character seemed to be swiftly answered by the public enjoyment of its novelty of style and color." Then Mr. Henderson went on to say: "The chief charms of the opera are its incessant flow of charming melody, of fresh and piquant character, its bright and vivacious pictures of Bohemian life, its captivating dances, its excellent character sketches, its simple yet unctuous comedy, and its admirable instrumentation. As a specimen of genuinely artistic comic opera, it takes commanding position." On that occasion the opera was performed in German. But on May 16, 1936, the Metropolitan Opera revived *The Bartered Bride* in an English translation by Madeleine Marshall.

In a Bohemian village, a century ago, Marie is in love with Hans. Her parents, however, want her to marry Wenzel, an idiotic, stuttering boy, son of Micha, a wealthy landowner. Kezal, the marriage broker, tries to convince Hans to foresake Marie. Hans finally consents to do so in return for a payment of three hundred crowns—but also on a contractual stipulation that Marie be allowed to marry Micha's son. Marie is heartbroken to discover that Hans proved so willing to exchange her for pieces of gold, and reconciles herself to becoming Wenzel's wife. But Hans has pulled a fast one on the marriage broker. Since Hans is a stranger in town, nobody knows that he is actually Micha's long-lost son. Consequently, according to the terms of the contract he had signed with Kezal, he can marry Marie and keep the three hundred crowns. Everybody (except the defrauded marriage broker) is delighted with this turn of events—even Wenzel, who by this time has fallen in love with a dancer, Esmeralda.

The orchestral excerpts are the most familiar pages of the score: the overture and the folk dances. The overture was so dear to the heart of Gustav Mahler that he often conducted it as the introduction to the second act (instead of the first) because he did not want latecomers to miss hearing it. The first theme is presented without introduction: a brisk tune for the strings and woodwinds against brass chords. A fugal treatment of the tune follows. After a climax and a repetition of this subject, a second melody is stated by the oboe. There is still a third theme, heard in the violins and cellos, but only after the first theme has received considerable attention. Many conductors—Mahler was one— like to perform the overture at a breathtaking tempo.

The folk dances are "The Dance of the Comedians," "Furiant," and "Polka." The first is used in the third act to accompany the feats of acrobats—a traveling company of performers come to the village to do a show in the public square. The furiant is a spirited Bohemian folk dance in ¾ time characterized by cross rhythms; the one in Smetana's opera appears as an orchestral interlude in the second act. The polka, to which the villagers dance, concludes the first act.

Of the vocal numbers, the following are a few of the more attractive ones: Marie's tender love song to Hans, "Gladly Do I Trust You," in the first act; Wenzel's stuttering tune, "Ma, Ma, Mama So Dear," and Hans's recollection of his faraway home, "Far From Here Do I Love," in the second act; and Hans's poignant entreaty to Marie in the third act, "My Dearest Love, Just Listen."

Bastien and Bastienne [*Bastien und Bastienne*] by Wolfgang Amadeus Mozart.

Singspiel in one act with text by Friedrich Wilhelm Weiskern, based on *Les Amours de Bastien et Bastienne* by Charles Simon Favart. First performance: Vienna, October, 1768 (private). First American performance (probable): Empire Theater, New York, October 26, 1916 (in English).

Mozart, at age twelve, paid a visit to Vienna, where he was commissioned to write this delightful one-act travesty. The commission came from Dr. Anton Mesmer, a specialist in magnetic therapy, from whose name the word "mesmerism" is derived. Dr. Mesmer owned a little theater, which was situated in the garden of his house, and it was for this theater that he asked the child Mozart to write him an opera. The composer's choice fell upon the German adaptation of a parody of Rousseau's comic opera, *Le Devin du village* (which see). Mozart had seen a performance of this parody in Paris, and was enchanted with the way in which it reduced Rousseau's naturalism to absurdity. This French parody, performed for the first time in 1752 at Fontainebleau before King Louis XIV, had been so successful that it was given a public performance in Paris on March 1, 1753. In 1764, Weiskern prepared a German translation which, with some minor modifications, served as Mozart's text.

Mozart's *Bastien and Bastienne* is a Singspiel—a kind of musical comedy that was the forerunner of German comic opera. But Mozart's musical style is more French than German, and his version differed from the French parody in that it was more pastoral than burlesque.

Only three characters are involved in the story. Bastienne, a shepherdess, is in love with young Bastien, but she feels she has lost him. She enlists the aid of Colas, a magician, who drops a hint to Bastien that his beloved shepherdess has found another lover. Aroused to jealousy, Bastien insists he must hear this from the lips of Bastienne herself before he will believe a word of it. When Bastienne appears, she is at first sulky, but on seeing the boy she loves, she forgets her grief and doubts and falls into his arms.

Mozart's score consists of sixteen numbers—arias, duets, and a trio. (In 1769, a year after he wrote the opera, he added recitatives.) The beauty is on the surface. There is nothing subtle or profound in the emotion or feeling. But Mozart's way with a mobile, graceful, caressing melody is already evident: in Bastien's love song, *"Meiner Liebsten schoene Wangen,"* and Bastienne's little lament, *"Wenn mein Bastien einst im Scherze";* in Colas' air, *"Diggi, daggi, Schurry, murry"*—in which he goes through the motions of casting a spell—where the cliché of the big opera seria aria is delightfully mocked.

The awkwardness in this little opera resides, as Nathan Broder has pointed out, "in a certain lack of variety in mood and pace—most of the numbers are in a moderate two-four or three-four meter." Mr. Broder adds: "But within this limited sphere the boy writes some charming melodies. Many of them, as was to be the case whenever Mozart set German texts, have a folk-like flavor."

One of the interesting features of the little orchestral introduction (*"intrada"*) with which the opera opens is the principal theme which bears a striking resemblance to the one used many years later by Beethoven in the first movement of the *Eroica* Symphony.

(The) Bat by Johann Strauss II. *See (Die) Fledermaus.*

Beatrice and Benedick [*Beatrice et Benedict*] by Hector Berlioz.

> Opéra-comique in two acts with text by the composer, based on Shakespeare's comedy, *Much Ado About Nothing.* First performance: Baden-Baden, Germany, August 9, 1862 (in German). First American performance (probable): New York City, March 21, 1960 (concert version).

In August, 1858, Bénazet, director of the Baden-Baden Casino, informed Berlioz of his plan to build a new theater in the German resort. He commissioned Berlioz to write an opera for it, and suggested a text based upon some incident during the Thirty Years' War. But this idea resembled another of Berlioz's operas (*Les Francs juges*) too closely and he rejected it. Berlioz suggested instead, a light comedy based on Shakespeare's *Much Ado About Nothing.*

After preparing his own libretto, Berlioz worked on the score between the end of 1859 and the early part of 1862. These years happened to be particularly depressing for the composer. He was beset by harrowing problems of all sorts, including domestic ones. Yet not the slightest shadow passes over this sunny music.

On July 26, 1862, Berlioz invited the press, and several prominent French musicians, to a private performance of his new opera—and the one that was destined to be his last. It made a forceful impression. It proved even more successful when Berlioz conducted its première in

Baden-Baden. A few months after that, in 1863, it was given in the German language in Weimar, with Berlioz once again conducting.

In adapting the short version of Shakespeare's play, Berlioz stressed comedy rather than romance and intrigue. Shakespeare's sub-plot involving Beatrice and Benedick is emphasized; the central love story of Claudia and Hero, and their harassment at the hands of Don John, is glossed over. Berlioz's opera begins with the return of the victorious troops, among them Claudio and Benedick who are awaited by their loved ones, Hero and Beatrice. The romance of Beatrice and Benedick refuses to run a smooth course, since both are hot-tempered and quarrelsome and each is reluctant to reveal to the other the true state of his or her feelings. Their friends, however, arrange it so that each manages to overhear the other confessing his or her love for the other. Thus they are finally united.

Berlioz introduces a character not found in Shakespeare: Somarona, an orchestral conductor. For him, Berlioz wrote a delightful parody of a sixteenth-century madrigal in *"Mourez tendres époux."* To heighten the local color, Berlioz also interpolated into his score several colorful Sicilian dances.

The overture begins with an introduction, the first theme of which is a spirited subject in triple time. After that comes an orchestral version of Beatrice's beautiful song, *"Il m'en souvient."* The main body of the overture projects a strong, brassy melody and a contrasting theme.

Besides the vocal passages already mentioned, the most important in the opera include the nocturne that concludes the first act; Beatrice's song, *"Dieu! viens-je d'entendre,"* probably the most celebrated single aria in the entire opera; a delightful duet, *"Vous souprize, madame!"*; Hero's affecting aria, *"Je vais la voir"*; and the charming travesty, the "Wedding Cantata," with its "unanswerable logic of the text," in the words of W. H. Hadow, "and the angular trills and flourishes of its oboe obbligato."

America had to wait a long time to hear an opera which the composer himself once described "as one of the most spirited and original I ever wrote." There is no record of an American performance before March 21, 1960, when the Little Orchestra Society, under Thomas Scherman, presented it in a concert version at Carnegie Hall, New York. On that occasion, Louis Biancolli described the opera in the *New York World Telegram* as "music of incomparable glow . . . a romantic comedy of idyllic and haunting beauty." He added: "What genius overflows in the writing of this score—always the right touch in the orchestra; the broad, soaring writing for voice; the matchless duets and trios—and over it all a gossamer mood of fantasy."

Beautiful Galathea by Franz von Suppé. *See (Die) Schoene Galatea.*

Beautiful Helen by Jacques Offenbach. *See (La) Belle Hélène.*

(The) Beggar's Opera by John Christopher Pepusch.

> Ballad opera in three acts with text and lyrics by John Gay. First performance: Lincoln's Inn Fields, London, February 9, 1728. First American performance: New York, December 3, 1750.

The Beggar's Opera was the first ballad opera ever written. As such, it marked the beginning of English comic opera. John Gay was probably sparked into the writing of this text by Jonathan Swift who (as reported by Alexander Pope) happened to remark that "a Newgate pastoral might make an odd pretty sort of a thing." (Newgate, until it was demolished in 1902, was London's prison where criminals awaited trial.) If this is fact, then a chance remark was responsible for one of the epochal events in the English theater.

Gay planned his text as a parody on grand opera, Handelian opera specifically, then in such vogue in London. Handel's operas were usually based on glamorous heroic characters and historic episodes. To give point to his parody—and to give free rein to his satire—Gay went for his material to the lowest strata of English society: thieves, harlots, a highwayman, a beggar, and so forth. But as the text took shape, Gay went far beyond his original intention of merely poking fun at opera. He also succeeded in writing a brilliant political and social travesty in which the-then Prime Minister, Sir Robert Walpole, and his satellites were broadly caricatured; current political corruption was heavily underscored; the predatory habits of English society were mocked; the prevailing callousness toward poverty and human suffering was exposed; and the pretensions of so-called high society laughed at.

He entitled the play *The Beggar's Opera* because in the prologue a beggar comes out to explain to the audience that the text was written to celebrate the marriage of two ballad singers. The beggar then describes the play itself and makes some derogatory remarks about opera in general. His prologue ended, the beggar withdraws, and he is never again seen or heard from.

The play recounts the story of Polly Peachum who, against her parents' objections, secretly marries the highwayman, Captain Macheath. When the parents discover this, they manage to get the highwayman arrested. Macheath is in a tavern, boasting of the delights he has enjoyed with women, when Polly's father appears with a constable and has him seized. In prison, Lucy, daughter of the jailer, falls in love with Macheath and even contrives to have an affair with him, with the result that she becomes pregnant. Macheath—now torn between his love for his wife and for his mistress—manages, with Lucy's connivance, to escape from prison. But his freedom is short-lived. Once again Peachum manages to get the highwayman back into jail. His sentence is execution. Both Lucy and Polly are prostrate with grief. At this point in the play, one of the actors remarks that were Macheath to be hanged, as now appears inevitable, the play would be transformed from a comedy into a stark tragedy. For this reason, and this reason alone, Macheath must get a reprieve.

The Beggar's Opera is a spoken play with many interpolated tunes. John Christopher Pepusch's score consists of only one piece of music of his own invention, the overture. The rest is made up of his adaptations of sixty-nine tunes: mostly English and Scottish ballads popular in the eighteenth century (including the still familiar "Greensleeves"); French airs; street songs; borrowings from Handel (a march from *Rinaldo*) and Purcell (in "When Young at Bar" and "Virgins are Like Flowers of May"). For all these melodies, Pepusch prepared the figured basses, but no formal harmonizations.

When first produced, *The Beggar's Opera* was a sensation. It received the-then unprecedented (for the English stage) initial run of sixty-two performances, thirty-two of them consecutive. The production brought fame and fortune to Lavinia Fenton, who created the role of Polly, the first step in a glamorous and much-toasted career which saw her marry the Duke of Bolton and sit for a painting by Hogarth. The producer, Rich, profited to the tune of four thousand pounds, and the author, John Gay, seven hundred pounds. In the words of a saying that made the rounds of London at the time: "*The Beggar's Opera* made Rich gay and

Gay rich." A passion for ballad operas was thus aroused which continued in London for over a decade: about 120 ballad operas were produced in that city between 1728 and 1738. And the popularity of the ballad opera spread—to Paris, the West Indies, and even the American colonies.

Long after many of the topical allusions in Gay's text lost their point, *The Beggar's Opera* continued to prosper. Through the years—up to the present—this ballad opera has been seen in numerous different versions and adaptations. The most famous of all is *The Three-Penny Opera* (which see), text by Bertolt Brecht and music by Kurt Weill. Another notable version was seen in London in 1920, in which the text was revised by Arnold Bennett and the music harmonized, orchestrated, and adapted by Frederick Austin. This, a rather refined, elegant, and polished replica of the original product, was so successful that it enjoyed a run of about two and a half years. In 1940, the Glyndebourne Opera of England presented still another version, produced by John Gielgud. This one departed from Austin's prettified adaptation in favor of a more realistic treatment, more in line with Gay's intentions. In 1948, in collaboration with Tyrone Guthrie, Benjamin Britten, England's leading twentieth-century opera composer, prepared a version for the English Group Opera. Once again the emphasis was on the stark, the sordid, the realistic. As Britten himself said, he tried to make it "the expression of people made reckless, even desperate, by poverty, but in whose despair there is nonetheless a vitality and gaiety that the art of elegant and fashionable people often misses." For his music, Britten went back to Pepusch's score instead of adapting the music as freely as Austin had done. He used sixty-six of Pepusch's sixty-nine tunes (Austin had used only forty-five). "Apart from one or two extensions and repetitions," says Britten, "I have left the tunes exactly as they stood." When the New York City Center revived *The Beggar's Opera* in New York, on March 14, 1957, they used still another version: that of Richard Baldridge. Meanwhile, a fine motion picture was made in England with Laurence Olivier as Macheath and the musical adaptations by Sir Arthur Bliss.

Pepusch's score is such a plentiful source of delightful tunes that it is impossible to single out all the highlights. The following, however, are a few random representatives: Filch's song to Peachum, " 'Tis a Woman that Seduces All Mankind"; the love duet of Polly and Macheath, "Pretty Polly Says"; Macheath's recital of the hazards of his profession, "If the Heart of Man"; the political tune, "Lillibullero"; Macheath's complaint on his unhappy plight. "Man May Escape from Rope and Gun"; and the duet of Lucy and Polly in which they confess they preferred their own deaths to that of their beloved highwayman, "Would I Might Be Hanged."

In 1729, Gay and Pepusch wrote a sequel to *The Beggar's Opera*, and called it *Polly*. Largely in reprisal for the biting political and social satire in *The Beggar's Opera*, the censors refused to permit *Polly* to reach the stage. Publication, however, was allowed, and through this means *Polly* became known and popular long before it was finally produced, at the Haymarket Theater on June 19, 1777. It was such a failure that it had to be withdrawn after a few performances. *Polly* was revived in 1782 and again in 1813, but with no change in its fortune. A modernized version was introduced at the Kingsway Theater in London on December 30, 1922, text revised by Clifford Bax and music arranged by Frederick Austin.

(The) Beggar Student [*Der Bettelstudent*] by Karl Milloecker.

> Operetta in three acts with text by F. Zell and Richard Genée. First performance: Theater-an-der-Wien, Vienna, December 6, 1882. First American performances: Thalia Theater, New York, October 19, 1883 (in German); Casino Theater, New York, October 29, 1883 (in English).

A classic among Viennese operettas, *The Beggar Student* was acclaimed not only at its world première in Vienna but immediately thereafter in New York and London. Indeed, in New York it was produced in both German and English within the space of ten days, and after that is was frequently revived. Among the more successful revivals were those in 1910 and 1913 with Rudolph Kolch and De Wolf Hopper, respectively, in the role of Ollendorf.

In Cracow, Poland, in the early eighteenth century, General Ollendorf is spurned by Laura, the attractive daughter of a countess. The general decides to avenge himself on Laura by perpetrating an unkind trick. He arranges for Symon, a humble beggar student, to assume the part of a wealthy gentleman. Then he has him come to court Laura, accompanied by his friend Janitsky, assuming the identity of a secretary. The two men are warmly welcomed within the Countess' household, and Laura falls in love with Symon. But before long, Symon's conscience troubles him to a point where he must confess to Laura who he really is. The General manages to intercept his explanatory letter, and thus the romance is allowed to develop until it reaches the stage of matrimony. The General now exposes the young man as a fraud. Disgraced, Symon contemplates suicide. But when Janitsky, aided by Symon, helps the king regain his lost Polish throne, the grateful monarch elevates both men to high stations. Now a member of the titled nobility, Symon can rightfully claim his bride.

The opera's most celebrated excerpt is General Ollendorf's entrance waltz, since become a favorite with German concert bassos. It is *"Ach, ich hab' sie ja nur auf die Schulter gekuesst,"* sometimes known as the "Kiss on the Shoulder" waltz. Effective use is made of it as the first-act climax. Also popular are Symon's two principal arias. The first is a mazurka-type romance, *"Ich knuepfte manche zarte Bande,"* in which he recounts his various adventures (amatory and otherwise) in strange lands. The second is his poignant confession to Laura that he is, after all, only a beggar student, *"Ich hab' kein Geld, bin vogel-frei."*

(La) Belle Hélène [*Beautiful Helen*] by Jacques Offenbach.

Opéra-bouffe in three acts with text by Henri Meilhac and Ludovic Halévy. First performance: Théâtre des Variétés, Paris, December 17, 1864. First American performances: New York, December 3, 1867 (in German); New York, March 26, 1868 (in French); New York, April 13, 1868 (in English).

This was a studied effort on the part of its authors to copy, and perhaps repeat, the success of their earlier opéra-bouffe, *Orpheus in the Underworld*. Here, as in their previous masterwork, they reverted to mythology for their text, arriving at the subject of Helen of Troy and her illicit romance with Paris. The librettists decided to treat this material with the same kind of malice and mockery, parody and satire that had made *Orpheus in the Underworld* so provocative and successful six years earlier. The Helen of Troy story was used to point up, and laugh at, some of the frivolities of the Second Empire whose accent was ever on pleasure and a relaxed moral code. Greek kings are presented in a contemptible light. The soothsayer is made to symbolize sacrilegious priesthood and is little better than a cheat. Helen succumbs to Paris' wooing because of her revulsion to her own surroundings, and absolves her conscience for this adulterous practice with a flimsy bit of feminine logic. But *La*

Belle Hélène not only put a mirror up to the face of the Second Empire. It was also a prophetic warning of the decline and fall of that empire, in the ominous feeling of doom that seemed to hover over the entire opera.

In ancient Sparta, Paris, son of Priam, comes to the high priest Calchas with a message from Venus. The goddess demands that Paris be given the beautiful Helen of Greece. Paris comes to Greece disguised as a shepherd, but his true identity becomes apparent when he wins three prizes in a competition. By this time Helen has come to realize that she is destined to go off with Paris, even though she is married to Menelaus. She crowns Paris victor. After Paris has contrived to send Menelaus off to Crete on a war mission, he makes love to Helen. Although strongly attracted to him, she tries at first to resist his advances. Realizing that Helen is the victim of her conscience, he tries to placate it by returning to her late one night after she has fallen asleep and, upon awakening her, trying to convince her that she is only dreaming. This ruse apparently satisfies Helen, who is now ready to succumb to Paris' ardent love-making. At this point Menelaus unexpectedly returns, but Paris effects his escape. Before long he returns, disguised as a priest, and abducts the all too willing Helen.

Although the beloved and glamorous Parisian stage star, Hortense Schneider, played the title role and *La Belle Hélène* was one of Offenbach's best scores, this opéra-bouffe was not at first successful. Indeed, history was destined to repeat itself. The reception accorded *La Belle Hélène* in Paris was pretty much like that previously encountered by *Orpheus in the Underworld*. Once again, with *La Belle Hélène* as earlier with *Orpheus in the Underworld,* the critics denounced it soundly as a desecration of antiquity. Once again, audiences were puzzled by the strange mixture of classical settings and characters with nineteenth-century frivolity. But with *La Belle Hélène,* as with *Orpheus in the Underworld,* articles in the press began to whet the interest and curiosity of Parisians in this provocative and somewhat scandalous production. *La Belle Hélène* soon became the rage, the thing to see, quote, discuss.

Offenbach's score runs the gamut from sentimentality to mockery, from pure and shining lyricism to frivolous accents, from the dramatic to the humorous. "Really," said the distinguished critic, Camille Bellaigue, "I do not know any music on earth which contains such a striking mixture of extremes. It is impossible to choose between the sentimental Offenbach and the other, or even to know them from each other, they are so completely fused."

The lyrical Offenbach is found in the haunting invocation, *"On me nomme Hélène"* (which all Paris sang in the middle 1880's), *"Amours divins,"* the air with which the queen and her entourage make their first-act entrance, and two celebrated airs of Paris, *"Le Jugement de Paris"* (also known as *"Au Mont Ida"*) and Paris's entrance song. The lighter side of Offenbach is encountered in the delightful Can-Can, one of the high spots of the whole production. The dramatic Offenbach is heard in two of Helen's second-act songs: *"La vrai! je ne suis pas coupable"* and *"Un mari sage est en voyage."*

(Der) Betrogene Cadi by Christoph Willibald Gluck. *See (Le) Cadi Dupé.*

(Der) Bettelstudent by Karl Milloecker. *See (The) Beggar Student.*

(The) Bird Dealer by Karl Zeller. *See (Der) Vogelhaendler.*

Bitter Sweet by Noël Coward.

> Operetta in three acts with text and lyrics by Noël Coward. First performance: His Majesty's Theater, London, July 18, 1929. First American performance: Ziegfeld Theater, New York, November 5, 1929.

For many years Noël Coward nursed the ambition to write an operetta in the grand romantic tradition of Vienna. One day, during the summer of 1928, while visiting friends in Surrey, he listened to a recording of Johann Strauss's *Die Fledermaus.* That was when he decided at long last to get to work on a Strauss-like operetta. After leaving his friends, he drove over the Wimbledon Commons. Suddenly he drew his car to the side of the road. "In the shade of a giant horse-chestnut tree," he recalls, "I mapped out vaguely the story of Sari Linden.

He finished the first act aboard the *Berengaria* bound for New York. The rest of the text went easily and was completed in New York City early in 1929. The writing of the music, however, proved a trial. In fact, even before he could get started on his score he seemed to reach a dead end. One day, in New York, the taxicab in which he was traveling became snarled in a traffic jam. All around him the angry horns of impatient drivers were sounding. Out of this pandemonium emerged in Coward's consciousness the refrain of a waltz tune. Back in his apartment he sat down at the piano and played the whole waltz melody from beginning to end. It was "I'll See You Again," the main musical number of his operetta. Once he put this song down on paper, the rest of the score went quickly.

Coward had hoped to get Gertrude Lawrence to star as Sari, but on mature reflection he came to the conclusion her voice was too small for the numbers she would be required to sing. Evelyn Laye was his second choice, but, regrettably, she was unavailable at the time. The final selection was Peggy Wood.

Sari, the heroine of the operetta, is an English lady of high social position who falls in love with her music teacher, Carl. On the eve of her marriage to a man in her own social world, she impetuously decides to elope with the humble musician. They come to Vienna where they lead a gay life in the city of wine and song and café-houses. But tragedy strikes, with the sudden death of Carl in a duel. Sari goes on to become a famous singer, her culminating triumph occurring in London, where she returns after an absence of half a century.

Noël Coward has singled out the moments in the operetta he likes best—and they are undoubtedly those which made the operetta so popular on both sides of the Atlantic. They include the first-act finale, in which Carl and Sari elope; the café-house scene in Vienna, when Carl's death is announced as the curtain slowly descends; and the closing scene when, to the final chords of "I'll See You Again," Sari (now an old woman) walks proudly off the stage.

Everything about this operetta is in the sentimental and nostalgic vein of typical Viennese productions, especially Noël Coward's music. Besides the waltz, "I'll See You Again," which Sari and Carl first sing in the second scene of the first act, the main numbers include, "If Love Were All," Sari's stirring gypsy song, "Zigeuner," "Tokay," "Tell Me, What Is Love?", and "Dear Little Café."

When *Bitter Sweet* came to New York late in 1929, Evelyn Laye finally played Sari, and this performance became one of the outstanding triumphs of her magnificent career. She stopped the show regularly with the number, "Tell Me, What Is Love?," and from then on the enthusiasm for her performance kept mounting until the final curtain, when pandemonium broke loose. Coward himself said that never before or since had he heard such prolonged outbursts of cheering in the theater as took place at the New York première. "It was Evelyn's night from the first to the last."

"Of all the shows I have ever done," wrote Coward, *"Bitter Sweet* gave me the greatest personal pleasure." And there can be little argument that its great waltz, "I'll See You Again," is the most formidable song success of Coward's entire career.

Bitter Sweet was twice made into motion pictures. The first time was in England in 1933 with Evelyn Laye as Sari. The second production, made in Hollywood in 1940, starred Jeanette MacDonald and Nelson Eddy.

(The) **Black Domino** by Daniel François Esprit Auber. *See (Le) Domino noir.*

(The) **Black Forest Maid** by Leon Jessel. *See Schwarzwaldmaedel.*

Bluebeard by Jacques Offenbach. *See Barbe-bleu.*

Boccaccio by Franz von Suppé.

> Operetta in three acts with text by F. Zell and Richard Genée. First performance: Karlstheater, Vienna, February 1, 1879. First American performances: Chestnut Street Theater, Philadelphia, April 15, 1880 (in English); Thalia Theater, New York, April 23, 1880 (in German).

The libretto of Suppé's most popular operetta is based on the romance of Boccaccio and Fiametta as described in the biography of Boccaccio, *L'Amoroso Fiametta.* Pietro, Prince of Palermo, is ordered by his father to proceed to Florence for the purpose of marrying Fiametta, illegitimate daughter of the Duke of Tuscany, who had been raised in childhood by a humble grocer. Boccaccio and Fiametta are in love, but unable to pursue their romance since Boccaccio is lustily hated throughout Florence for his novels ridiculing many of its citizens. When Pietro appears in Florence, and spends an evening carousing with students, he is mistaken for Boccaccio and is soundly beaten. On the occasion of Pietro's betrothal to Fiametta, Boccaccio presents a play in which he lampoons Pietro's many amatory escapades and points up the folly of two people marrying who do not love each other. The play convinces Pietro to give up Fiametta to Boccaccio, and to find consolation in an affair with a cooper's wife.

These are some of the highlights of Suppé's tuneful score: Fiametta's lyrical song, *"Hab' ich nur deine Liebe"*; the waltz, *"Wonnevolle Kunde"*; a first-act instrumental march; a rousing students' drinking song; the tuneful second-act ditty, *"Immerzu undici, dodici, tredici"*; and the duet, *"Florenz hat schoene Frauen."*

On January 2, 1931, the Metropolitan Opera revived this operetta for its glamorous prima donna, Maria Jeritza; it was the first occasion upon which this company produced a Suppé operetta. For this presentation, the spoken dialogue was replaced by recitatives; also a soaring waltz melody was concocted from two melodies of two other Suppé operettas (*Donna Juanita* and *Pique Dame*) to provide Mme Jeritza with a big third-act number.

(The) Bohemian Girl by Michael Balfe.

Romantic opera in three acts with text by Alfred Bunn, based on a ballet-pantomime, *The Gypsy,* scenario by Jules Henri Vernoy de Saint Georges. First performance: Drury Lane, London, November 27, 1843. First American performance: Park Theater, New York, November 25, 1844.

Balfe wrote about thirty operas in Italian, French, and English styles. Only one of these is still remembered: *The Bohemian Girl,* an outstanding example of romantic English opera, and the most successful English opera given in the first half of the nineteenth century.

The action takes place in Pressburg, Hungary, in the eighteenth century. Arline, daughter of Count Arnheim, has been kidnapped by gypsies, who raise her as one of their own. Now a woman, Arline is falsely accused of having stolen a medallion from the Count's palace and is imprisoned. When she comes before the Count to plead for mercy, by means of a scar on her arm he recognizes her as his long-lost daughter. The Count surrounds her with luxury, but Arline cannot forget her gypsy friends; she pines for Thaddeus, a young Polish exile, who as a gypsy had helped to raise her. But when the discovery is made that Thaddeus is really a Polish nobleman, the Count is happy to accept him as a match for Arline. With Thaddeus as her husband, Arline is ready and able to adjust herself to her new environment.

While in the tradition of grand opera, *The Bohemian Girl* is so rich with delightful, easily assimilable tunes that it is justly classified as a light opera. The most famous of these tunes is, to be sure, "I Dream'd That I Dwelt in Marble Halls," the one number above all others that helped keep the names of the opera and the composer alive to the present day. The melody is sung by Arline while she is still a gypsy, as she recounts to Thaddeus a dream in which she saw wondrous marble halls as the setting of her childhood. "The Heart Bowed Down," in which the Count recalls his long lost daughter while gazing at her picture, and Thaddeus' third-act song to Arline, "Then You'll Remember Me," are also celebrated.

The outpouring of wonderful lyricism made *The Bohemian Girl* an immediate favorite not only in London but also (in foreign translations) in France, Italy, and Germany. When *The Bohemian Girl* was revived in Paris in December, 1869, such was its success that it brought Balfe two high honors: Napoleon III made him a Chevalier of the Legion of Honor and the Regent of Spain made him Commander of the Order of Carlos III.

Bruder Straubinger [*Traveling Artisan*] by Edmund Eysler.

Operetta in three acts with text by M. West and J. Schnitzer. First performance: Vienna, January 20, 1903.

Eysler was one of Vienna's most prolific operetta composers. He created over sixty works for the stage. *Bruder Straubinger* was his first successful operetta, is his best operetta and the one work for which he is remembered today in Germanic countries, where it has enjoyed many revivals.

A little Rhine town in the eighteenth century is festive because Landgrave Philipp is about to come home from the wars. Schwudler, a traveling showman, is performing at the town gate. Among the many visitors pouring into the town for the celebration is Straubinger, a gardener, come to find a job on the Landgrave's estate. Having traveled a goodly distance, he is weary, and has fallen asleep at the town gate. An army deserter, Boniface, robs him of his identification papers, then utilizes them to get the gardener's job sought by Straubinger. Bereft of his identification papers, Straubinger seeks employment in a local museum supervised by Schwudler. When the wily Schwudler discovers that Straubinger has an army pass left him by a grandfather, he decides to capitalize on this situation. He disguises Straubinger as that old army veteran and has him appeal to the Landgrave for a pension. Young, lovely Oculi, eluding Boniface's advances, makes believe she is in love with the "old, venerable army man." As it turns out, she is really Straubinger's long-missing intended bride. When Oculi learns of the true identity of the old army man, she surprises everybody by her willingness to marry him. By now, Straubinger is reconciled to the necessity of playing the part of an old man for the remainder of his days. But his identity papers are finally recovered, and he can once again be a young man, and a young husband to Oculi.

The spine of Eysler's score is a wonderful waltz melody, *"Kuessen ist keine Suend,"* an admonition (if such be needed) that it is no sin to kiss. This melody captured the hearts of Europeans in the early twentieth century and it is still alive and vital in the repertory of café-house orchestras. Another delightful waltz is used with telling effect in the second-act finale, *"O suesse Sommernacht."* In addition, the score boasts a lilting tune for Straubinger, *"In Muenchen eine Kellnerin,"* and a lovely melody for Oculi *"Man nennt das wilde Maedchen mich."*

(La) Buona Figliuola or **La Cecchina** [*The Good Girl* or *Cecchina*] by Niccolò Piccinni.

> Opera buffa in three acts with text by Carlo Goldoni, based on Samuel Richardson's novel, *Pamela,* or *Virtue Rewarded.* First performance: Teatro delle Dame, Rome, February 6, 1760.

While this opera buffa is almost never performed today (this editor has not been able to uncover a single performance in the United States!) it is nonetheless a landmark in comic opera literature. Few eighteenth-century opera buffas were as successful as this one. After its première, it enjoyed an uninterrupted run of two years in Rome, after which it was seen throughout Europe. "In Rome," says Mrs. Julian Marshall, "it was played not only at all the principal theaters, but at the most insignificant, even that of the *burattini,* or marionettes, and all classes of people were equally delighted with it. Fashions were all *alla cecchina:* inns, shops, villas, wines—in fact, all things that could be named—were called after it." For many years, composers everywhere regarded it as a model for emulation. Paul Henry Lang has described it as a "comedy in music . . . of humorous and human qualities—here sentimental to evoke tears, there comic to rouse unbridled laughter."

To meet the specific needs and demands of opera buffa, Goldoni made many changes in Richardson's novel about the poor and humble Pamela whose virtue finally brought her the reward of becoming her master's wife. Opera buffa audiences in the eighteenth century did not look with favor on a heroine of lowly station. In the opera, therefore, she becomes the daughter of a poor teacher who turns out to be a count—a Scottish nobleman formerly exiled for revolutionary involvements. The father eventually gets a pardon from the king, and Pamela can now marry her master as a social equal.

In the opera buffa, Milord Bonfil (Mr. B.) of the Richardson novel becomes Il Marchese della Conchiglia; Miledi Duari (Lady Devers), La Marchesa Lucinda; and Pamela, La Cecchina. New characters are invented—some of them, such stock opera-buffa characters as scandal-mongering servants (Paoluccia and Sandrina) and basso buffos (Tagliaferro, a swashbuckling soldier, and Mengotto, a gardener).

In the Goldoni adaptation, Mengotto is in love with Cecchina, but knowing she is out of his reach—since her own master has designs on her —he compromises by accepting the love of the servant, Sandrina. Cecchina goes on to marry her master.

The most famous aria is that of Cecchina, *"Una povera ragazza,"* in which she explains that she is only a poor, misunderstood child. The leading buffo aria is that of Tagliaferro, *"Star trompetti."*

Of particular musical interest are the extended finales for each of the acts (a quintet for the first and second, and an octet for the third), which helped to develop and crystallize a tradition in comic-opera writing carried on with great success in Mozart's masterworks.

(Le) Cadi dupé or Der betrogene Cadi [*The Deceived Cadi*] by Christoph Willibald Gluck.

> Comic opera in one act with text by Pierre René Lemonnier. First performance: Burgtheater, Vienna, December 1761. First American per-

formance (probable): Rochester, New York, May 16, 1932 (in English).

The name of Gluck is prominent in opera history by virtue of the revolution he effected in departing from Italian clichés and traditions toward the creation of a new musical-dramatic form in operas like *Orfeo ed Euridice* and *Alceste*. But Gluck also wrote numerous operas in the more formal, and then familiar, French and Italian styles. Some of these are comic operas, of which one of the most delightful is *Le Cadi dupé*.

Zelmire, in love with Nuradin, has aroused the interest of the Cadi who wants her for himself. An elaborate ruse must be devised to discourage the Cadi from seeking out Zelmire and thus allow her to get married to Nuradin: convincing the Cadi that Zelmira is in reality the plain-looking, stammering daughter of Omar the tentmaker.

Of Gluck's score, Alfred Einstein wrote: "From many conventionalities emerge little melodic blossoms, tiny melodic piquancies, of the utmost charm. The spirit which Rousseau called 'the return to nature' is to be perceived everywhere; in the orchestra, nature's way is painted by means of figuration and tone color."

Cagliostro im Wien [*Cagliostro in Vienna*] by Johann Strauss II.

Operetta in three acts with text by F. Zell and Richard Genée. First performance: Theater-an-der-Wien, Vienna, February 27, 1875. First American performance (probable): Chicago, Illinois, 1886 (in English).

Johann Strauss's masterwork, *Die Fledermaus*, was first produced in 1874. *Cagliostro im Wien* was its immediate successor, coming less than a year later.

The principal character, Cagliostro, is an Italian wizard and imposter who, in the middle of the eighteenth century, comes to Vienna to promote the sale of love elixirs and to perpetrate various other frauds. He interests the Austrian Empress in a philosopher's stone which he claims can transform base metal into gold. When the Empress arrives at his laboratory to witness the experiment, Cagliostro is ready for her: Having acquired a good deal of gold through his sale of elixirs, he is able to change copper into gold before her very eyes. Thus Cagliostro acquires in the Empress a powerful ally in his fight against the police and his enemies. Meanwhile, Cagliostro gets involved in a plot to prevent the marriage of the Archduke Leopold and the Spanish Infanta, Marie Louise; indeed, to thwart the marriage, he even goes so far as to put the Infanta under an hypnotic spell. Secret papers involving Cagliostro in this plot fall into the Empress' hands. But the wizard works his wiles and charms upon her to elude punishment. He is permitted to leave Vienna in peace on the condition that he release the Infanta from the spell. Cagliostro's departure takes place with typical dramatics: He sails away in a balloon, above cheering Viennese crowds.

The main melody, as one might expect from a Strauss operetta, is a waltz: the "Cagliostro Waltz" (*"Koennt ich mit Ihnen fliegen durch Leben"*), sung by Blasoni, one of Cagliostro's confederates, as he dances a waltz. No less exciting a page from the score is a sensual dance tune, a czardas. These and other melodies from *Cagliostro im Wien* were adapted by Strauss himself into the *Bitte Schoen Polka*, opus 372.

Good as the principal waltz and the czardas are—and the first night audience in Vienna acclaimed both—*Cagliostro im Wien* hardly finds Johann Strauss at his best; and it was not a success. "For," explains H. E. Jacob, "*Cagliostro im Wien* needed the very finest tapestry. Moving crowds, vivandières, town-criers, soldiers, and a chorus of citizens had to be woven into the music. . . . Because Johann Strauss had not mastered this art he had to revert to German simplicity in the first act. He underwrote the mob movements and the choruses in elementary fashion with no stylistic transformation. What was gross in the subject matter remained gross in the music." Then Mr. Jacob adds: "The vulgarities of the mob that Strauss forced himself to depict do not come honestly from him. They bring him down to a lower plane. Not till the Italians appear does he come into his own. Humor, spirit, characteristic traits, emerge as soon as the proximity of Italy is apparent."

Cagliostro im Wien received a highly successful revival in Danzig on May 8, 1941. The libretto on this occasion was rewritten by Gustav Quedenfeldt, and the music adapted by Karl Tutein. In these performances, Strauss's famous concert waltz, the *Kaiserwalzer*, was effectively interpolated into the score.

(The) Caliph of Bagdad [*Le Calife de Bagdad*] by François Boieldieu.

Opéra-comique in one act with text by Claude Godard d'Aucour de Saint-Just. First performance: Opéra-Comique, Paris, September 16, 1801. First American performances: Park Theater, New York, August 27, 1827 (in French); New York, October 14, 1829 (in English).

This was the composer's fifth opera and his most successful up to that time. The vociferous expression of enthusiasm on the part of the audience attending the première completely upset Cherubini, the distinguished Italian-born composer of French operas. To Cherubini, a work so slight in structure and so light in style as *The Caliph of Bagdad* debased the high standards of French opera. When Cherubini met Boieldieu in the lobby of the theater immediately after the première, he inquired ungraciously: "Unhappy man, aren't you ashamed with such undeserved success?" Boieldieu's reply was a humble one: a request that he be allowed to study counterpoint with Cherubini. (Boieldieu actually did become Cherubini's pupil.)

In ancient Bagdad the Caliph, Isaaum, enjoys perpetrating tricks and pranks. One of his favorites is to parade around the city in disguise. In the uniform of an army officer he meets and makes love to Zeltube. The girl's mother objects to the officer and tries to get him arrested. At this point the Caliph is forced to reveal his real identity. He also discloses that he is truly in love with Zeltube and desires to marry her.

The overture is a perennial favorite of salon and pop orchestras. It begins with a stately melody for the strings. A change of tempo leads to a vivacious tune again in the strings. The music is brought to a climax, after which the mood becomes dramatic and stormy, but relieved occasionally by sensitive lyrical interludes.

Two vocal numbers are of particular appeal: *"D'une flame si belle"* and *"Depuis le jour où son courage."*

(La) Cambiale di Matrimonio [*The Marriage Contract*] by Gioacchino Rossini.

Opera buffa in one act with text by Gaetano Rossi, based on a comedy by Camillo Federici. First performance: Teatro San Moisè, Venice, November 3, 1810. First American performance: New York, October 14, 1829 (in English).

Beyond its interest as a frothy, vivacious little comic opera, *La Cambiale di Matrimonio* is historically significant as the first of Rossini's operas to be performed. The composer had recently finished his musical training at the Liceo Musicale in Bologna when, in the fall of 1810, he found an opportunity to make his debut as opera composer. Morandi, a friend of the Rossini family, was employed at the San Moisè Theater in Venice, which was planning to present an evening of one-act operas. The composer of one of these operas failed to complete his assignment, and Morandi suggested to Cavalli, director of the opera company, that he gamble on the unknown and inexperienced Rossini for a substitute work. Cavalli turned over to the young man the libretto of *La Cambiale di Matrimonio* which Rossini, with what was soon to become his characteristic dispatch and facility, finished setting within a couple of days. For his overture he borrowed an orchestral item he had previously written as a student at the Liceo. The opera was successful, although perhaps more for the excellent performance than for Rossini's music.

The text concerns the efforts of a Mr. Slook, a rich Canadian business man, to work out a business deal with his English agent, Tobias Mill, whereby he might win Mill's favor and thus be allowed to marry his daughter. The deal falls through when Mill's daughter is captured by another man, with whom she has fallen in love.

Francis Toye notes that Rossini's score is outstanding for "gaiety and high spirits," and maintains that it is doubtful if any earlier comic opera except for Mozart's *The Abduction from the Seraglio* and Cimarosa's *Il Matrimonio segreto* had been characterized by "such sparkle, such a wholly irresponsible sense of fun."

The overture, though slight in content, is pleasant to listen to and uses for one of its more charming subjects the melody of *"Dunque io son, tu non m'inganni"* which was to appear in the same composer's masterwork, *The Barber of Seville,* written a few years later. Other highlights, according to Toye, include "two attractive arias, a first-class trio with musical subjects and characters admirably contrasted, and a duel scene which for comic martial swagger could not well be bettered."

The first performance of *La Cambiale di Matrimonio* outside Italy took place in Barcelona, Spain, on April 26, 1819. When given in London on May 11, 1819, and in New York, on October 14, 1829, the opera was heard in an English translation by J. J. Dibdin. A new English translation was provided when *La Cambiale di Matrimonio* was given one of its rare New York revivals on February 27, 1961, in a performance by the Little Orchestra Society under Thomas Scherman. On this last occasion, Ross Parmenter reported in the *New York Times:* "Even at so youthful an age, Rossini's style was already fully formed. It is a most attractive work, with one lively number after another."

The first complete recording of *La Cambiale di Matrimonio* was released in 1961 by Mercury Records.

(Il) Campanello di notte [*The Night Bell*] by Gaetano Donizetti.
Opera buffa in one act with libretto by the composer based on a French
vaudeville by L. L. Brunswick, M. B. Troin, and V. Lhérie, *La Sonnette
de noir*. First performance: Teatro Nuevo, Naples, June 1, 1836. First
American performance (probable): Lyceum Theater, New York, May
7, 1917 (in English).

Donizetti wrote this opera in an attempt to save an opera company from
financial ruin. At the time he was one of Italy's most successful and
prolific composers for the stage, having completed over fifty operas, including such favorites as *Lucia di Lammermoor*, *Lucrezia Borgia*, and
Anna Bolena. When the Teatro Nuevo in Naples was faced with imminent collapse, its director approached Donizetti for a light, popular
work which might win public favor and thus help rehabilitate the depleted fortunes of the company. Donizetti complied with a one-act opera
buffa which he described as "a gay melodrama," completing the assignment in a single week. His opera proved so successful that the revenue
at the box office helped put the company back on a solid footing. The
opera was also heard soon afterward in France, Russia, Spain, and
Belgium. The United States, apparently, had to wait until 1917 to hear
it. On that occasion, the Society of American Singers produced it in
New York in an English translation; David Bispham was featured in the
leading male role.

Il Campanello di notte is a farce in the style of *La Serva padrona* and
Il Matrimonio segreto. In Naples, Don Annibale Pistacchio is an elderly
apothecary who marries young and lovely Serafina. He gives voice to his
delight in being married to one so desirable (*"Bella cosa, amici cari"*).
The dashing, young Neapolitan, Enrico, long in love with Serafina, seeks
to avenge himself on his successful rival. On Annibale's wedding night,
Enrico disturbs the newly married couple by several times ringing their
doorbell which (as local law demands) must be answered personally by
the apothecary. The first time, Enrico comes in the guise of a Frenchman
seeking spirits with which to settle a disturbed stomach. Then he appears
as a singer who had just lost his voice and must have soothing throat
lozenges (*"Ho una bella, un' infedele"*). A third time he is a senile old
fellow wanting pills for an ailing wife (*"La povera Anastasia"*). Thus Annibale is unable to enjoy the bliss of his wedding night. And, to add

more salt to his fresh wounds, at dawn he is summoned from home to travel by coach to Rome to help settle a will!

(**La**) **Cecchina** by Niccolò Piccinni. *See* (*La*) *Buona Figliuola.*

(**La**) **Cenerentola** or **La Bontà in Trionfo** [*Cinderella,* or *The Triumph of Goodness*] by Gioacchino Rossini.

> Opera buffa in two acts with text by Jacopo Ferretti based on a libretto by Charles Guillaume Étienne. First performance: Teatro Valle, Rome, January 25, 1817. First American performances: Park Theater, New York, June 27, 1826 (in Italian); New York, January 24, 1831 (in English).

Ferretti's libretto for Rossini follows that of Étienne so closely that it almost seems to be its Italian translation. But both of these versions travel far afield from the original fairy tale of Perrault on which they were based. All fairy elements are eliminated. The fairy godmother is replaced by Alidoro, a genial philosopher employed by the Prince. The personality of Cinderella herself is considerably revamped, and so are many of the basic elements in the fairy story. In the Rossini opera, Cinderella is a young lady well informed about fashions in Paris and Vienna. She is a helpless victim of abuses by her two stepsisters, Clorinda and Thisbe, and by her stepfather, Don Magnifico. Alidoro, a philosopher in the Prince's court, comes to Cinderella's home disguised as a beggar. The two cruel sisters drive him away. But Cinderella, touched by his poverty, foregoes her own meal to feed him. Alidoro is struck by Cinderella's beauty as well as her generosity. Meanwhile, the Prince of Salerno, Don Ramiro, is compelled by his father to marry on a specific day; but the Prince is insistent upon marrying only a girl who loves him for himself alone, and not for his high station. Alidoro arranges for Cinderella to attend a ball in the Prince's palace; but before this happens, Cinderella met the Prince when he came to her house disguised as a valet. At the ball, Cinderella still believes the Prince to be a valet and gives him one of her two bracelets as a token of her interest. During the festivities, the real valet passes himself off as the Prince, and in this guise tries to make love to Cinderella, who rejects him emphatically. Thus the real Prince becomes finally convinced that Cinderella loves him, not his royal station.

Several days after the ball, the Prince seeks shelter from a storm at Cinderella's home. He identifies Cinderella by matching the bracelet she had given him at the ball with the one she is wearing, and announces that she is the one he has chosen to be his bride. Only because Cinderella insists upon it are Don Magnifico and her two cruel stepsisters forgiven for having mistreated Cinderella so long.

Among Rossini's comic operas, *La Cenerentola* is second only to *The Barber of Seville* in vivacity, melodic charm, and lightness of touch. He wrote this score in less than a month, borrowing an overture he had used earlier for *La Gazzetta*. Rossini was confident that his new opera would be outstandingly successful—and for a practical reason. He knew that mezzo-sopranos everywhere would go to any length to win for themselves the title role.

The opera opens with two exceptionally fine lyric episodes. As the curtain rises, Cinderella tells the tale of a king weary of single blessedness (*"Una volta c'era un re"*), after which Don Magnifico arrives in a huff, having been aroused from his deep sleep by outlandish noises (*"Miei rampolli"*). Later significant arias include that of Don Magnifico in the second act, *"Sia qualunque delle figlie";* Cinderella's coloratura aria, *"Non più mesta accato al fuoco";* and the closing air of Cinderella in which she beseeches the Prince to forgive both her stepsisters and her father, (*"Ah prence, Io cado ai vostri piè"*).

When *La Cenerentola* was first heard in the United States in 1826, it was given by the Manuel Garcia Company, with the renowned Mme (Maria) Malibran in the title role. In London, in 1830, the fairy elements of the original tale were restored to the text. After 1860, the opera disappeared for several decades from the boards, largely because good mezzo-sopranos capable of singing the title role were not available. A remarkable revival of the opera took place in London in 1934, with Conchita Supervia as Cinderella, and after that the role was assumed by many notable singers including Jennie Tourel and Giulietta Simoniato. In this country, *La Cenerentola* was successfully revived by the New York City Opera Company on March 26, 1953.

(The) **Chimes of Normandy** [*Les Cloches de Corneville*] by Jean-Robert Planquette.

Operetta in three acts with text by Clairville and Charles Gabet. First performance: Théâtre des Folies-Dramatiques, Paris, April 19, 1877.

First American performances: New York, October 22, 1877 (in English); New York, May 13, 1878 (in French); New York, October 1, 1881 (in German).

This is Planquette's masterpiece. In his lifetime it made the rounds of the world capitals, and was acclaimed everywhere; since his death it is the only one of his operettas to be consistently revived.

The operetta provides an evocative picture of peasant life in the Normandy region of France during the reign of Louis XV. Henri, Marquis of Villeroi, returns to Corneville after a long absence and is welcomed by village festivities. Germaine, ward of the miser Gaspard, decides to find a job in the château of the Marquis. Her aim is to shake off the miser's tyrannical rule and at the same time avoid marrying the man Gaspard had selected for her, the local sheriff. For Germaine is in love with Grenicheux, a young fisherman who had once saved her life. After the return of the Marquis to his château, the place becomes the scene of an elaborate fête. But the villagers cannot forget that during their master's absence the château had been suspected of being haunted. Actually, during that time, the château had been used by the miser to hide his gold; and the sudden appearance of the Marquis so disturbs Gaspard that he loses his mind. While employed in the château, Germaine is pursued by the Marquis himself, but she resists him with the explanation that as a servant girl she is too humble for his attentions. When Gaspard recovers his sanity, he reveals that Germaine is no servant girl at all, but the rightful heiress to his gold. Germaine by this time is deeply in love with the Marquis and is happy to find she can accept him as an equal. Grenicheux—Germaine's one-time sweetheart—has by now become interested in a village girl, Serpolette.

In addition to its expressive lyricism, Planquette's score is distinguished for its subtle characterizations. The personalities of Germaine and the servant girl, Serpolette, are vividly delineated in the music each sings. Germaine's most famous song (probably the most famous in the entire opera) is the so-called "song of the bells" with chorus, "*Nous avons, hélas, perdu d'excellence maîtres.*" Her aria in the same act, "*Ne parlez pas de mon courage,*" is hardly less arresting. Serpolette's best airs include her first act rondeau, "*Dans ma mystérieuse histoire*" and her saucy cider song, "*La Pomme est un fruit plein de sève.*"

Other appealing numbers include the Marquis' waltz-rondo, "*Même sans consulter mon coeur*" and Gaspard's nostalgic ballad of the good old days, "*Enfin nous voilà transporte.*" The operetta ends with the same bell refrain (*"Digue, digue don"*) first heard within Germaine's second-act "song of the bells."

(A) Chinese Honeymoon by Howard Talbot.

> Operetta in two acts with text and lyrics by George Dance. First performance: London, 1899. First American performance: Casino Theater, New York, June 2, 1902.

Howard Talbot was born in America (Yonkers, New York), but taken to England when he was still a child. There he received his education and went on to become a successful conductor in London theaters and a composer of several highly successful English musical productions. His greatest success was *A Chinese Honeymoon.*

This is more of a vaudeville show than an operetta, its various acts, routines, and breath-taking scenes being strung together on the slightest thread of a plot. The plot follows the adventures of Fi-Fi, an English slavey, condemned to live in China. But the emphasis of the production was not on story or characters, but on eye-filling scenes, costumes, and production numbers. On both sides of the Atlantic Ocean, *A Chinese Honeymoon* was a spectacular production, and in New York, as in London, it proved to be a huge box office success.

To the principal character of Fi-Fi, Talbot assigned two delightful cockney songs which regularly stopped the show: "I Want to Be a Loidy" and "The Twiddley Bits." The theme song, "Tell Me, Pretty Maiden" (not to be confused with the far more popular song of the same name in *Florodora*), and "The à la Girl" were other attractive numbers. In New York, some local tunes were interpolated. One of these became a decided hit in 1902: "Mister Dooley," lyrics by William Jerome and music by Jean Schwartz.

(The) Chocolate Soldier [*Der tapfere Soldat*] by Oscar Straus.

> Operetta in three acts with text by Rudolf Bernauer and Leopold Jacobson, based on George Bernard Shaw's comedy, *Arms and the Man.* First performance: Theater-an-der-Wien, Vienna, November 14, 1908. First American performance: Lyric Theater, New York, September 13, 1909.

A half century before Lerner and Loewe tapped a famous Bernard Shaw comedy (*Pygmalion*) for a musical play which was destined to become one of the triumphs of the New York stage (*My Fair Lady*), another Shavian stage comedy was transformed into an operetta classic. Leopold Jacobson—Straus's librettist for *A Waltz Dream*—was the one who first thought up the idea of making *Arms and the Man* into an operetta. The delicate negotiations with Shaw were entrusted to Siegfried Trebitsch, who had translated some of Shaw's plays into German. At first, Shaw refused to consider the idea, insisting that nobody remembered librettists and also that if a musical version of his play were to become highly successful, his own play would be doomed to oblivion. "Who is still interested in Sardou's *Tosca* since Puccini, or Verga's *Cavalleria Rusticana* since Mascagni?" Shaw asked. But Trebitsch refused to admit defeat and continued to argue with Shaw until he won his point. Shaw finally consented, provided several conditions were met: The plot could be used, but none of the dialogue; all advertising posters and announcements were to make it clear that the operetta was an "unauthorized parody of Mr. Bernard Shaw's play, *Arms and the Man*"; and Shaw would accept no payment, since he wanted to have no legal part in the whole disreputable business.

The Chocolate Soldier, as Shaw's play was finally renamed for the musical stage, eventually became one of the supreme triumphs of the Viennese musical theater. It would be impossible to compute the number of performances it has received in all parts of the civilized world, even the number of companies that have performed it. Yet, strange to say, it started out in life limping. Vienna was at first cool to it because of the combustible situation then prevailing in the Balkans, and thus was unsympathetic to an operetta with a Balkan setting. But, somehow, after an unimpressive première before an apathetic audience, the operetta began to command interest as the weeks passed. Nobody knew just why, but it finally caught on, sold out performance after performance, and went on to achieve a sensational run in Vienna.

In New York, Fred C. Whitney bought the play before the Vienna opening, and had Stanislaus Stange adapt it for the American stage. With his enthusiasm considerably dampened by Vienna's initial indifference, he tried to get out of the contract. Unable to do so, he tried out the show in Philadelphia where, much to his amazement, it was a triumph. With a cast including Ida Brooks, J. E. Gardner, and William Pruette, *The Chocolate Soldier* had a prosperous New York run of almost three hundred performances. It was subsequently given thousands of performances by ten American touring companies; it was successfully revived in New York in 1921 and 1930. In London, its initial run at the Lyric Theater, begun on September 9, 1910, lasted five hundred performances. *The Chocolate Soldier* also became a successful motion picture in 1941, starring Risë Stevens and Nelson Eddy. During the negotiations between MGM and Bernard Shaw for clearance rights for the screen production, a colloquy took place, which has since been frequently quoted. When Shaw made financial demands Mayer considered excessive, Mayer remarked: "We are men of good will, Mr. Shaw. Surely we can come to an agreement." "Never," insisted Shaw, "because you, Mr. Mayer, are an idealist and I am a business man." Incidentally, it brought Shaw no little anguish to see the operetta become a world triumph and to realize how great a fortune he had lost by waiving his rights to royalties. But on one count he could rest content. The fame of the operetta did not in any way decrease the fame or popularity of his play *Arms and the Man*. When Trebitsch pointed this out to Shaw, the venerable playwright lifted an eyebrow and exclaimed haughtily: "Of course not! Do you put me in the same class as Sardou or Verga?"

The setting of the operetta is the Balkans in 1885. Bulgaria is at war with Serbia. Bumerli is a Serbian officer nicknamed "the Chocolate Soldier" because of his sweet tooth. Fleeing from the enemy, he takes refuge in the home of Colonel Casimir Popoff of the Bulgarian army. Three women of the household fall victim to his charms: Nadina, the Colonel's daughter; her mother; and Mascha. They contrive to effect Bumerli's escape by disguising him in Colonel Popoff's coat, in the pocket of which each of the women slips a photograph of herself. When the Colonel comes home from the war, he is accompanied by Nadina's fiancé, the conceited Alexius. Before long, to the embarrassment of the three women the Colonel asks for his coat. Fortunately, just then Bumerli slips back into the house, bringing the coat with him. Once the women get their hands on it, they try to retrieve their respective photographs, only to have each come up with the picture of one of the others. After all these minor complications are straightened out, Nadina and Bumerli are united as lovers, and Alexius consoles himself with Mascha.

One song, above all others, stands out prominently: Nadina's waltz, "*Komm, komm, Held meiner Traeume*," better known to the English-speaking world as "My Hero." "This one song," once said Franz Lehár, "has done more than hundreds of others to make operetta what it is today, a work of art." Straus himself once revealed: "I liked the melody as it came to me in a single flash, but never in my wildest dreams did I suspect it was destined for the popularity it has been lucky enough to achieve. Had I known that, you can be quite sure I should never have used it at the very beginning of the first act." There is hardly a concert soprano anywhere—including such glamorous prima donnas as Maria Jeritza and Grace Moore—who has not sung it publicly. The distinguished contemporary modernist, Arnold Schoenberg, thought its construction so perfect he sometimes had his pupils analyze its structure.

Other musical delights include the march of the Bulgarian soldiers, a travesty on military pomp and circumstance; the waltzes, *"Tiralala, tiralala"* and *"Pardon, pardon";* and Nadina's charming second-act letter song.

Cinderella by Gioacchino Rossini. *See (La) Cenerentola.*

(The) Circus Princess [*Die Zirkusprinzessin*] by Emmerich Kálmán.

Operetta in three acts with text by Julius Brammer and Alfred Gruenwald. First performance: Vienna, March 26, 1926. First American performance: Winter Garden, New York, April 25, 1927.

This popular Kálmán operetta opens in St. Petersburg where the Stanislawski Circus is giving performances. One of its attractions is a masked Mr. X, who performs equestrian daredevil tricks. Prince Sergius has brought the lovely widow, Fedora, to see the show. There he proposes to her and is rudely rebuffed. To avenge himself for this indignity, the Prince prevails on Mr. X of the circus to pose as the nobleman, Prince Korosoff, at a supper party. As he had planned and hoped, Prince Sergius sees Fedora become attracted to the fake nobleman. The two fall in love, and arrange to get married. During the wedding festivities, the circus colleagues of Mr. X come to congratulate their friend and co-worker; only then does Fedora discover who her future husband really is. She breaks away in horror, refuses to have any further communication with him, and takes off for Vienna. There she enjoys the company of Prince Sergius, who still harbors the hope of marrying her. Upon learning that the Russian circus has come to the Austrian capital, Fedora insists upon attending a performance. There she meets Mr. X again, realizes she really is in love with him and that, despite his background, she still wants to marry him. A new marriage date for Fedora and Mr. X is set, after the latter has given his beloved a promise that he will give up his career in the circus.

When *The Circus Princess* was given on Broadway in 1927 (adaptation by Harry B. Smith, and a cast including Desirée Tabor and Guy Robertson), the "circus" in the title was strongly accentuated through the introduction of aerialists, equestrians, and the clown Poodles Hanneford in some elaborate and stunning circus sequences.

Both in Vienna and New York, one musical number was especially popular: the passionate song *"Zwei Maerchenaugen"* (in America, "Dear Eyes That Haunt Me"). There are two other additional outstanding selections in the Kálmán score, both of them Viennese waltzes: *"Leise schwebt das Glueck vorueber"* and *"Im Boudoir der schoensten Frau."*

(The) **Clandestine,** or **Secret, Marriage,** by Domenico Cimarosa. *See (Il) Matrimonio Segreto.*

(Les) **Cloches de Corneville** by Jean-Robert Planquette. *See (The) Chimes of Normandy.*

(Le) **Comte Ory** [*Count Ory*] by Gioacchino Rossini.

> Opera buffa in two acts with text by Eugène Scribe and C. G. Delestre-Poirson, based on a one-act vaudeville which, in turn, came from a ballad by Picardy. First performance: Opéra-Comique, Paris, August 20, 1828. First American performance: New York, August 21, 1831.

This was one of two operas that Rossini wrote for Paris, and the next to the last of his operatic creations; his last stage work was *William Tell*. *Le Comte Ory* proved inordinately popular in France. In the half century following its highly successful première it received almost five hundred performances in Paris alone. In that time, it had also been heard and acclaimed in New York, and London, coming to the former city in 1831, and to the latter on June 20, 1849. For a long time after 1880, *Le Comte Ory* went into discard until 1952 when Vittorio Gui, a passionate Rossini fan, revived it for the 15th Maggio Musicale in Florence, Italy, on May

10. Two years later, it was once again successfully revived, this time by the Glyndebourne Opera Company at the Edinburgh Festival in Scotland, on August 23, 1954. On the latter occasion, D. Shawe-Taylor reported: "If for nothing else, the current festival will be remembered for its revival of Rossini's neglected masterpiece."

The long neglect of *Le Comte Ory* after 1880 was due mainly to its libretto which was confused, obscure, naïve and trite. In early thirteenth-century Touraine, Count Ory, a middle-aged Don Juan, stops at nothing to gain his nefarious ends with women. In his efforts to seduce the lovely Countess Adele, he appears in various disguises. In the first act—where presumably the Count is off with the Crusades—he poses as a hermit who brings people's wishes to realization. When his page, Isolier, and Countess Adele visit him at his hut with their respective problems, they discover that the hermit is none other than Count Ory himself. In the second act, he and his followers appear at Adele's castle disguised as nuns. When they get drunk, they betray their true identities. Now Isolier and Adele reveal that they are in love with each other, and the Count remains permanently frustrated.

If the plot is silly, the episodes beyond credibility, and the denouements of the Count's escapades exceedingly lame, Rossini's music, on the other hand, finds him at the height of his creative powers. D. Shawe Taylor says that in this opera buffa, the composer is "not only . . . at his best, but virtually a new Rossini, writing for the more cultivated French taste with the finesse and delicacy not to be found in his Italian operas." Hector Berlioz—not a particular Rossini admirer—once said that *Le Comte Ory* had enough good music in it for three operas.

The following are some of the best musical episodes: the duet of Isolier and the Count, *"Une dame de haut parage"*; Adele's aria, *"En proie à la tristesse"*; the duet of Adele and the Count, *"Ah, respect, Madame"*; the Count's air, *"Dans ce lieu solitaire"*; the drinking song, *"Buvons, buvons, soudain"*; and the trio, *"À la faveur de cette nuit obscure."*

Conversation Piece by Noël Coward.

Operetta in three acts with text, lyrics, and music by Noël Coward. First performance: His Majesty's Theater, London, February 16, 1934. First American performance: 44th Street Theater, New York, October 23, 1934.

One of Noël Coward's best loved songs, "I'll Follow My Secret Heart," comes from this operetta. The writing of this celebrated number has had a curious history. Coward was working on the score of *Conversation Piece* at his home in Kent, England, when he came to a dead-end because he was unable to come up with a tune suitable for the principal waltz. For hours he sat at the piano, but no ideas came. Thus stymied for about ten days, he became convinced that his creative well—as far as music went—had run dry. He decided to postpone the completion of his operetta for another half year. One evening, just as he was about to relay the decision of the delay to his producer (Charles Cochran) and star (Yvonne Printemps), he sought consolation in several whiskeys. Each drink plunged him into an ever deeper depression. Deciding to go to sleep, he went to the piano to turn out the light there. Suddenly and mechanically he sat down at the keyboard and played the entire song "I'll Follow My Secret Heart" from beginning to end and without hesitation; to add further mystery to this creative act is the fact that he played the tune in the key of G-flat, a key he never before had employed in working out his compositions.

"I'll Follow My Secret Heart" became the *tour de force* of the operetta, one of several reasons why *Conversation Piece* became so popular. Another reason was the star, Yvonne Printemps, for whom the song was written and who introduced it so excitingly. Coward created a second important song for Miss Printemps, "Nevermore," and a third significant number is a "period quartet" entitled "Regency Rakes."

Described by its author as a "romantic comedy with music," *Conversation Piece* is an old-fashioned type of operetta—sentimental, nostalgic, glamorous. The action takes place in 1811. To Brighton, come Paul (enacted by Noël Coward) and his ward, Melanie (the role assumed by Yvonne Printemps). A duke by birth but an adventurer by circumstances, Paul had discovered Melanie in a Parisian café-chantant, taken her under his wing, invented for her an aristocratic background, and coached her in the ways of nobility. By the time they arrive in Brighton, they are very much in love, but Paul's stern parents refuse to consider their marriage. To help the romance on, Paul prevails on his friend, Lady Julia Charteris, to give a grand ball. But there Melanie shocks the distinguished guests by extending a warm welcome to two ladies of the town. Paul's friends and relatives leave the ball in a huff, a development that creates a violent altercation between himself and Melanie. They separate, refusing to have any further contact with each other. But when Paul hears that Melanie is about to embark on a long voyage, he rushes to her apartment. There he finds only emptiness. Convinced that he has lost his beloved for good, he looks out of the window disconsolately. Suddenly Melanie appears from the shadows. Her supposed departure had been only a ruse contrived to bring Paul back to her. The operetta thus ends on the exultant, sentimental chord of a passionate reconciliation.

Così fan tutte [*Women Are Like That*] by Wolfgang Amadeus Mozart.

Opera buffa in two acts with text by Lorenzo da Ponte. First performance: Burgtheater, Vienna, January 26, 1790. First American performance (probable): Metropolitan Opera, New York, March 24, 1922.

This is the last of three great Mozart operas in Italian with texts by Da Ponte, all with comic overtones. Of the three masterworks, this one is the lightest in mood, gayest in feeling, and most easily assimilable. The other two are among the greatest operas ever written—*The Marriage of Figaro* (which see) and *Don Giovanni* (which because of its more serious intent and greater artistic scope, does not come in for discussion within a book on the lighter musical theater). *Così fan tutte*, while being a crowning masterpiece in its own right, is consistently light theater, both in text and music.

Although the text is based on a series of impossible situations and the two leading female characters are utterly unbelievable in their volatile irresponsibility, Mozart was stimulated to write one of his most inspired scores. The music is an endless reservoir of wonderful lyricism; it is a fount of charm and grace; it is filled with the most subtle musical characterizations and the most deft artistic touches.

Undoubtedly, Da Ponte intended his play to be a merry satire on woman's infidelity, but all he succeeded in writing was a slight little intrigue utilizing the all too familiar device of mistaken identity. In a café, in eighteenth-century Naples, two soldiers, Ferrando and Guglielmo, express the conviction that their respective sweethearts, the sisters Dorabella and Fiordiligi, would be faithful to them, come what may. Don Alfonso, an elderly bachelor, is skeptical, since it is his belief that there is not a woman alive who is not fickle. He wagers with the two soldiers that their sweethearts would succumb to the attractions of two presentable men, if the opportunity arose. The two soldiers take the bet eagerly, convinced of a happy resolution.

In the garden of their villa, Dorabella and Fiordiligi reveal how deeply they love their respective men (*"Ah guarda, sorella"*). Suddenly, Don Alfonso arrives with a carefully prepared plot to test the real moral fiber of these women. He informs them that Ferrando and Guglielmo are about to rejoin their troops. These two soldiers soon appear to bid their sweethearts a most tender farewell (*"Al fato dan legge"*). After the soldiers leave, Despina, the maid, describes the trials and tribulations of a humble servant's life (*"Che vita maledetta"*). When Dorabella gives voice to her own sad fate of so suddenly losing her beloved—in a brilliant mock-heroic aria, *"Smanie implacabili"*—Despina fails to respond sympathetically to her woes, since to Despina's mind no man can be trusted (*"In uomini, in soldati"*). At this moment, Ferrando and Guglielmo make an entrance disguised as Albanian noblemen. They proceed to woo Dorabella and Fiordiligi most ardently. The women resist their advances. Fiordiligi protests her faithfulness to Guglielmo in no uncertain terms (*"Come scoglio"*). The soldiers are beside themselves with delight, convinced that their sweethearts have remained true to them. Indeed, Fernando lapses into a sentimental mood over the girl he loves (*"Un' aura amorosa"*). But the test must still continue. After the two women speak once more of their deep love for their men and of how they miss them (*"Ah! che tutta in un momento"*), Ferrando and Guglielmo reappear, still in Albanian disguise. They inform the women that, because of frustrated love, they have taken poison; even now they are beginning to suffer the pangs of death. A "doctor" is summoned—he is none other than Despina in disguise, recruited for this purpose by Don Alfonso. Through various incantations (*"Questo e quel pezzo"*), and the aid of a magnet, Despina helps bring the "stricken" men from the shadows of death. Restored to health, they can now pursue their love suits even more passionately than before. Despina tries to convince her mistresses that a little harmless flirtation is no shame, and she goes to great length to describe the art of love (*"Una donna a quindici anni"*). Before long, the two women come to the conclusion that, with their men away, a flirtation with the Albanians might prove diverting. Upon the reappearance of the Albanians, the two men serenade their women (*"Secondate, aurette amiche"*). The two couples pair off. Guglielmo gives voice to words of passion to a sympathetic Dorabella (*"Il core vi dono"*). But Ferrando is less successful with Fiordiligi, a fact that causes him no little anguish (*"Ah! io veggio quell'anima bella"*). Suddenly Fiordiligi confesses that she is not altogether unmoved by Ferrando's protestations of love (*"Per pietà, ben mio, perdona"*). When Ferrando explains he is ready to destroy himself if Fiordiligi remains indifferent to him, she is ready to succumb.

The two love affairs now progress so swiftly that marriage is contemplated. Despina appears in the guise of a notary. She has hardly been able to complete the reading of the marriage contract when a roll of drums announces the return of the troops to Naples. In the ensuing confusion, the "Albanians" disappear, and Ferrando and Guglielmo arrive in their soldiers' uniforms. They feign surprise that their sweethearts suddenly appear so distant to them, and when they see the marriage contracts they grow violent with rage. But in the end both men confess that they are, indeed, the Albanians. The sisters, humiliated at this discovery, swear to love their men faithfully and permanently. They insist that it is Don Alfonso who is the real villain, but Don Alfonso benignly encourages the lovers to profit from their experience, philosophizing that what has happened has been for the best for all involved.

Surely there is not much here to send a great composer's imagination winging, not much that had not been used many times before in opera buffas. Yet Mozart was inspired by this nonsense to produce a score remarkable not only for its melodic beauty and profound psychological insight, but also for its very sensitive adjustment to the stage business. He is nobly lyrical when the play grows sentimental and delightfully witty when satire or burlesque are called for. The trivial, even the absurd, in the text becomes in Mozart's score, rich in tenderness and piquant in irony. Mozart's music, and that alone, transforms Da Ponte's play into operatic comedy on the highest possible level. Eric Blom wrote: "Mozart infallibly hits upon the truth of his characters—the truth of their stage existences, which is all there is to them. And he does it by means of parody that has both infinite gusto and endless sympathy in it. Laughing at them, he is never cruel, and takes away the sting of the satire by making game, at the same time, of the musical mannerisms of his time, including his own."

The overture is one of Mozart's wittiest. Says Donald Francis Tovey: "Its themes, alternating their whisperings and chatterings with a hilarious kind of Hallelujah Chorus, tells us in Mozart's language that the persons of this drama are, humanly speaking, rubbish, but far too harmless for any limbo less charitable than the eternal laughter of Mozart." A few chords preface and follow a mock-sentimental subject in the oboe. After this comes a motto phrase in descending low strings, heard again within the opera (Act II, Scene 3) when all three male characters exclaim: "All women are like that!" The main body of the overture now emerges— swift, sprightly, effervescent. The main melody passes through the strings, then the woodwinds, like quicksilver.

When *Così fan tutte* was first produced in Vienna, Italian opera buffa was on its last legs, and the opera was not successful. For some years after the première, it remained something of a stepchild among Mozart's stage works, occasionally revived with various alterations in the text, but rarely admired. Actually, not until the last years of the nineteenth century, when Richard Strauss conducted it in Munich, did it begin to make an impression on opera goers.

When *Così fan tutte* entered the repertory of the Metropolitan Opera in 1922 (the cast including Florence Easton, Lucrezia Bori, and Giuseppe De Luca, with Artur Bodanzky conducting), Richard Aldrich commented: "It may be said that the opera itself enchanted the ear and the musical sensibilities of the listener. In fact, it seemed wholly delightful; the music, characteristic of Mozart . . . and, in fact, showing some delicate traits, suitable to this opera. It is not to be expected that a public used to the more sweeping and varied effects of modern music drama will at once discern all the beauty of this fragile opera buffa."

In a revival by the Metropolitan Opera in 1951–52, *Così fan tutte* was given in English, the translation having been done by Ruth and Thomas Martin. For this production, the distinguished Broadway actor, Alfred Lunt, was recruited as stage director.

In passing, it is interesting to note the many varieties of translations given to the Italian title of *Così fan tutte*. In 1922, the Metropolitan Opera called it *So Do They All*, and in 1951–52, *Women Are Like That*. In France, the translations include the French equivalents of *The Chinese Laborer* and *Love's Labor Lost;* in Germany, the German equivalent of *Who Won the Bet?* and *The Girls' Revenge;* and in Denmark, the Danish equivalent of *The Flight from the Convent*.

Count Ory by Gioacchino Rossini. *See '(Le) Comte Ory.*

(The) Count of Luxembourg [*Der Graf von Luxemburg*] by Franz Lehár.

> Operetta in two acts with text by A. M. Willner and Robert Bodanzky. First performance: Vienna, November 12, 1909. American première: Amsterdam Theater, New York, September 16, 1912.

Although Lehár himself is believed to have regarded the music of *The Count of Luxembourg* with a healthy measure of condescension—he had dashed off the whole score in about three weeks—it is one of his best operettas. Like *The Merry Widow*—for whose world-wide popularity *The Count of Luxembourg* has proved, through the years, a formidable rival —this operetta is set in Paris at the turn of the present century. Prince Basil is in love with Angele, a singer. Since he does not want to marry a commoner, he offers to pay René, an impoverished count from Luxembourg, to marry Angele, share his title with her, and then divorce her without consummating the marriage. René and Angele have never met, nor do they know each other's identity. The Count insists that this anonymity be maintained through the marriage and divorce. Thus, when Angele and René are married, each is disguised. Before their divorce separates them, René goes to the theater, where he succumbs to the spell of the leading singer. She is Angele, but since René has not the least idea that she is his wife, he makes strenuous efforts to meet her. When they get acquainted they fall in love. Only then do they discover, to their amazement, that they are married. Angele is bitter that René should have been willing to sell himself for money. But as matters develop, the Prince cannot have Angele after all, since the Czar has ordered him to marry a real Countess. Thus René and Angele become reconciled and are now prepared to enter upon a happy marital state in earnest.

In this operetta we find one of Lahár's best loved and universally acclaimed waltzes. It is *"Bist du's lachendes Glueck,"* a duet of René and Angele, staged picturesquely with the principals descending a huge flight of stairs. Angele has a delightful waltz melody of her own in *"Lieber Freund, man greift nicht nach den Sternen."* Two other numbers are of especial appeal: an exciting mazurka (*"Unbekannt, darum nicht minder interessant"*) and an amusing little ditty (*"Maedel klein, maedel fein"*).

When the *Count of Luxembourg* first played in London (May 20, 1911), it became the first foreign stage offering to receive the patronage of King George V and the Queen. Its London run of 340 performances represented a solid success. The first New York engagement lasted only 120 performances. The book was adapted for the American stage by Glen MacDonough, with Adrian Ross and Basil Hood providing the lyrics. The cast was headed by Frank Moulan and Ann Swinburne. *The Count of Luxembourg* was revived in New York on February 17, 1930.

Countess Maritza [*Graefin Mariza*] by Emmerich Kálmán.

Operetta in three acts with text by Julius Brammer and Alfred Gruenwald. First performance: Vienna, February 28, 1924. First American performance: Shubert Theater, New York, September 18, 1926.

Kálmán had a personal gift in being able to pass flexibly from the gypsy sensuality of Hungarian folk music to the lilt and lightness of the Viennese waltz. And in none of his operettas is this gift more prominent than in *Countess Maritza*. The setting is Hungary in modern times. Count Tassilo, a former army officer—now impoverished—seeks a job with Countess Maritza under the assumed name of Torok. His aim is to save enough money to provide his sister, Lisa, with a dowery. Countess Maritza, absent from her estates for a long time, returns to celebrate her "betrothal" —actually a hoax she has devised to ward off suitors. But one of the guests at her party—Baron Koloman Zsupán—insists he is the man to whom the Countess is betrothed. Rather than create a scandal, Countess Maritza does not contradict him. As the party progresses, she ignores him to pay increasing attention to her hired hand, Torok. An intercepted letter from Torok to a friend reveals Torok's true identity to the Countess. She is convinced that he also is a fortune hunter, come to work for her only to win her confidence and love. Angrily she orders him to leave the house. When Torok, now assuming his real identity, comes to bid the Countess farewell, his aunt arrives. She is Princess Bozena Guddenstein, a woman of considerable means who has paid off all of her nephew's debts and has helped to make him financially independent. Since this change of circumstances makes it impossible for Countess Maritza to suspect Count Tassilo's designs, she confesses she is in love with him and very much wants to be his wife.

Perhaps the most popular melody Kálmán ever wrote is in this operetta: Tassilo's air, "*Komm, Zigan, komm Zigan, spiel mir was vor*," familiar in the United States as "Play Gypsies, Dance Gypsies." It begins moodily and with languor but before long relaxes in gypsy abandon. If this song is in Kálmán's familiar Hungarian gypsy idiom, others are in an identifiable Viennese style: "*Gruess mir die reizenden Frauen im schoenen Wien*," "*Einmal moecht ich wieder tanzen*," "*Sag ja, mein Lieb, sag ja*," and "*Schwesterlein, Schwesterlein*."

When first seen on Broadway, with book and lyrics by Harry B. Smith, *Countess Maritza* was presented with a remarkable cast that included Yvonne D'Arle in the title role, George Haskell, Odette Myrtil, and Walter Woolf. It became one of the leading box-office attractions of the season, with a run of 318 performances.

(The) **Country Philosopher** by Baldassare Galuppi. *See* (*Il*) *Filosofo di campagna*.

Crispino and the Fairy by Luigi and Federico Ricci. *See Crispino et la comare.*

Crispino e la comare or **Il Medico e la morte** [*Crispino and the Fairy or The Doctor and Death*] by Luigi and Federico Ricci.

> Opera buffa in three acts with text by Francesco Maria Piave, based on a comedy by S. Fabbrichesi. First performance: Teatro San Benedetto, Venice, February 28, 1850. First American performances: Academy of Music, New York, October 24, 1865 (in Italian); New York, November 13, 1882 (in English).

Each of the brothers, Luigi and Federico Ricci, was a successful composer of serious and comic opera in his own right. But their masterwork, their greatest box-office success, and the one work by which their names survive, came from a collaborative effort.

In seventeenth-century Venice, Crispino is a cobbler and his wife, Annetta, a ballad singer. They are about to be dispossessed by their landlord, Don Asdrubale, a miser who has been making advances to Annetta. In desperation, Crispino keeps hammering at shoes he cannot sell, while with no less a sense of futility, Annetta tries to get a job as a singer in a local café. Then, completely overwhelmed by despair, Crispino decides to commit suicide by drowning in a deserted well. From its depths there suddenly arises a fairy who promises to help him. First she brings him some money, then she transforms him into a celebrated doctor capable of effecting miraculous cures. Crispino now hangs up a physician's shingle outside his door, much to the amusement and derision of all his neighbors, including an apothecary. Crispino's first patient is a mason, so seriously hurt in an accident that other doctors have given up. But Crispino's medicines have magic powers; to the amazement of the townspeople, they see the stricken mason return to health. The neighbors are now more than ready to accept Crispino as a leader in the community. But with his sudden rise to high station, Crispino also acquires a temper and ugly moods. When he severely reprimands his good fairy, she retaliates with a sound blow on his arm. Suddenly both of them descend into the cavernous depths below earth, where the good fairy brings forth visions of Time and Judgment and, with them, candles representing human lives. The candle representing Crispino himself is burning low, an indication, the fairy explains, that he does not have much longer to live. That of Annetta, however, is burning brightly. Crispino falls to his knees and begs for an opportunity to see his wife and children once more. Suddenly Crispino espies them in a mirror; they are praying for him. After Crispino has recovered from a swoon, he finds himself home again, surrounded by family and friends. The good fairy has forgiven him.

The Metropolitan Opera first produced this charming opera buffa on January 18, 1919, with a cast including Frieda Hempel and Antonio Scotti. In this performance, Mme Hempel interpolated into the Ricci score the famous coloratura aria, "The Carnival of Venice" by Benedict.

Several of the more prominent and impressive vocal pages in the opera are these: the first-act cavatina, *"Io sono un po' filosofo"*; the duet of Crispino and Annetta in the first-act finale, *"Vedi, o cara, tel sacchetto"*; the duet of Crispino and the fairy in the scene by the well, *"Fermo da, che cosa fai?"*; and Annetta's beautiful song, *"Io non sono più l'Annetta."*

(The) **Crown Diamonds** by Daniel François Esprit Auber. *See* (*Les*) *Diamants de la couronne.*

(The) **Crown Prince** by Franz Lehár. *See* (*Der*) *Zarewitsch.*

(The) **Czar and the Carpenter** by Albert Lortzing. *See Zar und Zimmermann.*

(Die) **Czárdásfuerstin** [*The Gypsy Princess*] by Emerich Kálmán.

> Operetta in three acts with text by Leo Stein and Béla Janbach. First performance: Vienna, November 13, 1915. First American performance: New Amsterdam Theater, New York, September 24, 1917, under the title *The Riviera Girl.*

The heroine of this popular Kálmán operetta is Sylva Varescu, a Hungarian cabaret star making her farewell appearance in Budapest before embarking on an American tour, in the period just before World War I. Prince Edwin, of Vienna, is one of her many admirers. When the Prince's father orders him to break off with the singer and marry Countess Stasi, the young man refuses and, instead, signs a contract with the cabaret star to marry her as soon as his army service is ended. However, the singer soon learns that the contract is worthless, that the Prince's marriage to the Countess has been set by royal decree. Some months later, Sylva, posing as the wife of Count Boni, appears at a party honoring the engagement of the Prince and the Countess. Seeing her again revives the Prince's interest, and he begs Sylva to divorce the Count and marry him. Sylva then angrily reminds him of his worthless contract which, indeed, she has brought with her to the party and which she proceeds to tear into bits before his eyes. Then she flees from the palace. The Prince follows her to her hotel room to convince her that he is deeply in love with her and serious about marrying her. At last, after being reminded by a friend that long ago he, too, had once been in love with a seductive singer, the Prince's father becomes more tolerant toward his son's marrying a cabaret singer. The rejected Countess Stasi is consoled by the flattering attentions of the dashing Count Boni.

Once again, as in the even more famous Kálmán operetta, *Countess Maritza,* the score is a delightful marriage of Hungarian and Viennese styles. It is Viennese in its waltz music—in *"Machen wir's den Schwalben nach,"* *"Tausend kleine Engel singen,"* and *"Weisst du es noch?"* And it is Hungarian in the fiery czardas first heard in the overture. Two provocative little march tunes contribute some more piquant spice to this tasty musical dish: *"Ganz ohne Weiber geht die Chose nicht"* and *"Ja, so ein Teufelsweib faengt dich mit Seel' und Leib."*

This Kálmán operetta, adapted for Broadway by P. G. Wodehouse and Guy Bolton, was presented under the title of *The Riviera Girl,* with Wilda Bennett in the leading female role. Jerome Kern had two songs interpolated into the Kálmán score.

(La) Dame Blanche [*The White Lady*] by François Boieldieu.

Opéra-comique in three acts with text by Eugène Scribe, based on two romances by Sir Walter Scott, *The Monastery* and *Guy Mannering.* First performance: Opéra-Comique, Paris, December 10, 1825. First American performances: New York, August 24, 1827 (in French); New York, April 23, 1832 (in English); New York, January 15, 1864 (in German).

When first produced, *La Dame blanche* was a triumph. It came comparatively late in the composer's career, but when it finally did it proved to be the resplendent crown to all his earlier operas. In consequence of its enormous success during its baptismal year, *La Dame blanche* earned for its composer a handsome pension. Still more indicative of its popularity was the frequency with which it was parodied: in 1826 by *La Dame à la mode* and *La Dame jaune*, in 1827 by *La Dame noire*. Nor did this popularity prove fleeting. It was seen in the French capital about 1500 times in its first fifty years, 1675 times by 1914. Meanwhile it had come to other European capitals to be no less enthusiastically received; the English première took place at Covent Garden on January 8, 1827.

Boieldieu modestly tried to minimize his share in this formidable success by explaining that the main reason Parisians took so warmly to his opera was, first, because they were weary of the Rossini-type Italian opera, and, second, because they were sympathetic to Sir Walter Scott's romances. But, whether he would confess it or not, a lion's share of responsibility for the opera's triumph belonged to the remarkable score— some of it in imitation of old French chansons, some influenced by Scottish tunes, but all of it infectious in spirit, tuneful, and irresistible.

The White Lady in the title is a ghost haunting a castle in Scotland. When Julius, Laird of Avenel, falls into disrepute following the battle of Culloden, he has Gaveston, his steward, conceal all his jewels within the castle. Greedily, Gaveston tries to gain possession of the jewels legally by purchasing the castle, but his effort is thwarted when a stranger named George Brown arrives and—with the aid of Anna, Gaveston's ward—outbids Gaveston. Then George Brown reveals himself to be Julius, Laird of Avenel. Anna has a revelation of her own to make, namely, that she is the White Lady who has been "haunting" the castle. Julius and Anna, now in love, decide to get married and establish their home in this long-neglected castle.

The popular overture is made up of several melodies from the comic opera. The overture begins with a melody from the first-act finale. After that comes the lovely first-act ballad of the White Lady. A faster section brings on a robust drinking song from the first act, and with it some tunes from later acts, including a quotation of the popular Scottish air, "Robin Adair," which appears in the opera during George's first-act revery, and returns in an instrumental version in the third act.

Among the other outstanding numbers in the opera are the following: George's first-act entrance aria on the joys of being a soldier, *"Ah, quel plaisir d'être soldat!";* George's cavatina from the same act calling to the White Lady to make an appearance, *"Viens, gentille dame";* the duet of George and Anna, *"Ce domain";* George's third-act reverie with chorus, *"Chantez joyeux ménestral";* and Anna's lovely air, *"Enfin, je vous revois."*

When *La Dame blanche* was first given in English in New York, in 1832, the adaptation was made by John Howard Payne, author of "Home, Sweet Home." On that occasion Boieldieu's score was supplemented by songs, arias, and other musical episodes from the works of Rossini and Auber, among others. The first Metropolitan Opera performance of *La Dame blanche,* on February 13, 1904, was in the German language. The cast was headed by Johanna Gadski and Louise Homer, and Felix Mottl conducted. This was the only Boieldieu opera ever performed by the company.

(The) Dancing Years by Ivor Novello.

Operetta in two acts with text by Ivor Novello and lyrics by Christopher Hassall. First performance: Drury Lane, London, March 23, 1939. First American performance: St. Louis, Missouri, 1947.

Like Noël Coward, Novello wrote the music to his own texts, and then went on to star in the leading role. In *The Dancing Years,* he gave still further evidence of his remarkable versatility. He also played the piano, and in one of the scenes he conducted the pit orchestra with professional competence.

The Dancing Years was introduced in London a half year before the outbreak of World War II. Its initial Drury Lane run was only 187 performances. But on March 14, 1942, it reopened at the Adelphi Theater where it lasted for almost a thousand performances. To bomb-stricken Londoners, *The Dancing Years* proved a welcome ivory tower to which to flee from war's grim realities.

The operetta spans three eras in Vienna. The first is the pre-World War I period. Rudi Kleber, a young composer, is performing his most recent effort, "The Waltz In My Heart," for some actresses and officers in a small inn on the outskirts of the city. Maria Ziegler, Vienna's most celebrated stage star, becomes so enthusiastic over this waltz that she decides to include it in her forthcoming operetta, *The Lorelei.* Later, she decides to use even more of Kleber's songs in her show. After the opening night of *The Lorelei,* Rudi and Maria realize that they are in love.

Three years later, they spend a holiday in a Tyrolean chalet. Rudi's one-time sweetheart, Grete, now a stage star in her own right, suddenly appears. To impress Rudi, she sings for him "Primrose," the principal number from her next production. Once they are alone, Grete laughingly reminds Rudi of a promise he had once made: never to marry anybody before first asking her and allowing her to turn him down. In mock solemnity, Rudi goes through the motions of asking her to marry him. Maria happens to overhear him, and, thinking Rudi is serious, leaves the chalet in a huff.

Several more years pass before the paths of Rudi and Maria cross again. At a party at the Belvedere in Vienna, Rudi has Grete explain to Maria what really had transpired during the ill-fated "proposal." But the explanation comes too late; Maria is now married to her one-time lover, Prince Charles.

During the post-World War I era, Rudi becomes the musical idol of Vienna. He meets Maria in one of the city's fashionable restaurants. He is still very much in love with her, and he entreats her to desert her to desert her husband and run off with him. But Maria now discloses that she is the mother of Rudi's son, whom Prince Charles has generously accepted as his own child. For the sake of the boy's happiness, her marriage with Prince Charles must not be broken.

The final scene takes place in 1938, soon after the Nazis have occupied Austria. Rudi is seized by Brown Shirts, but is saved from concentration camp through Maria's intervention. The scene darkens; shadows engulf the stage. Through the haze, dancing couples are seen to the strains of a waltz, just as Viennese couples used to do in happier and more peaceful days.

"Mr. Novello's waltzes," said the critic of the *London Times,* "cleverly echo the authentic waltz songs of Vienna." The main one—besides "The Waltz In My Heart" from the opening scene—is "The Leap Year Waltz" during the Belvedere party. There are other equally memorable numbers: the already-mentioned "Primrose"; the love duet of Rudi and Maria, "My Heart Belongs to You"; and the Tyrolean dance music in the chalet scene. A beautiful ballet, "Masque of Vienna"—choreographed by Suria Magito—evokes, in terms of the dance, the spirit of Vienna preceding World War I. For the rest (and beyond the altogether captivating per-

formance of the American musical-comedy star Mary Ellis, as Maria),
there was Novello himself, always "in superb form," as the critic of the
Times noted, "whether playing the piano, singing, conducting the orchestra, or being happy or miserable in love."

In 1950, *The Dancing Years* was made into a British motion picture
starring Dennis Price and Giselle Preville. In July, 1954, it was produced
as an ice spectacle at Wembley Pool, London.

(The) Daughter of Madame Angot by Alexandre-Charles Lecocq. *See*
(La) Fille de Madame Angot.

(The) Daughter of the Regiment [*La Fille du Régiment* or *La Figlia*
del Reggimento] by Gaetano Donizetti.

> Opéra-comique in two acts with text by Jean-François Alfred Bayard
> and Jules Henri Vernoy de Saint-Georges. First performance: Opéra-
> Comique, Paris, February 11, 1840. First American performances: New
> Orleans, Louisiana, March 6, 1843 (in French); New York, June 5,
> 1844 (in English); New York, May 15, 1855 (in German).

Donizetti's first "French" opera, *The Daughter of the Regiment*, is a favorite of the French lyric theater. By World War I, it had been given
over a thousand performances by the Opéra-Comique, and it has proved
hardly less popular in Italy and Germany in translation.

Henry Simon, in *The Festival of Opera*, does not hesitate to describe
it as "a musical comedy." In its original French version it had, says Simon, "a good deal of spoken dialogue, and its plot, in any language,
retains the classical pattern of light opera and old-fashioned musical
comedy—that is, boy-meets-girl, boy-loses-girl, and boy-gets-girl."

The heroine, Marie, is a *vivandière* (canteen manager) of the 21st
French Regiment during the French invasion of the Tyrol in or about
1815. She is in love with the Tyrolean peasant, Tonio, whom the French
suspect of being a spy. Nevertheless, when they learn from Marie that
he had once saved her life, they accept him as a recruit in their regiment. Then the Countess of Berkenfeld uncovers the fact that Marie is
her long-lost niece. She insists that the girl leave the regiment for good

and live with her in her castle and be tutored in the ways of a highborn lady. But in the castle Marie cannot forget her French friends, nor her beloved Tonio; and the fact that her aunt insists that she marry a Duke deepens her depression. When the French troops storm the Berkenfeld castle Marie and Tonio are reunited. The Countess now informs Marie's French friends that the girl is not her niece, but her daughter, and consequently must do her bidding. The soldiers shout their disapproval, insisting that they will never allow their lovable *vivandière* to marry anyone but the man she really loves. The Countess is finally forced to give in, much to the joy of all the regiment.

Donizetti originally wrote this comic opera for Naples. When another of his operas had antagonized Neapolitan authorities by its political overtones, Donizetti left Italy for France and had his new opera performed there in French, with Sophie Anna Thillon appearing as Marie. When the opera was first heard in Italy (at La Scala), spoken dialogue was replaced by recitatives.

Much of the excitement of Donizetti's music comes from its stirring martial tunes, such as *"Rataplan, Rataplan,"* a hymn to war and victory sung by the French troops; Marie's rousing tribute to her regiment, *"Ah, chacun le sait, chacun le dit";* and the powerful salute to France with which the opera closes, *"Salut à France."* Because of its martial character, performances of this opera have had particularly timely interest for the United States in each of the two world wars. When revived by the Metropolitan Opera in 1917–18, Frieda Hempel interpolated into the score the popular World War I ballad, "Keep the Home Fires Burning." And during World War II—soon after the Nazi occupation of France—Lily Pons draped a French flag around herself and rendered the *Marseillaise.*

Stirring martial melodies are supplemented by romantic ones, of which two by Marie in the first act are of particular appeal: when she speaks of her love for Tonio in *"Depuis l'instant où dans mes bras,"* and when she bids a poignant farewell to her regiment with *"Il faut partir."* Also in an ardent romantic vein are the love duet of Marie and Tonio (*"Tous les trois réunis"*) and Marie's love song to Tonio (*"Quand le destin au milieu"*). Charm rather than passion can be found in the delightful second-act orchestral entr'acte, *"Tyrolienne."*

(The) Deceived Cadi by Christoph Willibald Gluck. *See (Le) Cadi dupé.*

(Le) **Devin du village** [*The Village Soothsayer*] by Jean-Jacques Rousseau.

Intermezzo in one act with text by the composer. First performances: Fontainebleau, France, October 18, 1752 (private); Opéra, Paris, March 1, 1753 (public). First American performance: New York, October 21, 1790.

It is not generally known by the average opera-goer that one of the earliest and most successful comic operas ever written was the work of the distinguished French philosopher, Jean-Jacques Rousseau, who wrote both text and music. Rousseau's stimulation came from a hearing of Pergolesi's *La Serva padrona* (which see), history's first comic opera, which was a sensation in Paris when heard there for the first time. Many Parisian music lovers had grown weary of French operas with such strong emphasis on mythology, fables, and ballets. These music lovers yearned for something simpler, truer to everyday life. Thus Pergolesi's *La Serva padrona* became for them something of a revelation. Almost immediately there sprang up a school of theorists in Paris who proclaimed Pergolesi's opera buffa the only true operatic art, the example to be followed. The school also set itself as the enemy of the more formal French operas glorified by Lully and Rameau. The bitter conflict which ensued between those who sided with Pergolesi and those who remained faithful to Rameau and Lully has become known in the history books as the "war of the buffoons" (*"la Guerre des Bouffons"*).

Rousseau, who believed passionately in a return to nature, and was an apostle of simplicity and humanity, stood in the vanguard of those who championed Pergolesi and *La Serva pardona*. "It is necessary," he said, "for music to return to Nature." To clarify his ideas, he wrote in November, 1753, the *Lettre sur la musique français*, a devastating attack on French opera. "There is neither time nor melody in French music," he wrote, "because the language is not capable of either: French song is a continuous bark, its harmony crude and suggestive of the work of a student; French airs are not airs at all, nor French recitative worth anything. And so I conclude that the French have no music at all."

Rousseau went beyond the writing of a letter to the creation of a comic opera in the style of Pergolesi, in which pastoral scenes and rural settings were predominant. Colette, a village girl, hearing that her beloved Colin has been unfaithful to her, consults a soothsayer. He tells her that Colin is still very much in love with her and wants her back. But the sooth-sayer also advises Colette to arouse Colin's love still further by feigning indifference to him. As part of this plan, the soothsayer informs Colin that Colette has fallen in love with another man. Distraught, Colin seeks the help of the soothsayer, who, by necromancy brings Colette on the scene. When she arrives she poses as a prude who has lost all interest in Colin. But in the end they become reconciled, to the delight of the villagers.

When *Le Devin du village* was first presented—to the court at Fontainebleau—it was heard with supplementary music by Pierre de Jélyotte (an overture and some recitatives). But when Rousseau's comic opera was given publicly at the Paris Opéra soon after that, only Rousseau's music was used, the composer providing for this occasion the recitatives and a new overture. Rousseau's little opera proved a sensation. On March 4, 1753, it was presented in the private theater of the Bellevue Palace, with Mme Pompadour herself enacting the role of Colette. On April 20, 1779, *Le Devin du village* was produced in Paris with six new airs. By 1829 the opera had been presented over four hundred times in Paris alone. In that year a wag in the audience (believed to be Berlioz, although he has denied this stoutly in his *Memoirs*) ridiculed the opera during a performance by throwing an old wig on the stage. This gesture helped relegate the work to oblivion. But by then its influence as the cornerstone of French comic opera had been fully acknowledged.

There is neither variety nor subtlety in Rousseau's airs, and this is the main reason why the opera is rarely revived. The tunes are pretty enough, but they hardly stir the emotions. The best are those of Colette *"J'ai perdu tout mon bonheur," "Si des galants de la ville," "Avec l'objet de mes amours,"* and *"Allons danser sous les ormeaux."* Pleasing, too, are the following: *"L'art à l'amour est favorable," "Que le jour me dure,"* and Colin's song *"Je vais revoir ma charmante maîtresse."* The opera also boasts some delightful orchestral music accompanying a dance pantomine.

For a parody of *Le Devin du village*, see *Bastien and Bastienne*.

(Les) Diamants de la couronne [*The Crown Diamonds*] by Daniel François Ésprit Auber.

Opéra-comique in three acts with text by Eugène Scribe and Jules Vernoy Henri de Saint-Georges. First performance: Opéra-Comique,

Paris, March 6, 1841. First American performances: New York, July 13, 1843; Boston, Massachusetts, 1854 (in English).

This is one of several masterworks with which the composer achieved world-wide recognition as "the last great representative of opéra-comique".

The time is the eighteenth century, the place, Lisbon. The Queen of Portugal, assuming the identity of Theophila, has come to a lair of counterfeiters for the purpose of having them replace the crown diamonds with counterfeit jewels. Don Enriquez, who has stumbled into the hideout, comes upon the imitation jewels and believes them to be the real ones, stolen from the king's palace. When the news is circulated in Lisbon that the crown diamonds have disappeared, Theophila is suspected, and Don Enriquez, now deeply in love with her, tries to save her from disgrace. Only then is the truth told, that Theophila and the Queen are the same person; that, as Theophila, the Queen had sold the crown diamonds to save her treasury from ruin. When the matter has been cleared up, the Queen announces her forthcoming marriage to Don Enriquez.

The characteristic Auber melody—suave, supple, sedate, lyrical, derived mainly from the old French chanson—elevates this comic opera to a place of significance in the French light theater. The overture begins with an extended melody for strings. A rhythmic section introduces a virile tune for brass, and this is followed by several more robust ideas. After the development of these thoughts, lyricism returns in two eloquent melodies, the second of which is opulently harmonized in the strings. A vigorous melody for full orchestra brings the overture to a dramatic end.

Three other orchestral episodes are of interest: two entr'actes, and the stately saraband of the second act.

Auber's aristocratic lyricism can be found in two of the Queen's main arias: the ballad, "*Le beau Pedrille*," and the haunting cavatina, "*Non, non, fermons l'oreille*." Don Enrique's song, "*Vivent la pluie*," and the bolero, "*Dans les défiles des montagnes*," also command attention.

(The) Doctor and the Apothecary [*Doktor und Apotheker*] by Karl Ditters von Dittersdorf.

Singspiel in two acts with text by Gottlieb Stephanie, probably based on a French play, *L'Apothicaire de Murcia*. First performance: Kaernthnerthor Theater, Vienna, July 11, 1786. First American performance: Charleston, South Carolina, April 26, 1796.

Karl Ditters von Dittersdorf, a contemporary of Haydn, wrote a good deal of music in all forms, but he was probably best writing comic pieces for the stage—the *Singspiel,* an early variety of German musical comedy. His masterwork was *The Doctor and the Apothecary,* and it is his only stage work that is still occasionally revived in Europe. Here, as Karl Ferdinand Pohl remarked, the composer "reveals a real vein of comedy, vivacity, and quick invention, bright spontaneous melody, original instrumentation, and breadth in the concerted numbers and finales." In its own day, *The Doctor and the Apothecary* was so popular that it made its composer an idol of the music-loving public and won for him a commission to write three more light operas in similar style. In 1789, Dittersdorf was invited by the German Emperor to Berlin to conduct a special performance of this gem. Since Dittersdorf's time, the comic opera has been periodically revived both in Europe and America.

When first heard in the United States—in Charleston, South Carolina, in 1796—the opera was given in a version in which the score was adapted by B. Bergman. In short order, this lovable opera traveled to other parts of America, to Philadelphia on May 20, 1796, and to New York on March 3, 1798.

At the London première, on October 25, 1788, the opera was given in an English translation (the work of J. Cobb) and with some additional music by S. Storace. It proved to be so appealing that it was presented thirty-six evenings.

Gotthold (son of Dr. Krautmann) and Leonore (daughter of Stoezel, the apothecary) are in love in a little eighteenth-century European town. But the fathers are mortal enemies, and, in addition, Leonore's father is determined to have her marry Captain Sturmwald. When Gotthold attempts to elope with his sweetheart and is frustrated, he performs all kinds of tricks on his bewildered rival in an effort to discourage him from taking Leonore as his bride. Gotthold also arrives in various disguises to try to steal her away. Only after Leonore's mother becomes Gotthold's ally are the two fathers reconciled and the lovers permitted to get married without interference. A subsidiary love plot runs contrapuntally to the major one; it involves Sichel, a surgeon, and Stoelzel's niece, Rosalie.

Dittersdorf's score is a reservoir of delightful melodies, of which the following are the best: those of Leonore (*"Wie kann ich Freude noch in meinen Blicken zeigen"*), Gotthold (*"Wann hoerst du auf, verliebte Qual"*) and Rosalie (*"Verliebte brauchen keine Zeugen"*); the duet of Sichel and Gotthold, *"Wenn man will zum Maedchen gehn"*; the orchestral intermezzo between the first and second acts; and the amusing second-act exchange between the doctor and the apothecary, *"Sie sind ein Charlatan."*

Doctor Cupid by Ermanno Wolf-Ferrari. *See* (*L'*)*Amore medico.*

(The) Doctor in Spite of Himself by Charles Gounod. *See* (*Le*) *Médecin malgré lui.*

(The) Dollar Princess [*Die Dollarprinzessin*] by Leo Fall.

> Operetta in three acts with text by A. M. Willner and Fritz Gruenbaum, based upon a comedy by Gatti-Trotha. First performance: Vienna, November 2, 1907. First American performance: Knickerbocker Theater, New York, September 6, 1909.

While European operettas were generally set in some glamorous or exotic locale or in a mythical kingdom, that of Leo Fall's most celebrated operetta was unusual in utilizing the background of New York and Canada. The period is just prior to World War I. John Couder, a widower, is a New York millionaire seeking a wife. He dispatches his brother to Europe for the purpose of finding him a lady of noble birth. The brother brings back Olga, a woman reputed to be a Russian countess, but who is actually a cabaret singer. Two people recognize her at once. One is Freddy Wehrburg, who is in love with Couder's daughter, Alice, the "Dollar Princess"; the other, Baron von Schlick, is master of the Couder stables. Both men promise Olga to remain silent about her real background and profession. Couder's engagement to Olga is announced at a lavish party. At the same time, Alice, without consulting Freddy, makes a public announcement that she is engaged to him. Freddy is repelled by this blunt announcement and by Alice's bland assumption that her wealth makes it impossible for him to reject her. He leaves the estate in a huff, and makes an equally hasty departure from New York to find a new home in Canada, where he becomes a highly successful business man. However, he cannot forget Alice. He invites Couder to Canada to discuss a business deal, urging him to bring along Alice and Olga (the latter by now Couder's wife). Alice is contrite. Since Freddy is rich in his own right, she can no longer be so self-assured and smug about her wealth. Things, then, turn out well for Freddy and Alice. But this does not hold true for Couder and Olga. Couder is convinced Olga has married him for his money alone, and arranges a handsome financial settlement on her in exchange for a divorce.

While *The Dollar Princess* differs from most European operettas in setting, it remains true to tradition by making a waltz the high point of both play and score. In this case, the waltz is a soaring melody, *"Will sie dann lieben treu und heiss,"* which became so popular throughout Vienna, and then Europe, that it played a major role in making *The Dollar Princess* an international favorite. These tunes are hardly less delightful: Olga's *"Kosakenlied";* the title number; the flippant, *"Wigl, wagl, wigl";* and the haunting duet, *"Wir tanzen Ringelreih'n einmal hin und her."*

The American première starred Donald Brian (then a Broadway matinee idol by virtue of his recent triumph in *The Merry Widow*). The American adaptation was made by George Grossmith, Jr., and the original score was supplemented by two popular songs by the young and still unknown Jerome Kern. "Exquisite and dainty from first to last as far as Mr. Fall's music is concerned," as one New York critic reported, *The Dollar Princess* had a highly successful initial New York run of over two hundred performances.

(The) Doll of Nuremberg by Adolfe Adam. *See (La) Poupée de Nuremberg.*

Die Dollarprinzessin by Leo Fall. *See (The) Dollar Princess.*

(Le) Domino noir [*The Black Domino*] by Daniel François Esprit Auber.

Opéra-comique in three acts with text by Eugène Scribe. First performance: Opéra-Comique, Paris, December 2, 1837. First American performances: New Orleans, Louisiana, November 1839 (in French); New York, July 18, 1843 (in English).

Le Domino noir ranks high with *Les Diamants de la couronne* among Auber's opéra-comiques: By 1882 it had been performed a thousand times at the Opéra-Comique alone. The opera opens with a gala masked ball at the palace of the Queen of Spain. Horatio, who, one year earlier, had succumbed to the charms of Lady Angela, meets her again at the ball without recognizing her, since she is wearing a "black domino" disguise. Finding the lady unusually appealing, Horatio looks forward to the midnight hour when she will unmask. But at midnight, Lady Angela refuses to reveal herself; instead, she flees from the palace and makes her way to the convent where she is a sister preparing to become Lady Abbess. Because of the late hour, she is unable to gain access into the convent. She finds refuge with Claudia, housekeeper for Juliano, one of Horatio's friends. When several of Juliano's friends arrive, and with them Horatio, Angela assumes the part of a peasant girl. As such, she proceeds to charm the men—particularly with the rendition of a folk song—and especially Horatio, who finds that she continually reminds him of his lost Lady Angela. Embarrassed by Horatio's interest and attentions, Lady Angela sneaks out of the house and prevails on the doorkeeper of the convent to let her in. When next Horatio sees her, she is wearing the robes of the Lady Abbess, although she has not as yet taken her vows. Once again Horatio is mystified to see how much the Lady Abbess reminds him of Angela, until he learns that she is, indeed, the girl for whom he has so long been searching. When the Queen of Spain compels Angela to leave the convent and her office and to seek out a husband, the happy union of Horatio and Angela becomes inevitable. Ursula, a young girl to whom Horatio has all the while been betrothed, succeeds Angela as Lady Abbess.

Several orchestral episodes are particularly attractive: the melodious overture, the entr'acte between the first and second acts, and, in the second act, the "*March militaire*" and "*Ronde aragonaise.*" Two of Angela's airs are among the vocal high spots: "*Une fée, un bon ange*" in the first act, and, in the last, "*Ah, quelle nuit, le moindre bruit me trouble.*" The first-act cavatina, "*Quel bonheur,*" and the beautiful third-act air, "*Pour toujours, disait-elle, je suis à toi,*" are also noteworthy.

Donna Diana by Emil Nikolaus von Reznicek.

Comic opera in three acts with text by the composer, based on *El Desden con el Desden* by Moreto y Cavaña. First performance: Prague, December 16, 1894.

Emil von Rezniček's most famous and successful opera was the one which, ironically, cost him the least effort and pains to create. He completed his score in a few weeks' time.

Toward the close of the nineteenth century, in Barcelona, Princess Diana is pursued by three lovers. One is Don Caesar, who feigns indifference to her in order to fan her interest. The ruse works. But as the Princess begins to show Don Caesar how much he appeals to her, he grows increasingly apathetic and aloof. In desperation, the Princess tells him she has decided to marry Don Louis. Don Caesar accepts this news calmly, and counters with the revelation that he is thinking of marrying Donna Laura. So deep grows Princess Diana's despair that Don Caesar takes pity on her, tells her he has loved her all the while and wants very much to make her his wife.

In Rezniček's own day, and for a short time afterward, *Donna Diana* enjoyed considerable popularity in the Austrian and German theaters. But more recently, only its lively, lilting overture has remained a favorite, and is frequently played. A sustained introduction precedes the vivacious main melody in the strings. Sprightly countersubjects weave themselves around this tune. The second theme then appears in violins and violas, accompanied by winds and horn. The mood now grows intense, but the note of levity with which the overture opened helps to bring it to a merry conclusion.

The style of the overture is essentially Viennese in its deftness and charm. Within the opera itself, the composer often injects Spanish color and personality into his music through the interpolation of Spanish melodies and rhythms. Nevertheless, the Viennese spirit remains dominant through most of the opera, particularly in the seductive first-act waltz and the second-act ballet music.

Two arias are in a similarly light and appealing vein: *"Muetterchen, wenn's in Schlaf mich sang"* and the *"Narren-Lied,"* or *"Die Narrenglocken klingen Tag."*

Donna Juanita by Franz von Suppé.

Comic opera in three acts with text by F. Zell and R. Genée. First performance: Karlstheater, Vienna, February 21, 1880. First American performances: New York, May 16, 1881 (in English); New York, September 27, 1881 (in German).

This was Suppé's last successful comic opera. "Donna Juanita" is actually a man masquerading in woman's clothes. In San Sebastian, Spain, toward the end of the eighteenth century, Gaston, a young French officer, is the prisoner of Sir Douglas. Gaston is in love with Petrita, who is also attractive to Sir Douglas; and just to balance the scales, Sir Douglas' wife, Lady Olympia, is interested in Gaston. René, Gaston's brother, penetrates the Spanish garrison by disguising himself as a seductive Spanish wench, Donna Juanita. When Petrita sees "her" talking to Gaston, her jealousy is aroused to the point where she refuses to have any further traffic with her sweetheart. René continues to fill the role of the exciting and irresistible Donna Juanita, to the delight of all the soldiers. At an elaborate Spanish festival, Petrita learns the truth, that Donna Juanita is Gaston's brother in disguise. When the French capture the garrison, Gaston is promoted to lieutenant and Sir Douglas becomes a prisoner of the French.

Almost half a century after its American première, *Donna Juanita* was first seen at the Metropolitan Opera—on January 2, 1932. It was revived at this time for the glamorous prima donna Maria Jeritza, who played the part of René masquerading as Donna Juanita. For these performances the text was livened up with gags and broad burlesque episodes—one of which included Mme Jeritza dancing an Adagio—to emphasize the comic element in the opera.

Several appealing numbers in the score are for orchestra, including an ebullient overture, a melodious intermezzo, and brilliant ballet music for the third act. Of the vocal highlights, four striking arias by René can be singled out: *"Ha-ha-ha," "Mein Vaterland das lieb ich sehr," "Ist man verliebt,"* and *"Ob unter Herrn, unter Damen, man ist, man kuesst."* No less attractive is a Spanish choral number, *"Dann hebt sich froehlicher Sang."*

(Le) Donne Curiose, or Die Neugierigen Frauen [*The Inquisitive* [*Women*] by Ermanno Wolf-Ferrari.

Opera buffa in three acts with text by Luigi Sugana, based on a comedy of the same name by Carlo Goldoni. First performance: Hofoper, Munich, November 27, 1903 (in German). First American performance: Metropolitan Opera, New York, January 3, 1912 (in Italian).

This is one of several works with which Wolf-Ferrari brought the opera buffa into the twentieth century.

In Venice, in the eighteenth century, several noblemen have formed a club to which women are denied access. This restriction has piqued the curiosity of the women about the goings-on within those secret walls. In their vivid imaginations, the wives or sweethearts of these noblemen conjure up pictures of wild orgies. Rosaura, betrothed to Florinda, is perhaps the most curious of all. But when they manage to get a set of duplicate keys for the club and plan an invasion, they insist Rosaura stay at home since she is too young, and unmarried to boot, to witness the orgies. Rosaura, however, prevails on Florinda to turn the keys over to her. All the women now, and Rosaura with them, finally gain admission into the club where they find their men partaking of an innocent meal. Their suspicion finally appeased, the women join the men in a lively dance.

Translated into a musical motive is the club's motto, "No Women Admitted" (*"Bandie ne le donne"*), which appears throughout the score as a connecting musical link.

In the first scene of the third act, Wolf-Ferrari quotes a popular Venetian barcarolle, *"La Biondina in gondoletta."* (It is interesting to note that some years earlier this same melody was occasionally interpolated into the "Lesson Scene" of Rossini's *The Barber of Seville.*) One of the loveliest of Wolf-Ferrari's own melodies is the second-act duet of Rosaura and Florinda, *"Il cor nel contento."* Among the more popular instrumental episodes are two charming old-world dances, a minuet and a forlana, the latter being a lively Italian dance in 6/4 and 6/8 time.

When given its world première in Munich, Germany, the opera was heard in a German adaptation by H. Teibler. The reason it was given in German—and in a German city—was because Wolf-Ferrari's publisher was German. The first time *Le Donne Curiose* was given in the original Italian was at the American première by the Metropolitan Opera Company in 1912. Toscanini conducted, and the cast was headed by the glamorous prima donna Geraldine Farrar. On that occasion Richard Aldrich said in the *New York Times*: "One feature of the opera is the frequent use of vocal ensemble. . . . [Wolf-Ferrari] is a master of moods in musical representation, and sentiment is expressed with direction and without sentimentality. He has treated the orchestra with remarkable skill and refinement. This orchestra is almost the antithesis of the Wagnerian orchestra. It is concerned little, or not at all, with the development of leading motives. The scoring is very light, with subtle refinements; it is an example of what a master can do with comparatively few resources."

Don Pasquale by Gaetano Donizetti.

Opera buffa in three acts with text by Giacomo Ruffini and the composer, based on *Ser Marcantonio* by Angelo Anelli. First performance: Théâtre des Italiens, Paris, January 3, 1843. First American performance: Park Theater, New York, March 9, 1846.

All the choice ingredients that go into making an opera-buffa dish succulent can be found in *Don Pasquale*, Donizetti's greatest opera and the last success he was to enjoy in a long and rich career. The characters include many favorites in opera buffa: the fat, old, lecherous bachelor; the busybody who sets the plot into motion; thwarted lovers. Deception, disguises, and a mock marriage are basic to the story, even as they are to most of the popular opera buffas of the eighteenth and nineteenth centuries.

Don Pasquale is a fat, old bachelor—in Rome in the early nineteenth century—who is violently opposed to a marriage between his nephew, Ernesto, and the lovely widow, Norina. Since the old bachelor is eager to end his own single blessedness, he is amenable to a suggestion by his physician, Dr. Malatesta, that he consider the physician's beautiful sister, Sofronia. Norina disguises herself as Sofronia, enchants Don Pasquale, and easily gets him to propose marriage. As soon as the marriage contract is signed, Sofronia becomes a shrew who makes poor old Don Pasquale sick to his stomach with her vicious tempers, whims, extravagances, even suspicions about his fidelity. In despair, Don Pasquale summons Dr. Malatesta to ask him to set things right. Only then does Pasquale discover how he had been duped by both the good physician and Norina; further, he is actually not married at all, since his marriage had been a mock one. This news so delights the old bachelor that he no longer stands in the way of the courtship of Norina and Ernesto.

The opera puts forth its best foot without preliminaries with one of Donizetti's most delightful overtures. Several descending chords lead to a beautiful song in the cellos. This is followed by a gay, insouciant tune for strings. After some transitional material, usually more dramatic than humorous, there comes a second sprightly melody, in woodwinds and strings. The treatment is light and effervescent, and the overture ends on a note of levity.

The contrast between tender and beautiful melodies, sentimental and vivacious tunes which characterizes the overture also prevails within the opera. Italian bel-canto at its noblest and most expressive, indeed some of the finest melodies Donizetti ever wrote, can be found in this score. In such a style are Norina's lovely first-act aria, "*So anch'io la virtù magica*" (in which she echoes her thoughts while reading a novel), with its enchanting cavatina, "*Quel guardo, il cavaliere*"; two laments by Ernesto—the poignant voice of a frustrated lover being kept from the woman he seeks—"*Sogno soave e casto*" in the first act and "*Chercherò lontana terra*" in the second; and Ernesto's rapturous serenade to Norina in the third act, "*Com'è gentil.*"

The vivacious, light-hearted numbers, of which there are an abundance, include the following: the first-act exchange between Norina and Malatesta in which they connive to dupe old Pasquale, "*Vado carro, si vado corro*"; Malatesta's description to Pasquale of his "sister," "*Bella siccome un angelo*"; the gay second-act finale, a vivacious quartet in which Pasquale bemoans the fact that he has been betrayed, "*Son tradito*"; the duet-nocturne, "*Tornami a dir*"; and the third-act finale which points up the moral that it is best for Pasquale to remain a bachelor after all, "*Bravo, bravo Don Pasquale.*"

At its world première, this comic opera was performed by a truly incomparable cast of artists. Lablache was Pasquale and at once became the foremost interpreter of this role in his generation; Tamburini was Malatesta; Grisi portrayed Norina; and Mario was cast as Ernesto.

One of the most successful interpreters of the role of Pasquale nearer our own time was the rotund Salvatore Baccaloni, for whom the opera was revived by the Metropolitan Opera on December 21, 1940. Virgil Thomson in the *Herald Tribune* called Baccaloni's performance "the finest piece of lyric acting in the comic vein I have ever seen, not excepting Chaliapin."

(Die) **Dreigroschenoper** by Kurt Weill. *See* (*The*) *Three-Penny Opera.*

(Das) Dreimaederlhaus [*The House of the Three Girls*] by Heinrich Berté.

Operetta in three acts with text by H. M. Willner and Heinz Reichert, based on a novel by R. H. Bartsch. Berté's music was adapted from compositions by Franz Schubert. First performance: Raimund Theater, Vienna, January 15, 1916. First American performance: Irving Place Theater, New York, 1917.

Sigmund Romberg's American operetta *Blossom Time*, based on the life and music of Franz Schubert, was an adaptation (though a very free one) of this extremely popular Austrian operetta, which is still often given in Europe. In London, on December 22, 1923, it was presented under the title of *Lilac Time* in an English version by G. H. Clutsam.

The three girls in the title are Hannerl, Hederl, and Haiderl. The last two are secretly engaged to young men without the knowledge of their father. They come to the courtyard of Franz Schubert's house where he is entertaining some friends, one of which is Franz von Schober. Hannerl confides to Schober that her father has put a spy on her trail, and Schober advises her to tell her father that she has come to take music lessons from Schubert. Indeed, Hannerl then and there does make arrangements to study with the great composer. Just then the girls' father arrives and meets Schober, who is finally able to persuade him to permit the two girls to marry the men of their choice.

In honor of the girls' marriage, their father gives a party. Schubert is one of the guests, and part of the evening's entertainment is a performance of some of his songs. Hannerl, who is deeply moved by Schubert's music, comes to realize that she is in love with her music teacher. Schubert returns her love, but he is too shy to make his feelings known. Schober's girl friend, Grisi, is led to suspect that her sweetheart is interested in Hannerl. Slyly, she approaches Hannerl to confide to her that Franz is a wastrel, liar, and cheat—referring, of course, to Schober. But Hannerl thinks she is describing Schubert. Disillusioned and heartbroken, she refuses to see Schubert and seeks solace and comfort in Schober's friendship. In time, Schober and Hannerl fall in love, a development that breaks poor Schubert's heart.

Surely no emphasis is required to the statement that this contrived plot has no basis whatever in biographical truth. Actually, although Schubert had been a victim of frustrated love, his friend Schober was never the cause; and although there had been one or two girls with whom Schubert had been diffidently in love, there was no Hannerl among them. But this manufactured yarn served a purpose: to offer Schubert's wonderful music in a popular format. Some of Schubert's incomparable Lieder are used by Berté, among them "The Erl King," "Serenade," "The Trout," and *"Ungeduld."* Some less familiar Schubert compositions also appear, including the lovely *Trauerwalzer.*

The American première at the Irving Place Theater in New York in 1917 was faithful to the original language, title, text, and music. Romberg's *Blossom Time*—heard at the Ambassador Theater on September 29, 1921—was something else again. None of the Berté score was used by Romberg, who preferred to make translations of Schubert selections of his own choice. The plot also underwent radical transformation at the hands of Dorothy Donnelly.

Das Dreimäederlhaus was made into a color motion picture in Austria in 1938, starring Johanna Matz and Karlheinz Boehm.

Drei Walzer [*Three Waltzes*] by Oscar Straus.

> Operetta in three acts with text by Paul Knepler and Armin Robinson. Music based partly on compositions by Johann Strauss, father and son. First performance: Zurich, Switzerland, October 5, 1935. First American performance: Majestic Theater, New York, December 25, 1937.

Here one great Viennese waltz king pays tribute to two earlier ones. Oscar Straus does homage to Johann Strauss, father and son, by adapting some of their music and combining it with his own. Father Johann Strauss's music is used in the first act to recreate the atmosphere of Vienna in 1865. The son Johann Strauss's compositions help to evoke the Vienna of 1900 in the second act. Only in the third act, the Vienna of 1935, does Oscar Straus fashion his own melodies.

The operetta opens in mid-nineteenth century. Fanny Pichler, a Viennese ballerina, and Lieutenant Rudi are in love. Marriage is out of the question, since a ballerina-wife would jeopardize Rudi's future in the army, as well as compromise his high social station. In order not to stand in the way of his social progress, Fanny signs a contract to dance in Paris. One evening in Vienna, Rudi and Fanny bid each other a tender farewell. They are never again destined to meet.

Thirty-five years have elapsed when the second-act curtain rises. A new operetta is being introduced in Vienna, and its star is Charlotte, daughter of Fanny Pichler, who is the recipient of a thunderous ovation. Later that evening, she meets Rudi's son, Otto, to whom she is immediately attracted. They go off to Sacher's. But, even as her mother had once been, Charlotte is doomed to frustration as far as romance is concerned. After hearing about Otto's numerous love escapades, she decides to reject him, aware that at best she can only become a fleeting incident in his life.

In the third act, we are plunged into the Vienna of 1935. A motion picture dramatizing the love of Rudi and Fanny is in production. The female lead is being played by Franzi, who happens to be Fanny's granddaughter and Charlotte's daughter. During a rehearsal of one of the scenes, Count Ferdinand (Rudi's grandson and Otto's son) is a fascinated spectator. The director prevails upon him to play the role of his grandfather. Before long, Franzi and Ferdinand are very much in love. And this romance achieves fulfillment in marriage.

The three main waltzes of the title are: "*Wien ist ein Liebeslied,*" the duet of Fanny and Rudi in the first act; "*Ich liebe das Leben,*" the duet of Charlotte and Otto in the second act; and in the third act, the duet of Franzi and Ferdinand, "*Man sagt sich beim Abschied Adieu.*"

The Broadway première of *The Three Waltzes* starred Kitty Carlisle and Michael Bartlett; the American adaptation of the text was made by Claire Kummer, and the English lyrics were written by Roland Leigh.

(The) Du Barry [*Graefin Du Barry*] by Karl Milloecker.

Operetta in three acts with text by Paul Knepler and J. M. Welleminsky, based on a libretto by F. Zell and R. Genée. First performance: Vienna, October 31, 1879. First American performance: George M. Cohan Theater, New York, November 22, 1932.

When Milloecker's *Grafin Du Barry* was first seen, in 1879, it was a dismal failure and went into discard. But on August 14, 1931, in Berlin, the operetta was revised, with a revamped text by M. Cremer and the musical score adapted by Theo Mackeben. Renamed *Die Du Barry*, Milloecker's operetta now proved a triumph. It was this same freshened and revised version of the operetta that was the source of the American version introduced on Broadway in 1932.

The setting is Paris and its environs during the latter half of the eighteenth century. As an employee in a Parisian millinery shop, Marie Jeanne meets the artist, René. When some hats are stolen from the store, Marie is falsely suspected. She quits her job and sets up house in René's studio as his mistress. Count Du Barry becomes interested in her and tries to make love to her in the studio. Rebuffed, the Count, hoping to inflame René's suspicions, leaves behind him a purse filled with money. The trick works: René drives Marie Jeanne away, swearing never again to see her. Marie Jeanne now supports herself by appearing as an entertainer in a gambling establishment. When she gets involved in gambling debts, Count Du Barry comes to her financial aid, then takes her home with him. Soon, using her as a pawn to further his own ambitions, Du Barry arranges for Marie Jeanne to marry his brother. Then, as a Countess, Marie Jeanne is invited to the court at Versailles where she interests the elderly monarch, who takes her on as his mistress. Although the Duke of Choiseul tries to bring about her ruin, Marie Jeanne's hold on the king's affections remains secure and she becomes firmly entrenched in her position as Madame Du Barry, the first lady of France.

René's infectious air, *"Wie schoen ist alles,"* runs throughout the score as a kind of catalytic agent. The two main waltzes—*"Es lockt die Nacht"* and *"Ob man gefaellt oder nicht gefaellt"*—are supplemented by several other highly delectable tunes. The best are: *"Ja, so ist sie, die Du Barry";* Marie Jeanne's lovely song, *"Ich schenk' mein Herz nur dem allein";* and the duets, *"Wenn Verliebte bummeln gehn"* and *"Reisen wir durchs Liebesland."*

(L') Éclair [*Flash of Lightning*] by Jacques Halévy.

Opéra-comique in three acts with text by Jules Henri Vernoy de Saint-Georges and F. A. E. de Planard. First performance: Opéra-Comique, Paris, December 16, 1835. First American performance: New Orleans, Louisiana, February 16, 1837.

Jacques Halévy first came to the attention of French opera lovers in 1835 with a serious opera in one hand and a comic opera in the other. As it turned out—although he wrote over twenty more operas in the next half-century—each of these 1835 works proved to be the composer's masterpiece in its category. The serious opera was *La Juive,* a classic of the French lyric theater. The comic opera was *L'Éclair,* which proved so popular that in less than half a century it was given over three hundred performances in Paris.

L'Éclair is something of a curiosity among the products of the lighter European theater in that both the settings and some of the principal characters are American. The action takes place in 1797 in a town near Boston. Madame Darbel, a young widow fond of city life, and her sister, Henrietta, an advocate of country life, learn that their British cousin, George, has come into a considerable fortune. But before George can collect his inheritance, the will specifies, he must marry one of his two American cousins. Lionel, an American naval officer, is rescued from a stormy sea by Henrietta. Temporarily blinded, he cannot see the one who has thus saved his life. When his sight is restored, he mistakenly believes that his benefactor had been Madame Darbel, a fact that distresses Henrietta no end since by this time she is in love with the young man. Of course, Lionel eventually realizes his mistake and proceeds to return Henrietta's love; and George and Madame Darbel turn out to be a willing, happy pair.

The leading aria of the first act is a barcarolle by Lionel in which he describes the beauty and majesty of the sea: *"Parlons la mer est belle."* After a melodious orchestral entr'acte preceding the second act, we hear a beautiful rondo by Madame Darbel, *"Eh! mon soeur jolie,"* followed soon thereafter by a moving duet by Lionel and Henrietta,*"Comme mon coeur bat."* A second orchestral entr'acte precedes the third act, in which the principal vocal number is Lionel's poignant romance, *"Quand de la nuit l'épais nuage."*

Eine Nacht in Venedig by Johann Strauss II. *See One Night in Venice.*

Ein Walzertraum by Oscar Straus. *See (A) Waltz Dream.*

(L') Elisir D'amore [*The Elixir of Love*] by Gaetano Donizetti.

Opera buffa in two acts with text by Felice Romani, based on *Le Philtre*, a libretto by Eugène Scribe. First performance: Teatro della Canobbiana, Milan, May 12, 1832. First American performances: Park Theater, New York, June 18, 1838 (in English); Palmo's Opera House, New York, May 22, 1844 (in Italian).

Donizetti wrote thirty-two operas before achieving his first success, which came in 1830 with *Anna Bolena*. Two years and five operas later, Donizetti wrote his first masterwork in the buffa style, *L'Elisir d'amore*. "I am obliged to write an opera in fourteen days," he informed his librettist, Romani. "I give you a week to do your share. . . . But I warn you, we have a German prima donna, a tenor who stutters, a buffo with a voice like a goat, and a worthless French basso. Still, we must cover ourselves with glory."

Despite the haste with which it was written, *L'Elisir d'amore* is one of the handful of works by which Donizetti is still represented most often in the world's opera houses. Here he reveals a remarkable gift for affecting, soaring lyricism and an incomparable talent for the delineation of humorous characters.

Despite Donizetti's qualms about the cast selected for his new opera, it stirred the first-night audience to an overwhelming demonstration of enthusiasm. So popular did the opera become that it had to be repeated on thirty-two consecutive evenings, and wherever it was heard after that, it invariably inspired ovations. There could be little question but that Donizetti and his librettist had truly covered themselves with glory!

In this country, of all Donizetti operas, only the serious opera *Lucia di Lammermoor* has been heard more often (although there is little question that Donizetti's *Don Pasquale* is a much finer buffa opera than *L'Elisir d'amore*). *L'Elisir d'amore* was a particular favorite with Enrico Caruso, for whom the Metropolitan revived the work in 1904. Caruso invariably brought down the house with his poignant and incomparable rendition of the aria, *"Una furtiva lagrima,"* certainly the most remarkable aria in the whole score. And it was while appearing in this very opera—in Brooklyn, New York, on December 11, 1920—that Caruso was stricken with the throat hemorrhage that later proved fatal.

In a small Italian nineteenth-century village, young and wealthy Adina is being courted by two men, Nemorino, a young farmer, and Belcore, and army sergeant. Capriciously, she favors now the one, now the other, to the despair of Nemorino who expresses his feelings for her in the eloquent aria, *"Quanto è bella."* Dr. Dulcamara arrives to sell his quack medicines and elixirs (*"Udite, udite"*). Nemorino purchases an elixir of love, which is nothing but inexpensive wine. He sings rhapsodic praises to the powers of this magic potion (*"Dell' elisir mirabile"*) and is under its intoxicating spell when he discovers that Adina has decided to marry Belcore after all. The whole village has been invited to witness the signing of the marriage contract. Nemorino entreats Dulcamara to provide him with another elixir, with which he hopes to arouse Adina's passion for him. When the quack turns him down because he has no money to pay for it, Nemorino enlists in the army in order to get the bonus given to all recruits. He is now able to buy the precious elixir. Poignantly he entreats Adina to delay her marriage, hoping to gain time for the elixir to work its magic upon her ("*Adina credimi*"). To the distress of Belcore, Adina agrees. Just then the news reaches town that Nemorino's uncle has died, leaving him a fortune. These tidings send the girls of the village swarming around Nemorino in admiration, arousing Adina's jealousy no end. Nemorino first tries to console her ("*Una furtiva lagrima*"), then becomes convinced that it is Dulcamara's elixir that has suddenly made him so irresistible to women. When he realizes he is heir to a fortune, and has been freed from his army duties through Adina's intercession, he can proceed to the serious business of winning the woman he loves.

Enrico Caruso made his debut at the Metropolitan Opera during the 1903–04 season. It was because of his presence that the Metropolitan decided that season to include *L'Elisir d'amore* in its repertory for the first time. In this performance (January 23, 1904), Sembrich appeared as Adina. But it was Caruso as Nemorino who stole the show, and the tumult following his rendition of "*Una furtiva lagrima*" made it necessary for him to repeat the entire aria.

(The) **Elixir of Love** by Gaetano Donizetti. *See* (*L'*) *Elisir d'amore.*

(Die) **Entfuehrung aus dem Serail** by Wolfgang Amadeus Mozart. *See* (*The*) *Abduction from the Seraglio.*

Erminie by Edward Jakobowski.

> Operetta in two acts with text by Claxson Bellamy and Harry Paulton, based on a melodrama by Robert Macaire. First performance: Comedy Theater, London, November 9, 1885. First American performance: Casino Theater, New York, May 10, 1886.

When first produced in London in 1885, *Erminie* was only a modest hit, with a run of less than two hundred performances. But in America a half year later, with a cast headed by Pauline Hall and Francis Wilson, it proved a triumph. Its run of 759 performances was one of the longest of any musical production in Broadway history up to that time. The composer (who came to New York for the première) received royalties in excess of $100,000. *Erminie* also enjoyed immense success in extended engagements in Boston and Philadelphia, and several road companies toured the country for a few years; there were even pirated versions. On Broadway, *Erminie* was revived in 1897, 1898, and 1899. As late as January 31, 1921, it was again seen in New York, with Francis Wilson from the original Broadway cast and De Wolf Hopper.

An unusual episode occurred during that first New York engagement. The blizzard of 1888 forced a temporary suspension of its performances. On the night the storm reached its peak, only two members of the cast showed up, and of the two only one was well enough to perform. There were only three people in the audience, all of them Canadians.

Ernest, a young nobleman, is on his way to meet his betrothed, Erminie, whom he has never seen. He is waylaid by two vagabonds, who tie him to a tree and steal his clothes and belongings. One of these vagabonds, Ravennes, assumes Ernest's identity, while the other, Cadeaux, poses as a "friend." When Ravennes comes to Erminie's house she becomes considerably upset to see the kind of man her prospective husband is. Besides, she is already in love with Eugene, her father's secretary. A party at Erminie's house is suddenly interrupted by the appearance of the real Ernest in ragged clothes. He is forthwith denounced as a fraud. Meanwhile, Ravennes has worked himself into the family's good graces, a convenience enabling him to rob the place before his true identity is revealed. By then the marriage of Erminie with Eugene, the man she loves, has become a foregone conclusion, a fact that causes Ernest no pangs because he is in love with Cerise.

Three songs became outstanding hits in the United States in 1886 and remained popular for several years after that: "At Midnight On My Pillow," "Darkest the Hour," and "Dear Mother in Dreams I See Her." Also popular were Erminie's two songs in the first act, "Ah, When Love Is Young" and "Dream Song"; the love song of Erminie and Eugene, "There Is Sweet Remembrance of the Past"; and a gavotte with which the operetta ends.

Fatinitza by Franz von Suppé.

> Operetta in three acts with text by F. Zell and R. Genée, based on
> *Circassienne*, by Eugène Scribe. First performance: Karlstheater, Vienna,
> January 5, 1876. First American performances: New York, April 14,
> 1879 (in German); New York, April 22, 1879 (in English); New York,
> October 14, 1887 (in French).

Fatinitza was the first comic opera to make Suppé world famous. Much
of its comedy comes from the stale business of having a man masquerade
as a woman. Vladimir, a lieutenant in the Bulgarian army, is in love with
Princess Lydia. Her uncle and guardian, General Kantschukoff, is not
kindly disposed toward him. To keep close to his beloved, Vladimir assumes the dress of a Turkish girl and, assuming the name of Fatinitza,
gets a job as Lydia's lady companion. This disguise was even more successful than the lieutenant had dared to hope: the General himself falls
in love with Fatinitza. One year later, at a Turkish fortress where
Vladimir is stationed with his regiment, he entertains his fellow soldiers
by performing in a play written for the occasion by his friend and
starring the Turkish girl, Fatinitza. During rehearsals, General Kantschukoff appears for a tour of inspection and, seeing Vladimir in costume,
is delighted to see his Fatinitza again. Princess Lydia has accompanied
her uncle. When an attack by the Turks appears imminent, the General
insists that Fatinitza and Lydia seek refuge in a nearby convent. While
there, they are captured by the Turks and brought before the governor
of the Turkish fortress. He is so pleased with Lydia that he decides to
take her on as a concubine. The first time Vladimir and Lydia manage
to be alone together Vladimir discloses that he is no Turkish girl at all.
After effecting his escape, Vladimir leads a successful attack on the
Turkish fort and liberates Lydia. Several months later, Lydia is about to
marry one of her uncle's cronies. Once again Vladimir appears as
Fatinitza, this time to use seductive feminine wiles on the old General
in order to get him to change his mind and permit Lydia to marry a
man of her own choice.

   Among the leading musical numbers are two waltzes: *"Silbergloeck-
chen klingt so helle"* (also known as the "Bell Sextet") and *"Woll'n
sie mich lieben."* A pert little march tune that accompanies the entrance
of the General (*"Himmel Bomben, Element"*) became popular with
salon and café-house orchestras throughout Europe in the late nineteenth

century. Also strongly favored by audiences are these numbers: Lydia's "Bell Song" (*"Glockenklaenge kuenden"*); her "Sleigh Song" (*"Theurer O heim laenger konnt"*); Vladimir's "Dream Song" (*"Sie, die ich nie darf nennen"*); and the chorus of the cadets (*"Erwache frei"*).

A successful revival of *Fatinitza* took place in Munich, Germany, on October 20, 1950. The book was radically altered by Eduard Rogati; new lyrics were provided by Herbert Witt, and the production was under the direction of Bruno Uher.

(Die) Fenster by Ferruccio Busoni. *See Arlecchino.*

(La) Figlia del reggimento by Gaetano Donizetti. *See (The) Daughter of the Regiment.*

(La) Fille de Madame Angot [*The Daughter of Madame Angot*] by Alexandre-Charles Lecocq.

> Opéra-bouffe in three acts with book by Paul Siraudin, Clairville, and Victor Koning, based on a French vaudeville by A. F. E. Maillot. First performance: Théâtre Alcazar, Brussels, December 4, 1872. First American performances: New York, August 25, 1873 (in French); New York, September 29, 1873 (in English); New York, April 17, 1874 (in German).

In the writing of opéra-bouffes, Lecocq was both a successor to and rival of Offenbach. But the two men had quite different concepts of what this form of theater should be. Perhaps because he was born crippled, Lecocq preferred an escapist theater in which romance, glamour, and dreams replaced the harsh realities of life as he knew it. He had no patience with Offenbach's acidulous satire. He did not care to debunk anything. He rejected Offenbach's indefatigable efforts to uncover human foibles.

Lecocq's masterpiece was *La Fille de Madame Angot,* set in Paris during the French Revolution when a directory, with Barras as head, had been established. Clairette ("the daughter of Madame Angot") is in love with the poet, Ange Pitou, but her mother wants her to marry

Pomponnet, the hairdresser. In a desperate attempt to avoid this marriage, Clairette contrives to get herself arrested, which she does by singing in a public square a satirical song by Pitou mocking Mlle Lange, an actress who has become Barras' favorite: *"Jadis, les rois, race proscrite."* After Clairette is dragged off to prison, Mlle Lange becomes interested in her through Pomponnet's intercession and arranges to have the girl visit her. They recognize each other at once as old-time schoolmates. Mlle Lange promises to free Clairette and to see to it that she gets to marry the man she loves. But what Mlle Lange does not know is that Pitou, Clairette's sweetheart, is the same man to whom she herself has become attracted. During a ball at Mlle Lange's house, the two women discover for the first time that they are rivals for Pitou. But Clairette, now wiser and more mature, has decided that she should marry Pomponnet after all, and thus she leaves the field clear for Mlle Lange.

One of the most effective emotional scenes comes in the second act when Pomponnet comes to Mlle Lange to convince her of Clairette's innocence and to gain the actress' support for his sweetheart. Here we find perhaps the most moving aria in the entire score, Pomponnet's romance, *"Elle est tellement innocente."* The sweetness and purity of such a melody won for its composer the sobriquet of "the Massenet of comic opera." Similarly moving in its affecting lyricism is the duet of Mlle Lange and Clairette recalling their childhood, *"Jours fortunes de notre enfance."* The third-act gavotte and the ballet music are outstanding instrumental excerpts.

When *La Fille de Madame Angot* first came to Paris (February 23, 1873), it enjoyed such public favor that it ran for more than five hundred consecutive performances.

(La) Fille du régiment or **La Figlia del regimento** by Gaetano Donizetti. *See (The) Daughter of the Regiment.*

(Il) Filosofo di campagna [*The Country Philosopher*] by Baldassare Galuppi.

> Opera buffa in one act with text by Carlo Goldoni. First performance: Teatro San Samuele, Venice, October 26, 1754. First American performance: WCBS-TV, February 7, 1960.

This opera buffa, its composer's masterwork, is a classic of early Italian comic opera. The collaboration of playwright Goldoni and composer Galuppi resulted in several operas responsible for bringing greater refinement, dignity, and restraint to the opera-buffa form; but nowhere were they more successful than in *Il Filosofo di campagna*. The principal character, Don Tritemo, is a foolish old man who devises various machinations and schemes whereby his lovely daughter, Eugenia, can be kept from marrying Rinaldo. He fails, to be sure. A secondary plot embroils Eugenia's friend, Lesbina, and Nardo.

In its own day, *Il Filosofo di campagna* was a tremendous favorite not only with Italian opera audiences but also with people in other European countries. It first came to London in 1761, and to Dublin in 1762. On both occasions it was presented under the title of *The Guardian Trick'd*. Probably no opera buffa between the time of Pergolesi's *La Serva padrona* and Piccinni's *La buona Figliuola* was held in higher esteem anywhere. Nevertheless, this opera had to wait more than two centuries before being seen and heard in the United States; and this happened not on a traditional stage but over television. At that time, Howard Taubman wrote in the *New York Times:* "It is a sprightly piece brimming with cheerful tunes. Galuppi . . . was a glib composer, but he also had knowledge and sophistication. He had a gift for building up a finale. . . . His tender numbers lacked depth, but he knew how to be crisp and gay."

The most tuneful arias in the score include three by Lesbina and one each by Rinaldo and Nardo. Two of Lesbina's airs appear successively, early in the opera: *"Quando son giovine"* and *"Son fresca, son bella"; the third is *"Compatite, signor."* That of Rinaldo is *"Anima vile,"* and that of Nardo, *"Vedo quell'albero."*

Il Filosofo di campagna has been edited on two different occasions by two outstanding Italian composers, Ermanno Wolf-Ferrari and Gian Francesco Malipiero. The Wolf-Ferrari version received its world première in Venice on August 25, 1954.

(La) Finta giardiniera [*The Pretending Gardener*] by Wolfgang Amadeus Mozart.

> Opera buffa in three acts with text by Raniero de Calzabigi, altered by M. Coltellini. First performance: Munich, January 13, 1775. First

American performance (probable): Mayfair Theater, New York, January 18, 1927 (in English).

This is one of several operas Mozart wrote in his boyhood, youth, and early manhood in imitation of the Italian opera buffa. He was commissioned to write *La Finta giardiniera* for the Carnival of Munich, completing his score in 1775, when he was nineteen. The first performance went off very well, indeed. "It is impossible for me to describe the tumult of applause," Mozart wrote to his mother. One can well understand the reason for his enthusiasm. Mozart wrote as effortlessly and as naturally in the opera buffa style as if he were an Italian himself. The score is a geyser eruption of the loveliest tunes, but it is much more than that. As W. J. Turner said, the music is "entrancing . . . without reserve," with "inimitable charm and gaiety, tenderness and fertility of invention." Beyond its wonderful lyricism and infectious good humor, the score boasts a real dramatic power (sometimes even touched with tragic feeling) such as is rarely encountered in the Italian comic opera form. Indeed, one of Mozart's biographers once complained that the music of *La Finta giardiniera* is "more powerful and passionate than the situations demand," and that its comic arias are "too subtle, elaborate, ingenious, and clever for the words."

If the music is highly distinctive, the plot and characterizations are stereotypes. Marchesa Violante has been slighted by the man she loves, Count Belfiore. She and her valet disguise themselves as gardeners and seek employment at the palace of the Podesta, ruler of Lagonero. The Podesta finds Violante most charming; and the Podesta's maid is strongly attracted to the valet. Meanwhile, Count Belfiore is about to marry the Podesta's niece who, in turn, is being pursued by Ramiro. Thus the various love-plot threads become hopelessly entangled. Before the final curtain, however, Violante and the Count, the valet and the maid, and Ramiro and the Podesta's niece are joined together in pairs by mutual love. Only the Podesta himself remains without a mate.

Especially beautiful in lyricism and touching in emotion are two of Violante's arias: "*Noi donne poverine*" and "*Geme la tortorella.*" Similarly attractive is a duet of Violante and Count Belfiore, "*Dove mai son*" with its lovely section "*Lei mi chiama.*"

After this opera was first introduced in Munich in the original Italian, it was translated into German by an actor named Stierle, for a touring company managed by Johann Boehm. The first performance of this

German version, named *Die verstellte Gaertnerin,* took place in Augsburg on May 1, 1780. After 1791, the opera went into complete discard until almost a century later when it was revived by the Vienna Royal Opera on December 25, 1891, the music edited and revised by J. N. Fuchs.

(La) Finta Semplice [*The Pretending Simpleton*] by Wolfgang Amadeus Mozart.

> Opera buffa in three acts with text by Marco Coltellini, based on a libretto by Carlo Goldoni. First performance: Salzburg, Austria, May 1, 1769.

La Finta semplice was Mozart's first opera, written when he was only twelve. He had come with his father to Vienna where he startled the court with his prodigious musical feats. The Emperor commissioned him to write a comic opera for a theater leased and managed by Affligio. A text was provided by Coltellini, theatrical poet in Vienna. Mozart completed his entire score in about four months: twenty-one arias, three finales, one duet, and one chorus. But getting the opera performed was another matter. Intrigues both at court and in Affligio's theater—particularly among those resenting the performance of an opera by a child—led to one postponement after another. "The court cannot say a word," wrote Mozart's father to a friend, "as he [Affligio] takes all the risks. . . . The singers, who, in any case, scarcely know their notes . . . and must learn by ear now began to say they could not sing their arias (which they had already heard in our room, approved of, and applauded) as they were not suitable, the orchestra that it would not be conducted by a boy, etc, etc. . . . Meanwhile others declared the music was not worth a groat . . . because the boy did not sufficiently understand Italian." At last, Affligio decided he would not produce the opera at all and warned Mozart's father that if he was stubborn about sticking to the contract, Affligio would see to it that the opera was hissed off the stage. The première, when it finally did take place, was given not in Vienna but in Mozart's birthplace and hometown, Salzburg.

It was an amazing libretto for a child of twelve to try setting to music —involving a woman-hater, a philanderer, and various love intrigues. The main plot concerns the efforts of two bachelors—Cassandro and Polidoro—to prevent their sister from marrying an officer. The bachelors are eventually outwitted by the officer's sister.

But if such goings-on are beyond the everyday experience of a child, there is nothing in Mozart's music to betray this fact. The score is witty and sophisticated, especially brilliant in its depiction of the bachelors and in its humorous treatment of intrigues and disguises. "Here," says Nathan Broder, "are touches that point to the future master, like Cassandro's aria, '*Ella vuole ed io torrei*,' whose text, with its opportunities for fooling, might have delighted the high-spirited boy; or Rosina's '*Amoretti*,' which in spirit anticipates some of the lyric moments in *Così fan tutte*; or Cassandro's '*Ubriaco non son io*' with the violins reeling around in their ritornel as drunk as the singer; or the pantomime bit in Act II, where the music, subdued and poetic, is on a much higher level than the silly scene being enacted."

A complete recording of *La Finta semplice* was issued by Epic Records in 1960 in a Salzburg performance.

Flash of Lightning by Jacques Halévy. *See* (*L'*) *Éclair*.

(Die) Fledermaus [*The Bat*] by Johann Strauss II.

> Operetta in three acts with text by Karl Haffner and Richard Genée, based on *Le Réveillon*, a French vaudeville by Henri Meilhac and Ludovic Halevy, which in turn was derived from *Das Gefaengnis* by Roderich Benedix. First performance: Theater-an-der-Wien, Vienna, April 5, 1874. First American performances: Thalia Theater, New York, November 21, 1874 (in German); Casino Theater, New York, March 16, 1885 (in English).

Johann Strauss II had already reigned for many years as waltz king in Vienna when he finally decided to write his first operetta. That was in 1871, with *Indigo und die vierzig Rauber*, written at the instigation of Offenbach (then visiting Vienna) and Strauss's wife, Jetty. *Indigo* was a failure, nor did its immediate successor, *Der Karneval in Rom* in 1873, do much better. But in 1874, Johann Strauss wrote and had produced *Die Fledermaus*. The composer, who had previously acquired a unique place in Vienna's musical life through his incomparable quadrilles, polkas, and waltzes, had now become the foremost Austrian operetta composer of his time.

When his collaborators first brought him the libretto of *Die Fledermaus*,

Strauss instantly fell in love with it. He was impatient to get pen to paper. Shutting himself up in his study in his Hietzing villa, he became a recluse from all save his wife. He often refused food and drink, as he continued writing in a white heat. It took him forty-three days to complete his entire score.

Die Fledermaus appeared at a black moment in Vienna's history. Austria had been stricken by an economic crisis in 1873, the effects of which were still strongly felt a year later. People were not in the mood for the kind of frivolity, gaiety, and froth offered by a stage work like *Die Fledermaus*, and they rejected the new operetta after an initial run of only sixteen performances. But soon after that, it was given in Berlin, where it ran for a hundred performances. Then, returning to Vienna later in 1874, it finally became a triumph. Within six months of the Vienna première, *Die Fledermaus* was performed in over one hundred and fifty theaters in Germany alone. It came to New York in 1874 and to London in 1876. In 1894 it entered the permanent repertory of the Vienna Royal Opera, where it was given a stunning performance under the musical direction of Gustav Mahler. Since then *Die Fledermaus* has become one of the most celebrated and one of the most frequently performed operettas in the world; token of its artistic and musical significance is the fact that it is heard as often in the world's leading opera houses as it is in popular theaters.

Since its American première in 1874, *Die Fledermaus* has been a frequent visitor to the opera houses and popular theaters of the United States. A Broadway production in 1942, renamed *Rosalinda* and starring Dorothy Sarnoff and Everett West, had over five hundred performances. The Metropolitan Opera first introduced it into its repertory on February 16, 1905, with Marcella Sembrich as Rosalinda—the first time that this Johann Strauss operetta was heard in America with a cast of opera singers. In this performance, the wonderful second-act finale was extended to include a café-chantant spectacle in which some of the greatest stars of the Metropolitan Opera (including Caruso, Eames, Fremstad, and Journet) made brief appearances in concert or operatic numbers. Another unorthodox performance was the gala revival of *Die Fledermaus* by the Metropolitan Opera during the 1950–51 season. The operetta was heard in a new English translation by Howard Dietz; Garson Kanin, heretofore identified exclusively with Broadway and Hollywood, served as stage director; the role of Frosche, the jailer, was played by a nightclub comic, Jack Gilford.

The action takes place in Vienna in or about 1870. Baron Eisenstein, guilty of some minor offense, is to be sentenced to a prison term of five days. His friend, Falke, convinces him to delay serving long enough to attend a gala masked ball at Prince Orlofsky's palace. During the Baron's absence from home, his wife, Rosalinda, entertains at supper her lover, a handsome young singer, Alfred. When the police arrive to arrest the Baron, Rosalinda is reluctant to confess that Alfred is not her husband, and so it is Alfred who is dragged off to prison. Rosalinda, with her maid Adele, now decides to go to Prince Orlofsky's ball. There Baron Eisenstein flirts with, then tries to make love to, his own wife without realizing who she is—much to Rosalinda's chagrin. The party over, the Baron goes off to the jail where Alfred is incarcerated. It is only then that the Baron discovers that his wife has a lover. When Rosalinda arrives to try to effect Alfred's release, the Baron and his wife exchange heated accusations over each other's infidelity. But Falke, the Baron's friend, comes to the rescue by taking full responsibility for what has transpired and saying he had planned it all as a practical joke.

It is not too much to say that *Die Fledermaus* is the first authentic Viennese operetta. It set a standard and established a style and a tradition which all later Austrian operettas were to emulate. A basic element of this new style was the grand finale pivoted on a waltz. In *Die Fledermaus* it occurs at the conclusion of the second act, at Prince Orlofsky's masked ball. First Orlofsky and the chorus sing a hymn to champagne, "*Im Feuer-strom der Reben.*" The guests pledge brotherhood as they lift wine glasses high in air, "*Bruederlein, Bruederlein, und Schwesterlein,*" culminating with the refrain, "*Du, du.*" After that comes a ballet scene (for which it is now customary to utilize the music of Johann Strauss's immortal waltz, "The Blue Danube"). The ballet over, the Prince invites his guests to dance. They do so to the pulsating rhythms of one of Strauss's greatest waltz melodies, the one used so prominently in the overture.

That overture is a kind of resumé of essential musical materials from the rest of the opera. First we hear three subjects from the last-act prison scene; then, the monumental second-act waltz; after that, in contrast, the lugubrious strains with which Eisenstein bids farewell before departing for prison.

Strauss's score is a cornucopia of melodic riches. Here, as Bruno Walter once wrote, "we have beauty without heaviness, levity without vulgarity, gaiety without frivolity, and a strange mixture of exuberant musical richness (somewhat resembling Schubert) and popular simplicity." The overture and the grand second-act finale have already been commented upon. In addition to these, the following excerpts are worthy of note: Alfred's drinking song in the first act, *"Trinke, Liebchen, trinke schnell"*; in the second act, Prince Orlofsky's air to his guests, *"Ich lade gern mir Gaeste ein,"* Adele's laughing song mocking her employer, *"Mein Herr Marquis,"* and Rosalinda's blood-warming czardas, *"Klaenge der Heimat."* The introduction of a czardas (one of the several high peaks in the score) into a Viennese operetta was made logical by having Rosalinda presented to the company as a Hungarian countess, a role in which she decides to entertain her friends with a rendition of authentic Hungarian music. "No genuine Hungarian music," says Ernest Newman, "could sing more movingly of the pain of separation from the beloved homeland or of the fires in the Hungarian breast that drive them to the dance."

Florodora by Leslie Stuart.

> Operetta in two acts with text and lyrics by Owen Hall. First performance: Lyric Theater, London, November 11, 1899. First American performance: Casino Theater, New York, November 10, 1900.

"Tell me, pretty maiden, are there any more home like you?" This catch question was often bandied about by young men of the town both in London and New York at the turn of the present century. It is also a line from a song which was probably the greatest single factor in the triumph of *Florodora* in both England and the United States. In London, *Florodora* had a run of 455 performances; in the United States (where it profited from an all-star cast that included R. E. Graham, Fannie Johnstone, Edna Wallace Hopper, and Cyril Scott, together with the celebrated "Florodora Sextet"), it ran for 505 performances in New York, and then was revived there in 1902, 1905, and 1920. It also enjoyed an eight-year run on the road which touched practically every major American city.

The play itself was a rather silly concoction, sillier even than those found in other operettas. The first part takes place in a Philippine island called Florodora. Cyrus W. Gilfain, a rich American manufacturer, has stolen a perfume formula named after the Philippine island, from Dolores' deceased father, and Dolores is reduced to earning her living in the factory. Anthony Tweedlepunch is bent on restoring the formula— and the rights to its manufacture—to their rightful owner. In the second part of the play, the scene shifts to a castle in Wales, ancestral home of Gilfain's manager, Frank Abercoed. All the principals are present. Abercoed, in love with Dolores, joins Tweedlepunch in the search for some evidence among Gilfain's belongings proving Dolores' right to the perfume. Failing that, Tweedlepunch comes upon an ingenious scheme: invoking a ghost who frightens Gilfain to the point at which the millionaire is ready to admit his sin and do right by Dolores. Their mission ended, Dolores and Abercoed can devote their time to each other.

The Sextet, which made audiences in London and New York swoon with delight, occurs in the first act, on the island of Florodora. Six ravishingly attractive girls (advertized in New York as "the most beautiful girls in the world") are employed in Gilfain's factory as typists (or as they were known at the turn of the century, "typewriter girls"). They are tall, willowy, lithe. Some are brunettes, others red heads. They come out on the stage followed by six swains who inquire: "Tell me, pretty maiden, are there any more home like you?" The girls reply modestly, "There are a few." For the sake of the record, the Florodora sextet of girls in New York were Marie Wilson, Agnes Wayburn, Marjorie Relyea, Vaughn Texsmith, Daisy Green, and Margaret Walker. Three of these girls married millionaires, thereby probably being responsible for inaugurating a trend long persistent on Broadway of chorus girls seeking out and winning men in high social and financial positions.

Besides this sextet, Stuart's score included a beautiful song in "The Shade of the Palm" (in many ways more haunting than the much-publicized tune of the sextet) and two other fine numbers presented by Dolores, "The Silver Star of Love" and "The Island of Love."

(The) **Four Ruffians** by Ermanno Wolf-Ferrari. *See (I) Quattro rusteghi.*

Fra Diavolo or **L'Hôtellerie de Terracine** [*Fra Diavolo* or *The Inn of Terracine*] by Daniel François Esprit Auber.

Opéra-comique in three acts with text by Eugène Scribe. First performance: Opéra-Comique, Paris, January 28, 1830. First American performances: Chatham Theater, New York, October 17, 1831 (in French); New York, June 20, 1833 (in English); New York, November 16, 1858 (in German); New York, December 21, 1864 (in Italian).

The composer's masterwork, *Fra Diavolo*—which came two years after his highly successful and historically significant *La Muette de Portici*—is one of several creations in which the opéra-comique form was crystallized and perfected. It proved the most successful of all of Auber's comic operas, having received over one thousand performances at the Opéra-Comique by the time of World War I.

In preparing his script, Scribe bore in mind the popularity in Paris for texts utilizing brigands, highwaymen, forgers, and other disreputable members of nineteenth-century society. His hero is Fra Diavolo, an Italian bandit chief, who terrorized the countryside. Despite a much publicized reward for his capture, Fra Diavolo manages to elude his captors by assuming various disguises. He comes to Matteo's tavern in a small Terracine village, dressed as the Marquis of San Marco. Lorenzo, an officer, dreams of capturing the highwayman and using the reward money as bait with which to capture Zerlina, the innkeeper's daughter. After the arrival of the "Marquis," an English Lord announces he has been robbed. He also complains that his wife is being relentlessly pursued by a marquis who, as a matter of fact, is even then paying her marked attention at the dinner table. Later on, Fra Diavolo and two of his henchmen hide in Zerlina's bedroom. After Zerlina has fallen asleep, they try to rob the English lord in a nearby bedroom, but manage only to arouse the whole household. The culprits escape. Fra Diavolo, reassuming the pose of a marquis, explains his presence in Zerlina's room by revealing he had had a rendezvous with her. This infuriates Lorenzo, who challenges Diavolo to a duel. Later on, in a forest, Diavolo reassumes his bandit's outfit and waits for Lorenzo, who manages to lure Diavolo and his men into a trap in which the bandit chief is killed.

Although there is a good deal of Rossini sparkle and gaiety in Auber's musical writing, his style is nevertheless essentially French, deeply rooted in French popular melodies and rhythms. The overture has dash and vivacity. It opens with a quiet drum roll that leads to a brisk little march tune for strings. The tune is taken over by the other instruments and is built up into a climax for full orchestra. After that comes a succession of pleasing melodies, all of them derived from the material of the first act.

The most popular melody in the opera is Zerlina's second act aria: In her bedroom, unaware that Fra Diavolo and his men are hiding there, she speaks of her happiness in loving Lorenzo (*"Quel bonheur"*). She renders another distinguished aria in *"Voyez sur cette roche"*—ending with the exclamation *"Diavolo! Diavolo!"*—in which she tells the "Marquis" about the infamous Diavolo.

Mention should also be made of Diavolo's delightful second-act barcarolle, *"Agnès la jouvencelle";* the melodious orchestral intermezzo between the second and third acts; the choral third-act episode, *"O sainte vierge";* and Lorenzo's beautiful romance, *"Pour toujours disait-elle."*

In the 1930's, *Fra Diavolo* was made into a Hollywood farce starring Laurel and Hardy.

Frasquita by Franz Lehár.

> Operetta in three acts with text by A. M. Willner and Heinz Reichert. First performance: Vienna, May 12, 1922.

The "Frasquita Serenade" is one of Lehár's best-known melodies. This is a romantic song which the hero, Armand, sings to Frasquita, the gypsy girl: *"Hab ein blaues Himmelbett."* The world-famous concert violinist Fritz Kreisler made a fine arrangement of it for violin and piano and performed it at many of his concerts, besides recording it for R.C.A. Victor. An orchestral version is in the repertory of most "pop," light, or café-house orchestras. If for no reason other than this one melody, *Frasquita* deserves to be remembered.

The setting is Paris and Barcelona; the time, the early 1920's. Armand comes to Barcelona to visit his uncle and is honored with a gala reception. The party is interrupted by the arrival of a band of gypsies, headed by the mercurial, fiery Frasquita. Frasquita and one of her friends get involved in a heated fight. Armand finally manages to break it up, but in doing so, he loses his golden cigarette case, which he accuses Frasquita of having stolen. It is not long before Armand falls a victim to the spell of Frasquita's beauty and charm. Frasquita, however, cannot forget how unjustly Armand had accused her of being a thief; in an effort to avenge herself she lures him into believing that she is in love with him. In a nightspot where Frasquita is the star performer, Armand confronts her in her dressing room, where she is entertaining several men. Seized by an uncontrollable fit of jealousy, he showers abuse on Frasquita who, at that moment, suddenly realizes that she is in love with Armand after all. Back in Paris, Armand cannot forget Frasquita; his friends try to relieve his black mood by inviting him to a carnival. Unexpectedly, Frasquita comes to his apartment to confess she has made the trip from Spain to tell him how much she loves him. Armand, skeptical, is cold to her ardent expressions of tenderness, even orders her to leave his house.

But Armand's uncle realizes that the two were meant for each other and he brings about their reconciliation.

Besides the "Frasquita Serenade," the best-known vocal numbers include the following waltzes: *"Weisst du nicht, was ein Herz voller Sehnsucht begehrt," "Wo du weilst, was du immer tust,"* and *"Du siehst auf jedem kleinen Blatt."*

Frau Luna [*Lady Moon*] by Paul Lincke.

Operetta in two acts with text by H. Bolten-Baeckers. First performance: Berlin, Germany, December 31, 1899.

To Americans, the name of Paul Lincke is known best through his song "The Glow Worm" which first appeared in the operetta, *Lysistrata* (1902), and then went on to become famous throughout the world. In 1952 it once again became a leading American song hit with new amusing lyrics by Johnny Mercer. Europeans know Lincke best not only for "The Glow Worm" (or *"Gluehwuermchen"*), but also for several of his operettas, the most famous of which was *Frau Luna.*

Long before a trip to the moon became the serious project of missile scientists and engineers, long before even such a voyage was a favored subject for science-fiction writers, a lunar expedition served as a theme for one of the most successful German operettas in the closing years of the nineteenth century. Entitled *Frau Luna,* it had an initial run of six hundred performances. The setting was divided boldly between the Berlin of 1899 and the moon. Fritz Steppke, a mechanic, wants to build a balloon capable of reaching the moon. He is encouraged by Laemmermeier, a tailor, and Pannecke, a wealthy merchant engaged to Mrs. Pusebach, Fritz's landlady. Mrs. Pusebach, however, considers the entire venture mad. She insists that the mechanic vacate his room, and she cautions her niece, Marie, who is in love with Fritz, to warn the mechanic he must make a choice between Marie and his wild dreams. Laemmermeier and Pannecke come to Fritz's attic to inform him that all is in readiness for the flight. They are followed by the landlady, who tries to dissuade them from making the foolhardy attempt. But all four are within the balloon when it begins its upward flight. The passengers reach the moon where they are met by Theophilus, caretaker of that domain. He promises Mrs. Pusebach he will get her back on earth with the help of Prince Shooting Star, who has come to the moon in his space automobile to court the queen of the moon, Lady Luna. Theophilus places the others under arrest and brings them to trial before Lady Luna. The latter falls in love with Fritz and tries to seduce him. Theophilus conceives a plan to break up this romance. He advises Prince Shooting Star to go to earth and bring Marie back with him to the moon. When this has been accomplished, and Fritz has had a glimpse of the girl he loves, he forgets the Queen completely. Lady Luna consoles herself with Prince Shooting Star, and the five earthly people are brought back to earth in his space ship, since Fritz's balloon is no longer capable of functioning.

The subject lent itself to spectacular scenes, one reason why *Frau Luna* had such powerful audience appeal. A second reason for the show's success were three hit songs which all Berlin was singing, or listening to, at the turn of the twentieth century: *"Schloesser, die im Monde liegen," "Schenk mir doch ein kleines bisschen Liebe, Liebe,"* and *"Lass den Kopf nicht haengen."*

Friederike [*Frederika*] by Franz Lehár.

Operetta in three acts with text by Ludwig Herzer and Fritz Loehner. First performance: Berlin, Germany, October 4, 1928. First American performance: Imperial Theater, New York, February 4, 1937.

The protagonist in this minor Lehár operetta is Goethe, the distinguished German poet-philosopher. In the play he is at first still a law student in Strasbourg. On a visit to a rector in another town, he falls in love with the rector's daughter Frederika. But Goethe warns his beloved that he may not be able to see her again for a long time since he must concentrate on his studies. Back in Strasbourg, the girl's aunt, Mme School, is giving a party honoring Goethe. Several of Goethe's friends, and Frederika, have been invited. She suspects Goethe of infidelity when she espies him in the company of several lovely ladies, but she becomes reassured when he presents her with a ring as a token of his love and informs her he has just been appointed to the Weimar court. Captain Knebel from Weimar insists that Goethe leave for his new post without delay. When Goethe refuses to do so, since he wants time to marry Frederika, she tells him lightly that she does not love him and frees him from his promise to marry her. Unaware that her real intention had been to prevent him from losing his valuable post, Goethe is overwhelmed by her seeming callousness and departs for Weimar without so much as bidding her farewell. Eight years elapse. Goethe, a famous poet now, revists the parish where Frederika resides and discovers that she has never married, that, indeed, she still nurses a frustrated love for him. Only now does Goethe discover what a sacrifice she had made for the sake of his career. But it is too late for amends: Goethe no longer loves her. Sadly, Goethe leaves town and Frederika forever, leaving behind him a good part of his past.

Friederike contains several fetching Lehár melodies, the best of which is Goethe's waltz, "*O wie schoen, wie wunderschoen*," and Frederika's rapturous song with which the operetta sweeps to a climax, "*Warum hast du mich wachgekuesst?*" Also of more than passing appeal are the duet of Goethe and Frederika when they meet for the first time, "*Blicke ich auf deine Haende*"; and three Goethe songs, "*O Maedchen, mein Maedchen*," "*Sah ein Knab' ein Roeslein steh'n*," and "*Liebe, gold'ner Traum*."

When *Friederike* appeared on Broadway as *Frederika* in 1937, the text had been adapted for American audiences by Edward Eliscu, who was also the author of the lyrics. The cast was headed by Dennis King and Helen Gleason.

(La) Gazza Ladra [*The Thieving Magpie*] by Gioacchino Rossini.

Opera buffa in two acts with text by Giovanni Gherardini, based on *La Pie voleuse*, a French melodrama by Jean Marie Théodore Baudouin d'Aubigny and Louis Charles Caigniez. First performance: La Scala, Milan, May 31, 1817. First American performances: Philadelphia, October 1827 (in French); New York, November 18, 1833 (in Italian); New York, January 14, 1839 (in English).

Although there are some highly dramatic, even tragic, episodes in *La Gazza ladra,* the opera contains enough opera buffa touches to place it solidly in the comic-opera category. Rossini wrote it for La Scala after he had suffered two successive failures in Milan. Never reluctant to stoop to conquer, and determined to turn the tide of his Milan fortunes, he made every effort to cater to public taste. Because Milan had begun reacting favorably to German operas, Rossini emulated the Germans by using a larger orchestra and assigning to it a greater importance that he had been accustomed. Since a prayer in another opera had recently brought down the house at La Scala, Rossini included a prayer in *La*

Gazza ladra. These may have been some of the reasons why *La Gazza ladra* proved a monumental success. Stendhal called the opening night one of the most successful he had ever seen. The opera stayed in the La Scala repertory the entire season.

But a much more salient reason for the opera's success has been presented by Francis Toye. It had "something for everybody: pathos, tragedy, tenderness, and gaiety."

Ninetta, a servant girl, has been accused of stealing a silver spoon. Although innocent, she refuses to clear herself, for by doing so she would have to give information leading to the arrest of her father, an army deserter. In the end, she is completely cleared: the silver spoon had been lifted and secreted by a pet magpie. The main love interest engages Ninetta and Fernando, and much of the humor comes from the cumbersome efforts of a lecherous old Podesta to gain Ninetta's favor.

The overture is now famous. In its time, it caused quite a stir because it opens unorthodoxly with rolls from two snare drums, placed at opposite sides of the orchestra. This seemed such a scandalous procedure that a story was circulated that the concertmaster planned to murder the composer. The irate musician, however, was dissuaded from this crime only by having Rossini promise never again to make a similar offense in an overture.

After these unusual drum rolls, the orchestra enters with a stout march tune. A return of the snare drums, and five strong chords for full orchestra, bring on the main portion which begins with a graceful melody from the third act. A transition for wind instruments leads to the second melody, after which both main subjects are amplified and repeated.

Several of the most poignant melodies of the opera are assigned to the heroine, Ninetta: the first-act aria, "*Di piacer mi balza il cor*"; her first-act duet with Fernando, "*Come frenare*"; and her second-act aria, "*Deh! tu reggi in tal momento.*"

These vocal excerpts are also noteworthy: in the first act, the air of the Podesta, "*Il mio piano è prepara*," and that of Isacco, a minor character, "*Stringhe e ferri da calzete*"; and in the second act, Fernando's air, "*Accusata di furto.*"

Rossini's wit is best revealed in some of his dexterous characterizations, most notably in that of the lecherous Podesta. One of his best dramatic pages is the so-called Judgment Scene," described by Toye as "one of the very best examples of power and dignity in Rossini's writing for the stage."

(The) Geisha by Sidney Jones.

> Operetta in two acts with text by Owen Hall and lyrics by Harry Green-
> bank. First performance: Daly's Theater, London, April 25, 1896. First
> American performance: Daly's Theater, New York, September 9, 1896.

The Geisha—in which Marie Tempest was starred in an exotic operetta
set in Japan—is the composer's most popular operetta and one of the most
successful in the English theater of its time. It ran for 760 performances
in London. After that it was performed in Vienna in a German version
by C. M. Roehr and Julius Freund, and was presented in New York with
an all-American cast in which Isadora Duncan, later the world-famous
dancer, made her first appearance as a ballerina.

At the close of the nineteenth century, Lieutenant Reggie Fairfax, an
English naval officer, is stationed in Japan. On shore leave, he meets and
pays attention to the attractive geisha girl, O Mimosa San, although his
betrothed, Molly, is also in Japan. Molly decides to teach Reggie a lesson. Disguising herself as a geisha, Molly gets a job in the very teahouse where O Mimosa San is employed, and as a geisha makes advances
to Reggie. Just then, the chief of police—himself in love with Mimosa
—orders the teahouse to be closed and the geisha girls to be sold at auc-
tion. Molly, dressed as a geisha, is bought by the chief of police, while
Mimosa becomes the acquisition of an English lady. For the rest of the
play, Molly tries to extricate herself from this strange predicament until
she is able to effect her escape. After that she and Reggie square matters
between them. Mimosa finds happiness with her true lover, a Japanese
named Katana, while the chief of police is consoled by a French girl,
Juliette.

"The Amorous Goldfish" is one of several delights in the score, intro-
duced in London by Marie Tempest in the role of O Mimosa San, and in
America by Dorothy Morton. Among the other musical highlights are
"Kissing" and "Toy Monkey," both of them duets of Mimosa and Fairfax;
Mimosa's song about her profession, "A Geisha Girl"; Fairfax's song,
"Star of My Soul"; and the chorus "Chin, Chin, Chinaman." Two other
numbers were especially popular in the United States: "Chon Kina" and
"The Jewel of Asia."

In New York, *The Geisha* was revived on March 27, 1913, with a cast
including Lina Abarbanell and James T. Powers.

Gianni Schicchi by Giacomo Puccini.

Opera buffa in one act with text by Giovacchino Forzano. First performance: Metropolitan Opera, New York, December 14, 1918.

Toward the end of his magnificent career as the foremost composer of Italian operas since Verdi, Puccini completed a trilogy of one-act operas. One of these was a tragedy (*Il Tabarro*); the second was a religious opera with overtones of mysticism (*Suor Angelica*). The third, in sharp contrast to the other two, was *Gianni Schicchi,* an opera buffa in the style of Rossini and Wolf-Ferrari. All his life Puccini had nursed an ambition to write a comic opera. When Forzano brought him the libretto of *Gianni Schicchi,* Puccini could hardly wait to get to work on it. Into this one-act work he not only poured his wonderful gift for sensitive lyricism, but he also tapped for the first time a rich vein of mockery, satire, laughter, and buffoonery. Puccini even went so far as to parody the sentimental style for which he himself had become famous in his serious operas.

In discussing *Gianni Schicchi,* George R. Marek said in his biography of Puccini: "Puccini mixes short, mordant phrases with long, leisurely melodies, giving the opera fine variety. The lights go on and off, though it never gets dark. Altogether this is a real comedy and possesses that special brand of Mediterranean merriment which is half good nature and half spite."

In *Gianni Schicchi* we get one of the composer's rare successful male characterizations; heretofore his talent had flourished with heroines. The central character is a wily old fox who appears briefly in Dante's *Divine Comedy.* In Florence, in Dante's time, a wealthy Florentine by the name of Donati dies, leaving all his possessions to charity. His relatives are flabbergasted to discover that they have been neglected and are determined to contrive some legal way of circumventing Donati's last wishes. Young Rinuccio consults Gianni Schicchi, a sly fellow who happens to be the father of Lauretta, with whom Rinuccio is in love. Schicchi comes posthaste to the dead man's house to concoct an ingenious scheme. He has the dead body removed. Since no one in town has as yet learned that Donati is dead, Schicchi slips into Donati's sickbed to impersonate him. First he fools Donati's doctor by imitating the dead man's voice, then he calls a notary to draw up a will. But Schicchi is nobody's fool. Realizing he is in full control of the situation, he dictates a will in which

Donati's entire estate is bequeathed to—Gianni Schicchi. All of Donati's relatives are furious at this trick, but since they were all willing partners to a fraud in the first place, they must remain silent.

When the opera was given its world première—not in Italy, but at the Metropolitan Opera in New York—Giuseppe De Luca was cast as Schicchi and Florence Easton as Lauretta. The bill was filled out with the world premières of Puccini's two other one-act operas of his trilogy. The critical reaction to the serious one-act operas was reserved, but for the comic opera there were only expressions of delight. Henry Krehbiel wrote: "An invigorating breeze blew through the theater when the curtain rose. . . . This comedy is so uproariously funny, the music so full of life, humor, and ingenious devices that . . . it was received with uproarious delight."

Two of its arias belong among Puccini's greatest melodies. One is an eloquent hymn to the city of Florence delivered by Rinuccio, *"Firenze è come un'albero fiorito."* The other is the popular and familiar aria of Lauretta, *"O mio babbino caro."* Hardly less appealing is the love duet of Rinuccio and Lauretta, *"Lauretta mia."*

Giroflé-Girofla by Alexandre-Charles Lecocq.

Opéra-comique in three acts with text by Albert Vanloo and Eugène Leterrier. First performance: Théâtre Alcazar, Brussels, March 21, 1874. First American performances: New York, February 4, 1875 (in French); New York, March 10, 1875 (in German); New York, May 19, 1875 (in English).

The names in the title represent a pair of twins in a mid-nineteenth-century North African colony belonging to Spain. They are so identical that each must wear a scarf of different color to be recognized. Giroflé is to be married to Marasquin, a wealthy banker, a union encouraged by her father as a convenient means to relieve his financial distress. Her sister, Girofla, is betrothed to a fire-eating Moorish chieftain, Mourzouk. En route to the wedding of Giroflé and the banker, Girofla is seized and abducted by a band of pirates. When the Moor, Mourzouk, arrives at the ceremony, he mistakes the bride for his own betrothed and insists upon marrying her forthwith. To placate him, Giroflé poses as her twin sister and goes through a marriage ceremony for the second time. Then, fearing the secret might leak out, the mother of the twins locks the bride in a closet, leaving the ceremony with two husbands and no bride. Matters get even more complicated when one of the bride's relatives releases her from the closet, plies her with wine until she is inebriated, then brings her out in a completely befuddled state to confront her two husbands. Each husband claims her as his wife. The matter gets completely out of hand, and the bride's father is forced to reveal what has taken place. The aroused Moor is about to inflict physical harm on the father when, suddenly, Girofla reappears, having been rescued from the pirates and seemingly none of the worse for her experience. A real marriage between Girofla and the Moor can now take place.

These are a few of the many musical bon bons in this delightful comic-opera dish: the tongue-in-cheek pirates' chorus when they capture Girofla, *"Parmi les choses délicates"* Giroflé's sparkling drinking song, *"Le punch scintille"* the love duet, *"O ciel!"* and the affecting ballad, *"Lorsque la journée est finie."*

(The) Gondoliers or **The King of Barataria** by Gilbert and Sullivan.

Comic opera in two acts with text and lyrics by W. S. Gilbert and music by Arthur Sullivan. First performance: Savoy Theater, London, December 7, 1889. First American performance: New Park Theater, New York, January 7, 1890.

The Gondoliers—one of the merriest of the Gilbert and Sullivan inventions, which enjoyed a profitable London run of 554 performances—is the last of the famous Savoyard operas. Only two works came from Gilbert and Sullivan after that; both were failures and both have been heard only rarely, *Utopia Limited* in 1893 ,(which see) and *The Grand Duke* in 1896.

"In spite of their complexities," writes Audrey Williamson about *The Gondoliers,* "none of its characters seem to feel . . . the slightest touch of real grief. Even the parting of the husbands and wives has a shade of tenderness, no more." In the same way the Gilbertian satire has, perhaps, less of a sting here than in earlier masterworks—confined most often to an occasional song or ditty rather than a situation, or to a sly, swift nudge at equality and republicanism. The topsy-turvy world of Gilbert and Sullivan here has a much greater semblance of order. The characters are less zany, the plot less complicated.

As the title suggests, Gilbert and Sullivan bring their frolicking to the Italian dream city of Venice. Antonio, a gondolier, gives voice to the happy estate of someone in his profession ("For the Merriest Fellows Are We, Tra La"), after which Marco and Giuseppe, brothers and gondoliers, arrive in a gondola to provide a further commentary on the gondoliering trade ("We're Called Gondolieri"). They proceed to select their wives through a game of blind man's buff. Thus Marco wins Gianetta, and Giuseppe, Tessa. This matter satisfactorily consummated, all depart. At this point, and with a courtly flourish, there appear the Duke of Plaza-Tora and his entourage: the Duchess, their daughter, Casilda, and the drummer, Luiz. In a pompous narrative, the Duke speaks of his powers ("In Enterprise of Martial Kind"), then sets forth to visit the Grand Inquisitor and his wife. Left alone, Casilda and Luiz reveal how much they love each other ("There Was a Time") and how their love can never be consummated in marriage, since in babyhood Casilda had been married to a Prince of Barataria whom she must now rejoin after the lapse of many years. The Prince has grown up to become a gondolier, although, as the Grand Inquisitor discloses, who this gondolier is nobody seems to know ("I Stole the Prince").

Just then Marco and Giuseppe arrive with their brides. Tessa ruminates over marital bliss ("When a Merry Maiden Marries"). After that, the Grand Inquisitor informs those present that one of these two gondoliers is the real Prince who must forthwith assume the office of king. Since nobody really knows whether the real king is Marco or Giuseppe, both men must go to Barataria and rule that kingdom jointly. The gondoliers promise to do so in a truly democratic fashion. Bidding farewell to their wives, they depart for Barataria where they are rousingly welcomed. Just as Marco is voicing his pain at missing his beloved wife ("Take a Pair of Sparkling Eyes"), the two young wives arrive to join their husbands. But the joy of reunion is short-lived. When the Grand Inquisitor comes to relate the fact that one of the two gondoliers had been married to Casilda in childhood, Marco and Giuseppe insist that such a situation is highly absurd, since both of them are already married. There seems no solution to this mess until Inez, one-time nurse to the Prince, volunteers the information that neither Marco *nor* Giuseppe is the long-lost Prince. Luiz, the drummer, is the man! Since Luiz and Casilda are in love anyway, they accept the news with considerable éclat—as do the two gondoliers, only too happy to return to Venice, to their profession, and to happy domesticity with their wives.

To Isaac Goldberg, the opening scene is "one of the most splendid . . . in all Gilbert and Sullivan." He goes on to say: "It is comparable, as scene, action, wedding of sound to sense, and dramatic fusion of the successive numbers, to the rare finale of the first act of *The Mikado*. Here is Sir Arthur frankly donning the costume of his gondolieri and singing, in his English voice, the songs of an Italy that is not altogether imaginary." Rarely before had Sullivan been as inspired in his lyricism as in this score; and it is easy to understand why its writing cost him more pain and effort than that of any other comic opera.

(The) **Good Girl** by Niccolò Piccinni. *See (La) Buona Figliuola.*

(Der) **Graf von Luxemburg** by Franz Lehár. *See (The) Count of Luxembourg.*

Graefin Du Barry by Karl Milloecker. *See (The) Du Barry.*

Graefin Mariza by Emmerich Kálmán. *See Countess Maritza.*

(The) **Grand Duchess of Gerolstein** [*La Grande Duchesse de Gérolstein*] by Jacques Offenbach.

> Opéra-bouffe in three acts with text by Henri Meilhac and Ludovic Halévy. First performance: Théâtre des Variétés, Paris, April 12, 1867. First American performances: French Theater, New York, September 24, 1867 (in French); New York, April 23, 1868 (in English); New York, January 12, 1870 (in German).

In 1867, Bismarck was the man-of-the-hour in Europe. Bismarck's policies were carrying Europe to the brink of war. With such a cataclysm hanging over their heads, Frenchmen were in the mood for an operetta like *The Grand Duchess of Gerolstein* which treated war frivolously, discussed militarism with levity and laughter, described royal courts, diplomats, autocracy, and petty princelings with mockery and malice.

When *The Grand Duchess of Gerolstein* was first given it was, however, not received enthusiastically—even though that darling of the Parisian stage, Hortense Schneider, was cast in the title role. This was no surprise to Offenbach himself, since there was a good deal in the libretto he did not favor: its loose construction; its complicated and at times confused third act; its attempt to parody grand opera, specifically Meyerbeer's *Les Huguenots.* After opening night, therefore, the third act was completely rewritten the opera parody was omitted; a considerable amount of humor was introduced. The third performance of the opéra-bouffe, and the first of the revised version, became a sensation. From then on it progressed quickly, becoming one of Offenbach's most provocative and most successful creations. By 1873 it had been produced by 65 French theaters and on 117 foreign stages!

In the United States, *The Grand Duchess of Gerolstein* had a particularly eventful early history. Its première in 1867—with the lovely French soprano, Lucille Tostée, making her American debut—was largely responsible for initiating in New York a craze for opera-bouffes in general and Offenbach in particular; and the craze continued for the next decade until supplanted by that for the comic operas of Gilbert and Sullivan. *The Grand Duchess of Gerolstein* was the first opera to be performed in Salt Lake City (June 1, 1869). On August 30, 1875, the comic opera was performed at the Fifth Avenue Theater in New York by a children's troupe from Mexico, the Mexican Juvenile Opera Company.

The story takes place in one of those mythical foreign kingdoms so dear to the hearts of European operetta composers. Fritz, an army recruit, is favored by the Grand Duchess of Gerolstein, but he is in love with a peasant girl, Wanda. When Fritz draws up a campaign for waging war that meets with the full approval of the Duchess, he is elevated to the rank of general, thus replacing the stupid, and overbearing General Boum. As a general, Fritz becomes a hero by winning the war. The Grand Duchess tries to win his love, but finds him cold to her. The fury of a woman scorned leads the Duchess to join up with Fritz's enemies in an effort to destroy him. But before long, the Duchess marries Prince Paul, and is now ready to forgive Fritz and to try frustrating all attempts at his ruin. On the evening he is to marry Wanda, Fritz's enemies waylay him and administer a severe beating. No longer a general, and in addition now a sad and forlorn creature, Fritz reverts to his former humble status as a mere recruit. But he does get to marry Wanda, which, after all, was what he had wanted most of all.

The devastating characterization of the pompous, bombastic, foolish, and vain General Boum gives the operetta much of its satirical punch.

The General wants war, then loses all interest in the purpose of that conflict; the military campaign he devises is a travesty on all military expeditions. The General is the kind of man who, instead of taking snuff, fires a pistol and inhales its smoke; a man who has no qualms about starting a war in order to provide the Duchess with some welcome distraction. And if this General is a caricature of military heroes, then Prince Paul, the Duchess's suitor and later her husband, is an unforgettable portrait of a dim-witted princeling and the Duchess herself a take-off on volatile and pampered royalty.

The text is notable not merely for its sharp characterizations, but also for its many brilliant political allusions, topical remarks, and, most of all, for its many telling asides on the hollowness of court life, stupidity of court gossip, bombast of military folk, complexities of court intrigues. It is a thinly disguised satire on Russia and the court of Catherine the Great. But in its cynicism, and its flight from reality, it is also a mirror of the Second Empire. S. Kracauer says: "In 1867, *La Grand Duchesse [de Gerolstein]* represented the last sunset glory of the Second Empire."

Three important arias are assigned to the Grand Duchess: the "Saber Song," *"Voici le sabre";* the "legend of the glass," *"Il était un de mes aïeux";* and the beautiful second-act love song described by Halévy as a "jewel," *"Dites-lui qu'on l'a remarqué."* Other striking excerpts include the song of the knife grinders, *"Tournez, tournez";* the regimental chorus, *"Ah, c'est un fameau regiment";* and a galop used as entr'acte music before the rise of the third-act curtain.

(The) Gypsy Baron [*Der Zigeunerbaron*] by Johann Strauss II.

Operetta in three acts with text by Ignaz Schnitzer, based on *Saffi,* a story by Maurus Jókai. First performance: Theater-an-der-Wien, Vienna, October 24, 1885. First American performances: Casino Theater, New York, February 15, 1886 (in English); Thalia Theater, New York, April 1, 1886 (in German).

During a visit to Budapest to conduct a performance of one of his operettas, Johann Strauss met the celebrated Hungarian playwright and novelist, Maurus Jókai. Jókai outlined to Strauss the plot of *Saffi,* a novelette he was completing. The story delighted Strauss because, like so many of his fellow Viennese, he was an addict to all things Magyar—its food, wine, folk music, and settings. He suggested to Jókai that the story be adapted for an operetta libretto. Jókai, in turn, turned the project over to Ignaz Schnitzer. Thus *The Gypsy Baron* came into being.

The Gypsy Baron, produced almost a dozen years after *Die Fledermaus*, is second only to that masterwork in public favor among Strauss's operettas. It was first given in Vienna on the eve of the composer's sixtieth birthday, which was being celebrated throughout Vienna with pomp and ceremony. Thus the première of *The Gypsy Baron* was a special event, and its first-night audience responded with appropriate affection and enthusiasm. Contemporary records describe the tears and cheers greeting the new operetta. It was given eighty-four performances in succession in Vienna, and in short order made the rounds of the world's capitals. In Vienna, it remained a hardy, enduring classic; by 1910, it had received there over a thousand performances.

The initial New York run, begun on February 15, 1886, was only eighty-six performances, but a return engagement not long afterward managed to accumulate over five hundred. On February 15, 1906, *The Gypsy Baron* entered the repertory of the Metropolitan Opera. This was an elaborate production in which (during the third-act festivities) members of the regular company appeared as guest performers in special arias and songs (including Caruso, Fremstad, Eames, and Journet). Elaborate, too, was the production of the operetta by the Metropolitan Opera during the 1959–60 season. Cyril Ritchard and Walter Slezak were drafted from the Broadway stage, the former to serve as stage director and the latter to appear in the role of Kalman, the wealthy pig farmer. From the world of ballet came Alexandra Danilova to perform in the third-act ballet. The libretto was newly translated into English by Maurice Valency, a version which shifted the time of the play to 1848; made Saffi the daughter of Prince Rakóczy; and transferred the third-act setting from a public square to the royal palace of Emperor Ferdinand.

The original setting of Strauss's operetta was Hungary at the end of the eighteenth century. Sandor Barinkay returns to the estates which his parents lost during the Turkish wars. The castle lies in virtual ruin and much of the family grounds have been confiscated by Kalman, a wealthy pig farmer, who is searching for treasure he is sure the Turks had secreted in the recent war. Barinkay wishes to lay claim to this estate; he is also seeking the hand of Arsena, Kalman's daughter. But Arsena is in love with the handsome Ottokar, and she uses the specious argument that she is unable to marry Barinkay because he is no longer a baron. The gypsies of the neighborhood, headed by old Czipra, welcome Barinkay back warmly, hailing him as their gypsy baron. Once again

Barinkay tries to win Arsena's hand and heart, and once again he is rejected. But Barinkay is now able to accept his rejection stoically since he has just learned that Arsena and Ottakar have been having an affair and, besides, he has become attracted to a lovely gypsy girl, Saffi. As a member of the gypsy band, Sandor Barinkay finds the hidden Turkish treasure in a tower near his ruined castle. The police invade the gypsy haunt, then reproach Sandor and Saffi for being lovers without the sanctification of marriage. Sandor is about to be arrested and his treasure about to be confiscated, when the news arrives that Saffi is really the daughter of the noble Pasha. Just then a squadron of Hungarian Hussars passes by en route to battle the Austrians; Sandor and the gypsies join them. For his bravery in action, Sandor Barinkay is decorated and is elevated to the rank of baron. A magnificent feast now celebrates the Hungarian victory, at which the Emperor himself is present. The Emperor stands ready to fulfill any wish Sandor may make. Sandor wants and gets Saffi; he also arranges for Arsena and Ottokar to be married.

None of Strauss's operettas cost him so much pain and effort as this one. He spent two years writing the music, aspiring to make his score the meeting ground for the best in Hungarian and Viennese popular music; or, to put it another way, to effect a marriage of the czardas and the waltz. There can be little question that this is one of Strauss's best stage scores, perhaps not as consistently brilliant, fresh, and inspired as *Die Fledermaus*, but, nonetheless, in its best pages, its artistic equal.

The overture, using material from the operetta, combines Hungarian and Viennese elements. It begins with vigorous gypsy music (that which accompanies the arrival of the gypsies in the first-act finale). We then hear in the strings Saffi's famous gypsy air, "*So elend und so treu*," in praise of the loyalty of the gypsy clan. A climax is reached with a rousing statement of the famous second-act "*Schatz*" or "Treasure" waltz.

Early in the operetta we hear one of Strauss's most radiant melodies. It is Sandor's entrance song with chorus with which he greets his Hungarian home after his return from foreign lands. The song begins with "*Als flotter Geist*" and reaches a climax with the sensual waltz "*Ja, das alles auf Ehr*." Strauss originally planned writing a czardas for this scene, but his librettist convinced him that a waltz at this point would have greater musical interest and dramatic validity. This song was a particular favorite with the beloved Austrian tenor Richard Tauber, who often sang it at his concerts.

Another rapturous Strauss waltz is heard in the second act, the "Treasure" or "*Schatz*" waltz. This is a trio sung by Saffi, Sandor, and Kalman when they discover the treasure hidden in a tower near the castle (*"Ha, seht es blinkt"*).

There are still several more musical episodes worth singling out for special attention: the so-called "Bullfinch Song," a duet of Sandor and Saffi (*"Wer uns getraut?"*); the trio of Sandor, Saffi, and Kalman as they greet the dawn (*"Mein Aug' bewacht"*); the second-act czardas; and the brilliant "Entry March" in the third act (*"Hurrah! Die Schlacht!"*).

Gypsy Love [*Zigeunerliebe*] by Franz Lehár.

> Operetta in three acts with text by A. M. Willner and Robert Bodanzky. First performance: Vienna, January 8, 1910. First American performance: Globe Theater, New York, October 17, 1911.

This Lehár operetta, set in early nineteenth century Rumania and Hungary, has been produced as an operetta in Vienna, as a grand opera in Budapest (1943), and as a Broadway musical. The last was adapted by Harry B. and Robert B. Smith and starred Marguerite Sylva.

Dragotin, a landed proprietor, wants his daughter, Zorika, to marry Jonel, a young man of established social position. But Zorika is sure she can find happiness only with the gypsy violinist, Jozsi. Her plan to elope with Jozsi is, however, frustrated by her old nurse. Zorika flees from a party celebrating her engagement to Jonel and hides near the bank of a river. There she is reminded of an old legend: Whoever drinks the river's waters can look into the future. She takes a drink and falls into a deep sleep. In her dreams she sees herself foresaking Jonel for the gypsy violinist. The couple are doomed to wander from town to town, in each of which Jozsi is pursued by seductive women. Nevertheless, Jozsi is willing to enter upon a gypsy marriage with Zorika, despite the fact that Zorika is the victim of derision by all of the violinist's friends and relatives. It is not long before Jozsi embarks upon a tempestuous love affair with the wealthy Lady Ilona. Suddenly Zorika awakens. Jonel is at her side, come to fetch her back to the party. There she finds Jozsi flirting with a girl named Ilona. Zorika suddenly realizes that she has had a glimpse into the future. She is now happily willing to accept Jonel as her prospective husband.

Jozsi's first-act gypsy song to his own violin accompaniment is one of the operetta's best melodies in a Hungarian style, *"Ich bin ein Zigeunerkind."* The best Viennese waltzes are Jozsi's unforgettable waltz-song,

"Und nenn' mein Lieb' dich," "Gib mir dort vom Himmelszelt," and *"Nur die Liebe macht uns jung."* Still another delightful tune is Jonel's ditty, *"Zorika, kehre zurueck."*

(The) Gypsy Princess by Emmerich Kálmán. *See (Die) Czardas-fuerstin.*

H.M.S. Pinafore or The Lass That Loved a Sailor by Gilbert and Sullivan.

> Comic opera in two acts with text by W. S. Gilbert and music by Arthur Sullivan. First performance: Opéra-Comique, London, May 25, 1878. First American performance: Boston Museum, Boston, November 25, 1878.

It was with *H.M.S. Pinafore* that the craze for Gilbert and Sullivan first seized and held both the English and Americans. Before *H.M.S. Pinafore*, Gilbert and Sullivan had written *Trial by Jury* (which see), in which English law was satirized, and *The Sorcerer* (which see), with its tongue-in-cheek evaluation of English country-estate life. In looking about for a new subject to lampoon—and one close to the hearts of Englishmen—Gilbert seized upon the idea of the British Admiralty and the sea. He selected a specific target, however: W. H. Smith, publisher, recently appointed by Disraeli as First Lord of the Admiralty. Smith had risen to this proud estate from the humble status of a newsboy, and he had succeeded in becoming Lord of the Admiralty without ever having gone to sea. Once having decided upon the Royal Navy as a fit subject for mirth and satire, Gilbert went on from there to deride patriotism, politics, and social snobbery. "It has been our purpose," explained Gilbert, "to produce something that should be innocent but not imbecile."

He finished his text by the end of 1877 and sent it on to Sullivan with the following comment: "I have very little doubt whatever but that you will be pleased with it." Indeed, so pleased was Sullivan that, although he was very ill at the time, he started working on the music immediately. He continued writing at a breathless pace, all the while afflicted by paroxysms and pains.

When finally produced, *H.M.S. Pinafore* proved a shocker—not only because of its irreverent and iconoclastic treatment of the Royal Navy (an institution dear to the heart of every true Englishman), but also because it reduced to absurdity some of the high ideals, principles, and social pretensions jealously guarded by the English everywhere. It instantly became a subject for discussion in drawing rooms, but at first did not do well at the box office. The summer of 1878 had been particularly hot and humid; so wilted did the box-office receipts become that on several occasions plans were made to close the show. Then two things helped to stimulate business. At a Promenade concert at Covent Garden, Sullivan performed a potpourri from *H.M.S. Pinafore* that proved so attractive that many in the audience were encouraged to see the production. Then came the news from across the ocean of the way *H.M.S. Pinafore* had conquered the hearts and enthusiasm of Americans. More and more English people now wanted to see for themselves what this provocative operetta was all about. Performance after performance was sold out—the run lasted for about seven hundred evenings—and before the end of the century, it had been given a thousand times. Sullivan's tunes and Gilbert's lines were on everybody's lips. The Gilbert and Sullivan madness had begun.

That sensational American première at the Boston Museum in 1878 was a pirated performance, given without sanction from—or payment to—the authors. *H.M.S. Pinafore* took Boston by storm, then developed into a typhoon that swept the entire country. When it came to San Francisco on December 23, it helped open the new Tivoli Opera House. (In this production Alice Oates was cast in the male role of Ralph Rackstraw!) Philadelphia saw the comic opera on January 6, 1879, and New York nine days later. In a single season, ninety different companies gave *H.M.S. Pinafore* throughout the United States; New York had five companies running simultaneously. *H.M.S. Pinafore* was given by children's groups, Negro companies, religious organizations. Barrel organs ground out the melodies in the city streets; sheet music of the main airs flooded the stores and decorated the pianos in the nation's parlors. People considered it smart to sprinkle their conversations with such catch phrases from the play as "What never? No, never!" or "For he himself has said it."

To protect their copyright interests, Gilbert and Sullivan came to the United States to offer an "authorized" version of their comic opera at the Fifth Avenue Theater, on December 1, 1879. Sullivan conducted, and it is said that Gilbert appeared on the stage as one of the sailors. The evening was a triumph of the first magnitude.

Since then, *H.M.S. Pinafore* has become more popular with amateur groups, schools, and semiprofessional companies than any other Gilbert and Sullivan comic opera. In the 1940's, a Yiddish parody became exceedingly popular in New York, and was recorded. In 1960, a modernized and freshly staged version of *H.M.S. Pinafore*, by Tyrone Guthrie, was introduced at the Stratford (Ontario) Festival, and subsequently in an off-Broadway production in New York.

The action takes place aboard the *H.M.S. Pinafore*, anchored off Portsmouth, England. After the opening sailors' chorus ("We Sail the Ocean Blue"), Little Buttercup, a bumboat woman, comes aboard to sell her wares ("For I'm Called Little Buttercup"). Buttercup is upset to discover from Ralph Rackstraw, a handsome seaman, that he is in love with Josephine, the daughter of Captain Corcoran ("A Maiden Fair to See"). Captain Corcoran now makes his entry, introduces himself ("I am the Captain of the *Pinafore!*") and reveals to Buttercup he wants Josephine to marry Sir Joseph Porter, First Lord of the Admiralty. Josephine is heartsick at the thought, since she loves another man ("Sorry Her Lot Who Loves Too Well"). The arrival of Sir Joseph—followed by his sisters, cousins, and aunts—is greeted with a loud fanfare. He speaks of his high station ("I Am the Monarch of the Sea") and of his lowly origins ("When I Was a Lad"). In return, Ralph and his mates sing a ditty written by Sir Joseph describing the qualities that go into the making of a true sailor lad ("A British Tar is a Soaring Soul"). Ralph then confides to Josephine how much he loves her. Too proud to admit that she returns this love, Josephine at first is distant and aloof. But when, in despair, Ralph threatens to take his life, she breaks down with the confession of the true state of her feelings. Everyone seems exultant at this development ("Oh Joy, Oh Rapture Unforeseen!")—all save the villain, Dick Deadeye, who is determined to smash this budding romance.

That night the Captain is on the poop deck wondering over the strange sadness that has suddenly seized him ("Fair Moon, to Thee I Sing"). Nor is his depression dispelled by Buttercup with her vague allusions to how deceptive things sometimes appear ("Things Are Seldom What They Seem"). Josephine is also sad, her conscience disturbed over the fact that her impending elopement violates her father's wishes. But that elopement never takes place. Dick Deadeye, who had overheard the plans, breaks the news to the Captain, who in turn intercepts the fleeing pair and reprimands them soundly. Ralph's mates defend him stoutly by pointing to his nationality ("He is an Englishman!"), but Sir Joseph orders his imprisonment. It is only then that Buttercup comes forth with a startling piece of news. Years back, when she had been the nurse for both the Captain and Ralph, she had mixed them up, and it is Ralph who is really the captain of the ship and Corcoran a lowly seaman ("A Many Years Ago"). With the tables thus neatly turned, there is nothing standing in the way of Ralph and Josephine getting married, for Sir Joseph would never consider demeaning himself by taking as wife the daughter of a humble seaman.

H.M.S. Pinafore, says Isaac Goldberg, "stands among the most felicitous creations in the history of comic opera. In it, Gilbert and Sullivan sparkle with a spontaneity and with high spirits that they are not often to attain in after years. In essence, [H.M.S.] *Pinafore* is no more a mere satire of the nautical drama then, let us say, *Patience* is merely a satire upon the extravagances of the youthful Oscar Wilde and his coterie. The ostensible target is but a blind: the jester's shaft cuts through its core and finds its proper mark in a human foible that is timeless."

Hansel and Gretel [*Haensel und Gretel*] by Engelbert Humperdinck.

> Fairy opera in three acts with text by Adelheid Wette based on the fairy tale of the brothers Grimm. First performance: Hoftheater, Weimar, Germany, December 23, 1893. First American performances: Daly's Theater, New York, October 8, 1895 (in English); Metropolitan Opera, New York, November 25, 1905 (in German).

In style, structure, and aesthetics, *Hansel and Gretel* is essentially a product of the Wagnerian school, and thus cannot accurately be classified as a light or comic opera. Nevertheless, because its text is a famous fairy tale, because it boasts some delightful musical passages, and because it is so easily assimilable at first hearing, it has become a favorite with young and old. As such an attraction, it is given so many performances by school and amateur groups that it deserves as much attention as any of the lighter productions enjoyed by the masses.

Humperdinck, who had never before written anything for the stage, had not originally planned this work as an opera. His sister, Adelheid Wette, adapted the fairy tale as an evening's entertainment for the children of the Humperdinck family, and she asked the composer to write one or two tunes for this presentation. He complied and was so delighted with the results that he hit upon the plan of setting her *entire* text to music—still for home presentation. As Humperdinck progressed with the writing of his score, he became increasingly impressed with the potential held of the libretto for an operatic production. He, therefore, extended the scope of his writing to operatic dimensions. When Richard Strauss saw the completed score he wrote Humperdinck: "It is a masterwork of the first order." And it was Strauss who conducted the world première of the opera in Weimar.

Hansel and Gretel made its composer famous. It is still the one work by which Humperdinck is remembered. It was a sensation not only in Weimar but throughout Germany, and after that in the rest of Europe. The first performance in England took place in London on December 26, 1894.

The American première was less than a year later. The opera was brought to the United States by Sir Augustus Harris, an English impresario, in a production in English conducted by the distinguished Wagnerian, Anton Seidl. The following day, the *New York Herald* reported: "When Sir Augustus stepped in front of the curtain at Daly's Theater last evening and in an amusing speech impressed upon his listeners that in *Hansel and Gretel* he had brought to this country not only a novelty but what was abroad considered the most important lyric work of the last decade, he told the truth if ever a man did." The opera had a six-weeks' run. It was not seen again in New York until November 29, 1906, when the Metropolitan Opera revived it in the German language, in a remarkable performance directed by Alfred Hertz. Since that time, Hansel and Gretel has become a favored Christmas attraction for children—although precisely why tradition should have married the Christmas season to this fairy opera has never been clarified.

As a devoted Wagnerian, Humperdinck leaned heavily on concepts and techniques of the music drama. Nevertheless, *Hansel and Gretel* managed to open up vistas of its own in German opera. It was the first successful German opera on a fairy-tale subject, thus establishing a school in German opera extremely popular in the early twentieth century.

Hansel and Gretel are two poor children who are hungry in their hut. To distract her little brother, Gretel teaches him to sing and dance (*"Bruederchen, komm tanz' mit mir"*). When their mother finds them playing this way, she reprimands them sternly for neglecting the housework, and sends them off to the woods to pick strawberries for the evening meal. The father soon returns from the town where he has been selling brooms. Both he and his wife become apprehensive about the fate of their children and go off to search for them. Meanwhile, Hansel and Gretel have gone into the forest in their search for strawberries. Gretel rests momentarily under a tree, entertaining herself by singing a little folk song (*"Ein Maennlein steht im Walde"*). When Hansel joins her with a basket full of strawberries, the hungry children gobble up the fruit voraciously. Suddenly night falls. The children cannot find their way home and are terrified. When they become drowsy, the Sandman appears to put them to sleep with a poignant lullaby (*"Der kleine Sandmann bin ich"*). The children say their prayers (*"Abends will ich schlafen gehen"*) and fall into a sound sleep. Angels surround them with a ring to watch over them and protect them from harm (*"Dream Pantomine"*). The following morning, after the Dewman sprinkles dewdrops on the children (*"Der kleine Taumann heiss' ich"*), they awaken to find themselves outside a gingerbread house. Ravished, they rush inside and begin to gobble up morsels of the house. Suddenly a witch seizes them, imprisons Hansel within a cage and orders Gretel to do the housework. The children are further terrified by her weird chant (*"Hurr, Hopp, Hopp, Hopp"*). Gretel manages to steal her wand and with it to free her brother from his cage. Then, when the Witch commands Gretel to look inside a flaming oven, Gretel innocently inquires for further instructions. As the Witch shows her how to attend to the oven, Hansel and Gretel push her into the fire. They are overjoyed at being freed from the toils of the evil woman (*"Gingerbread Waltz"*), and happier still to see all the gingerbread—victims of the Witch—suddenly revert to its original state as children. The parents of Hansel and Gretel arrive on the scene to find all the freed children celebrating joyously.

The tuneful overture is made up of several main excerpts from the opera. It opens with the second-act prayer of the children, presented by horns and bassoons. A change in tempo and rhythm tells of the fright of the children in the Witch's presence. Later material incorporates the third-act Dewman's song to the children, the happy dance of the children after they destroy the Witch, and a return of the children's prayer melody. The overture, the "Dream Pantomime," the "Gingerbread Waltz," and an orchestral entr'acte between the first and second acts, entitled "Witch's Ride," are frequently played by symphony and "pop" orchestras and semiclassical organizations.

Harlequin by Feruccio Busoni. *See Arlecchino.*

(The) Haunted Castle by Karl Milloecker. *See (Der) Verwunschene Schloss.*

(L') Heure espagnole [*The Spanish Hour*] by Maurice Ravel.

> Comic opera in one act with text by Franc-Nohain (Maurice Legrand), based on his play of the same name. First performance: Opéra-Comique, Paris, May 19, 1911. First American performance: Chicago, Illinois, January 5, 1920.

This is the most successful opera by France's foremost twentieth-century composer and one of the most sparkling and effervescent French comic operas of our time. Ravel described it as "a conversation in music," and as Madeleine Goss wrote in her biography of Ravel, "it is completely different in form from the classical opera, containing few if any of the traditional arias, choruses, and orchestral interludes, and recalling rather the old Italian opera-buffa—comedy which is close to farce and at times approaches caricature. It is really an opera in miniature, where the characters resemble marionettes, and everything is compressed into the smallest possible space. The orchestra remains in the background throughout the opera, and the vocal parts are written in such a way that they seem to be spoken rather than sung—*récitatif quasi parlando.* The resulting effect is as natural and unforced as that of an ordinary play or drama, yet more vivid and colorful because of the musical accompaniment which enhances the general effect without ever obtruding."

In a clockmaker's shop in Toledo, Spain—sometime during the eighteenth century—Concépcion is busy entertaining her lovers while her husband, Torquemada, is absent. First one (Gonsalve, a poet), then a second (Ramiro, a muleteer), and after that a third (Don Inigo, a banker) arrive. Since Torquemada is due back soon, Concépcion conceals each of them in one of the huge grandfather clocks. When Torquemada finds them there, the lovers explain they are customers come to inspect the insides of the clocks before purchasing them. The opera concludes with a gay quintet in which the characters remind the audience that all that has happened represents only a mild flirtation.

The way in which Ravel gives voice and identity to the various clocks and mechanical toys in his music almost brings to these inanimate objects life and personality. These musical representations of clocks and toys are heard in the opening prelude, or overture, which Émile Vuillermoz described as "a chorus of little voices of the clocks" and as "a delicate prelude from which comes the harmonious exhalation of the singing soul of familiar things where . . . the poetic and remote mystery of minute steel mechanisms is evident."

Although Ravel completed the opera in 1908, he had to wait three years for its première. Once performed, it was an immediate hit, although one critic regarded it only as a "miniature pornographic vaudeville." More typical of the critical evaluation was the comment of Henri Ghéon in the *Nouvelle revue française:* "It is miraculous to see how Franc-Nohain's buffoonery, whose comedy lies in gestures rather than words, becomes the jumping-off ground for those unexpected and unrestricted arabesques, based on the spoken word, but melodic all the same; to see how an art so concentrated and absorbed by the problems of expression can give the impression of being so natural. His grace and gaiety, in my opinion, are supremely vocal." *L'Heure espagnole* was given ten times at the Opéra-Comique that season, and on December 5, 1921, it entered the repertory of the Paris Opéra. It was also given successfully at Covent Garden in 1919, Chicago and New York in 1920, Brussels in 1921, and Hamburg in 1925. On November 7, 1925, it was presented by the Metropolitan Opera in a dual bill that included Cornelius' *The Barber of Bagdad* (which see). Olin Downes said at that time in the *New York Times:* "There is not a measure that fails to tell its tale; not an innuendo of a racy text which fails to find its echo in the score. The opera is a masterpiece in the little. . . . *L'Heure espagnole* accomplishes perfectly its purposes and this with a distinction of workmanship past describing. Every event of that Spanish hour . . . is depicted by the orchestra with humor as adroit as it is inspired in its craftsmanship."

In 1936, *L'Heure espagnole* was presented at the Juilliard School of Music in New York in an English translation by R. A. Simon.

(The) **House of the Three Girls** by Heinrich Berté. *See (Das) Dreimaederlhaus.*

If I Were King by Adolfe Adam. *See Si j'étais roi.*

Im Weissen Roessl by Ralph Benatzky. *See (The) White Horse Inn.*

(The) Impresario or **The Music Master** by Wolfgang Amadeus Mozart. *See (Der) Schauspieldirektor.*

(The) Inquisitive Women by Ermanno Wolf-Ferrari. *See (Le) Donne curiose.*

Iolanthe or **The Peer and the Peri** by Gilbert and Sullivan.

> Comic opera in two acts with text by W. S. Gilbert and music by Arthur Sullivan. First performance (dual): Savoy Theater, London, and Standard Theater, New York, November 25, 1882.

Iolanthe is perhaps the most underestimated and the most underappreciated of the Gilbert and Sullivan comic operas. The brilliant satire on the English parliament, on party politics, and on the law in general, is in Gilbert's best vein. His darts fly with deadly accuracy toward the bull's-eye. Nothing is more Gilbertian and topsy-turvy in concept than gathering into a single improbable play members of fairyland and the House of Peers, nor, for that matter, in presenting a hero who is half-human and half-fairy. As for Sullivan, his invention was rarely richer and more varied, rarely more neatly attuned to Gilbert's whims, moods, and vivacious verses.

To Isaac Goldberg, *Iolanthe* is a "fairy of operettas. . . . It preserves a virginal freshness that maintains it well in the forefront of the inimitable series. As words, as music, it is in its own right a peer among its kind. . . . The Gilbertian conflict between reality and fantasy is mirrored in detail great and small—in scene, costume, in line, in gesture."

Fairies in "an Arcadian landscape" come forth in the opening scene to explain who they are ("We Are Dainty Little Fairies") and to entreat their Queen to forgive Iolanthe who had been banished from fairyland a quarter of a century ago for marrying a mortal. Iolanthe appears, bearing the news that she now has a son, Strephon. When the latter arrives, he tells his mother that he is about to marry Phyllis, a ward in the Chancery ("Good Morrow, Good Mother"). After Strephon and Phyllis have exchanged tender sentiments ("Thou the Tree and I the Flower"), the proud procession of the British Peers ("Loudly Let the Trumpet Bray") takes place. The Lord Chancellor loses no time in introducing himself ("The Law Is the True Embodiment"). Two of these Peers—the Earl of Mount Ararat and the Earl of Tolloler—try in vain to gain Phyllis' interest. When the Lords depart, they leave the stage to the Lord Chancellor, who gives Strephon an insight into his legal modus-operandi ("When I Went to the Bar as a Very Young Man"). Since Phyllis does not know that Strephon's mother is Iolanthe, a fairy—nor, for that matter that he himself is half-human and half-fairy—her jealousy is aroused upon espying him in the company of lovely Iolanthe. In despair, she decides to give up Strephon and to accept the wooing of one of the Lords. Strephon now calls upon the fairies to help him out of his plight. In reply, the Fairy Queen commands him to become a member of Parliament and do what he can to create havoc and confusion there.

Outside the Houses of Parliament, a lonely sentry is soliloquizing on party politics ("When All Night Long a Chap Remains"). The Fairies and the Peers are soon on hand to remark on the disaster caused by Strephon's presence in Parliament. Mount Ararat seizes this opportunity to voice his patriotic ardor ("When Britain *Really* Ruled the Waves"). The fairies, meanwhile, have begun to grow interested in the Peers, and the Fairy Queen has come to find the sentry uncommonly attractive ("Oh, Foolish Fay!"). The Lord Chancellor describes the horrors he has just experienced during a nightmare ("When You're Lying Awake With a Dismal Headache"), after which Mount Ararat and Tolloler urge him to marry Phyllis himself. But by this time, Phyllis and Strephon are reconciled ("If We're Weak Enough to Tarry"). Iolanthe makes the disclosure that her mortal husband is none other than the Lord Chancellor and that the fairies are married to the Peers. To meet such a dramatic turn of events, fairy law is revised to read that any fairy *not* marrying a mortal is doomed to death. Thus Iolanthe is completely exonerated, and the Fairy Queen is able to marry the sentry with a free conscience.

Iolanthe is one of the rare instances in which Sullivan himself wrote the overture (*The Yeomen of the Guard* is another), an earnest of how highly he regarded the score. It is an uncommonly distinguished score, as a matter of fact, even for Sullivan. Audrey Williamson points up some of its salient attractions: "The musical characterization is highly developed, and distinctive motives—an equivalent of the Wagnerian Leitmotiv—are used not only for Iolanthe, Phyllis and Strephon, but also for the Lord Chancellor himself. . . . For sheer joyousness and vivacity the comedy waltz trio, 'Faint Heart Never Won Fair Lady,' is not surpassed in any of the operas. . . . The haunting tenderness of the Invocation to Iolanthe, and her own wistful motif, deepen into poignancy in the choral writing after Iolanthe's vain appeal to the Lord Chancellor. Sullivan . . . in this wailing cry of lament on two sets of three notes . . . came, perhaps, as near as he ever did to suggesting the tragic in atmosphere. . . . Best of all in the vigorous line is the magnificent chorus of peers, with its trumpet fanfares, martial pomp, and typical flowering into humor, in the skittish accompaniment to the solemn choral, 'Pillars of the British Nation.' "

(**L'**) **Italiana in Algeri** [*The Italian Girl in Algiers*] by Gioacchino Rossini.

> Opera buffa in two acts with text by Angelo Anelli. First performance: Teatro San Benedetto, Venice, May 22, 1813. First American performance: Richmond Hill Theater, New York, November 5, 1832.

Rossini was only twenty-one when, suddenly, he became the idol of Venetian opera lovers—and with two different operas. One was a serious work, *Tancredi*, introduced on February 6, 1813. The other, an opera buffa, arrived less than four months later. It was *L'Italiana in Algeri*. In the latter, Rossini profited from a first-rate comic text, "a very good farce," as Francis Toye described it, "abounding in funny situations, wily stratagems, and ridiculous expedients." Rossini fully met the comic demands of the play. His rare gift in provoking laughter in music could be found in the tongue-in-cheek hymn of praise to the Mustapha in the first-act finale; in the sparkling duet of Lindoro and the Mustapha, "*Oh, che muso?*"; in the broad burlesque treatment of the absurd initiation scene to the Pappataci, especially in the accompaniment.

In eighteenth-century Algiers, Mustapha, the Bey, has grown weary of his favorite, Elvira. He decides to give her over in marriage to Lindoro, an Italian slave, even though the latter is in love with a wealthy Italian girl, Isabella. Isabella is en route to Algiers to meet Lindoro when her ship is wrecked near shore. Ali, looking for a new favorite for the Mustapha, comes upon her and decides she is a likely candidate. He brings her back to the Mustapha's palace, where the Bey is instantly taken with her. When Isabella learns that Lindoro must marry Elvira, she tries to persuade the Mustapha to change his mind about this arrangement. Making no headway, she meets Lindoro secretly to plan an elopement. With Elvira's cooperation, they work out a wily scheme. They form a secret society named the Pappataci, to which they offer the Mustapha membership. He is delighted to join, and all too willing to perform all the secret rites required in the initiation—including drinking considerable quantities of intoxicating liquor. When he is reduced to a stupor, Lindoro and Isabella are able to flee. After recovering from his binge, the Mustapha welcomes Elvira back as his favorite.

The score, which Rossini completed in about a month, never reveals the haste with which it had been prepared. The overture is a particular joy, familiar to all Rossini admirers. It begins slowly with a sensitive song for the oboe. A crescendo leads to the main section, where two bright, sprightly melodies are heard in the woodwinds. The overture comes to an exciting conclusion after a dramatized crescendo.

One of the most beautiful arias in the opera is that which Lindoro sings in the first act, *"Languir per una bella."* Two arias of Isabella are no less touching. In the first, *"Cruda sorte!,"* she reveals that she knows how to get whatever she wants, while the other, *"Per lui che adoro,"* is her avowal of love for Lindoro. In addition to these outstanding episodes, three other vocal excerpts are of particular fascination: a duet of Isabella and the Mustapha, *"Ai capricci della sorte";* the duet, *"Se inclinassi a prender moglie";* and the Mustapha's second-act air, *"Le Femmine d'Italia."* In Rossini's best comic style are the *"Pappataci"* trio and the vivacious ensemble number, *"Va Sossopra il mio cervello."*

Francis Toye considers the first-act finale the high musical point of the entire score, with a concluding *Vivace* section "which positively takes one's breath away, so madly, so swiftly it rushes along."

L'Italiana in Algeri entered the repertory of the Metropolitan Opera on December 5, 1919. The cast included Charles Hackett, Marie Sundelius, and Giuseppe De Luca; Gennaro Papi conducted.

Jenny's Wedding by Felix Marie Massé. *See (Les) Noces de Jeannette.*

(A) King in Spite of Himself by Emmanuel Chabrier. *See (Le) Roi malgré lui.*

(The) King Said So by Léo Delibes. *See (Le) Roi l'a dit.*

King's Rhapsody by Ivor Novello.

> Operetta in three acts with text by Ivor Novello and lyrics by Christopher Hassall. First performance: Palace Theater, London, September 15, 1949.

In its choice of plot, characters, and setting, this is old-hat operetta. Nevertheless, it proved to have such surpassing charm and appealing sentiment that it enjoyed a run of 839 performances. Nikki, Prince of Murania, renounces his rights to the throne so that he might go off to Paris with Marta. A marriage, however, is being arranged for him with Princess Cristina of Norseland. When Nikki's father dies, the Queen Mother, Elana, comes to Paris to insist that Nikki desert his mistress for good, return to Murania to marry Cristina, and ascend the throne. After Cristina arrives in Murania to marry Nikki, she is determined to have visible proof that Nikki will no longer have any associations of any kind with his one-time mistress. She invites Marta to a court ball, a fact that so infuriates Nikki that he invites Marta to share the opening dance with him. Once he is married to Cristina, Nikki continues to carry on his affair with Marta. He arouses the anger of the people until he is compelled to abdicate and go off into permanent exile, leaving behind both his wife and their child. Ten years later, the son is crowned. Although warned that if he dared set foot within Murania he would be killed, Nikki returns in disguise to watch the coronation, and, from a distance, to take one more look at his wife and son. Cristina senses his presence and drops a white rose for him. He picks it up tenderly, then, as the curtain falls, he kneels in prayer at the foot of a high altar.

The high spots of Novello's popular score are two songs ("Someday My Heart Will Awake" and "Take Your Girl") and the background music for a stunning ballet, "Muranian Rhapsody."

Lady Madcap by Paul Rubens.

> Operetta in two acts with text by Paul Rubens and Newnham Davis, and lyrics by Paul Rubens and Percy Greenbank. First performance:

Prince of Wales Theater, London, January 1905. First American performance: Casino Theater, New York, September 20, 1906 (under the title *My Lady's Maid*).

One English critic described *Lady Madcap* as an updated *She Stoops to Conquer* by Oliver Goldsmith. The "madcap lady" in the title is Lady Betty Claridge, daughter of Lord Fralingham. A spoiled brat, she likes nothing better than to fabricate lies, perpetrate deceit, and indulge in escapades. She invites the officers of the East Anglican Hussars to her home, Egbert Castle; at the same time, to get rid of her father, she sends him a fake telegram summoning him to town. The father, aware of her rare gift for getting into trouble, locks her in her bedroom to keep her from harm while he is gone. But Lady Betty effects her escape through an open window. To get a richer measure of delight from entertaining her soldiers, Betty masquerades as a maid, while her maid, in turn, impersonates Betty. But when Lady Betty falls in love with Trooper Smith, she reveals her true identity in order to persuade him to give up soldiering and take on a job as butler in her castle. Meanwhile, an advertisement she has placed in the newspaper for a millionaire suitor has brought several candidates. By this time, the father has returned from his wild-goose chase, irate to discover the castle swarming with strangers, and, worse still, to see his daughter in love with a soldier. But when he learns that Trooper Smith is a millionaire, he regains his composure.

Three of Rubens' songs helped spell success for this operetta: "Her Little Dog," "I Like You in Velvet," and "The Beetle and the Boot."

When given in the United States as *My Lady's Maid*—text adapted by Eduard Paulton and R. H. Burnside—Madge Crichton created the role of Lady Betty for New York, just as she had done previously in London. The Rubens score was supplemented in New York by several numbers by local composers, including some by Jerome Kern.

Lady Moon by Paul Lincke. *See Frau Luna.*

(Das) Land des Laechelns by Franz Lehár. *See (The) Land of Smiles.*

(The) **Land of Smiles** [*Das Land des Laechelns*] by Franz Lehár.

Operetta in three acts with text by Ludwig Herzer and Fritz Loehner, based on a libretto by Victor Léon. First performance: Metropole Theater, Berlin, October 10, 1929. First American performance: Shubert Theater, New York, September 5, 1946 (under the title *Yours Is My Heart*).

On February 9, 1923, Lehár's operetta *The Yellow Jacket* (*Die gelbe Jacke*) was introduced unsuccessfully in Vienna. One of its songs was *"Dein ist mein ganzes Herz,"* sung by the heroine, Lisa. This song made as little impression upon critics and audiences as did the operetta as a whole. The star playing the role of Lisa had even tried to get the song removed from the show.

When Richard Tauber, the celebrated Austrian opera and concert star, heard this number he was so taken with it that he decided to feature it at his recitals. In time, he helped make the song phenomenally popular throughout Europe, so much so that song and singer became inextricably associated in the minds of concertgoers.

Then in 1929, Lehár decided to revise both the score and the text of *The Yellow Jacket;* the revamped version was baptized *The Land of Smiles*. Lehár assigned the main love song to the hero (instead of the heroine) and made it the climax of the second act. This decision made many a critic shake his head sadly, recalling how dismally the song had failed in *The Yellow Jacket*.

Lehár also prevailed on Tauber to star in *The Land of Smiles*—as the hero, Prince Sou-Chong. He was a sensation. After the extended Berlin engagement, Tauber appeared in this operetta in virtually every part of the civilized world: It has been computed that in all he must have appeared over three thousand times as the Prince. By now, too, *"Dein ist mein ganzes Herz"* ("Thine Is My Heart Alone") was *Tauber's* song. He rarely gave a concert anywhere without singing it either on the program itself or as an encore. And when *The Land of Smiles* was finally produced on Broadway—once again starring Tauber—the production was renamed *Yours Is My Heart,* in deference to the singer and his song. (The play was adapted for Broadway by Harry Graham, Ira Cobb, and Karl Farkas, and Lehár's music was edited by Felix Guenther.) The New York critics

did not find much to praise in this operetta; everything about it seemed
"corny." But they expressed unqualified admiration for the title song and
for the way Tauber sang it. On opening night, the song received such
an ovation that Tauber repeated it four times, in as many different
languages (English, French, Italian, German). Because of the song, and
because of Tauber's popularity, *Yours Is My Heart* seemed destined for
a long run, the critics notwithstanding. Unfortunately, the star fell sick
soon after the show had opened, and since the operetta was nothing at
all without Tauber, it had to close down.

The Land of Smiles has, for the most part, an Oriental setting, but it
opens in the Viennese salon of Count Lichtenfels. His daughter, Lisa,
falls in love with a Chinese diplomat, Prince Sou-Chong. When he is recalled home, she decides to marry him. For a while, Lisa is completely
happy in Sou-Chong's palace in Pekin. But she is held in suspicion, even
hated, by most of the diplomats surrounding her husband. Gustav von
Pottenstein, long in love with Lisa, arrives from Austria to fill the office
of military attaché in Pekin, where he finds a new love in Mi. Meanwhile,
Sou-Chong, according to family custom, has to take on four more wives,
thus relegating Lisa to the humble status of fifth wife. This development,
combined with Gustav's presence, suddenly awakens in Lisa an over-
powering nostaglia for Vienna and home. When her husband refuses to
give her permission to leave China, Lisa discovers to her horror that she
has come to hate him. She gains the cooperation of Gustav and Mi in
planning her escape, but while fleeing she is caught red-handed by Sou-
Chong. The Prince has it in his power to condemn his wife to death.
Instead, with royal magnanimity, he not only forgives her, but also asks
Gustav to conduct her safely back to Vienna. Sou-Chong and Mi remain
behind in Pekin, each heartbroken at the loss of his and her respective
loves.

The song, *"Dein ist mein ganzes Herz"*, is a radiant song with which
Prince Sou-Chong tries to convince his wife, Lisa, that, although she
is to become his fifth wife, she remains the one he loves best. Sou-Chong
has two other fine numbers: *"Immer nur laecheln"* and *"Von Apfelblueten
einen Kranz."* Other outstandingly effective musical excerpts include
Lisa's beautiful song of nostalgia for Vienna and home, *"Ich moecht
wieder einmal die Heimat seh'n"* and the love duet of Gustav and Mi,
"Meine Liebe, deine Liebe."

(**Die**) **Landestreicher** [*The Vagabonds*] by Karl Ziehrer.

Operetta in two acts and prologue, with text by L. Krenn and C. Lindau. First performance: Vienna, July 26, 1899. First American performance: Knickerbocker Theater, New York, June 24, 1901 (under the title, *The Strollers*).

Of the twenty-nine operettas Karl Ziehrer wrote in Viennese style and tradition, *Die Landstreicher* was the most popular. Selections from its score have helped make Ziehrer one of the most popular composers of Viennese light music since Johann Strauss II.

The operetta's main characters are August Fliederbush and his wife, Bertha. They are vagabonds who stroll the byways of Bavaria, living entirely by their wits. Having found a pearl necklace and a thousand-mark bank note, they indulge in a lavish repast, then are arrested on suspicion of robbery. When they manage to escape from their cell they are confronted by Prince Adolar Gilka and his girl friend, Mimi, a dancer; they have come to report the loss of a pearl necklace. Fliederbush, pretending to be a magistrate, conducts Gilka and Mimi to his own cell where he asks them to await developments, then expropriates their outer clothes. Thus elegantly attired, they come to a fashionable resort where they pass themselves off as Prince Adolar Gilka and Mimi until the Prince himself arrives to brand them as frauds. Once again Fliederbush and Bertha face arrest and once again their ingenuity makes it possible for them to evade the long arm of the law. Prince Gilka, impressed by Fliederbush's resourcefulness, engages both him and Bertha to recover the pearl necklace which, by now, has been stolen by Mimi. Bertha comes to a lavish masquerade disguised as a Moroccan magician. She performs an act, during which she gains from Mimi possession of the pearl necklace. As a reward, Prince Gilka takes Fliederbush and Bertha into his service. Only then is the discovery made that the pearl necklace which caused all the trouble is an imitation.

One of Ziehrer's most famous waltzes is found in the first-act finale, "*Sei gepriesen, du lauschige Nacht.*" If any one melody helped spell success for this operetta, this is the one. Another attractive musical episode occurs as background music for Bertha's exhibition of legerdemain at the masquerade ball.

Harry B. Smith adapted both book and lyrics for the American stage, where it was produced in 1901 as *The Strollers*. For this occasion an entirely new domestic score replaced that of Ziehrer, the work of Ludwig Englander. Francis Wilson, Irene Bentley, Harry Gilfoil, and Eddie Foy were in the cast.

(The) Last Waltz [*Der letzte Walzer*] by Oscar Straus.

Operetta in three acts with text by Julius Brammer and Alfred Gruenwald. First performance: Berlin, February 12, 1920. First American performance: Century Theater, New York, May 10, 1921.

The two operettas that made Straus immortal in the Viennese popular theater—*The Chocolate Soldier* and *A Waltz Dream*—were both produced before World War I. Of Straus's postwar operettas, the most significant and the most successful was *The Last Waltz*. It was written while composer and his librettists were residing in Bad Ischl, Austria. One day, after their operetta had, to all practical purposes, been completed, the librettists met the beloved Austrian stage star, Fritzi Massary, on a street in Bad Ischl. They told her about Straus's new operetta and inquired if she might be interested in starring in it. She promised to come the next day to Straus's studio to hear text and music. The librettists rushed over to a club where they knew Straus was at that moment playing poker and told him of their encounter with Massary. All of them decided to make immediate changes in the text in order to stimulate her interest in the operetta, especially in the matter of expanding her role. The authors of the text spent most of that night making the necessary revisions, and the composer devoted himself to writing a new number for Massary. The next day Fritzi Massary was so impressed by the operetta that she consented to appear in it—and she was a triumph.

The Last Waltz was as popular outside of Berlin as in it. Soon after the Berlin première, Sir Charles Hawtrey produced it at the Gaiety Theater in London with formidable success, the cast there headed by Bertram Wallis and José Collins. For the American production, book and lyrics were adapted by Harold Atteridge and Edward Delaney Dunn; the cast included Eleanor Painter, James Barton, and Walter Woolf.

The setting of the operetta is Poland. The forthcoming marriage of General Karsinski and Vera Lisaweta is being celebrated. Within the General's castle, Count Dimitri is being held prisoner, sentenced to death the following morning for having dared to protect a beautiful young woman from the unwelcome advances of the Prince. After promising he would make no attempt to escape, Dimitri is allowed one last dance at the General's party. While there he recognizes Vera as the young girl whom he had shielded from the Prince. On seeing Dimitri again, Vera realizes she is in love with him. She decides to break her engagement to the General and entreats Dimitri to flee with her. At first Dimitri is tempted to do so. But after some vacillation, his sense of honor triumphs over his instinct for self-preservation, and he insists upon going back to his cell. In her determination to save Dimitri's life, Vera visits the Prince and coquettishly arouses his desire for her. She then asks the Prince to turn over to her the command of the castle for a single day, a request he is unable to refuse. Vera's first order is to bring Dimitri to her; her second, that Dimitri marry her. Faced with a *fait accompli*, the Prince generously permits the loving couple to leave Poland safely.

The most popular musical number is that which Straus wrote so hurriedly for Fritzi Massary to gain her interest in his operetta. It is a light, delicate little number called "Oo-La-La." The big title waltz—with its spacious thirty-bar melody—is the one to which Dimitri and Vera dance at the General's party.

(Der) Letzte Walzer by Oscar Straus. *See (The) Last Waltz.*

(Der) liebe Augustin [*Dear Augustin*] by Leo Fall.

> Operetta in three acts with text by Rudolf Bernauer and Ernst Welisch. First performance: Berlin, February 3, 1912. First American performance: Casino Theater, New York, September 3, 1913.

In the Balkans, Bogumil tries to stave off financial ruin by having his niece, Princess Helene, marry Prince Nicola, wealthy regent of a neighboring country. Such a marriage of convenience is utterly distasteful to the young lady, who is deeply in love with her piano teacher, a Viennese musician by the name of Augustin Hofer. To complicate matters further, Hofer is engaged to Anna, daughter of Helene's steward. When Prince Nicola comes to claim Helene, his high-handed attitude, lack of civility, and stuffed-shirt formality antagonize her completely. Nevertheless, the wedding arrangements are made. Just then, it is discovered that Helene and Anna were born on the same night during a storm twenty years earlier—and in the same place, a nearby monastery. At birth, a mix-up occurred in which Anna, really the daughter of royalty, was passed off as a commoner, while Helene, a commoner, was assumed to be of royal blood. With this dramatic turn of events, Helene is able to marry Augustin; and Augustin—who never really had much interest in Anna—is delighted to see Anna marry Prince Nicola.

Leo Fall's score passes nimbly from Viennese frivolity to Viennese sentiment. The most important number has a sentimental touch: *"Lass dir Zeit,"* notable for its seductive waltz interlude, *"Was es Schoenes gibt, das nimm dir."* The following are some other distinguished selections: *"Anna, was ist denn mit dir?"*; the duet, *"Und der Himmel haengt voller Geigen"*; *"Wenn die Sonne schlafen geht"*; and *"Wo steht denn das geschrieben?"*

Der liebe Augustin was produced in New York in 1913 under its German title. Book and lyrics were adapted by Edgar Smith, and the cast was headed by Roszika Dolly and De Wolf Hopper.

(The) Lily of Killarney by Sir Julius Benedict.

Romantic opera in three acts with text by John Oxenford and Dion Boucicault, based on Boucicault's play *Coleen Bawn*. First performance: Covent Garden, London, February 8, 1862. First American performance: Academy of Music, New York, January 1, 1868.

A most engaging sentimentality, an infectious Irish charm, and a heart-warming tenderness are the winning suits of an opera that is not only the composer's best work but also one of the best operas by an Englishman in the latter half of the nineteenth century.

It is set in nineteenth-century Ireland. Hardress Cregan, a wealthy Irishman, is secretly married to Colleen Bawn, who is known as "the lily of Killarney." But Corrigan, an upstart who holds the mortgage on the vast Cregan estate, is bent on having Cregan marry Ann Chute, an heiress. To keep his marriage with Colleen secret, Cregan is compelled to feign he is wooing Ann. Meanwhile, Colleen Bawn has disappeared, arousing the suspicion that Cregan has murdered her. Cregan is cleared only after Colleen reappears. On this occasion, Cregan confesses that she is his wife, much to Corrigan's displeasure.

The highly popular air, "Colleen Bawn," sung in the second act by

Danny the Boatman, and Cregan's song in the third act, "Eily Ma-voureen," are both characteristic of the folklike simplicity and charm of the composer's lyricism. The same qualities can also be found in two more appealing numbers: "It Is a Charming Girl I Love" and "Your Slumbers." The first-act music for the fox hunt and the first-act aria, "The Cruiskeen Lawn," are also familiar.

The Lily of Killarney was an overwhelming success not only at Covent Garden but also outside England. Within six years of its première, the opera had been introduced and acclaimed in Germany, Australia, and the United States.

(Die) lustigen Weiber von Windsor by Otto Nicolai. *See (The) Merry Wives of Windsor.*

(Die) lustige Witwe by Franz Lehár. *See (The) Merry Widow.*

Madame Pompadour by Leo Fall.

> Operetta in three acts with text by Rudolph Schanzer and Erich Welisch. First performance: Vienna, March 2, 1923. First American performance: Martin Beck Theater, New York, November 11, 1924.

Leo Fall's special gift for writing music in tune with a rococo setting is particularly pronounced in *Madame Pompadour*. The time is the middle eighteenth century; the place, Paris; the heroine, the mistress of King Louis XV. Bored by the routines of a gala court ball, Madame Pompadour flees to a carnival hoping to find some distraction. In a public inn, she meets Count René, a fugitive from his wife, Madeleine; since Madame Pompadour is masked, the Count does not know who she is. He falls in love with her at once. At the inn, Calicot, the Count's friend, sings a satirical ditty ridiculing Madame Pompadour, not realizing, of course, that she is close at hand. Hardly has he finished when the chief of police breaks into the inn. He knows Madame Pompadour is there, and he has come to find evidence of her infidelity to the king and thus bring about her ruin. Madame Pompadour manages to convince him that she has come here, not for an escapade, but to gain firsthand information about the revolutionary activities within the city. The police chief then arrests René and Calicot as traitors to the crown, but Madame Pompadour uses her influence, not only to free them, but also to gain for René an appointment as a member of her regiment, and to make Calicot court poet. When Madeleine arrives at court to get information about her husband, Madame Pompadour discovers they are half sisters. And when the chief of police brings the king evidence that Madame Pompadour and René are in love, she is able to confuse the issue by stoutly maintaining that her interest in René stems entirely from the fact that he is the husband of her half sister. René and Madeleine are now free to go home, and the idyllic affair between king and mistress can continue without further interruption.

The song hit of this score is an amusing tidbit, the duet *"Joseph, ach Joseph"* ("Joseph, oh Joseph, why are you so chaste?"). Another pleasing tune is in a similar tone of levity: *"Dem Koenig geht's in meinem Schachspiel schlecht."* These are the principal waltz melodies: *"Heut koennt einer sein Glueck bei mir machen"* and *"Mein Prinzesschen, du."* Mention should also be made of two instrumental delights, a march and a gavotte.

For the American première in 1924, *Madame Pompadour* was adapted by Clare Kummer, while the cast included Wilda Bennett, John Quinlan, and Louis Harrison.

(The) Magic Flute [*Die Zauberfloete*] by Wolfgang Amadeus Mozart.

> Comic opera in two acts with text by Emanuel Schikaneder. First performance: Theater auf der Wieden, Vienna, September 30, 1791. First American performances: Park Theater, New York, April 17, 1833 (in English); German Opera House, New York, November 10, 1862 (in German); Metropolitan Opera, New York, March 30, 1900 (in Italian).

Mozart was in the last year of his life when Emanuel Schikaneder asked him to write the music for *The Magic Flute*. Schikaneder was a singer, actor, writer, and impresario who had recently acquired the Theater auf der Wieden in Vienna where he hoped to recoup his sadly depleted fortunes by presenting popular musical productions. For his first venture, he decided to do *The Magic Flute,* a libretto which he himself had prepared from a story named *Lulu,* or *The Magic Flute,* by Liebeskind.

Shrewd showman that he was, Schikaneder was convinced that this tale was a stew with many of the ingredients the Viennese public found so succulent: a fairy-tale with an Oriental setting and spectacular scenes; characters that included an evil magician, a wronged queen, and a comic simpleton. As Schikaneder worked out his text, he transmitted finished portions to Mozart for musical setting. Then, after they had completed one full scene and were working on the second, they were confronted with a rival production in Vienna, based on the same *Lulu* story, which contained most of the elements Schikaneder had been planning for his adaptation. A radical change had to be made in the libretto; the story was changed into an allegory of Masonic ideals and aspirations filled with Masonic ritual and symbolism (both Schikander and Mozart were Masons). The wronged fairy queen became a villain, and the evil magician was transformed into an Egyptian high priest embodying the highest ideals of Masonry. The hero, Tamino, was made to represent the Austrian Emperor; his beloved, Pamina, symbolized the Austrian people. Only the tomfoolery of the comic character, Papageno, was allowed to stand pretty much as originally planned.

Neither Schikaneder nor Mozart planned *The Magic Flute* as an opera. They were writing a Singspiel, the German form of musical comedy that included light, gay, popular tunes, with spoken dialogue. Mozart's score overflows with melodies that have the character of folk music or tunes of a popular nature. But the touch of genius elevated what was intended as a slight little musical comedy into one of the greatest comic operas ever written. Together with lilting melodies, particularly those for Papageno, which are of the Singspiel variety, Mozart created some of his noblest music. Bernard Shaw once said that the two arias of Sarastro are the only compositions he knew that could come from the lips of God himself. But there are many other pages that ascend the heights—wonderful love songs, duets, choruses; the two arresting coloratura arias of the Queen of the Night; the delightful orchestral "March of the Priests." The score as a whole has such variety and majesty of style, such elevated sentiments, and such wondrous beauty that it has placed *The Magic Flute* among the most exalted works for the stage ever written, as well as one of the most amusing. It was Beethoven's favorite among all the Mozart operas, *Don Giovanni* not excluded; and Eric Blom has said that this opera "contains elements of greater idealistic aspiration than any other stage work of Mozart's . . . a single gem of many facets—and of inestimable value."

In the world première, Schikaneder himself played the part of the comic Papageno; Mozart's sister-in-law, Josefa Hofer, created the role of the Queen of the Night. Although Mozart did not live to see it happen (he died thirty-seven days after the première of his opera), *The Magic Flute* became a formidable success. Largely from the profits reaped from this one opera, Schikaneder was later able to build for himself a new theater in Vienna, in front of which he appropriately placed a statue of himself in his Papageno costume.

France first became acquainted with *The Magic Flute* through a curious hodgepodge named *Les Mystères d'Isis,* produced in Paris in 1801, and made up of sections from four Mozart operas (*The Marriage of Figaro, Don Giovanni, La Clemenza di Tito,* besides *The Magic Flute*). In London, *The Magic Flute* received a highly successful première in 1811, while in Vienna a decade later Wilhelmine Schroeder-Devrient, the world-famous prima donna, made her stage debut as Pamina. America first became acquainted with the opera in 1833 in an English translation. The first time the opera was performed by the Metropolitan Opera, in 1900, it was given in Italian, but a revival there in 1941 used a new English translation by Ruth and Thomas P. Martin.

The famous overture opens with three stately chords in full orchestra, which are again heard within the opera as introductory measures to Sarastro's aria, *"O Isis und Osiris"* and "The March of the Priests." The whole introductory section has an exalted character. A change of pace and mood is made by a delightful little melody presented in the strings. This is the main subject of the overture. It receives fugal treatment, is repeated, and then is subjected to elaborate development.

The curtain rises on a bleak landscape. Tamino, a prince, is saved from a serpent by the three attendants of the Queen of the Night. When Papageno, a birdcatcher, appears and identifies himself (*"Der Vogelfaenger bin ich ja"*), Tamino showers gratitude on him in the mistaken belief that this fellow had been his savior. Flattered by all this attention, Papageno does nothing to set Tamino straight. The attendants of the Queen of the Night punish him by sealing his lips with a padlock. Then they present Tamino with a picture of beautiful Pamina, daughter of the Queen of the Night, over whose beauty the prince grows ecstatic (*"Dies Bildnis ist bezaubernd schoen"*). Suddenly the Queen of the Night arrives. She informs Tamino that Pamina is being held captive by "the evil" Sarastro, begs Tamino to save her, and promises him Pamina's hand in marriage as a reward (*"Zum Leiden bin ich auserkoren"*). When Tamino consents, the Queen presents him with a magic flute which, when played upon, will keep him from harm. Since Papageno is recruited to accompany Tamino on this mission, his lips are unsealed, and he is given a set of magic chimes.

Both men come to Sarastro's palace where Pamina is being guarded by the Moor, Monostatos. When the latter catches a glimpse of Papageno, he flees with terror, believing the visitor to be a devil. This offers Papageno the opportunity to reveal to Pamina that she is soon to be liberated by a handsome prince; for Pamina and Papageno to sound a hymn to the powers of love (*"Bei Maennern, welche Liebe fuehlen"*); and for the two of them to try to effect their escape.

In a grove outside the Temple of Isis, Tamino learns that Sarastro is no villain at all, but a man of the highest principles, and that there is good reason why he is holding Pamina captive, although that reason will not yet be made known to the prince. Suddenly Papageno and Pamina are dragged in by Monostatos and his slaves, having been caught red-handed in their escape. Now Sarastro himself makes an appearance. He explains to Tamino and Pamina that they must perform a number of rites to prove their courage and their devotion to each other.

The second act opens with the appearance of Sarastro and his High Priests to the stately measures of a march. Sarastro entreats the Priests to permit Tamino to be initiated into the mysteries of their holy order so that he might be able to marry Pamina. After the Priests give their consent, Sarastro prays to his gods that Tamino and Pamina meet their tests successfully (*"O Isis und Osiris"*).

And now Tamino, Pamina, and Papageno must pass their first test. Tamino is not allowed to speak to his beloved, however much she may entreat him to do so, and by the same token Papageno must not say a word to the bride Sarastro has chosen for him. The ordeal proves too much for poor Papageno. When he starts talking to an old woman, come to bring him water, a clap of thunder sends her scurrying away. But Tamino is more successful. After summoning Pamina, he refuses to say a word to her even though she gives vent to her grief over Tamino's sudden coldness (*"Ach, ich fuehl's"*). Meanwhile, the Queen of the Night appears before Pamina and urges her to avenge herself on Sarastro by killing him with a dagger (*"Der Hoelle Rache"*). Pamina recoils in horror at the suggestion; later, she begs Sarastro to forgive her mother, which he does magnanimously, since at the holy Temple there is room for neither hate nor vengeance (*"In diesen heil'gen Hallen"*).

As new trials await Tamino and Papageno, Sarastro assures the prince and his beloved that all will turn out well in the end, and conducts Tamino away. Papageno staggers in, weary and thirsty, to find welcome relief in a huge jug of wine. After drinking his fill, Papageno expresses the wish for a wife (*"Ein Maedchen oder Weibchen"*), in response to which an old, haggard woman makes an appearance. With broken heart, Papageno accepts her as his wife, since the alternative for him is a lonely life on bread and water. Suddenly the old woman sheds her disguise and becomes the lovely bird-girl, Papagena. The birdcatcher is about to take her in his arms when he is summoned by a voice to undergo one or two ordeals.

Convinced she has lost Tamino's love, Pamina decides to commit suicide, but at the zero hour the pages of the Queen of the Night save her life and assure her of Tamino's eternal devotion. Tamino himself, come to provide her further proof of this, embraces her. Now, led by Pamina, Tamino is ready to go through caverns of fire and water, playing his magic flute for protection as he proceeds. Tamino's success is hailed by the priests.

For a while, Papageno is completely miserable, believing he will never again see Papagena. He contemplates hanging himself. Then the Queen's pages remind him of the magic power of his chimes, and no sooner does Papageno sound the first notes when, to his great delight, Papagena comes to join him.

The powers of evil, however, have not yet been completely vanquished. In a gloomy grove, the Queen and her attendants make a last effort to abduct Pamina and destroy Sarastro, but to no avail. A crash of thunder and a flash of lightening send these evildoers scurrying in defeat into the depths of the earth. Now Tamino and Pamina are brought triumphantly before Sarastro and initiated into the mysteries of the order, as all present raise their voices in a hymn to Isis and Osiris.

Mam'zelle Nitouche by Hervé.

> Opéra-bouffe in three acts with text by Henri Meilhac and A. Millaud. First performance: Théâtre des Variétés, Paris, January 26, 1883. First American performance: Wallack's Theater, New York, 1886.

Hervé (more officially Florimond Ronger) was one of Offenbach's most important predecessors in writing opéra-bouffes. The fifty or so works he completed in this genre may well be regarded as the beginnings of French operetta.

SCENES FROM
METROPOLITAN OPERA
PRODUCTIONS

Louis Mélançon, Metropolitan Opera House

L'Elisir d'amore, Act I

The Magic Flute, Finale, Act II

Louis Mélançon, Metropolitan Opera House

Louis Mélançon, Metropolitan Opera House

Die Fledermaus, Act II

Gianni Schicchi

The Gypsy Baron, Act III

Martha, Act I

Louis Mélançon, Metropolitan Opera House

Cosí fan Tutte, Act I

The Marriage of Figaro, Act I

The Barber of Seville (Rossini), Act II

La Périchole, Act I

Hansel and Gretel, Act II

Louis Mélançon, Metropolitan Opera House

For his setting for *Mam'zelle Nitouche,* his masterwork, Hervé went to a small French provincial town, in or about 1850. Celestin, an organist and music teacher in a convent school, is the composer of an operetta about to be produced in a nearby town; its star is his sweetheart, Corinne. Celestin's favorite pupil at the school is Denise. To the casual observer she might appear to be a pious and disciplined young girl, but inwardly she is restless for love and adventure. She is delighted to discover that she must leave the convent to marry Count Fernand, a young army officer, since this will allow her to attend with him the première of her teacher's operetta. When Corinne sees Celestin in a hotel with an attractive young lady, she becomes suspicious and outraged; during the intermission of her performance, she refuses to continue. Denise now assumes the identity of a mythical actress, "Mam'zelle Nitouche," and as such she substitutes for Corinne and scores a triumph. Count Fernand, who is in the audience—and who does not know that it is Denise who is performing—falls in love with this "Mam'zelle Nitouche." Later in the evening, Celestin and Denise are arrested as suspicious characters and brought for judgment before Count Fernand. He recognizes the girl as the star of the evening, without realizing that she is also Denise. After Celestin and Denise are freed, the latter returns to the convent, since Fernand is no longer interested in marrying her. Only after Fernand discovers that "Mam'zelle Nitouche" and Denise are the same person does he change his mind again.

Hervé wrote *Mam'zelle Nitouche* for the celebrated singing star of France, Mme Judic. And when *Mam'zelle Nitouche* was introduced to the United States in 1885, it was Mme Judic who once again filled the title role. A year after that, when the comic opera was revived at the Grand Opera House in New York, the title role was taken over by a Miss Lotta.

Bearing in mind the voice and personality of Mme Judic, Hervé assigned to Denise some of his most important arias. In the variety of their mood and style, these arias reflect the girl's spurious piety, on the one hand, and her vivacity and love of life, on the other. Her first-act air, "*Sous les vieux arceaux gothiques*"; her second-act rondeau, "*Ce n'est pas une sinecure*"; her second-act rondeau and song, "*La Voiture attendant en bas*" and "*À minuit après la fête*"; and her third-act couplets, "*Le long de la ru' Lafayette*" and "*Est-il possible?*"—all these represent the cream of the melodic crop in Hervé's bountiful score. To Celestin are assigned two other fine melodies, "*Pour le théâtre Floridor*" in the first act and, in the third, *"Je te plains, ma pauvre Denise."* The first act also boasts an outstanding duet between Celestin and Denise in *"Le Grenadier était bel homme."*

Maritana by William Vincent Wallace.

> Romantic opera in three acts with text by Edward Fitzball, based on *Don César de Bazan*, a French play by Adolphe Philippe d'Ennery and Pinel Dumanoir. Interpolated lyrics by Alfred Bunn. First performance: Drury Lane Theater, London, November 15, 1845. First American performance: Philadelphia, Pennsylvania, November 9, 1846.

William Wallace, acclaimed on three continents as a concert violinist, was for a long time much more famous as a virtuoso than as a composer. One day, in 1845, he paid a call upon the writer Edward Fitzball. He played for Fitzball some of his compositions, which made such an impression on the writer that he handed over to Wallace the first act of *Maritana*, a play on which he was then working. Wallace was impressed with what he read and told Fitzball he would like to set the completed play to music.

This was Wallace's first attempt to write an opera, but with it he realized international fame as a composer. He never again wrote anything as popular. When first produced in London, *Maritana* had a profitable run of fifty consecutive performances. It was staged in Vienna on January 8, 1848, where it received an ovation. That same year it was also heard in New York as well as in several other of the world's music centers. Before long it became a favorite production with English amateur companies.

In seventeenth-century Madrid, King Charles is attracted to Maritana, a gypsy he had heard sing and seen dance in the streets. To compromise the king, Don José conspires to get Maritana carried to Don César, who is in prison for having tried to fight a duel during Holy Week. Since Maritana is in love with César she is an all-too-willing partner to this conspiracy. After they are secretly married in prison, Don César is conducted to the courtyard to be shot. But he escapes unharmed, since Lazarillo has removed the bullets from all the guns of the firing squad. Meanwhile, Maritana is a guest at a sumptuous ball in the palace. César appears, demanding his wife from the king. Don José now insists that César must be apprehended as an escaped criminal. But José is proved to be the real traitor and is killed by César. The latter is now appointed by the king to be governor of Valencia, and his marriage to Maritana receives the royal blessing.

One of the most beautiful airs in the opera, indeed one of the most beautiful airs in all English opera—Maritana's first-act romance, "The Harp in the Air"—had an interesting history. Wallace had written it some years before he started work on his opera. In its original version, it was a piano composition written by Wallace for one of his pupils, Isabella Kelly, whose physical charm had inspired him. Wallace fell so deeply in love with Isabella that, to marry her in 1831, he converted to Catholicism. The marriage, however, was short-lived; they separated in 1835. Wallace then went to live with Helen Stoepel, another pianist, who bore him two sons. A decade after that, in preparing the score for his first opera, Wallace decided to exhume the piano piece inspired by his first wife and to transform it into a romantic aria.

Another highly popular air is that of Don César in the second act, just before he faces the firing squad, "Yes, Let Me Like a Soldier Fall." In the nineteenth century, this melody was sung and played in parlors throughout England.

Other prominent melodies include Don César's sentimental ballad, "There is a Flower"; Maritana's song, "Scenes that are Brightest"; and the male duet, "I am the King of Spain."

Mârouf, Savetier du Caire [*Mârouf, Cobbler of Cairo*] by Henri Rabaud.

> Comic opera in five acts with text by Lucien Népoty, based on a tale from *The Arabian Nights*. First performance: Opéra-Comique, Paris, May 15, 1914. First American performance: Metropolitan Opera, New York, December 19, 1917 (in French); New York, May 21, 1937 (in English).

This is one of the most significant comic operas of the twentieth century. Introduced when France was on the eve of plunging into World War I, *Mârouf, Savetier du Caire* was described by Camille Bellaigue as "the last smile of French music before the war."

In ancient Cairo, Mârouf's wife is a shrew who raises such a fuss when he brings her a cake of sugar (instead of one made from honey) that two policemen rush in thinking she is being beaten. They punish

poor Mârouf with a hundred lashes of the whip. This convinces the cobbler he must run away from home. He goes to sea, gets shipwrecked, and
is saved by wealthy Ali, Mârouf's one-time school chum. Ali brings his
friend to Khaitan, where he dresses him in style and passes him off as
"the wealthiest man in the world." The Sultan invites Mârouf to his
palace and offers him his daughter in marriage. But when Mârouf falls
in love with the princess, his conscience troubles him, leading him to
confess to her the true state of his affairs. His poverty and marriage seem
to make little difference to the princess, since she, too, is now in love,
and they elope. Upon coming to a plain not far from Khaitan, they find
a magic ring which, when rubbed, brings them immense wealth and a
sumptuous palace. The Sultan has come in pursuit, having learned
that Mârouf is a pauper. But seeing Mârouf and the princess in such for-
tunate circumstances, he once again is convinced that his prospective
son-in-law is fabulously wealthy and is happy to embrace him.

Rabaud's style skillfully combines orientalism with modernism, pure
French lyricism with the style of the German Romantic school. The
music is ever pleasing to the ear, rich in local color, filled with moments
of high dramatic appeal. Orientalism is pronounced in the sensual music accompanying the third-act ballet; French lyricism is found at its
best in three Mârouf arias, *"Il est des Musulmans,"* in the first act, *"La
Caravane"* (*"À travers le désert"*) in the second, and *"Viens, mon épouse
fleurie"* in the fourth.

When the Metropolitan Opera introduced *Mârouf, Savetier du Caire*
to American audiences in 1917, the cast included Giuseppe De Luca and
Frances Alda, while Pierre Monteux was the conductor. "There was much
to see and admire in the new opera," reported W. J. Henderson in the
New York Sun, "which is one of fancy, humor, and sentiment, without
a touch of the tragic. . . . Rabaud has treated the story in a thoroughly
modern manner. His voice parts move almost wholly in ariosos. . . .
Oriental color is laid on not merely with a brush but with a palette knife.
And the greatest amount of illustrative and descriptive detail is inevitably
given to the orchestra. . . . The greatest pleasure . . . will be obtained
by regarding the music as a colorful background for a legendary comedy."

(The) **Marriage Contract** by Giacchino Rossini. *See* (*La*) *Cambiale
di Matrimonio.*

(The) Marriage of Figaro [*Le Nozze di Figaro*] by Wolfgang Amadeus Mozart.

> Opera buffa in four acts with text by Lorenzo da Ponte, based on *Le Mariage de Figaro*, a play by Beaumarchais. First performance: Burgtheater, Vienna, May 1, 1786. First American performances: New York, 1799 (probable); New York, May 10, 1824 (in English); New York, October 24, 1831 (in French); New York, November 23, 1858 (in Italian); New York, December 18, 1862 (in German).

This is opera buffa *in excelsis*. It would not be too difficult to build a case for it as the greatest such work ever written, and one of the greatest in any style or form. It combines the most wonderful, expressive, and varied invention in lyricism with the most consummate skill in counterpoint, harmony, and orchestration; the music assigned to the principal characters is filled with subtle and profound insight into each personality; its extended finales are miracles of structure and content which carry on, in extended sequences, the dramatic action and provide us with a further understanding of the inner conflicts of the characters. No wonder, then that more than one critic looks upon *The Marriage of Figaro* as "the perfect opera buffa" and that Eric Blom said it represents "Italian comic opera in its final stage of perfection . . . as great as a whole as it is captivating in detail."

In their book *The Opera*, Wallace Brockway and Herbert Weinstock wrote: "It is a peerless *jeu d'esprit* which knows where it is going from the first note of the lightsome and exactly right, perfectly proportioned overture to the joyous finale, when the reconciled principals announce that they are about to turn night into day. Complex as the plot is, the opera proceeds to its destination as swiftly and as unerringly as a homing pigeon making its way back through the trackless mazes of the sky. Frivolous, impudent, and witty in every scene and situation, *Le Nozze di Figaro* carries the profound internal reality of its own made world and has the razor-sharp edge of seriousness that the mature satire of Beaumarchais deserves."

It is believed that it was Mozart himself who had chosen Beaumarchais' play as an opera text and had it brought to the attention of the Viennese court poet, Lorenzo da Ponte. It was a truly amazing choice. For the trilogy of plays which Beaumarchais built around the character of the valet, Figaro, were a thinly disguised attack against aristocracy and the social order of the day. The Emperor of Austria recognized this when he refused to give his consent for Da Ponte and Mozart to make one of these plays into an opera, and yielded only after both had promised to eliminate the social and political criticism and to emphasize the farcical elements. The farce is there—both text and music effervesce with gaiety and good spirits—but some of Beaumarchais' thrusts against the nobility and their dictatorial ways have not been completely eliminated.

After the brief and sprightly little overture, which sets the vivacious mood for what is soon to follow, the curtain rises on an apartment in the palace of Count Almaviva at Seville, Spain, in the seventeenth century. These are the quarters to be assigned to Figaro, the Count's valet, soon to marry Susanna, the Countess' first woman-in-waiting. Figaro is a bit concerned because he notes that this apartment is close to the Count's sleeping quarters, and the Count is rather kindly disposed to Susanna; nevertheless, Figaro soon insists he knows well how to handle his master (*"Se vuol ballare"*). However, Figaro has a far better reason to be upset. Some time ago he had borrowed money from Marcellina, promising to marry her if he failed to return the debt. Since the debt has not been repaid, Marcellina comes to discuss with Figaro arrangements for meeting the terms of the contract. When Susanna and Marcellina meet they forthwith reveal their dislike for each other (*"Via resti servita"*). Marcellina leaves in a huff. Cherubino, the Count's page, makes his appearance, with the complaint that he is about to be dismissed from the Count's service for having dared to flirt with Barbarina, the gardener's daughter. What the Count does not know is that Cherubino is secretly in love with the Countess. When the Count appears, Cherubino hides behind a chair, but is soon located there and is ordered by the Count to enlist in his regiment. With tongue in cheek, Figaro gives Cherubino instructions on how to behave as a soldier (*"Non più andrai"*).

Within her boudoir, the Countess bewails the fact that the Count has been unfaithful to her (*"Porgi Amor"*). She teams up with Susanna and Figaro to revive the Count's interest in her by fanning his jealousy. The Count will be made to find a letter intended only for the Countess' eyes, and at the same time a rendezvous will be arranged for the Countess, which Susanna will keep disguised as her mistress. Further, they intend to have the Count meet Susanna secretly for a love tryst, but with Cherubino impersonating Susanna. When Cherubino appears, singing poignantly about the meaning of love (*"Voi che sapete"*), he is hurriedly dressed in Susanna's clothes. But the precipitous and unexpected arrival of the Count forces Cherubino to hide in a closet; then when the Count is not looking, Cherubino escapes out the window while Susanna takes his place. Finding Susanna in the closet—instead of some lover—the Count is apologetic and contrite until he is informed by the gardener that somebody had just escaped from the window and dropped a piece of paper in the flower bed. That paper, Cherubino's commission in the Count's regiment, puts a finger on the culprit. The Count, fully convinced that Cherubino is the Countess' lover, vows vengeance. Marcellina now comes to the Count to demand that he compel Figaro to go through with his contractual bargain and marry her.

Susanna consents to a rendezvous with the Count under threat that if she declines, he will insist on Figaro's marrying Marcellina, which he intends to do anyway. The meeting is then arranged (*"Crudel! perchè finora"*). During detailed negotiations between Marcellina and her lawyer, and Figaro and the Count, the startling news is uncovered that Figaro is Marcellina's long-lost son; thus he is no longer required to marry her. Meanwhile, in her solitude, the Countess reminisces about the times long past when the Count was deeply in love with her (*"Dove sono?"*). When Susanna appears, the Countess dictates a letter in which Susanna invites the Count to a secret rendezvous (*"Che soave zeffiretto"*). It is the Countess' intention to go to that rendezvous disguised as Susanna. And now, without further ado, the marriage ceremony of Figaro and Susanna can take place, after which the Count invites everyone to a gala party.

Later the same evening, the Countess and Susanna come into the garden, each dressed in the other's clothes. Thus Figaro is tempted to believe that Susanna is planning to meet the Count, and he becomes further convinced of this when he hears her sing an invitation to her absent lover (*"Deh vieni, non tardar"*). When Cherubino steps into the garden he mistakes the Countess for Susanna and tries to steal a kiss, only to be discovered by the Count and rudely sent scurrying. Now the Count, thinking the Countess is Susanna, makes love to his own wife, until he is brought face to face with the truth. The Countess forgives her erring husband, and the entire assemblage returns to the palace to celebrate Figaro's wedding.

Mozart's enemies in Vienna, led by the redoubtable Antonio Salieri, did what they could, first, to prevent the première of *The Marriage of Figaro* and then, to sabotage it. But for the intervention of the Emperor himself, the opera might have died immediately after the first rehearsal. By the end of the second rehearsal, singers and musicians alike were completely won over to the new opera. "The performers on the stage and those in the orchestra," recalled Michael Kelly, Mozart's friend, "vociferated, *'Bravo, Maestro! Viva, viva grande Mozart!'* I thought the orchestra would never cease applauding, beating the bows of their violins against the music desks." The opera enjoyed an even greater triumph at its first performance at the Burgtheater: Almost every aria had to be repeated, and the Emperor himself rose to his feet to shout his approval. Such a formidable success made Mozart's enemies redouble their efforts to discredit the new opera. What they did was to present at the Burgtheater a catchy little opera by the name of *Una Cosa rara,* hoping its success would throw Mozart's opera in the shade. In this they succeeded all too well: *The Marriage of Figaro* was withdrawn from the repertory of the Burgtheater after only nine performances.

But in Prague, where there were no rivals or enemies to obstruct him, Mozart and his new opera met a far different fate. A visiting company performed it in the Bohemian capital toward the end of 1786, and the city went mad over the opera. In the cafés, at theaters, in the streets, its most famous arias were continually heard. With no little delight Mozart reported: "Here no one hums, sings, or whistles anything but airs . . . of *Figaro.* No other opera draws . . . but *Figaro.*" When Mozart conducted a concert on January 20, 1787, the audience shouted, *"Figaro!"* Forthwith, Mozart sat at the piano and improvised a dozen variations on the aria, *"Non più andrai,"* to receive a deafening ovation.

Martha or **Der Markt von Richmond** [*Martha* or *The Market at Richmond*], by Friedrich von Flotow.

> Comic opera in four acts with text by Friedrich Wilhelm Riese ("W. Friedrich"), based on *Lady Henriette,* a French ballet-pantomime with scenario by Jules Henri Vernoy de Saint-Georges. First performance: Kaernthnerthor Theater, Vienna, November 25, 1847. First American performances: Niblo Gardens, New York, November 1, 1852 (in English); New York, March 13, 1855 (in German); New York, January 7, 1859 (in Italian).

Although *Martha* enjoyed a prosperous career in the world's leading serious operatic theaters—and its composer himself designated the work as a "semi-serious opera"—it is more of an operetta than a grand opera by virtue of its infectious tunes and the light and often comic elements in the text. In their book *The Opera,* Herbert Weinstock and Wallace

Brockway consider it "as well contrived an operetta as *Blossom Time.*" And when *Martha* was revived with a new English text by the Metropolitan Opera on January 27, 1961 (after an absence from its stage of thirty-two years), Harold S. Schonberg said in the *New York Times:* "*Martha* is nothing more or less than musical comedy, with a plot as intellectually rigorous as that of most musical comedies." Louis Biancolli wrote in the *New York World-Telegram and Sun:* "Those who prefer their operas tuneful, romantic, colorful, well-dressed, and amusing, have one answer in . . . *Martha.* Only a heart of stone could resist its bland charms."

Martha is the composer's masterpiece, the one of his more than twenty-five stage works by which he is most often represented in the world's lyric theaters. Almost as if he were fully aware of its destiny, the composer expended on its score a considerable amount of time and effort. The opera was based on an earlier Flotow stage score: a ballet, *Lady Henriette,* on which Flotow had collaborated with two other composers and which had been produced at the Paris Opéra on February 22, 1844. In translating the ballet into an opera, Flotow rewrote his score four times before he was satisfied with it. Thus, because of its origin, *Martha* is essentially a *French* opera, although it was written by a *German* composer and is most often heard in the *Italian* language.

The opera was introduced in Vienna where it was an immediate success. Through the years it retained its popularity with Austrian audiences; by 1882, it had been given five hundred times in Vienna alone. It was equally successful in other world centers. When first heard in America, at Niblo Gardens, the role of Lady Harriet was assumed by Ann Bishop, former wife of Howard Payne, the composer of "Home Sweet Home." In 1886, *Martha* was produced in English (translation by Henry E. Krehbiel) at the Academy of Music in New York. It entered the repertory of the Metropolitan Opera during its first season of operation, on March 14, 1884, presented in Italian. The opera flourished at the Metropolitan between 1906 and 1908, profiting from a remarkable cast that was headed by Caruso, Sembrich, Plançon, and Edyth Walker.

The action takes place in Richmond, England, during the reign of Queen Anne. Lady Harriet and her maid, Nancy, decided to disguise themselves as peasant girls, assume the fictitious names of Martha and Julia, and go off to visit the Richmond Fair. There they meet two charming young men—Plunkett, a young farmer, and his foster brother, Lionel. The men hire the girls as servants on a one-year contract. Unable to break this agreement, the girls decide to make the lives of their masters as miserable as possible. The situation is further complicated by the fact that Lionel falls in love with "Martha" and Plunkett with "Julia."

The ladies manage to escape. Sometime later, at a hunting park in Richmond Forest, Plunkett espies Nancy, whom he recognizes as his servant "Julia," and Lionel comes upon Lady Harriet dressed up in the fineries of a great lady. When both men insist that the girls return into their service, Lady Harriet sees to it that Lionel is apprehended by the police. Bitter at this development, Lionel decides to forget Martha, even after she has come to him with the confession that she loves him. Plunkett and Nancy now join with Lady Harriet in a maneuver to win back Lionel. They set up a replica of the Richmond Fair, in the hope that if Lionel revisits the scene of his first meeting with "Martha" his love for her will be reawakened. To this simulated fair comes Lady Harriet, once again dressed in peasant garb. When Lionel sees her he takes her into his arms.

Two melodies above all others stand out in Flotow's score, but only one of these is the work of the composer. "The Last Rose of Summer" (*"Die letzte Rose"* or *"Qui sola, vergin rosa"*) is an old Irish air, "The Groves of Blarney," set to a poem by Thomas Moore. Flotow used this beloved Irish melody in the second act for Lady Harriet, when Lionel urges her to sing for him. The aria recurs in the first scene of the fourth act at the simulated fair, and with it Lady Harriet tries to reawaken Lionel's love for her. The melody is heard once again at the end of the opera as a duet of Lady Harriet and Lionel expressing the joy of reconciliation.

Flotow's own melody is the beautiful *"M'Appari"* (or, *"Ach, so fromm"*), sung in the third act by Lionel as he pines for Martha. This aria was one of Caruso's favorites; he never failed to bring down the house with it. When Berlioz first heard *Martha*, for which he manifested little admiration, he remarked of *"M'Appari"* that its "fragrance alone was sufficient to disinfect the rest of the work."

The coquettish "Good Night Quartet" of the four principals, in the second act (*"Schlafe wohl! und mag dich reuen,"* or *"Dormi pur"*); the drinking song of Plunkett and the farmers (*"Lasst mich euch fragen"* or *"Chi mi dira"*); and the quintet with chorus, *"Mag der Himmel euch vergeben,"* or *"Ah! che a voi perdoni Iddio"*—all these are also in Flotow's best melodic vein.

Masaniello by Daniel François Esprit Auber. *See (La) Muette de Portici.*

(La) Mascotte [*The Mascot*] by Edmond Audran.

Opéra-comique in three acts with text by Alfred Duru and Henri Charles Chivot. First performance: Bouffes-Parisiens, Paris, December 28, 1880. First American performances: Gaiety Theater, Boston, April 11, 1881 (in English); Abbey's Park Theater, New York, November 30, 1881 (in French); Thalia Theater, New York, December 5, 1881 (in German).

La Mascotte is one of the crowning successes of the French light theater. In its first five years it was given over a thousand performances in Paris; by 1897 it had been heard there 1700 times. It was a sensation when introduced in both London and America, less than a year after the world première. Its initial performance—in Boston in 1881—was followed a month later with presentations in Philadelphia and New York. New York also saw the French and German versions of the operetta, while a touring company brought it to other leading cities. To supplement all these productions, the London company came to tour the United States. *La Mascotte* was revived in New York on December 1, 1926.

In fifteenth-century Italy, in a town called Piombino, Rocco, a farmer, has suffered many setbacks in his personal fortunes. He sends a shepherd, Pippo, to find him some money. Pippo is unsuccessful, but he does manage to bring back with him Bettina, a young girl whom he describes as a "mascot" and who he is sure will bring Rocco luck. Lorenzo, Prince of Piombino, is on a hunting trip with his daughter, Fiametta, and her suitor, Frederick. They seek a respite in Rocco's humble abode, where Lorenzo is so taken by Bettina's beauty that he decides to take her back to his court. At the same time Fiametta falls in love with Pippo. At court, Bettina becomes the Countess Panada, and Rocco is given the post of court chamberlain. When Pippo appears in court disguised as a strolling player, he convinces Bettina to run away with him. Fiametta and Rocco also affect their escape, disguised as wandering minstrels. All are apprehended. Bettina and Pippo firmly announce their intent to get married, and Fiametta and Frederick are reconciled.

The choral passages are particularly effective. The best of these are: the first-act chorus, "*Les gens sages*"; the chorus of the Pages with which the second act opens; and the soldiers' chorus in the third act. In a more lyrical vein are Pippo's first-act aria, "*Légende de la mascotte*," and Bettina's second-act arietta, "*Laissez-moi seule*."

(Il) **Matrimonio segreto** [*The Clandestine,* or *Secret, Marriage*] by Domenico Cimarosa.

> Opera buffa in two acts with text by Giovanni Bertati, based upon *The Clandestine Marriage,* a play by George Colman and David Garrick. First performance: Burgtheater, Vienna, February 7, 1792. First American performance: New York, January 4, 1834.

Between Pergolesi's *La Serva padrona,* with which the opera buffa form as we know it today came into being, and Rossini's *The Barber of Seville,* with which the form climbed to the summits, stands Cimarosa's *Il Matrimonio segreto,* the only Italian comic opera of that period still performed. Verdi considered this to be the ideal of what opera buffa should be. And A. Maczewsky wrote: "Cimarosa was the culminating point of genuine Italian opera. His invention is simple, but always natural; and in spite of his Italian love for melody, he is never monotonous; but both in form and melody is always in keeping with the situation. . . . His real talent lay in comedy—in his sparkling wit and unfailing good humor. His invention was inexhaustible in the representation of that overflowing and yet naïve liveliness, that merry teasing loquacity which is the distinguishing feature of the genuine Italian buffo style. His chief strength lies in the vocal parts, but the orchestra is delicately and effectively handled, and his ensembles are masterpieces, with a vein of humor which is undeniably akin to that of Mozart." Professor Edward J. Dent goes so far as to say that Mozart learned much from Cimarosa, taking over "his conventions—his breathless back-chat in recitative, his charming tunes, his patter songs for the bass, his chattering ensembles—and added to them his own warmth of harmony and ingenuity of orchestration."

Cimarosa wrote *Il Matrimonio segreto* while filling the office of Kapellmeister for Leopold II of Austria. Thus it was in Vienna, and not in Italy, that this comic opera was introduced. It proved a sensation. At its second performance the Emperor himself was present and was so enthusiastic that after the final curtain he invited the members of the cast for supper, after which the entire opera was repeated for him.

The story follows the pattern of many others found in eighteenth-century opera buffa. In eighteenth-century Bologna, Carolina, daughter of the wealthy but avaricious merchant, Geronimo, is secretly married to Paolino. Paolino devises a plan to win the favor of his father-in-law and thus be in a more strategic position in which to confess that he is his son-in-law. He arranges a match between Carolina's older sister, Elisetta, and an Englishman, Count Robinson. But what Paolino had not reckoned with was that Elisetta would fall in love with the schemer herself and that Count Robinson would be similarly attracted to Carolina. There is only one way out of this mess, and that is for Carolina and Paolino to run away. But they are intercepted by Geronimo, who finally discovers they are man and wife. Geronimo reconciles himself to this situation, while Count Robinson and Elisetta finally realize that they are in love with each other after all.

The Mozart-like little overture begins with three chords as a preface to the first theme: a fleet, vivacious melody. The second subject is, by contrast, a lyrical and tender air for strings.

Principal vocal numbers alternate neatly from gay moods to sentimental ones. In the buffa style are two airs by Geronimo: *"Udite, tutti, udite,"* in which he informs Elisetta that a noble marriage had been arranged for her with a Count; and *"Un matrimonio nobile,"* in which he speaks of his joy that his older daughter is to marry someone of such a high social position.

The following are at times in a tender and lyrical manner, at others in a more dramatic vein: *"Questa cosa accordar,"* Carolina's attempt to dissuade Count Robinson from loving her by maintaining she does not deserve a nobleman; her sorrowful song to her father when Geronimo threatens to send her off to a convent, *"E possono mai nascere";* Paolino's beautiful air when he arranges to run off with Carolina, *"Pria che spunta in cielo";* and his poignant avowal to Carolina that he will be true to her forever, *"Ah! no, che tu così morir."*

Mavra by Igor Stravinsky.

Opera buffa in one act with text by Boris Koshno, based on *The Little House at Kolomna*, a fairy tale by Pushkin. First performance: Opéra, Paris, June 3, 1922, by the Diaghilev Ballet (public). First American performance: Philadelphia, Pennsylvania, December 28, 1934 (in English).

One does not usually associate Stravinsky, the iconoclast of twentieth-century music, with opera buffa; and *Mavra* is, indeed, a curiosity among Stravinsky's works. "I wanted merely to try my hand at this living form of opera buffa," the composer has explained. "My opera *Mavra* was conceived because of a natural sympathy I have always felt for the melodic language, the vocal style, and the conventions of the old Russian-Italian school."

The text is a merry little tale involving a man dressed in woman's clothes. Parasha is in love with the handsome Hussar, Basil. When the cook of Parasha's household dies, Parasha conceives of a novel way to get her beloved into her establishment on a permanent basis. She has him disguise himself as a female and gets him the job of cook in her home under the assumed name of Mavra. This ruse does not work out very well. One day, Parasha's mother surprises Basil while he is shaving himself. The mother goes into a dead faint, and Basil jumps out of the window and flees.

The Stravinsky score is unusual on several counts. It calls for an orchestra consisting of twelve woodwinds, twelve brasses, and a double-bass. The vocal score has no recitatives whatever. The music is an uninterrupted procession of airs and ensemble numbers, the melody found as often in the orchestra as on the stage. Generally speaking, Stravinsky's style is in the national Russian idiom of Glinka and Dargomyzhsky, but the composer also exploits the Italian *bel canto*, gypsy songs, and even American ragtime—the last found in the sprightly finale. Eric Walter White points out that the Russian-type lyricism is found in Parasha's air at the beginning of the opera, the Italian-type melody in the music devoted to Parasha's mother and neighbor, and the gypsy song in many of the Hussar's airs. White goes on to say that all three styles "seem to coalesce in his (the Hussar's) final air."

The performance at the Paris Opéra on June 3, 1922—by the Diaghilev Ballet—was not actually the world première, although it was the first *public* performance. Before that, the little opera was given in a private concert performance at the Continental Hotel in Paris for special guests.

The first public performance of *Mavra* made the composer very unhappy. The huge auditorium in which it was given and the spectacular numbers by the Diaghilev Ballet with which it was played, were not conducive to setting off this informal little piece to best advantage. "*Mavra,*" the composer wrote in his autobiography, "was regarded as a disconcerting freak of mine, and a downright failure. Such was also the attitude of all the critics, notably those of the prewar left. They condemned the whole thing then and there, attaching no importance to it, and regarding it as unworthy of closer examination. Only a few musicians of the younger generation appreciated *Mavra,* and realized that it marked a turning point in the evolution of my musical thought."

(The) Meadow of the Scholars by Louis Joseph-Ferdinand Hérold. *See (Le) Pré aux clercs.*

(Le) Médecin malgré lui [*The Doctor in Spite of Himself*] by Charles Gounod.

> Opéra-comique in three acts with text by Jules Barbier and Michael Carré, based on the play of the same name by Molière (with only slight alterations). First performance: Théâtre Lyrique, Paris, January 15, 1858. First American performance: New York, May 10, 1917 (in English).

Although Gounod certainly is remembered most often for his operas in the grand French romantic traditions—and especially for *Faust*—Martin Cooper is of the opinion that in a comic work like *Le Médecin malgré lui* (Gounod's first attempt in a lighter operatic style) the composer is "at his best—an elegant musician with a charming lyrical gift, a genuine instinct for what might be called 'chamber drama,' and a discreet and well balanced sense of the orchestra."

The librettists, in adapting the Molière comedy for the operatic stage, did not tamper greatly with the original product. And, in his music, Gounod captured much of Molière's wit and sardonic humor.

In a forest, at noon, Sagnarelle gives his wife a sound beating. She vows to seek revenge. When she learns that Lucinde, daughter of wealthy Géronte, is ill, she informs Géronte's servants that her husband, Sagnarelle, is a miracle-working physician disguised as a humble wood-chopper. Sagnarelle refuses to attend Lucinde, insisting he knows nothing about medicine. But the servants will not believe him and administer such a sound thrashing that the wood-chopper is finally willing to do anything asked of him. Meanwhile, at Géronte's palatial home, Leander is serenading Lucinde, a fact that arouses the old man to uncontrollable fits of anger, since he wants his daughter to marry Horace, a wealthy man. At this point, to the delight of old Géronte, Sagnarelle diagnoses Lucinde's case and prescribes a cure. When Sagnarelle leaves the house, Leander tells him that Lucinde has been merely pretending illness in order to avoid a marriage with Horace. Finally, Lucinde and Leander plan to elope. When this news reaches Géronte, the old man and his servants attack Sagnarelle, accusing him of being a fraud. The wood-chopper is saved by the sudden reappearance of Lucinde and Leander with the good tidings that Leander has just inherited his uncle's wealth. Of course, Géronte is now more kindly disposed toward Leander and gives his belated consent to the marriage. At the same time, Sagnarelle's wife finds it in her heart to forgive her wayward husband.

Among the more impressive lyrical or humorous episodes in Gounod's score are the following: Sagnarelle's first act air, *"Qu'ils sont doux"*; Leander's serenade to Lucinde with which the second act opens, *"Est-on sage?"*; Sagnarelle's hymn of praise to medicine that opens the third act, *"Vive la médecine!"*; the lovely air of Jacqueline (Géronte's nurse), *"D'un bout du monde l'autre bout"*; and the mock choral hymn to science with which the opera ends, *"Nous faisons tous ce que nous savons faire."*

The United States had to wait until 1917 for a local première of this comic opera. On that occasion it was heard in an English translation by A. Mattulath. The opera was revived in New York by the Juilliard School of Music in 1936, with a new English translation by A. Dean and the title changed to *The Frantic Physician;* Gounod's music was arranged by M. Bartholomew.

Meine Schwester und Ich [*My Sister and I*] by Ralph Benatzky.

Operetta in two acts, prologue and epilogue, with text by Blum, based on a French play by Berr and Verneuil. First performance: Berlin, Germany, March 29, 1930. First American performance: Shubert Theater, New York, December 30, 1930.

Of Benatzky's many operettas this is the one that holds second place in popularity to *The White Horse Inn.* The time is the present; the place, Paris and Nancy in France. Roger Fleuriot, a musicologist—possibly the only time this profession has been represented in operetta—wants a divorce from his wife, Dolly, a French girl of noble birth. When the divorce reaches the law courts, the story of their romance unfolds, and becomes the heart of the play.

Roger is the librarian in a French château belonging to Dolly's family. Dolly is being sought after by Count Lacy, but her heart belongs to Roger. While Roger reciprocates her love, he recognizes marriage is impossible because of their difference in social station. He decides to leave the château for good and become a professor in a music school. To frustrate these plans, Dolly devises a scheme. As Roger is about to leave the château, she entreats him to deliver a ring and letter to her sister Genevieve, who had cut herself off from her noble family to become a salesgirl in a Nancy shoe shop. Actually, there is no such person as Genevieve, but a role which Dolly has manufactured for herself. When Roger delivers the message, he falls in love with Genevieve at first sight, and before long asks her to marry him.

The epilogue carries the story back into the divorce court. Dolly now discloses that when Roger learned that she and Genevieve were one and the same person, he once again became inhibited by his humble social status, and insisted on breaking off their marriage. The judge, realizing that they are very much in love, advises them to go home and try to make a success of their marital state—advice which they follow eagerly.

Benatzky's score is made up not only of some delightful waltz music, as might be expected from a German operetta, but even of such essentially American popular idioms as the fox trot, shimmy, and tango. *"Um ein bisschen Liebe dreht sich die Welt"* and *"Ich war fruehr doch sonsts nicht so"* are tangos; *"Freunderl, mir is heut' so gut"* is a waltz; *"Ich bin verliebt"* (with the intoxicating refrain, *"Mein Maedel ist nur ein Verkaeuferin"*) is a slow fox trot; and *"Ich lade Sie ein, Fraeulein"* is a shimmy.

When produced in New York in 1930, the book was adapted for American audiences by Harry Wagstaff Gribble and the cast included Walter Slezak and Bettina Hall.

Merrie England by Edward German.

Operetta in two acts with text by Basil Hood. First performance: Savoy Theater, London, April 2, 1902.

When Sir Arthur Sullivan died in 1901, Edward German was called in to complete Sullivan's last opera, *The Emerald Isle*. Up to this point all German had written was some exceptionally fine incidental music for plays by Shakespeare and Anthony Hope, but no operas or operettas. But as soon as he finished work on the Sullivan opera, German wrote his first operetta—*Merrie England*. The first proved the best: *Merrie England* became one of the most successful English operettas of the twentieth century, so frequently revived that it is almost as familiar to present-day London theatergoers as it was half a century ago.

A simple text, set during the Elizabethan era, exposed love scandals at court, particularly one involving Sir Walter Raleigh and the Queen's Maid of Honor. This affair arouses the ire and jealousy of Queen Elizabeth, who has designs on Sir Walter herself, and the concern of the Earl of Essex, who hopes to win the Queen.

Edward German's thoroughly English score consists of delightful jigs, country dances, glees, and numbers imitating old-time madrigals. An unidentified London critic, reviewing the operetta after its première in 1902, thus described text and music: "The opera opens in the meadows at Dachet, with Windsor Castle in the distance. Here there are revels, the hunt of a witch . . . and a sort of open-air masque or entertainment given before Queen Elizabeth. The scene itself, under the Greenwood, with the River Thames and the Castle in the distance, the foreground peopled with a brightly dressed throng. In this act . . . there is some of the best music, including the weird ditty of 'Jill-All-Alone,' a drinking song of Sir Walter Raleigh, a capital glee, 'Hey, Jolly Little Love,' a ballad for the Maid of Honor, a love duet for her and Raleigh, a patriotic song, 'The Yeomen of England,' a fine song for Queen Elizabeth, 'O Peaceful England,' likewise of a patriotic character, and a very elaborate first finale. It contains an old English song, one theme of which is afterwards used in the Morris dance; a capital quartet for the four tradesmen of Windsor, two waltz songs for the supposed Witch, an old-fashioned and rather conventional operatic ensemble, and a duet for the two lovers. The interest in the second act is almost exclusively lyrical, pictorial, and humorous, for the story seems to be but very slowly advanced. Early in the act, where all the characters are gathered by Herne's Oak, there is an excellent jig; and shortly afterwards, when the May Queen is holding her revels, there is another jig, together with a rustic dance. In addition, there is a tenor song for Sir Walter, a waltz song for Bessie, a topical song, to say nothing of a burlesqued Masque and Fête before Queen Elizabeth. Some of the best music in this act is comprised in an old English duet and chorus, 'The Play of Robin Hood and Little John.'"

(The) Merry Widow [*Die lustige Witwe*] by Franz Lehár.

Operetta in three acts with text by Victor Léon and Leon Stein, based on a comedy by Meilhac. First performance: Theater-an-der-Wien, Vienna, December 28, 1905. First American performances: New Amsterdam Theater, New York, October 21, 1907 (in English); Weber's Theater, New York, November 15, 1911 (in German).

It is doubtful if there is a place in the civilized world that is not familiar with the romantic love story of Prince Danilo and Sonia, heiress of Marsovia; that does not know and love the strains of the unforgettable "Merry Widow Waltz." No operetta, past or present, has enjoyed such world-wide acclaim as *The Merry Widow*. There is perhaps not a single evening when this operetta is not performed somewhere on the globe. It has been given over six thousand performances since its première, wherever there is a stage, in twenty-four languages. It was seen over a thousand times in Vienna alone. Jan Kiepura and his wife, Marta Eggerth, have appeared over a thousand times in this operetta in Europe and America. *The Merry Widow* has been seen in several streamlined and in three burlesque versions; it has been given as a ballet. On three occasions it has been adapted for the screen in Hollywood: a silent version in 1925 starred John Gilbert and Mae Murray; a black-and-white singing and talking film came in 1934 with Maurice Chevalier and Jeanette MacDonald, directed by Ernest Lubitsch; a Technicolor extravaganza was produced in 1952 with Lana Turner and Fernando Lamas. This one operetta made its composer a millionaire several times over.

It was a triumph from the first evening. Following a sensational Viennese première in 1905, the operetta traveled around the world. In its initial New York presentation it had an impressive run of 416 performances and grossed about a million dollars. In London it lasted 778 performances. In Buenos Aires, in 1907, it played simultaneously in five theaters in five different languages. Women designers copied and made fashionable the huge ostrich-feathered hat and wasp-waisted gown worn by the heroine. "Merry Widow Shoes," "Merry Widow Gloves," "Merry Widow Undergarments" were marketed. As recently as 1951 an American company made a fortune through the distribution of "Merry Widow Corselets."

The Merry Widow was first brought to the American stage in 1907 by Henry W. Savage. The production made a matinee idol out of Donald Brian, playing Danilo, and it lifted the unknown and comparatively inexperienced Ethel Jackson to stardom as Sonia. At this American première, *The Merry Widow* was seen with some discreet omissions of lines and situations considered too risqué for American tastes. Even so, the *New York Times* said that "the moral atmosphere is by no means fragrant."

As one of the supremely successful musical attractions on Broadway, *The Merry Widow* helped to intensify local interest in foreign operettas, and was responsible for bringing on a new wave of importations from the European stage. As for its popular waltz—which everybody in 1907 was humming, playing on the piano, or dancing to—it sold hundreds of thousands of copies of sheet music and helped (as *Variety* said) to sweep off "the regimented convolutions that had hitherto passed for dancing and introduced a more intimate and appealing type of dance."

The Merry Widow undoubtedly has lost whatever capacity it once had to shock and outrage stern moralists, but its power to enchant audiences does not seem to have diminished. Alan Jay Lerner, Broadway's present-day eminent lyricist and librettist, once confessed that "not a month goes by that I don't play at least one *Merry Widow* record at home." And he is not the only one to whom this remarkable operetta remains a perpetual joy with its charm, gaiety, and love of life.

We find ourselves in Paris at the beginning of the twentieth century. At the Marsovian Legation, a party is in progress, celebrating the birthday of the ruler of that kingdom. Baron Popoff, Marsovian diplomat, is in a funk. Sonia, one of Marsovia's wealthiest women, has come to Paris and is being besieged by fortune hunters. What if she should decide to marry one of them? Her fabulous wealth might leave Marsovia and send that little country into bankruptcy. When Prince Danilo, Marsovian Minister of Finance, appears at the party and sings the praises of Paris, its wine and women, Baron Popoff hits upon a happy solution to his problem: He must convince the Baron to marry Sonia and thus keep her wealth at home. The Prince is reluctant to enter upon such a scheme, since he had once been in love with Sonia and had been rejected. But after Sonia makes her entrance and pays marked attention to him, Danilo changes his mind, although he pretends indifference to her interest. She later arranges a huge party in the garden of her Paris establishment, where she sings to her guests—more specifically to Danilo— the beautiful songs of her homeland. In the face of his continued aloofness, Sonia suddenly announces she is about to marry a Frenchman named Jolidon. Danilo does not know that she has made this announcement to save the reputation of Baron Popoff's wife, Natalie, who has been compromised by Jolidon. The news throws Danilo into despair, and he realizes he still loves Sonia passionately. Later on, at still another party —in Sonia's living room, arranged to simulate Maxim's, the famous Parisian restaurant—Danilo begs Sonia not to go ahead with her marital plans. It is then that Sonia reveals to him why she had announced this marriage in the first place, and confesses she has no possible interest in thé Frenchman. Danilo hesitates no longer to tell Sonia of his love. Baron

Popoff, secure in his ignorance about his wife's infidelity, can now also be at peace with the knowledge that Sonia's fortune will stay safely in Marsovia.

Lehár wrote two overtures, one in 1905 for the original production and a second in 1940 with a more ambitious orchestration and a more formal structure. In both cases, the overture is a potpourri of the operetta's principal melodies, with the famous waltz as its core.

That waltz, " 'Sfluestern Geigen, Lippen schweigen," is perhaps second only to Johann Strauss's "Blue Danube" as the most famous composition ever written in three-quarter time. Lehár's waltz occurs at a climactic moment in the play, during the first-act ball scene in the Marsovian Embassy. Sonia and Prince Danilo dance elegantly to its sweeping melody, and it is during this waltz that Sonia comes to realize for the first time how much she really loves him.

A second captivating waltz is "Vilia," one of the numbers sung by Sonia to her guests as a reminder of her native land. In addition to these two unforgettable melodies, the score also boasts the following: Danilo's sparkling hymn to Paris' night life, *"Dann geh' ich in's Maxim";* Sonia's sensual mazurka, *"Hab' in Paris mich noch nicht ganz akklimatisiert";* and a choral episode in march time, *"Ja, das Studium der Weiber ist schwer!"*

The Merry Widow acquired notoriety during the World War II era as Adolf Hitler's favorite operetta; apparently Der Fuehrer conveniently forgot the fact that both librettists were Jews. Because of Hitler's enthusiasm for the operetta, its composer was sometimes falsely accused of being a Nazi, which most certainly he was not. For one thing, Lehár was married to a non-Aryan; for another, he was once subjected to house arrest by the Gestapo because he refused to leave his wife. But the suspicion of his Nazi affiliations clung to him up to the time of his death in 1948, a fact that embittered him greatly.

(The) Merry Wives of Windsor [*Die lustigen Weiber von Windsor*] by Otto Nicolai.

Comic opera in three acts with text by Salomon Hermann von Mosenthal, based on Shakespeare's comedy of the same name. First performance: Hofoper, Blin, Germany, March 9, 1849. First American performances: Academy of Music, Philadelphia, March 16, 1863 (in German); New York, February 5, 1886 (in English).

Writing *The Merry Wives of Windsor* proved for its composer a labor of love and joy. "My new opera," as he said, "has in its composition made me very happy." This joyousness is reflected throughout the work, in the buoyant, effervescent, infectious spirit which pervades the music from beginning to end. This is one of the most sparkling and enduring comic operas in the German language. Nicolai completed it in 1844, but he had to wait five years for its première performance; written for Vienna, it had been turned down by the Vienna Royal Opera. Meanwhile, in 1847, Nicolai had received an appointment as Kapellmeister of the Opera and newly established 'Domchor' in Berlin. While holding this post, he was finally able to hear his opera performed (by royal request)—and none too soon; two months after its première the composer died of a stroke.

The Shakespearean plot is followed without much deviation. Mrs. Ford and Mrs. Page—who have received identical love letters from Falstaff—decide to play a trick on the fat lecher. Mrs. Ford invites Falstaff to her home, supposedly for a rendezvous. By prearrangement, Mrs. Page interrupts them by announcing that Mr. Ford is on his way home. Falstaff is hurriedly concealed in a basket of dirty clothes, then unceremoniously dumped out of the window into the Thames River. Later on, at the town inn, Falstaff boasts to his cronies that he has been propositioned by Mrs. Ford. He is interrupted by Mr. Ford, who comes to him disguised as a Mr. Bach, for the purpose of hiring Falstaff to woo Mrs. Ford on his behalf. Falstaff is delighted with this assignment and does not hesitate to reveal to "Bach" that he has already received an invitation to Mrs. Ford's house. Once again, at a planned rendezvous with Mrs. Ford, Falstaff is interrupted by the announcement of the precipitous appearance of the lady's husband. This time Falstaff disguises himself in women's clothes, but, after Mr. Ford has severely reprimanded his wife for her faithlessness, Falstaff is suddenly discovered by Ford, who thrashes him soundly. The two wives now concoct one more plot to trick Falstaff: they invite him to Herne's Oak in the woods where he is to appear disguised as Herne the Huntsman. Various cronies and friends of both the Fords and the Pages—disguised as wood sprites and elves—spring out of the woods to taunt him. They then reveal to poor Falstaff that all the while he has been the victim of a prank. All his tormentors then come forth to forgive him.

A more conventional love interest involves Anne Page and young Fenton. Anne, however, is being sought by two other suitors—Slender (favored by Anne's father) and Dr. Caius (preferred by Anne's mother). Anne frustrates the wishes of both by secretly marrying Fenton.

The melodious overture is a classic in the light-music repertory. It opens in stately fashion with a slow, expressive melody in the basses, soon thereafter repeated by other instruments. A graceful transition brings on the main part of the overture. Two delightful tunes are now prominent, the first in the strings and wood winds, the second in the violins; the latter is intended as a tonal portrait of vivacious Anne Page.

These are some of the principal vocal and choral numbers: In the first act, Mrs. Ford's recitative and coloratura aria as she plans to trick Falstaff, *"Nun eilt herbei!"*, and a duet of Mrs. Ford and Mrs. Page, *"Nein, das ist wirklich doch zu stark!"*; Falstaff's drinking song with which the second act opens, *"Als Bueblein klein"*—through the years a favorite with German bassos; Fenton's beautiful serenade to Anne, also in the second act, *"Horch, die Lerche singt im Haim"*; and in the third act, Mrs. Page's popular "Ballad of Herne the Huntsman." In the last scene some of the opera's principal melodies (first heard in the overture) are repeated in various choral and dance episodes.

After its highly successful Berlin première, it did not take this comic opera long to circle the globe. When first heard in Vienna on February 12, 1852, it was a triumph, and it has remained a strong favorite with Viennese audiences since that time. Americans first heard the work in Philadelphia in 1863; the first performance in London took place on May 3, 1864, when it was presented under the title of *Falstaff*. It received a solitary performance at the Metropolitan Opera in New York on March 9, 1900, revived for the convenience of the German baritone, Fritz Friedrichs, who apparently knew only three roles, one of these being that of Falstaff in this opera. A revival of *The Merry Wives of Windsor* was seen in New York in 1936, performed in English by the Juilliard School of Music.

(The) Mikado or The Town of Titipu by Gilbert and Sullivan.

Comic opera in two acts with text by W. S. Gilbert and music by Arthur Sullivan. First performance: Savoy Theater, London, March 14, 1885. First American performance: Grand Opera House, Chicago, July 6, 1885.

Interest in Japan, the Japanese people, and Japanese customs had been aroused in London through the creation of a Japanese village in the Knightsbridge section. The geisha girls, the exotic Oriental settings and costumes, Japanese food and way of life delighted the English people; all things Japanese became a favorite topic for discussion. Gilbert was also made Japanese-conscious by the Knightsbridge exhibit—and this, in all probability, was the direct stimulus for his writing the text of *The Mikado*. A story, long circulated, that he also received his inspiration from a Japanese sword which, hanging on the wall of his apartment, suddenly fell to his feet one day, is apparently apocryphal. When Gilbert explained to an interviewer how he came to write *The Mikado*, he made no mention of the sword incident. Instead, he said: "It has seemed to us that to lay the scene in Japan afforded scope for picturesque treatment, scenery, and costume, and I think that the idea of a chief magistrate, who is king, judge, and actual executioner in one, and yet would not hurt a worm, may perhaps please the public."

When introduced in London, *The Mikado* became the most successful of all the Savoyard operas, and ran for almost two years (672 performances); by 1896, it had been seen in London a thousand times. *The Mikado* proved still one more powerful stimulus to the Japanese craze then seizing London. The melodies were heard endlessly in music halls, drawing rooms, and on street corners. Yet for all its unqualified success —and despite the approbation of public and critics—*The Mikado* was not altogether free from attack. Queen Victoria called the plot "silly." The Japanese Ambassador to England tried to get the play suppressed on the grounds it subjected the Japanese Emperor to ridicule. Sir Arthur Quiller-Couch took Gilbert severely to task for permitting his cruel personal streak to assert itself in the malevolent portrait of an unsightly old woman (Katisha) and in his vivid description of torture in the song, "The Criminal Cried."

While the official American première of *The Mikado* took place at the Grand Opera House in Chicago on July 6, 1885, there actually had been an earlier performance of the comic opera in that city. On June 29, 1885, a company had presented *The Mikado* at the Museum Theater in Chicago in a strangely garbled and truncated version. A pirated performance of *The Mikado* also took place at the Union Square Theater in New York on July 20, 1885, but was closed down after a single presentation by a restraining order of Judge Wheeler, who sent its hapless producer, Sydney Rosenfeld, to jail. The official, authorized New York première opened at the Fifth Avenue Theater on August 19, a production put on by the visiting D'Oyly Carte Company which had come to America under a thick veil of secrecy. Since, at the time, it was general practice throughout the United States to give Gilbert and Sullivan comic operas in pirated productions—and since it was well known that Sydney Rosenfeld planned such an unauthorized showing in New York—the English company was dispatched across the Atlantic in great stealth to frustrate these efforts. The D'Oyly Carte production lasted in New York for 250 performances.

Whether in England or the United States, *The Mikado* has been the public's favorite among Gilbert and Sullivan comic operas, frequently revived. *The Mikado* was also the first Gilbert and Sullivan comic opera to come to the screen: in a British production in 1939 starring Kenny Baker, Jean Colin, and Martyn Green.

Nanki-Poo, son of the Mikado, has fled from the royal court to avoid marrying the homely and elderly Katisha. Disguised as a wandering minstrel ("A Wandering Minstrel I") he comes to Titipu and meets lovely Yum-Yum, ward of Ko-Ko, the Lord High Executioner. Nanki-Poo falls in love with her at once, and is horrified to discover that she is about to become the bride of her guardian ("Young Man, Despair"). A hymn of praise is now sounded to herald the approach of Ko-Ko ("Behold the Lord High Executioner!"), who explains that he has compiled a long list of victims for the execution block ("As Some Day It May Happen"). Now a train of ladies appears, headed by Yum-Yum and her two companions, Peep-Bo and Pitti-Sing ("Three Little Maids from School Are We"). Once Nanki-Poo and Yum-Yum manage to be alone, they exchange tender words of love ("Were You Not to Ko-Ko Plighted").

Upon returning to the scene, Ko-Ko discloses that a decree from the Mikado states that unless an execution were soon to take place in Titipu the office of Lord High Executioner would be abolished. This turn of events upsets Ko-Ko no end, for he must find a victim to behead. Only when he learns that Nanki-Poo is about to commit suicide because he can never get Yum-Yum does a solution to Ko-Ko's dilemma present itself. Ko-Ko proposes to turn Yum-Yum over to Nanki-Poo for a month if, at the end of that time, Nanki-Poo submits himself to execution. Pooh-Bah, the holder of many offices, is willing (for a bribe) to draw up the necessary legal papers.

Yum-Yum, preparing herself for her marriage to Nanki-Poo, suddenly finds the whole world glowing with beauty ("The Sun Whose Rays"). She joins her companions in singing a carol to her wedding day ("Brightly Dawns Our Wedding Day"). But an unforeseen development casts a shadow: Ko-Ko learns, through all of Pooh-Bah's official capacities, that an old law in Titipu requires that the widow of an executed man be buried alive ("Here's a How-De-Do").

With a loud fanfare, the Mikado and his entourage (among them

Katisha) enter. The Mikado introduces himself ("My Object All Sublime"). Since the Emperor has arrived at Titipu sooner than expected, Ko-Ko and Pooh-Bah must fabricate the fiction of an execution, and they specify that the victim was a troubadour by the name of Nanki-Poo. Then they learn to their horror that this Nanki-Poo is the son of the Mikado and that the punishment for killing a prince is to be boiled in oil. Necessity now compels Ko-Ko to admit that Nanki-Poo is still alive, but Nanki-Poo is willing to stay alive only on the condition that Ko-Ko marry Katisha and thus allow him to stay mated to Yum-Yum permanently. The marriage of Katisha and Ko-Ko, maintains Nanki-Poo, would be as welcome to him as are the flowers of spring ("The Flowers That Bloom in the Spring"). Although Ko-Ko is convinced a man can die of a broken heart ("Willow, Titwillow, Titwillow"), he reluctantly agrees to the bargain.

Text and lyrics find Gilbert at his sardonic best, while the character of Pooh-Bah is surely one of his rarest inventions. "He is," said Isaac Goldberg of Pooh-Bah, "the essence of cultivated diplomacy, behind which lurks the best motives. Every word of his is bought and paid for; every smile, every courtesy has its monetary equivalent." Subtle characterization can also be found in much of Sullivan's music, but affecting and poignant lyricism has not been sacrificed. Sullivan's haunting melodies are often touched with Oriental suggestions through a discreet use of the Oriental pentatonic scale.

Mister Bruschino by Gioacchino Rossini. *See* (*Il*) *Signor Bruschino.*

(Il) Mondo della luna [*The World of the Moon*] by Joseph Haydn.

> Opera buffa in three acts with text by Carlo Goldoni. First performance: Esterház, Hungary, August 3, 1777.

This delightful comic opera lay forgotten for almost two centuries. Then, through the efforts of H. C. Robbins, distinguished English musicologist, it was finally resuscitated. Robbins went to many different sources in all parts of Europe to piece together various fragments into a complete opera. This version was revived in 1959 in several European festivals (including those at Holland and Aix-en-Provence), and proved a completely ingratiating experience. Haydn's *Il Mondo della Luna* is perhaps the best of all the settings this text has received at the hands of such notable opera buffa composers as Galuppi, Piccinni, and Paisiello, among others. Paul Affelder found here some of Haydn's "most effective music for the lyric stage . . . music suprisingly Mozartean in character." Everett Helm called the opera "a winner . . . a thoroughly charming work."

Buonafede, an eccentric wealthy Venetian merchant interested in astronomy, tries to keep his daughter, Clarissa, from contacts with the world outside his own home. Dr. Ecclittico, an astrologer, devises a fraudulent telescope through which—he convinces Buonafede—the moon and its inhabitants could be seen. When the merchant is laid low by a sleeping pill, he is transported to Dr. Ecclittico's garden. Awakening suddenly, Buonafede is convinced he is on the moon itself. Completely involved in lunar matters, Buonafede loses all interest in the world below it, to the point where he permits Clarissa to marry her suitor, Leandro, and is even philosophical when his housekeeper, Lisetta, in whom he is more than passingly interested, is captured by Cecco.

In many ways, *Il Mondo della luna* is a traditional opera buffa—most characteristically so in Buonafede's buffa arias, some of which are the best vocal episodes in the entire opera.

Haydn's expressive lyricism can be found in several other memorable arias: that of Leandro, *"Und liegt auch zwischen dir und mir"*; an arietta of Cecco, *"Wenn das jetzt kein Narr'nturm ist"*; a duet of Leandro and Clarissa, *"Am Tor der himmlischen Freude"*; and an air of Clarissa, *"Wind der mich faechelt warm."*

Instrumental episodes are as notable as the vocal ones. In the first act, a brief orchestral interlude carries the audience into lunar regions; and in the first-act finale, the orchestra depicts realistically the sensation of a flight to the moon. The second-act prelude describes ceremonies attending the appearance of the moon's sovereign. There is one orchestral section for each of the three times that Buonafede looks through the fake telescope for glimpses of the moon, each amusingly interruped by appropriate commentary by Buonafede. Haydn was so partial to still another orchestral excerpt (the first-act overture) that he used it as the first movement of the Symphony No. 63, *La Roxolane*.

(La) Muette de Portici or **Masaniello** [*The Mute of Portici*] by Daniel François Ésprit Auber.

> Romantic opera in five acts with text by Eugène Scribe and Germain Delavigne. First performance: Opéra, Paris, February 29, 1828. First American performances: New York, August 15, 1831 (in French); Park Theater, New York, November 28, 1831 (in English); New York, November, 1854 (in German); New York, June 18, 1855 (in Italian).

It does not often happen that an opera has profound political repercussions. *La Muette de Portici* was such an opera. The text was drawn from incidents surrounding the successful revolt in Naples in 1647 against Spanish oppressors. Auber's opera proved so inflammatory when first performed in Brussels on August 25, 1830 that it inspired revolutionary riots among patriots opposing Dutch rule and was a leading influence in ejecting the Dutch from Belgium. *La Muette de Portici* also helped stimulate and intensify the revolutionary spirit in Paris just before the outbreaks in July, 1830.

The mute in the title is Fenella, who has been seduced and imprisoned by Alfonso, son of the Spanish Viceroy in Naples. After her escape, her brother Masaniello, leads a revolt against the despotic Spanish rule—a revolt that erupts when Selva, a Spanish captain, tries to arrest Fennella again and is killed by Masaniello. In the battle between the followers of Masaniello and those of Alfonso, Masaniello is killed. Hearing the tragic news, Fenella plunges to her death into the sea.

Auber's forte was the opéra-comique, in which he provided light texts with equally light and ingratiating melodies. But in *La Muette de Portici*, a romantic opera, his scope is larger and his musical style more serious and ambitious. In place of comic writings, we have dramatic episodes calling upon the fullest resources of his creative invention. The very first musical sound that came from the opera, the diminished seventh with which the overture opens, is "defiance hurled against conventionality," as Arthur Hervey has written. So forceful and original is Auber's writing in *La Muette de Portici* that Richard Wagner once praised it for "the bold effects in instrumentation, particularly in the treatment for strings; the drastic groupings of the choral masses which here take on an important role in the action; the original harmonies; and the happy strokes of dramatic characterization." *La Muette de Portici* has often been described as the foundation on which rests all later French grand opera. It was Auber's greatest success having had over a hundred performances by 1840 and more than five hundred by 1880.

For all its pronounced dramatic impact, *La Muette de Portici* is also a highly melodious opera, with the kind of ear-caressing lyricism for which Auber was famous in his lighter works. One such number—perhaps the most appealing in the entire score—is the "*Air du sommeil*" or "Slumber Song," a duet of Masaniello and Fenella in the fourth act. No less expressive or poignant are the second-act male duet, "*L'amour sacré de la patrie*," the third-act choral prayer, "*Saint bien heureux*," and Masaniello's fourth-act cavatina, "*Du pauvre seul ami fidèle*."

(The) **Music Master** by Wolfgang Amadeus Mozart. *See* (*Der*) *Schauspieldirektor.*

(The) **Music Miner** by Karl Zeller. *See* (*Der*) *Obersteiger.*

My Sister and I by Ralph Benatzky. *See Meine Schwester und Ich.*

(Eine) **Nacht in Venedig** by Johann Strauss II. *See One Night in Venice.*

(The) **Nautch Girl** or **The Rajah of Chutneypore** by Edward Solomon.

> Comic opera in two acts with text by George Dance and lyrics by George Dance and Francis Desprez. First performance: Savoy Theater, London, June 30, 1891.

Richard D'Oyly Carte, the celebrated producer of the Gilbert and Sullivan comic operas, achieved his greatest stage success in his post-Savoyard career with *The Nautch Girl*. The setting is India, where Indru, son of the Rajah, has fallen in love with Beebee, a lovely Nautch dancing girl. The Rajah refuses to consider such a marriage and plans to have Beebee sent out of the country. Meanwhile, a diamond, representing the eye of the idol Bumbo, has been stolen. When Beebee manages to retrieve it, the idol comes to life and Beebee wins his eternal gratitude. He grants her any wish, and she chooses, of course, to marry Indru with the Rajah's blessing.

The score overflows with delightful airs and duets. The best are these: the duet of Indru and Beebee, "When Our Shackles Are Undone"; the haunting Indian lullaby, "Gentle Bear My Lady"; Beebee's delicate air, "One, Two, Three"; Indru's poignant ballad, "The Sun Was Setting, Cool the Day," and his equally affecting tune, "When All the World Was Bright, Lover." In a more amusing vein is Punka's entrance song, "Room for Punka."

(Die) neugierigen Frauen by Ermanno Wolf-Ferrari. *See (Le) Donne curiose.*

(The) Night Bell by Gaetano Donizetti. *See (Il) Campanello di notte.*

(Les) Noces de Jeannette [*Jenny's Wedding*] by Felix Marie Massé.

> Opéra-comique in one act with text by Jules Barbier and Michel Carré. First performance: Opéra-Comique, Paris, February 4, 1853. First American performances: New Orleans, Louisiana, November, 1854 (in French); New York, April 9, 1855 (in English, under the title *Georgette's Wedding*).

This is the composer's most celebrated opéra-comique, as well as a classic in lighter French musical theater. By 1895 it had been given over a thousand performances at the Opéra-Comique in Paris. In England it was first seen in 1855 in an English translation by W. Harrison, and entitled *Georgette's Wedding*. In the United States, after the première in New Orleans and New York, it was successfully revived in 1861 with Clara Louise Kellogg as the star; and a few years after that it was again revived in New York by the American Opera Company directed by Theodore Thomas.

Jean, a boorish rustic, and Jeanette are about to get married. On the wedding day, however, Jean loses heart and runs away before the ceremony can be completed. Jeanette follows him to his bachelor quarters to seek an explanation for his strange behavior. She insists she does not want to marry him if he has changed his mind, but she also wants to save her face and reputation. She suggests that they sign a contract in which Jean agrees to marry her, after which she will publicly renounce him and destroy the contract. But once it is signed, Jeanette insists that Jean stick to it. In a fury, he proceeds to demolish the furniture in his place; then, out of sheer exhaustion, he goes to sleep. While he is sleeping, Jeanette patiently straightens out the house. Then, after he awakens, she greets him so sweetly and with such good humor that Jean becomes completely reconciled to marriage.

Both Jean and Jeanette have two fine airs, rich with emotional appeal. Those by Jean are *"Enfin, me voilà seul"* and *"Ah, vous ne savez pas ma chère";* those by Jeanette, *"Parmi tant d'amoureux"* and *"Il est au village."*

The creator of the role of Jeanette was Caroline Marie Felix Carvalho-Miolan, one of France's foremost dramatic sopranos. A few years after appearing in this light opera she also created the leading soprano roles in two outstanding grand operas by Gounod, *Faust* and *Romeo and Juliet.*

(Les) Noces d'Olivette by Edmond Audran. *See Olivette.*

(Le) Nozze di Figaro by Wolfgang Amadeus Mozart. *See (The) Marriage of Figaro.*

(Der) Obersteiger [*The Music Miner*] by Karl Zeller.

Operetta in three acts with text by M. West and L. Held. First performance: Vienna, January 5, 1894.

Two visitors come to a salt-mining district in mid-eighteenth-century Austria. One is Zwack, a mining director, who wants to investigate the causes of low production figures. The other is Countess Fichtenau, a refugee from an unwanted suitor, passing as Julia, a simple country girl. Zwack, although married to Elfriede, falls in love with Nelly, a lacemaker; and Nelly's fiancé, Martin, a miner, is attracted to Julia. During an industrial crisis, Martin loses his job and becomes the leader of a band of musicians made up of unemployed miners. After a tour, Martin and his band come home at festival time and join in the celebration. At this event, Zwack is faced with two disasters: both the loss of his job as mining director and his wife, who has become interested in Martin. A Prince, all the while appearing incognito as a volunteer worker, sets matters right. Zwack regains his old post and becomes reconciled with his wife; Nelly and Martin are also reunited after Martin has become reemployed. And the Prince now successfully woos Julia.

The plot may be somewhat overcomplicated and the situations somewhat stilted and contrived, but Zeller's music helps to introduce fresh breath and vitality into a lifeless body. Zeller had an uncommon gift for waltz music, with which his operetta overflows; the best waltz melody is *"Trauet nie dem blosson Schein."* The most popular song in the operetta is one by Martin, *"Wo sie war, die Muellerin zog es auch den Fischer hin"* with its intoxicating refrain *"Sei nicht boes, es kann nicht sein!"* The first-act finale is made up of several delightful folk tunes and marches.

Old Vienna by Joseph Lanner. *See Alt Wien.*

Olivette or **Les Noces d'Olivette** [*The Marriage of Olivette*] by Edmond Audran.

> Opéra-comique in three acts with text by H. C. Chivot and A. Duru. First performance: Bouffes-Parisiens, Paris, November 13, 1879. First American performances: Bijou Theater, New York, December 25, 1880 (in English); New York, December 6, 1881 (in French).

In Perpignan, during the reign of Louis XIII, Olivette is in love with Valentine. But her father compels her to consider the affluent Captain de Merimac as a husband. Olivette's life is further complicated by the fact that Valentine is being pursued by Countess de Rousillon. When Valentine tries to contact Olivette, he blunders into the Countess' room where he is discovered by the Duke des Ifs. The Duke, himself in love with the Countess, imprisons the intruder. Valentine effects his escape by disguising himself as the Captain de Merimac. When Olivette recognizes the disguise, she suddenly expressess to her father the desire to marry the man of his choice. Meanwhile, the Duke has abducted the Countess. In an effort to save her, Valentine and Olivette—both of them dressed as sailors—board the ship on which the Countess is imprisoned and help to free her. Valentine and Olivette now confess that they have long been married secretly. This information makes the Countess more amenable to accepting the Duke as her husband.

Olivette was a major success when first produced in Paris, and it has remained popular ever since. In London, where it opened on September 18, 1880, it was given in English, in a translation by H. B. Farnie; after the successful opening it had a run of 466 performances at the Strand Theater.

Audran's music is of the light, somewhat superficial kind that does not overtax the intelligence but gently woos ear and heart. These are among the finest numbers: Olivette's first-act song, "*Quand il s'était*"; the Countess' lilting first-act waltz, "*De cet accueil flatteur,*" and in the same act, her air, "*Vous êtes, dit-on*"; Olivette's rondeau, with which the second act opens, "*Se marier avec un vieux bonhomme,*" and in the same act Valentine's aria, "*Sur votre front où la beauté rayonne*" and that of the Countess, "*Par les rideaux de ma fenêtre*"; and two airs in the third act, the first by the Countess, "*Des caprices du jeu*" and the other by Olivette, "*Mes amis, qu'il était beau.*"

One Night in Venice [*Eine Nacht in Venedig*] by Johann Strauss II.

> Operetta in three acts with text by Richard Genée and F. Zell. First performance: Friedrich-Wilhelm Theater, Berlin, October 3, 1883. First American performances: New York, April 24, 1884 (in English); New York, January 8, 1890 (in German, under the title *Venetianische Naechte*).

There were some curious negotiations involving the libretto of *One Night in Venice*. The authors had completed two plays. One was *One Night in Venice* which they did not regard too highly, recognizing it as a curious jumble of coincidences and far-fetched episodes; for this text they sought a top-flight composer, specifically Johann Strauss II, the waltz king. The other play was *The Beggar Student* (which see). This they felt was first-rate, and for this reason they were willing to gamble on a young and still unknown composer, Milloecker. Strauss, however, was partial to *The Beggar Student,* a fact that upset the librettists no end. To team up a poor script like *One Night in Venice* with an unknown composer like Milloecker, they realized, could only spell disaster. They enlisted strategy and wile to change Strauss's mind by informing him that young Milloecker was so taken with *One Night in Venice* that he refused to give it up. This succeeded in whetting Strauss's interest, and he now insisted on having *One Night in Venice,* saying he was no longer interested in *The Beggar Student.* In choosing the former, Strauss had not even bothered to read the libretto!

Strauss recognized his mistake only after the operetta had suffered a most dismal failure at its première. He explained to a friend: "The nature of the book is such that with the best will in the world I could find no inspiration in it. Its coloring is neither poetic nor humorous. It is a scatterbrained, bombastic affair without a trace of action. Nor does it require any music. . . . I never saw the libretto, dialogue, only the words of the songs. So I put too much nobility into some parts of it and that was unsuitable to the whole. There is nothing in this book on which a noble interpretation could be put. At the last rehearsals, where I discovered the whole story, I was simply horrified. No genuine feeling, no truth, no sense, nothing but tomfoolery! The music has nothing in common with such crazy, inartistic stuff."

The plot, it is true, is sillier than most within the realm of operetta. In Venice, the Duke of Urbino, is taken with the beautiful Barbara, wife of the elderly Senator, Delacquas. The Duke is giving a grand ball in his palace. He asks his barber, Caramello, to go to Venice and bring Barbara to the ball. When Caramello returns, he is accompanied by his own girl friend, Annina, disguised as Barbara. And Barbara comes to the ball disguised as Annina. The Duke manages to find an opportunity to be alone with Annina, whom he believes to be Barbara. The tête à tête is interrupted when dinner is announced. Eventually, the Duke learns from Barbara herself how he had been duped, and he takes it all in good humor. The operetta ends with a ballet glorifying love and faithfulness in which the dancers personify doves.

Despite such nonsense, Strauss managed to create a score that was sheer magic; and it is Strauss's music, of course, that keeps the operetta alive in revivals. Two of Strauss's incomparable waltzes can be found here: the famous "Lagoon" or "*Lagunen*" Waltz ("*Ach wie so herrlich zu schau'n*") and Caramello's first-act waltz melody, "*Komm in die Gondel.*" There are still two other first-rate waltzes: Herzog's air,

"*Kommt, kommt ihr holden Frauen,*" and Caramello's beautiful hymn of praise to Venice, "*Sei mir gegruesst du mein holdes Venetia*" which is followed immediately by still another rapturous melody, "*Treu sein, das liegt mir nicht.*"

One Night in Venice was Strauss's first operetta to be introduced outside of Vienna, having been written to open a new theater in Berlin, the Friedrich-Wilhelm. But it was in Vienna that the operetta first became popular, when it opened there on October 9, 1883, less than a week after the Berlin première.

(Der) Opernball [*The Opera Ball*] by Richard Heuberger.

Operetta in three acts with text by Victor Léon and Hugo von Waldberg, based on *Die Rosa-Dominos*, a comedy by Delacour and Hennequin. First performance: Vienna, January 5, 1898. First American performances: Liberty Theater, New York, May 24, 1909 (in German);· New York, February 12, 1912 (in English).

Heuberger's first, and most successful, operetta takes place during carnival season in Paris in the 1890's. Paul Auber has come to the French capital with his wife, Angela, and they are staying at the home of their friend George. Marguerite, George's wife, is skeptical about the fidelity of husbands in general and her own in particular. Provoked by Angela's naïveté, she proposes to put both their husbands to the acid test. Two similar letters are dispatched to Paul and George inviting them to an opera ball for the purpose of arranging a rendezvous; the senders do not identify themselves, but describe the clothes they will wear. At the ball, Paul meets George's wife, and George meets Paul's wife, both women being in disguise. The men prove more than passingly interested in their charming companions and get involved in various complications, during which the women are able to escape and return home. The following day, George and Paul discover some of the notepaper on which their invitations from their women had been written and thus recognize the hoax. A bitter fight ensues between the husbands and their respective wives. After George and Paul promise never again to flirt, a sentimental reconciliation follows.

The major song is a waltz that took Vienna by storm. It was "*Komm mit mir ins Chambre séparée,*" which in the American production of the operetta was translated into, and become popular as, "Let Us Find a Charming Rendezvous." Popular and salon orchestras in Europe have also been partial to the vivacious and rhythmic overture.

When first given in New York in an English translation, in 1912, *The Opera Ball* was adapted by Clare Kummer and Sydney Rosenfeld; had some additional music written for Broadway by Heuberger (and an interpolated song by Chris Smith entitled "I Want a Little Lovin' Sometime"); and starred Marie Cahill and George Lydecker.

Orphée aux enfers or *Orpheus in der Unterwelt* [*Orpheus in Hades*] by Jacques Offenbach.

> Opéra-bouffe in two acts with text by Hector Crémieux and Ludovic Halévy. First performance: Bouffes-Parisiens, Paris, October 21, 1858. First American performances: Stadt Theater, New York, March 1861 (in German); New York, January 17, 1867 (in French); New York, April 22, 1874 (in English).

One of the reasons Offenbach wrote *Orphée aux enfers* was to rehabilitate his then sadly depleted fortunes. As director of the Bouffes-Parisiens, he had been so extravagant in mounting his productions that in time he was faced with bankruptcy. Creditors were hounding him, and it was in the hope of paying them off that he went to work on a new opéra-bouffe with popular appeal. But at the première, *Orphée aux enfers* was a dismal failure. Some felt it was sacrilegious for Offenbach and his librettists to satirize the Olympian gods so outlandishly. Others were shocked by some of the daring sex insinuations in the text. Still others were bored by what they regarded as a dull affair from first curtain to last. Curiously enough, a devastating review—of all things!—helped turn the tide. Jules Janin wrote a violent attack against it in the *Journal des débats* in which he described *Orphée aux enfers* as a "profanation of holy and glorious antiquity in a spirit of irreverence that bordered on blasphemy." The curiosity of many Parisians was piqued by Janin's attack; they wanted to see for themselves what had so aroused the ire of the eminent critic. Audiences now flocked to the Bouffes-Parisiens in increasing numbers, until *Orphée aux enfers* became the thing to do, to discuss, quote, ridicule, or admire. People began to hum its tunes; the light infantry marched to the brisk rhythms of one of its main melodies. And the can-can—a dance prominently featured in the comic opera—

suddenly became the rage. Seen right after a stately minuet—to point up the contrast between two periods in French history—the can-can was a sensation. "This famous dance," wrote an unidentified contemporary, "has carried away our entire generation as would a tempestuous whirlwind. Already the first sounds of the furiously playing instruments seem to indicate the call to a whole world to awake and plunge into the wild dance. These rhythms appear to have the intention of shocking all the resigned, all the defeated, out of their lethargy and by the physical and moral upheaval which they arouse, to throw the whole fabric of society into confusion."

So provocative, so exciting did *Orphée aux enfers* become in Paris that many saw the show not once but several times, and it enjoyed a highly profitable initial run of 227 consecutive performances. Actually it could have run much longer than that were it not for the fact that the cast was exhausted and insisted upon closing. Toward the end of April, in 1860, it was revived for a gala evening at the Italian Opera, put on at the special request of the Emperor. Once again *Orphée aux enfers* was a success; the profit from that evening alone exceeded 20,000 francs. A revival of *Orphée aux enfers* in Paris on February 7, 1874—now presented in four instead of two acts—was an even greater triumph. By the time of World War I, *Orphée aux enfers* had been given over a thousand times in Paris alone.

Orphée aux enfers was Offenbach's first important opéra-bouffe and it is extremely doubtful if, for all his later success, he ever wrote another quite so good. S. Kracauer goes so far as to maintain that Offenbach's later great operettas "were all derived from this one."

Orpheus and Eurydice have marital problems, since Orpheus has become interested in Chloe and Eurydice in the shepherd Aristeus. When Eurydice flees with Aristeus, Orpheus is overjoyed, for he is now rid of his wife and is free to follow his own love interest. But Popular Opinion insists that civic morality be maintained and that Orpheus go to Jupiter and beg him to restore his wife. Up on Mt. Olympus, a revolt is taking place: The gods are demanding more substantial food than mere ambrosia and nectar. The revolt is quelled with the appearance of Public Opinion and Orpheus. With mock seriousness, and with only half a heart, Orpheus entreats Jupiter to punish Aristeus and send Eurydice back to him. Aristeus (who is actually Pluto in disguise) refuses to cooperate. Jupiter, consequently, is forced to descend to the Underworld and investigate the situation for himself.

In the Underworld, Eurydice is being guarded by the idiot, John Styx.

Jupiter, disguised as a fly, makes love to Eurydice, who promises to go off with him to Olympus. On learning he had been tricked, Pluto tries to kill the fly but is thwarted when the entire palace swarms with flies and insects. Pluto now gives a farewell party for his visitors from Olympus, to which Orpheus comes with a half-hearted request for the return of his wife. Jupiter, however, reluctant to part with so delectable a woman, imposes a condition for Eurydice's return to Orpheus: If Orpheus can reach the river Styx without turning his head to look at his wife, she will once again be his. Orpheus is on the threshold of success when a bolt of lightning, hurled by Jupiter, terrifies him and makes him turn around instinctively. Thus Jupiter contrives to keep Eurydice for himself, a development that pleases Orpheus, saddens Public Opinion, and enrages Pluto.

Thus are the august gods of antiquity handled irreverently. And in his music Offenbach is equally impudent in his use of satire and burlesque. Songs of Cupid and Venus have an accompaniment that sounds like the snoring of the gods. Orpheus's half-hearted request for the return of his wife is a parody of the tender and eloquent lament of Orpheus from Christoph Willibald Gluck's opera about Orpheus, *"Che farò senza Euridice."* And in the final scene, after Eurydice's frenzied hymn to Bacchus (*"Evohé! Bacchus m'inspire"*), a staid minuet is, as we remarked earlier, immediately followed by a frenzied can-can performed by the gods and goddesses. The can-can was not new in 1858, having become popular in Paris immediately after the accession of Louis Philippe in 1850. But in *Orphée aux enfers* it was revived with such phenomenal success that it achieved a new and increased vogue in Paris.

These are some of the more memorable vocal pages in Offenbach's score: John Styx's air, *"Quand j'étais roi de Boétie,"* sometimes known as "The Song of Arcades," which he chants as he guards Eurydice in the Underworld; the delectable "flea duet" or *"Duo de la mouche"* of Eurydice and Jupiter (*"Il m'a semblé sur mon epaule"*); Aristeus' shepherd's song, *"Moi je suis Aristée";* Eurydice's hymn to Bacchus, *"J'ai vis le Dieu Bacchus";* and the lively choral drinking song, *"Vive le vin, vive Pluton!"*

Perhaps the most famous page of all is the overture, a perennial favorite with salon orchestras. After a vigorous introduction, a saucy tune is offered by the strings. After that comes a haunting song, first in solo violin and later in the full orchestra. This melody is the heart of the entire overture.

Orpheus in der Unterwelt by Jacques Offenbach. *See Orphée aux enfers.*

Paganini by Franz Lehár.

Operetta in three acts with text by Paul Knepler and Béla Jenbach. First performance: Vienna, October 30, 1925.

The hero is the nineteenth-century Italian violinist whose cadaverous appearance and fabulous musical virtuosity made him a legend in his own time. Some used to say that Paganini was the son of the devil; superstitious people would cross themselves when they saw him. In Paris he was dubbed Cagliastro; in Prague the rumor was circulated that he was the "Wandering Jew"; in Ireland they said he had come to their shores on the "Flying Dutchman." But for all the superstitious terror he inspired around him, he remained one of the most adulated musical virtuosos of his generation. Wherever he performed he achieved personal triumphs of the first magnitude. In Vienna, where he came in 1828, food, clothes, and delicacies were named after him. Even the most discriminating musicians were rapturous in their praise of his performances.

In this operetta, Paganini comes to a village near Lucca, Italy. The villagers flock outside his house to catch a glimpse of him, and among them is a mysterious lady come to express her adoration. Paganini becomes strongly attracted to her upon a first meeting; but only after he has kissed her does he discover that she is Princess Maria Anna Elisa, the wife of Prince Felix of Lucca and the sister of Napoleon. The Princess invites Paganini to be a guest at her palace in Lucca, an arrangement the Prince is willing to tolerate since he is carrying on an affair with the prima donna, Bella Giretti. But Paganini soon arouses the jealousy of both the Prince and the Princess by showing excessive interest in Bella. Elisa's love for Paganini now turns to hate, especially after she learns that a love song Paganini supposedly had written in her honor has been dedicated to the prima donna. At this point, an emissary from Napoleon arrives, demanding that Paganini leave the palace, his affair with Elisa having set European tongues wagging. Elisa orders Paganini's arrest, but then becomes so bewitched by his violin playing that she suddenly changes heart and helps him to escape from Lucca. Paganini seeks refuge in a smuggler's den on the Italian border, where he is followed by both Bella and Elisa. Each protests she is hopelessly in love with the violinist, and each in turn is rejected by him. For Paganini has now come to the irrevocable decision to forego women for good and devote himself entirely to his art.

Stimulated by both the personality and the music of his hero, Lehár wrote for this operetta some of the most freshly conceived and expressive melodies of his entire career. The best is *"Gern hab' ich die Frau'n gekuesst"* (a particular favorite with the famous Austrian tenor, Richard Tauber), in which Paganini maintains lightly that the women he has so fondly kissed have never troubled him to inquire if it were permissible. Three other songs are in an equally soaring lyrical style: *"Liebe, du Himmel auf Erden," "Niemand liebt dich so wie ich,"* and *"Toene, suesses Zauberlied,"* the first two being passionate love songs delivered by Paganini. In addition, the score boasts two lovely, duets, one in a jocular vein (*"Einmal moecht ich was Naerrisches tun"*) and the other in a sentimental mood (*"Hab' nur dich allein"*).

When *Paganini* was introduced in London in 1937 the leading roles were played by Richard Tauber and Evelyn Laye.

Parisian Life by Jacques Offenbach. *See (La) Vie parisienne.*

Patience or **Bunthorne's Bride** by Gilbert and Sullivan.

> Comic opera in two acts with text by W. S. Gilbert and music by Arthur Sullivan. First performance: Opéra Comique, London, April 25, 1881. First American performance: Uhrig's Cave, St. Louis, July 28, 1881.

Strictly speaking, *Patience* is the first of the Savoyard operas, since it was the first to be performed at the Savoy Theater which D'Oyly Carte had built for Gilbert and Sullivan. When *Patience* was first produced, the Savoy Theater was not yet ready and the comic opera had to be presented at the Opéra Comique, where it played to crowded houses until October 10. Only then was *Patience* transferred to the Savoy. Opening night at the new theater was a gala occasion attended by the Prince of Wales and others representing royalty, dignitaries of all sorts, high society, and leading figures from the artistic world. Sullivan conducted.

The theater itself was probably a greater attraction than the comic opera, since the latter had by now become familiar stuff to Londoners. But the Savoy, the first theater in London to be lit by electricity, aroused considerable interest and excitement. It was also at the Savoy that a tradition was established, since then become a practice in the London theater: the queue system for unreserved seats.

Gilbert's original plan in writing *Patience* was to spoof the clergy. But after he had written his play, he became exceedingly uncomfortable over his irreverent handling of religious figures, and worried over the effect such desecration might have on his audience. As a result, he decided to change the profession of his leading characters, while retaining most of the plot and stage business. "As I lay awake one night, worrying over the difficulties I prepared for myself," he wrote, "the idea suddenly flashed upon me that if I made Bunthorne and Grosvenor a couple of yearning aesthetes and the young ladies their ardent admirers, all anxieties as to the consequences of making them extremely ridiculous would at once be overcome. Elated at the idea, I ran down at once to my library, and in an hour or so I had entirely rearranged the piece upon a secure and satisfactory basis."

Once the idea about aesthetes had jelled in his mind, Gilbert had no difficulty in selecting the proper victims for his satire. Oscar Wilde, though only twenty-five at the time, had already become famous (and notorious) for his poses, epigrams, attitudes, fetish for the exotic and the esoteric, and flair for paradoxes. Wilde was choice meat for Gilbert's roasting, and Gilbert knew it. So was the Pre-Raphaelite movement that flourished in England between 1848 and 1854, with D. G. Rossetti and Millais as its earliest spokesmen. The Pre-Raphaelites propagandized a closer study of Nature, a return to simplicity, a rebellion against academicism. Here, then—in Wilde on the one hand and the Pre-Raphaelites on the other—Gilbert found his two principal protagonists, Bunthorne and Grosvenor.

Reginald Bunthorne is a "fleshly poet" whose aestheticism has made a pronounced impact upon twenty lovesick maidens ("Twenty Lovesick Maidens We"). They are no longer interested in their former lovers, the members of the Heavy Dragoons. But Bunthorne ignores these girls, since he is in love with the innocent milkmaid, Patience, who knows nothing about love or men ("I Cannot Tell What This Love May Be"). The officers of the Dragoon Guards appear ("The Soldiers of Our Queen") and provide a recipe of those ingredients that go into the making of a dragoon ("If You Want a Receipt"). They are upset to see their young ladies following Bunthorne as if in a trance, beseeching his love while he ignores them high-handedly. ("Now Is Not This Ridiculous?"). Once the ladies and the dragoons leave, and Bunthorne is alone, he soliloquizes that he is an aesthetic sham, that his cynicism and postures are just a pose; he also provides the rules for carrying on the aesthetic game ("If You're Anxious For to Shine").

Archibald Grosvenor, an "idyllic poet" of fatal beauty, is seeking to win Patience's love ("Prithee, Pretty Maiden"), but Patience, being a girl of extreme unselfishness, must reject him, since it would be most selfish of her to love one as perfect as he. Bunthorne, realizing Patience will never be his, and unable to choose for himself any one of the twenty lovesick maidens, decides to put himself up for raffle. At that moment, Patience decides she can love Bunthorne, since to love him would be an unselfish act; and the twenty lovesick maidens are about reconciled to return to their respective dragoons. Just then Grosvenor reappears and changes the situation, for, upon seeing him, the lovesick maidens transfer their adulation to him. Grosvenor explains to the girls why he can never love them ("A Magnet Hung in a Hardware Shop"). Patience is heartsick, for she is really in love with Grosvenor ("Love Is a Plaintive Song"). In an effort to woo the girls away from Grosvenor, the dragoons assume aesthetic garb, but the maneuver is doomed to failure. Bunthorne, by threatening Grosvenor with a terrible curse, has compelled the latter to become an "everyday young man"—a transformation to which Grosvenor readily acquiesces since as such he can win Patience ("Conceive Me If You Can"). The young ladies cease to interest themselves in aesthetic matters and turn their attention to things that are plain. But all comes out well in the end, that is, for everybody except Bunthorne. Grosvenor gets Patience, the dragoons return to their maidens. Bunthorne alone is left without a bride—only with a tulip or a lily in his hand as a consolation prize.

Patience is probably Gilbert's most brilliant text. His imagination here was alive, as never before or since, with contradictions, paradoxes, and absurdities. Since hero worship, sham, buncombe and artistic hokum are timeless, Gilbert's text remains as witty and as acid today as it was in 1881. As for Sullivan's music, it rarely proves a match for the inimitable Gilbert. As one of his contemporary critics remarked of Sullivan: "[He] has had to be content with an altogether subordinate position, as a sort of accompanist to the librettist." The parody of grand opera in the first-act finale and the take-off on the simplicities of English ballads are both good fun; for the rest, Sullivan is content to produce simple airs, tunes, and ballads which never seem to be ignited into a satirical bonfire by the brilliant sparks of Gilbert's wit and malice. If there is any single significant lack in Sullivan it is that he never really manages to convey the absurdities and contradictions of the aesthetic movement in musical terms the way Gilbert's satires and parodies do through verses and dialogue.

(Les) Pélerins de la Mecque by Christoph Willibald Gluck. *See (La) Rencontre imprévue.*

Perchance to Dream by Ivor Novello.

Operetta in three acts with text by Ivor Novello. First performance: Hippodrome, London, April 21, 1945.

With a run exceeding a thousand performances, *Perchance to Dream* was one of the triumphs of both Novello's career and of the London musical stage of the 1940's. Novello, besides writing music and text, was the star in three roles, which kept him on the stage for the greater part of the evening. A different period, a different set of characters, and a different love affair is presented in each of the three acts. But all of them are set against the background of the same old mansion, Huntersmoon.

In the first act the period is the Regency in 1818. The hero is an impoverished landowner, Sir Graham Rodney, who is reduced to highway robbery. He falls in love with his lovely cousin, Melinda, and dies in her arms.

The second act takes place during the Victorian period, in the middle 1800's. The hero is Valentine Fayre, a choirmaster, who falls in love with his wife's best friend, Melanie. But this love is doomed even before it begins.

In the final act we are carried to modern times. Bay is a dapper young man in love with Melody, whom he marries. Thus Huntersmoon, after a century, is finally able to witness a happy consummation to a love affair. In the final scene, the ghosts of Huntersmoon flit across the Great Hall to attend the marriage of Bay and Melody.

The hit song was "We'll Gather Lilacs."

(La) Périchole by Jacques Offenbach.

Opéra-bouffe in three acts with text by Henri Meilhac and Ludovic Halévy, based on a one-act play by Merimée, *Le Carrosse du Saint-Sacrement*. First performance: Théâtre des Variétés, Paris, October 6, 1868. First American performances: Pike's Opera House, New York, January 4, 1869 (in French); New York, March 11, 1874 (in German); New York, February 1, 1887 (in Yiddish); New York, December 21, 1925 (in Russian); Metropolitan Opera, New York, December 21, 1956 (in English).

In *La Périchole,* Offenbach departed from the satire and cynicism that had characterized his earlier opéra-bouffes and entered the more romantic, glamorous, and escapist world of the operetta. Like most operettas, it has a storybook setting: Peru in the eighteenth century; like most operettas, it boasts colorful characters. And its main plot deals with a love complication that is happily resolved before the final curtain.

La Périchole is a gypsy street singer in love with her singing partner, Paquillo. They plan to marry. During birthday festivities for the Viceroy, celebrated in the public square, La Périchole and Paquillo try, without success, to raise the money they need for a marriage license. Don Andres, the Viceroy, chances to see La Périchole, is stunned by her beauty, and persuades her to come to his palace as a lady-in-waiting. Since the Viceroy is a widower, and Peruvian law forbids having an unmarried woman live in his palace, he searches the streets for some likely candidate to marry La Périchole. He comes on Paquillo, who is in deep despair, since he has just received a note from La Périchole that she is leaving him forever. The Viceroy consoles Paquillo with wine. After Paquillo becomes inebriated, he is willing to be the husband of a woman the Viceroy has selected for him, even though her identity is not revealed. When Paquillo awakens the following morning, he is amazed to find himself in the Viceroy's palace, and more startled still to learn that he is married to the Viceroy's favorite. He joins other noblemen in singing the praises of womankind. Then, at a grand reception, he espies La Périchole for the first time. Realizing that it is she who is the Viceroy's favorite, he denounces her for her faithlessness. For this he is spirited off to a dungeon where he muses over the recent sorry events. La Périchole comes to him with a plan for escape. They find asylum in a café, where once they had appeared as humble street singers. There they are found by the

Viceroy, who is moved by pity to forgive them and give them their freedom.

The most famous single number in the operetta is La Périchole's letter to Paquillo in which she bids him permanent farewell: "*O mon chèr amant, je te jure.*" Of this celebrated melody, S. Kracauer has written: "The music was reminiscent of Mozart, and the words were a versification of Manon Lescaut's letter in Prévost's famous novel. It can be compared only to the song of Fortunio or the letter to Metella in *La Vie parisienne.*"

These are some of the other highly delightful excerpts from Offenbach's score: the air of the drunken Paquillo as he is about to marry La Périchole, in which he confesses he is in love with somebody else, "*Je dois vous prévenir*"; the sturdy hymn of praise to womankind by Paquillo and the courtiers, "*Et là maintenant*"; La Périchole's plea to Paquillo to be calm and sympathetic after he had denounced her for her faithlessness, "*Que veulent dire ces colères*"; Paquillos soliloquy in prison, "*On me proposait d'être infâme*"; and La Périchole's plan to escape with Paquillo, "*Tu n'es pas beau.*"

When first produced—Hortense Schneider was starred in the title role —*La Périchole* had only two acts. Offenbach later revised the operetta by adding a third act and about half a dozen new numbers. This version was first seen in Paris on April 25, 1874, once again with Hortense Schneider. *La Périchole* first came to the United States only a few months after its world première and has often been produced in this country since then. It was given for the first time by the Metropolitan Opera on December 21, 1956, when it was produced as a lavish spectacle. An English version had been prepared by Maurice Valency, and Cyril Ritchard (eminent English producer and actor) filled the dual role of stage director and actor (in the part of the Viceroy). The orchestration was revised to give it greater dimension and amplitude, in keeping with the spectacular nature of the production; and several ballet and circus episodes were interpolated, together with some vocal numbers, from other Offenbach operettas. "The trouble with this sort of thing," wrote Ronald Eyer in *Musical America,* "is that it makes the music, already slight enough, seems lost and rather insignificant in the grandeur of its new investiture. . . . The result is attractive, but should not be mistaken for true Offenbach."

Pinafore by Gilbert and Sullivan. *See H.M.S. Pinafore.*

(The) Pirates of Penzance or **The Slave of Duty** by Gilbert and Sullivan.

> Comic opera in two acts with text by W. S. Gilbert and music by Arthur Sullivan. First performance: Fifth Avenue Theater, New York, December 31, 1879. First performance in England: Opéra Comique, London, April 3, 1880.

The relationship between *The Pirates of Penzance* and the United States was an intimate one. When Gilbert and Sullivan came to this country late in 1879 to try to protect the copyright interests of *H.M.S. Pinafore*, they brought with them a copy of the completed text of a new comic opera, *The Pirates of Penzance*, for which Sullivan had thus far completed only a few random musical episodes. Most of his music was written in the United States—specifically at 45 East 20th Street, New York City, where Gilbert and Sullivan established residence. (A plaque commemorating this fact was placed on the building in 1927).

The Pirates of Penzance became the only Gilbert and Sullivan comic opera to receive an exclusive world première in the United States. (*Iolanthe* was introduced simultaneously in New York and London on the evening of November 25, 1882). Actually this world première in New York, now accepted as official, was not the first time *The Pirates of Penzance* had been performed. A single, unofficial, and quite haphazard presentation took place one night before the New York première, at the Bijou Theater in Paignton, Devon, England, for an audience numbering some fifty people.

Still one more point of American interest in *The Pirates of Penzance* is the fact that one of its airs was taken over by Theodore F. Morse, an American song composer. Dressed up with a new set of exuberant lyrics, it has since become a classic of American popular music (of sorts). Few, surely, need be reminded that the melody of "Hail, Hail, the Gang's all Here" is that of the pirates' chorus "Come Friends, Who Plough the Sea."

A highly successful revival of *The Pirates of Penzance*—with the freshly conceived stage direction of Tyrone Guthrie—was seen at the Stratford (Ontario) Festival in 1961 and brought to New York in an off-Broadway presentation on September 6, 1961.

The effervescence of Sullivan's music makes it hard to believe that he wrote the score in extreme haste; that—hounded as he was at the time by all kinds of social engagements and musical obligations—he wrote it in fits and starts; and that much of it was done while he was ill and in extreme pain. Indeed, he was unable to get around to writing the overture until the evening of December 30. *After* the dress rehearsal on that date, he went home and worked through the night, completing the chore by five in the morning. Then, overstimulated and overfatigued, he went to an all-night tavern for oysters and champagne. Weary beyond description, and ill, he still did not go to bed, but stayed up until the evening when he directed the première performance of his opera.

This business of protecting the copyright was a ticklish affair, since pirated performances of copyrighted works was the rule in the United States at the time. To protect themselves, Gilbert and Sullivan refused to allow either the libretto or the score of *The Pirates of Penzance* to be published before the première. They kept a vigilant eye on both the music and the musicians to make sure that neither text nor score strayed off to an unscrupulous competitor. After that, Gilbert and Sullivan themselves prepared the performances of several touring companies (rehearsing three or four such companies simultaneously) so that their "authorized version" might reach outlying districts before pirated ones. The strain of all this almost killed poor Sullivan.

The Pirates of Penzance was a sensation in New York, where for many months it did record business. Then it went on to conquer London, where, following its premièr on April 3, 1880, it stayed for 363 performances.

There is good reason to believe that Gilbert derived the idea for his libretto from an episode early in his life. As a child, while attended by a nurse, Gilbert had been kidnapped by bandits near Naples. But whatever the original source, the completed product proved to be *echt* Gilbert in its nonsense, paradox, topsy-turvy episodes; in its mix-up of children in the cradle; in its cruel delineation of an unattractive middle-aged woman.

On a rocky seashore on the coast of Cornwall, a band of pirates are raising their wine glasses to toast one of their number, Frederic ("Pour, Oh Pour the Pirate Sherry"). Frederic on this day has reached the age of twenty-one, and thus has outgrown his apprenticeship as a pirate and and is free to leave the band. His former nursemaid, Ruth, reveals that his long association with the pirates was due to a sorry mistake: When he was a child in the cradle she was told to apprentice him to a "pilot," but she had misunderstood that word to be "pirate" ("When Frederic Was a Little Lad"). Frederic is ready to forgive her, since he is convinced both that he loves her and that she is beautiful—Ruth being the only woman he thus far has seen. But he soon becomes filled with doubts about her pulchritude when a train of lovely maidens, all of them the daughters of Major General Stanley, come skipping in ("Climbing Over Rocky Mountain"). They are horrified to learn that Frederic is a pirate, but he soon manages to quell their fears with a heartfelt plea for sympathy ("Oh, Is There Not One Maiden Breast?"). One of them, Mabel, takes pity on him ("Poor Wandering One"). It is not long before Mabel and Frederic realize they are in love. They exchange tender sentiments, while Mabel's sisters try to ignore them by commenting upon the weather. When the rest of the pirates espy the delightful girls, they are tempted to abduct them, but are dissuaded from doing so after learning that their father is the Major General. The latter now comes upon the scene, identifies himself ("I Am the Very Pattern of a Modern Major General"), and elicits the sympathy of the pirates for himself and his daughters by revealing that he is an orphan—the pirates being notoriously partial and sympathetic to orphans.

But the Major General soon becomes the victim of a troubled conscience, for the truth of the matter is that he is no orphan at all, but had perpetrated a lie to save himself and his daughters. However, he is considerably heartened when a band of policemen arrive to engage the pirates in battle. The Sergeant of Police encourages his men with stirring martial tones ("When the Foeman Bears his Steel"), while Mabel exhorts them to fight the battle gallantly ("Go, Ye Heroes, Go to Glory!").

Within the pirate ranks an altogether unforeseen development takes place. Frederic discovers that while it is true his apprenticeship with the pirates ends on his twenty-first birthday, that birthday is still many, many years off. Paradoxically, he was born in a leap year and, counting by birthdays, he is still only a boy of five ("A Paradox, a Most Ingenious Paradox"). Thus Frederic must remain a pirate, and thus, too, he must reject Mabel, who is grief stricken at the news ("Oh Leave Me Not to Pine"). But as the war between the constabulary and the pirates becomes imminent, the Sergeant of Police reveals some of the problems of being a policeman ("When a Felon's Not Engaged in His Employment"). Meanwhile, on cat-like tread, the pirates arrive to attack, but go into hiding as soon as the Major General appears, the latter tormented by the anguish of having told a falsehood but momentarily assuaged by the beauty of the nocturnal scene ("Sighing Softly to the River"). Once he is gone, the battle erupts in earnest. Although the pirates are victorious, they yield to the conquered police when the latter exhort them to do so in the name of Queen Victoria. We now learn that the pirates are all ex-noblemen gone wrong. They receive official pardon, and each takes for himself one of the delectable daughters of the Major General. Mabel and Frederic are reunited and can look forward to their wedding.

Isaac Goldberg has pointed out, with penetration, that *The Pirates of Penzance* is "in almost every respect . . . [*H.M.S.*] *Pinafore* transferred from sea to land. In the one, it is the babes who are changed in the cradle; in the other, the future professions of the baby. *Pinafore* plays with the Navy and its administrators; *The Pirates,* with the police and with the army. The host of female relations that haunts the Admiral's presence—and his thoughts—is paralleled by the Major General's daughters. Ruth is Little Buttercup in pirate trappings, and like the bumboat woman, holds the fearful secret in her power. . . . The finale of *The Pirates,* it would appear, was written by Gilbert with the intention of salving the slight he had offered to the Queen in *Pinafore.*"

Sullivan, ever partial to poking fun at grand opera, pulled out all the stops in his satirical organ in *The Pirates.* The chorus that was later made into "Hail, Hail, the Gang's All Here" was really a parody of the "Anvil Chorus" from Verdi's *Il Trovatore;* Mabel's song, "Poor Wandering One," does a similar service for traditional coloratura arias, while the exchange between Frederic and Ruth ("Faithful Woman," "Master, Master") ridicules operatic recitatives. But oratorio as well as opera stimulates Sullivan's malice. The mock solemnity of "Hail, Poetry," with which the pirates express their weakness for things poetic, has some of Handel's pomp and ceremony, but with tongue-in-cheek.

(The) Poacher by Albert Lortzing. *See (Der) Wildschuetz.*

Polenblut [*Polish Blood*] by Oskar Nedbal.

> Operetta in three acts with text by Leo Stein. First performance: Vienna, October 25, 1913.

Of its composer's eight operettas, this is the most famous, made familiar to contemporary Austrian audiences through a highly successful revival in Vienna on October 10, 1954.

As the title indicates, the setting is Poland (in or about Warsaw); the time, just before World War I. Count Bolo Baranski hopes to rehabilitate his family fortune by marrying Helena, daughter of wealthy Jan Zaremba. But at a grand ball in Warsaw, the Count ignores Helena to pay attention to the strikingly beautiful ballerina, Wanda. She, in turn, is being pursued by Bronio von Popiel. Chagrined at being slighted, Helena conspires with Bronio to punish the Count. Through Bronio's influence, Helena, disguised as a peasant girl, gets a job as the manager of the Count's impoverished estate. She embarks on a wave of economy in which the liquor cabinet gets locked, the Count's dissolute companions discouraged from visiting him, and the Count himself compiled to seek work. Helena's regime proves most beneficial. At the Harvest Festival, the grateful Count crowns her queen. Wanda, the ballerina, is also a guest at this event; the reformed Count is delighted to discover she no longer appeals to him. He learns further that his peasant-girl manager is actually Helena, whom he had once spurned, but he does not hesitate to propose marriage. Wanda finds consolation in Bronio.

Nedbal, who was of Bohemian birth and training, filled his score with arresting dashes of folk flavors. Not the least of the attractions of his score are its Polish folk dances, notably the mazurkas and the polkas. But Nedbal is also a Viennese, having lived in the Austrian capital for most of his mature life. And as a Viennese he, too, had a passion for the waltz. Three are among the best vocal excerpts in the score: the Count's song, *"Maedel, dich hat mir die Gluecksfee gebracht"*; Helena's air, *"Ihr seid ein Kavalier"*; and *"Hoerren Sie, wie es singt und klingt."*

Polish Blood by Oscar Nedbal. *See Polenblut.*

(Le) Postillon de Longjumeau [*The Postillion of Longjumeau*] by Adolphe Adam.

> Opéra-comique in three acts with text by Adolphe de Leuven and Léon L. Brunswick. First performance: Opéra-Comique, Paris, October 13, 1836. First American performances: Park Theater, New York, March 30, 1840 (in English); New York, June 16, 1843 (in French); New York, December 9, 1870 (in German).

This is Adam's most famous comic opera, and it was given a gala performance at the Opéra-Comique on May 17, 1936, on the centenary of its première. Since Adam is one of the founding fathers of opéra-comique, the importance of this work can hardly be overestimated.

In the mid-eighteenth-century, at Madame de Latour's wealthy estate at Longjumeau, near Fontainebleau, France, Chappelou is employed as a postillion. A fine singer, he is discovered by the Marquis de Corcy who becomes impressed with his voice when Chappelou accompanies with a song the task of repairing a broken wheel on the Marquis' carriage. De Corcy offers Chappelou a job as a singer with one of the royal amusement groups he manages. Chappelou accepts this offer eagerly, although it means he must part with Madeleine, the woman he has just married. Chappelou goes on to become a famous singer under the assumed name of St. Phar. Meanwhile, his wife, Madeleine, has assumed a new identity of her own, that of the wealthy Madame de La Tour. As Madame de La Tour she flirts with and wins the love of St. Phar, who does not recognize her as Madeleine. Since the singer is already a married man, he cannot propose marriage to the desirable de La Tour; instead, he prevails on one of his friends, a fellow singer, to assume the guise of a priest and perform a mock marriage ceremony. Only then does Madame de La Tour reveal to St. Phar that she is really Madeleine, his wife. This disclosure delights the singer, but it causes the Marquis considerable grief since he has fallen in love with her.

The first-act postillion song, *"Mes amis, écoutez l'histoire"* (the most celebrated aria in the opera), has become identified with the nineteenth-century singer Theodore Wachtel. Wachtel used to delight New York audiences with his performances in this opera at the Stadt Theater in 1871–72 and at the Academy of Music in 1875–76. In all, he appeared in the role of the postillion over twelve hundred times. Wachtel, like the hero in the opera, had himself been a postillion before he achieved fame as a singer. In performing the postillion song, he introduced a routine which became an accepted procedure with many singers who followed him: He would provide an exciting rhythmic background to the refrain "Ho, Ho" by cracking a whip.

Three more arias are worthy of attention: Madeleine's beautiful first-act air, *"Mon petit mari"*; her second-act song in which she recalls her husband nostalgically, *"Je vais donc le revoir"*; and the postillion's romance in the same act, *"Assis au pied d'un hêtre."*

(La) Poupée de Nuremberg [*The Doll of Nuremberg*] by Adolphe Adam.

Opéra-comique in one act with text by Adolphe de Leuven and Léon L. Brunswick. First performance: Théâtre Lyrique, Paris, February 21, 1852.

Though this comic opera is most certainly not in the class of *Le Postillon de Longjumeau* described above, it has enjoyed considerable popularity in France and England.

The setting is Paris in the middle of the nineteenth century. Cornelius, dealer in toys, has manufactured a life-size doll that seems so animate that he is tempted to think of her as a living woman who will some day marry his son, Benjamin. On one occasion, his nephew, Heinrich, and a girl friend, Bertha, use the toy-maker's apartment while he is away. His sudden return sends Bertha hiding in the closet, where she finds the doll's clothes and puts them on. When Cornelius opens the closet and sees Bertha, he is sure his doll has come to life. But Bertha, acting as the doll, becomes such a nuisance to Cornelius that he begins to wish she would return to her former inanimate state. After Bertha has once again changed places with the doll and assumed her former identity, Cornelius destroys his creation, convinced that it is really the handiwork of the devil himself.

Two of the opera's most attractive melodies are assigned to Bertha: *"Où suis-je, quel prestige"* and *"Quand je commande, attention."* A third is delivered by Cornelius, *"Le rêve de tante ma vie."*

(Le) Pré aux clercs [*The Meadow of the Scholars*] by Louis Joseph-Ferdinand Hérold.

> Opéra-comique in three acts with text by François Antoine Eugène de Planard, based on a story by Merimée. First performance: Opéra-Comique, Paris, December 15, 1832. First American performance: New York, July 3, 1843.

Hérold made his position in the world of opéra-comique secure with two major achievements. One was *Zampa*, his first success. This was followed a year later by Hérold's last complete opera, *Le Pré aux clercs*. The Germans have always been more partial to *Zampa*, while the French have preferred *Le Pré aux clercs*. The latter has been one of the triumphs of the Opéra-Comique in Paris, where, by 1900, it had been given over fifteen hundred performances.

Although *Le Pré aux clercs* is a serious work on a historical subject, the musical score is written with a much lighter and more graceful hand than was that for *Zampa*. Much of *Le Pré aux clercs* is in the spirit of Rossini; *Zampa* is more in the romantic German style of Weber.

The text is so full of incident that the plot is often confusing. The story is basically the attempt of Mergy, a Bernese gentleman, to win the heart and hand of Isabella, a maid-of-honor to the Queen of Navarre. The Queen favors their union, but the king would like Isabella to marry someone of his choice. To frustrate the king, the young lovers get married secretly in the chapel of the Pré aux clercs.

The opera is characterized by "unity of style, variety of accent, and sustained inspiration, always kept within the limits of truth," according to Grove's *Dictionary of Music and Musicians.* The principal airs are: "*À la fleur du bel âge,*" Nicette's song in the third act; the first-act duet of Nicette and Girot, "*Le Rendezvous de noble compagnie*"; Mergy's aria in the same act, "*Ce soir*"; and Isabella's second-act romance, "*Jours de mon enfance.*"

Hérold knew that he was approaching the end of his career as composer with *Le Pré aux clercs.* When stricken by his last fatal illness—only a few weeks before the première—he remarked sadly: "I am going too soon. I was just beginning to understand the stage."

(The) Pretending Gardener by Wolfgang Amadeus Mozart. *See (La) Finta giardiniera.*

(The) Pretending Simpleton by Wolfgang Amadeus Mozart. *See (La) Finta semplice.*

Princess Ida or **Castle Adamant** by Gilbert and Sullivan.

Comic opera in three acts with text by W. S. Gilbert and music by Arthur Sullivan. First performance: Savoy Theater, London, January 5, 1884. First American performances: Boston Museum, Boston, and Fifth Avenue Theater, New York, February 11, 1884 (simultaneously).

Princess Ida differs from the other popular Gilbert and Sullivan comic operas in several important respects. It is the only one in three acts instead of two; the only one in which the dialogue is in blank verse; and one of the few whose source was not Gilbert's *Bab Ballads* (as was usually the case with the other operas), but an early Gilbert play, *The Princess,* a comedy version of Tennyson's narrative poem of the same name. "He has trimmed a dish removed from the table years ago," remarked the London *Musical World,* "and re-served it with sauce à la Sullivan."

Sullivan did not like the text when Gilbert showed it to him, a fact that created considerable antagonism between the two partners. They were still at odds when their opera went into rehearsal—and their tempers grew more explosive as the rehearsals went badly because the actors did not relish speaking lines in verse. Thus *Princess Ida* started off on a lame foot, and it never really did gain equilibrium. It was not particularly successful during its initial run, and it has not been particularly popular since either in England or the United States. The truth is that, in both plot and style, *Princess Ida* was a dated product—even in 1884. Having men cavort about in women's clothes, disporting themselves with obviously male behavior, was old hat. The satire on the feminist movement had little sting, particularly since some of the things mocked by *Princess Ida* (such as woman's right to be admitted into universities) had long since known reform. Moreover, within the framework of the blank verse, Gilbert strained to make his puns; and Sullivan's attempts to satirize grand opera and the Handelian oratorio were by now a thrice-told tale to audiences at the Savoy. Indeed, Sullivan's invention in *Princess Ida* was frequently as weak as Gilbert's. Arthur Jacobs goes so far as to maintain that "never in his stage works anywhere did he sink lower into trite sentimentality as he did in the love lyric, 'Whom Thou Hast Chained Must Wear His Chain.'"

In King Hildebrand's palace, King Gama and his daughter Ida are being awaited. Hilarion reveals that, during her infancy, Ida had been betrothed to him ("Ida Was Twelve Months Old") and that she is now coming to join him at last. The three ridiculous sons of Gama now make their appearance ("We Are Warriors Three"). They are followed by Gama himself ("If You Give Me Your Attention"). But Ida fails to arrive, since she has secluded herself at Castle Adamant as the head of a woman's university to which all men are denied access. This information infuriates Hildebrand, who decides to keep Gama and the three sons as hostages while Hilarion—and his friends Cyril and Florian—go forth to penetrate Castle Adamant.

At that university, the girls disclose the nature of their varied activities and the principles by which their school is run ("Man is Nature's Sole Mistake"). They hail Ida ("Mighty Maiden With a Mission"), who now makes an entrance. While all this is happening, Hilarion and his friends arrive on the university grounds where they don feminine robes and proceed to pass themselves off as girl students ("I Am a Maiden Cold and Stately"). When Ida sees them, she is fooled into believing they are females, but Psyche knows better, since she is the sister of one of the men. After Psyche has expressed the belief that man is inferior to woman ("With a View to Rise in Social Scale"), Lady Blanche, professor of abstract science, and her daughter, Melissa, also become aware that the intruders are male. They, however, remain silent, for Lady Blanche is eager to usurp Ida's position at the school, and can do so only if Hilarion is successful in abducting the young girl. A series of complications ensue. First Ida falls into a river and is saved by Hilarion ("Whom Thou Hast Chained Must Wear His Chain"). Then Hildebrand's forces attack the university. The girls stand ready to battle, but are too softhearted to inflict harm on the enemy. Only Ida is willing to engage Hildebrand's forces, spurred on by her father, Gama ("When'er I Poke Sarcastic Joke"). But Ida's three brothers insist upon making war. To facilitate their movements they remove their armor, which thus far has hampered them ("This Helmet I Suppose"). In the ensuing struggle, Hildebrand and his men are victorious and Ida must go off with Hilarion. Meanwhile, his two friends have become interested in Psyche and Melissa and have convinced the girls to accompany them home.

Prodaná Nevěsta by Bedřich Smetana. *See (The) Bartered Bride.*

(The) Quaker Girl by Lionel Monckton.

> Operetta in three acts with text by James T. Tanner and lyrics by Adrian Ross and Percy Greenbank. First performance: Adelphi Theater, London, November 5, 1910. First American performance: Park Theater, New York, October 23, 1911.

Together with *The Arcadians*, this operetta represents the leading stage success of its composer's career. It enjoyed a run of 530 performances in London and 240 in New York.

The girl in the title is Prudence, who has been ejected by the Quakers because she is in love with Tony Chute, an American naval officer. She finds a job as a model in a Parisian dressmaking shop, and experiences many adventures in the social whirl of Paris before she is permitted to marry Tony.

Prudence's entrance song, "A Quaker Girl," her second-act waltz "Come to the Ball," and her air "A Dancing Lesson" are the three main numbers in the score. "Tony from America" and "Just as Father Used to Be" are in a lighter vein. When *The Quaker Girl* was given on Broadway, Irene Claire was starred as the heroine in a cast that also included Percival Knight and Olga Petrova.

(I) Quattro Rusteghi [*The Four Ruffians*] by Ermanno Wolf-Ferrari.

Opera buffa in three acts with text by Giuseppe Pizzolato, based on a comedy by Carlo Goldoni. First performance: Munich, Germany, March 19, 1906 (in German). First American performance: New York City Center, October 18, 1951 (in English).

The four ruffians in the title are four Venetian merchants who treat their women handily. One is Lunardo, a boor to both his daughter, Lucieta, and his wife, Margarita. He arranges for his daughter to marry Filipeto, son of Maurizio the merchant, but he refuses to permit the two young people to meet until the wedding day. This arrangement bothers the boy's aunt, Marina, who contrives a plot whereby the young people might at least see each other, however briefly. The three ruffians and their wives come to dine at Lunardo's house. Filipeto appears disguised as a woman, and he is finally able to catch a glimpse of Lucieta, with whom he falls immediately in love. When invited to take some snuff, Filipeto is forced to remove his disguise. Lucieta can now see what he really looks like, and becomes an instantaneous victim of love at first sight. But the irate Lunardo, upset at being duped, announces angrily that all plans for the wedding are canceled. Now the wives of the ruffians go to work on their respective husbands, and they in turn convince Lunardo of the folly of his action. To the delight of the lovers, Lunardo announces that the wedding will proceed as scheduled.

The vivacious and brisk little overture, a highly melodious intermezzo preceding the second act, and Filipeto's rapturous air, "*Lucieta è un bel nome,*" are some of the musical delights of the merry score. Some of the ensemble numbers, as Cecil Smith remarked, are also of great appeal. "Wolf-Ferrari could write for three or four basses alone (the ruffians are all basses) without losing the thread of individual characterization in each part. The voices of the chattering, scheming ladies blend . . . delightfully. . . . The second-act sextet is meltingly lovely. There are, moreover, many instances of adroit musical characterization, the most affecting of which, perhaps, is the moment when the young couple, Lucieta and Filipeto, are rendered all but speechless at their first sight of each other."

(The) **Queen's Handkerchief** [*Das Spitzentuch der Koenigin*] by Johann Strauss II.

> Operetta in three acts by Heinrich Bohrmann-Riegen and R. Genée. First performance: Theater-an-der-Wien, Vienna, October 1, 1880. First American performances: Casino Theater, New York, October 21, 1882 (in English); New York, October 1, 1883 (in German).

Not the least of the important elements in this operetta is one of its vocal numbers, *"Wo die wilde Rose,"* which the composer used for one of his most celebrated instrumental waltzes, *Roses from the South* (*Roses aus dem Sueden*).

Bohrmann-Riegen originally wrote this text for Franz von Suppé, who had then been recently acclaimed in Vienna for *Boccaccio*. By the time the librettist was able to turn his text over to that composer, Suppé was busily engaged upon another comic opera. Rather than wait for Suppé, Bohrmann-Riegen asked Strauss to do the music.

The story is set in Portugal in the sixteenth century, and one of its main characters is the famous author of *Don Quixote*, Cervantes. At that time Portugal was dominated by Philip II of Spain. In an effort to strengthen his own position, the Prime Minister of Portugal tries to create dissension between Portugal's indolent king and the queen. The queen finds an ally in Cervantes, who, having been banished from Spain, is a member of the Portuguese guard. With the help of the queen's confidante, Cervantes conspires to break the Prime Minister. But before he can do so he gets into trouble with that official. A handkerchief presented to Cervantes by the queen—on which there is embroidered the legend, "the queen loves you, but you are not the king"—was found by the Prime Minister in a copy of *Don Quixote*. This handkerchief enables the Prime Minister to prove to the king that Cervantes and the queen are having an affair. Thrown into jail, Cervantes manages to escape. He joins a band of brigands who capture the queen. The king finds the queen at an inn, disguised as a maid. Their reconciliation is complete when Cervantes tells the king that the handkerchief had been intended for the king himself; that the slogan embroidered on it indicated that though she loves the king, he had not been performing his regal duties as Destiny intended him to do.

Beyond Cervantes' enchanting romance, *"Wo die wilde Rose,"* which later became *Roses from the South,* Strauss's excellent score includes the duet *"Bleib' dunkle Nacht";* Cervantes' delightful song, *"Lichter Glanz";* the enchanting aria, *"Du Maerchenstadt im Donautal";* the king's comic "truffle song"; the queen's humorous ballad describing a "wondrous fair and starry night," and her striking coloratura aria, *"Siebzehn Jahre."*

When this operetta was first seen in the United States, it was at the opening of the new Casino Theater, destined to be for many years New York's most important home for operettas and comic operas. In fact, the theater was not fully completed at the time of the première of the Strauss operetta. The heating system was not yet functioning, and the theater was so cold that the operetta had to close after several performances. For a few weeks it went on tour, returning to the Casino Theater on December 28 for a new opening and an extended run.

Renard by Igor Stravinsky.

> A burlesque in one act "to be sung and played," with text by the composer, adapted from Russian folk tales. First performance: Opéra, Paris, by the Diaghilev Ballet, June 3, 1922 (public). First American performance: New York, December 2, 1923 (concert version).

Renard is a burlesque of farmyard characters in song and dance; it takes about twenty minutes to perform. A cock, alight on his perch, is beseeched by a fox to descend to the ground. When he complies he is forthwith seized, but a passing cat and goat capture the fox, strangle him, and rescue the cock. All animals then join in a dance of celebration.

In a note to his published score, the composer explains that *"Renard* is to be played by clowns, dancers, or acrobats, preferably on a trestle stage with the orchestra placed behind. If produced in a theater, it should be played in front of the curtain. The players do not leave the stage. They enter together to the accompaniment of the little march that serves as introduction, and their exit is managed in the same way. The roles are dumb. The voices (two tenors and two basses) are in the orchestra."

Describing Stravinsky's music, Eric Walter White says: "The score is beautifully homogeneous on a miniature scale. The music, as is appropriate to the subject, has an almost human quality. . . . The cymbalom, percussion, and frequently plucked strings give the work a predominantly dry timbre and bouncing resonance." (Stravinsky had heard the cymbalom in a European restaurant and was so delighted with it that he bought one for himself, learned to play it, and then decided to incorporate the instrument into the orchestration of his *Renard*.)

André Schaeffner goes on to say: "Stravinsky extracts from his four singers a vocal virtuosity that is often irresistibly droll; it seems as if four animals with different voices are caged together in the orchestra pit and their cries sound as if a sleeping farmyard had been disturbed at midnight."

Stravinsky wrote *Renard* for Princess Edmond de Polignac, and before the little opera was given a public performance it was heard in the Princess' private theater. The first public performance was by the Diaghilev Ballet at the Paris Opéra, an occasion which also saw the première of another Stravinsky light opera, *Mavra*. "Alas," wrote Stravinsky in his autobiography, "I was deeply disappointed by the disastrous surroundings in which my poor *Mavra* and little *Renard* found themselves. Being a part of a Ballet Russe program, my two intimate acts were dwarfed when sandwiched between spectacular pieces which formed the repertory of Diaghilev's season and were the special attraction for the general public. This crushing environment, the enormous framework of the opera house, and also the mentality of the audience, composed mainly of the famous *abonnés*, all combined to make my two little pieces . . . seem out of place."

(La) Rencontre imprévue or **Les Pélerins de la Meque** [*The Unforeseen Meeting* or *The Pilgrims to Mecca*] by Christoph Willibald Gluck.

Comic opera in three acts with text by L. H. Dancourt, based on a French vaudeville by Lesage and D'Orneval. First performance: Burgtheater, Vienna, January 7, 1764.

While Gluck was serving as court Kapellmeister in Vienna he wrote several comic operas with spoken dialogue to French texts. The last and the most popular was *La Rencontre imprévue*, which has also been given under the alternate title of *Les Pélerins de la Mecque*.

Prince Ali, believing his mistress, Princess Rezia, is dead, wanders aimlessly with his servant, Osmin, until he reaches Cairo. There he learns that Rezia is still alive, that she is actually in Cairo, a member of the Sultan's harem. When Rezia learns that Ali, too, is in Cairo she decides to test his love for her and sends several harem girls to tempt him. Ali resists them all, and, convinced of his unwavering devotion, Rezia welcomes him back passionately.

Most of the best comic episodes in the opera involve minor characters: Ali's servant, Osmin; a whimsical painter named Monsieur Vertigo, who is pretty much of a fool; an amusing Dervish. Sentiment, and tenderness, and deep feeling assert themselves in the principal characters. F. Bonavia has written: "The charm of the opera is all in its melodies, in the arias in which Prince Ali bemoans his fate, in the arias in which, while praising their beauty, he resists the fascinating friends of Rezia (one aria with flute obbligato is a gem), and in the duets in which the lovers express their joys, their fears, their hopes. To Rezia are assigned two arias of great worth—one in the character of a minuet; another abounding in flourishes and roulades, is nevertheless essentially and beautifully lyrical."

The most appealing tunes in a lighter style include *"Castagno, Castagno"* and *"Il Pa Pa Pa"*. Among the more emotional or spirtual melodies are *"Un ruisselet bien clair,"* *"Les Hommes pieusement,"* and *"C'est un torrent impétueux."*

(The) Rise and Fall of the City of Mahagonny [*Aufstieg und Fall Der Stadt Mahagonny*] by Kurt Weill.

Opera in three acts with text by Bertolt Brecht. First performance: Leipzig Opera and Frankfurt Opera, March 9, 1930 (simultaneously).

Zeitkunst—"contemporary art"—was a vogue in Germany soon after the end of World War I. This art dealt with modern subjects in a racy, timely style filled with all kinds of present-day references and allusions. Kurt Weill was a leading figure in the movement. His most successful product of *Zeitkunst* was *The Three-Penny Opera* (which see), and probably the most provocative, *The Rise and Fall of the City of Mahagonny*. The latter originated in 1927 as a one-act "song play" made up of sprightly choruses and lyrics; its musical style embraced jazz, music-hall tunes, folk songs, and marching melodies. Introduced at the Baden-Baden Festival, Germany, this one-act play shocked the avant-garde audiences gathered to hear a festival of modern music featuring compositions of the most advanced tendencies. To these ultra-sophisticates, the popular, tuneful music of Weill's opus seemed an affront.

After *The Three-Penny Opera* had become a world triumph, Kurt Weill and Bertolt Brecht decided to expand their little one-act play into a full-length opera. The revised version was given a simultaneous première in Leipzig and Frankfort, and in both places it created a scandal. In Leipzig, the Nazis were particularly effective in provoking a riot in the theater. Stink bombs were dropped, boos and shouts of disapproval sounded, and fistfights were encouraged. The management had to keep the lights on in the theater to prevent chaos; and the conductor decided to shorten the finale. In Frankfort, things went just as badly. During an uncontrolled fight in the audience, one man was shot and killed; after that, the management decided to close down the show.

There was certainly much to shock an audience out of whatever complacency or equilibrium it may have had before entering the theater. A good deal in Brecht's text was obscene, irreverent, iconoclastic; much was off-beat. Described as a "morality play" about the wish dreams of modern ne'er-do-wells, *The Rise and Fall of the City of Mahagonny* was set in the fictional town of Mahagonny, Alabama, in the United States. Here, in the wilderness, three ex-convicts are stranded while fleeing from the law. They decide to build a new kind of society where people can do whatever they wish without regard to ethics or morality; where freedom is limited only by the law of supply and demand; where anything is pardonable, except the lack of money. Brecht's pronounced Leftist leanings led him to use the plot as a hook on which to hang his bitter social and political satire. He saw and lay bare the hypocrisy, corruption, and decadence of modern materialism. He caricatured the drives and rivalries of capitalism. He removed the mask of duplicity concealing the real grimaces and distorted features of modern society. A formidable economic crash and a devastating hurricane are two of the forces bringing about the destruction of Mahagonny. But Mahagonny withstands them, just as it withstands the corruption and vices of its citizens. The final irony, in a setting glorifying ironies, comes when Trinity's Moses tries to consign the degenerates of Mahagonny to Hell and finds he cannot do so since these people are already living in a Hell. "The atmosphere of Berlin of the 1920's," said H. W. Stuckenschmidt, "has found no more anguished expression than in this opera." Stuckenschmidt then goes on to describe the opera as a "document of its times."

Jazz, "pop" tunes, music-hall melodies, the blues, ragtime are some of the elements in Weill's racy score, which in its own way was no less iconoclastic, irreverent, and at times even shocking, than Brecht's text. A lively men's chorus in the fourteenth scene (*"Erstens, vergesst nicht, kommt das Fressen"*) admonishes the people of Mahagonny that first comes eating, then love, then boxing, then drinking—and that in this town people are permitted to do whatever they wish. A hit number (indeed, one of Germany's leading song hits in 1930) was the "Alabamy Song" which Jenny, the heroine, presents with a chorus of six girls. The title here is in English because the lyric is in English, that is, a gibberish English that makes no sense whatever and yet carries reminiscent echoes of Tin Pan Alley.

(The) Riviera Girl by Emmerich Kálmán. *See (Die) Czárdásfuerstin.*

(Le) Roi l'a dit [*The King Said So*] by Léo Delibes.

> Opéra-comique in three acts with text by Edmond Gondinet. First performance: Opéra-Comique, Paris, May 24, 1873.

Delibes, who made such a distinguished contribution to the French lyric theater with *Lakmé,* was also a composer of lovable light operas. He wrote twelve of them before he became successful in this style, and that first success came with *Le Roi l'a dit.*

In seventeenth-century Versailles, the Marquis de Moncontour, having successfully retrieved the favorite parrot of Madame de Maintenon, is presented to King Louis XIV. The audience so rattles the Marquis that he tells the King he has a son, whereas the truth is he has four daughters. When the King insists that the Marquis bring the son to court, the latter is in a terrible dilemma: A king's command cannot be disobeyed. The Marquis prevails on Benoît, a simple peasant boy, to pose as his son, a role for which he is given comprehensive training. Benoît enjoys being the son of a nobleman and to the Marquis' discomfort plays the part more than adequately. Indeed, Benoît makes such a nuisance of himself —even insisting upon marrying one of the Marquis' daughters—that the Marquis must find a way to get rid of him. When Benoît is wounded in a duel, the Marquis informs the King the boy is dead. The King consoles the "stricken" Marquis by making him a duke. And Benoît, recovering from his wound, is now willing to return to his former humble status and marry the peasant girl, Javotte.

The popular overture opens with a vigorous march, after which we hear a delicate melody in the strings. The march then returns to preface a romantic song for clarinets. The pace quickens and the mood lightens as a chattering figure is heard in the strings and woodwinds. The overture ends vigorously with a final recall of the opening march music.

The most famous vocal number—a favorite in the concert hall—is the first-act serenade, "*Déjà les hirondelles.*" In the same act we also find the delightful couplets of Mitou, "*Il vous conte fleurette.*" Subsequent acts bring us the merchants' chorus, "*Nous avons la dernière mode,*" and Javotte's charming cantabile, "*Ah! je n'avais qu'un courage.*"

(Le) Roi malgré lui [*A King in Spite of Himself*] by Emmanuel Chabrier.

> Opéra-comique in three acts with text by Émile de Najac and Paul Burani, based on a comedy by F. Ancelot. First performance: Opéra-Comique, Paris, May 18, 1887.

This is the composer's most famous work for the stage and the last to be produced in his lifetime. Although primarily an opéra-comique—and consequently in a style and mood lighter than those demanded by grand opera—*Le Roi malgré lui* is so striking for its original harmonic writing and orchestration that it is considered one of Chabrier's most important *serious* creations, much more distinctive and personal than a work such as *Gwendoline* in which the Wagner influence is so pronounced.

Le Roi malgré lui was extraordinarily well received by both critics and the public at its première at the Opéra-Comique, but misfortune aborted what undoubtedly would have been a successful season. One week after the première of the opera—and after its third performance—the opera house burned down. *Le Roi malgré lui* could not be given again until the Opéra-Comique found temporary quarters, late the same winter. But in time it became a classic, often performed and just as frequently acclaimed. Maurice Ravel once confessed that he would rather have written this opera than the entire Wagner Nibelungen trilogy!

The opera opens in 1574, as Henri de Valois is about to be crowned king. After enjoying some delightful escapades in Paris, he arrives for the coronation, surrounded by members of the French nobility. Informed that a conspiracy against his life has been hatched by some Polish noble-men, Henri assumes the identity of one of his friends, De Nangis. He makes it his business to become associated with some of the conspirators and in time gains their confidence to the point where they stand ready to let him slay the prospective king. When the real De Nangis appears in the conspirators' den, he is mistaken for Henri and thus is menaced by possible murder. Henri now makes an effort to disclose his true identity so that his friend's life might be spared. Nobody believes Henri, espe-cially after his one-time mistress, Alexina, insists he is really De Nangis. But in the end the conspirators are frustrated and Henri is crowned king.

Because of Chabrier's remarkable gifts as an orchestrator, some of the most effective pages in the opera are those either exclusively for or-chestra or in which the ochestra is particularly prominent. Three of these are the melodious overture, the *Danse slave,* and the *Fête polonaise,* for chorus and orchestra.

These are some of the distinguished vocal excerpts: Minka's first-act aria, *"L'amour se devint maître";* the king's Ceremonial and Romance, *"Beau pays!";* Fritelli's couplets, *"Le Polonais est triste et grave";* the second-act gypsy song, *"Il est un vieux chant de Bohème";* Nangis' French song, *"Je suis le roi";* and, in the final act, Fritelli's couplets, *"Je suis du pays des gondoles."*

Ruddigore or **The Witch's Curse** by Gilbert and Sullivan.

> Comic opera in two acts with text by W. S. Gilbert and music by Arthur Sullivan. First performance: Savoy Theater, London, January 22, 1887. First American performance: Fifth Avenue Theater, New York, February 21, 1887.

On November 22, 1869, there had been produced in London a one-act operetta, *Ages Ago,* text by Gilbert and music by F. Clay. Gilbert, who never hesitated to borrow from himself, used material from that operetta for the text of *Ruddigore,* which was the immediate successor to *The Mikado.* Upon *Ruddigore* the authors expended considerable creative pain, determined to follow the triumph of *The Mikado* with another no less striking. With a paradox worthy of a Gilbertian libretto, each of the two collaborators was convinced he himself was doing the best work of his career in *Ruddigore* and just as sure that his partner was letting him down. Sullivan resented the fact that Gilbert's text did not make more provision for music, while Gilbert grumbled that there was already too much music in the play. Sullivan, moreover, was not altogether sold on the merits of Gilbert's libretto and was particularly critical of the finale in which ghosts come back to life. In return, Gilbert whined that if Sullivan had been able to write music with a humorous bent, the last scene would have come off successfully; Gilbert insisted that Sullivan's tunes made the finale sound as solemn as a comedy in which lines from Milton's *Paradise Lost* were interpolated.

Notwithstanding their differences of opinion and their disagreements, they worked hard—and in great secrecy. Not only did they refuse to reveal the nature of their new comic opera, but they also held rehearsals behind bolted doors. Gilbert wanted to spring his new play as a complete surprise on his audience. Thus, at the première, few knew what *Ruddigore* would be about. But if that evening carried any surprises they were on the authors, who were astounded to hear the unwelcome sounds of hissing and booing after the final curtain. Apparently Sullivan had been right: the return of the ghosts to life had been just too much for the audience to accept. Or it may have been that some in the audience deeply resented the slur against the British Navy implicit in the sailor's song about "the darned Mounseer."

The morning after the première, the collaborators went to work to alter the text and music, especially the finale. But these changes did not do much to change the public reaction. Audiences as well as critics regarded *Ruddigore* as decidedly anticlimactic after a delight like *The Mikado*. Indeed, as with *Princess Ida*, this comic opera had one of the shortest runs of any of the better-known comic operas of Gilbert and Sullivan (283 performances); and it was regarded by D'Oyly Carte as a definite failure.

Nevertheless, since that first engagement, *Ruddigore* has come to be accepted as one of Gilbert's freshest and most original inventions: an unconventional, and at times rowdy, burlesque on old-fashioned English melodramas.

In Rederring, Cornwall, a group of bridesmaids are lamenting the fact that Rose Maybud, a neighborhood beauty, is still unmarried ("Fair Is Rose as the Bright May-Day"). Dame Hannah, Rose's aunt, is also unmarried, though she is now betrothed to the late Sir Roderic Murgatroyd, 21st Baronet of Ruddigore. Hannah explains that a curse has befallen Sir Rupert Murgatroyd, the first of the Baronets, and all his successors. This curse has made it necessary for each Murgatroyd to commit at least one crime a day or suffer death ("Sir Rupert Murgatroyd"). When Rose arrives, she bewails the fact that, living as she does by the book of etiquette, she is hampered in her courtships ("If Somebody There Chanced to Be"). She is really in love with the shy bumpkin, Robin Oakapple, with whom she exchanges tender sentiments ("I Know a Youth Who Loves a Little Maid"). Robin is none other than Sir Ruthven Murgatroyd in disguise. Thus he, too, is a victim of the curse compelling him to commit a daily crime—a fact well known to his foster brother, Richard Dauntless, a nautical lad just back from the seas ("I Shipped, D'Ye See, in a Revenue Sloop"). Richard offers to woo Rose for Robin ("My Boy, You May Take it From Me"), but in the process he falls in love with the girl ("The Battle's Roar Is Over"). The love intrigue is further complicated by the appearance of Mad Margaret ("Cheerily Carols the Lark"), who is in love with Sir Despard, still another of the Murgatroyds, a wicked baronet. To Sir Despard, Richard reveals that brother Ruthven is masquerading as Robin ("You Understand?"). During the marriage ceremony of Robin and Rose ("Where the Buds Are Blossoming"), Robin is unmasked. Rose deserts him for Richard, and Despard welcomes Margaret with open arms. Now appearing as Sir Ruthven, the oldest of the Murgatroyds he gives Richard and Rose his blessings for their forthcoming marriage ("Happily Coupled Are We"). Suddenly the pictures of the Murgatroyd ancestors on the wall, headed by Sir Roderic, come to life ("When the Night Wind Howls"). They taunt Ruthven for not having inflicted enough crimes. Ruthven stoutly defies them, and is joined by Despard and Margaret ("My Eyes Are Fully Open to My Awful Situation"). But a subtle bit of circumlocution and ratiocination on the part of Ruthven manages to outwit Sir Roderic. In the end Ruthven gets Rose back as his bride.

(The) Runaway Girl by Ivan Caryll and Lionel Monckton.

Operetta in three acts with text by Seymour Hicks and Harry Nichols, and lyrics by Aubry Hopwood and Harry Greenbank. First performance: Shaftesbury Theater, London, 1898. First American performance: Daly's Theater, New York, August 25, 1898.

With a London run of almost 600 performances, and with a full season's engagement on Broadway followed by an American road tour, *The*

Runaway Girl represents one of the major stage hits of the successful composing team of Caryll and Monckton. The central character, Winifred, is an orphan girl, who escapes from a convent to join a group of traveling minstrels as their "queen." When this troupe crosses paths with a Cook's Tour, she meets and falls in love with Guy Stanley. Actually, a match between Winifred and Guy had been prearranged long before this meeting, a match Guy had been scrupulously avoiding. Only after he meets her does he discover to his delight that she is his predestined bride.

The main song, "Soldiers in the Park," proved as popular in New York as in London. Other memorable tunes include the following: Guy's gay air, "Not That Sort of a Girl"; Winifred's song, "I'm Only a Poor Little Singing Girl"; the duet of Gay and Winifred, "No One in the World"; and Winifred's song with chorus, "Beautiful Venice."

San Toy by Sidney Jones.

Operetta in two acts with text by Edward Morton, and lyrics by Adrian Ross and Percy Greenbank. First performance: Daly's Theater, London, October 11, 1899. First American performance: Daly's Theater, New York, October 1, 1900.

Having scored so heavily in 1896 with his Japanese operetta *Geisha* starring Marie Tempest, Sidney Jones returned to an Oriental setting in *San Toy* and once again called upon Marie Tempest to be his heroine. The results were impressive, indeed. *San Toy* had a London run of 768 performances (eight more than *Geisha*).

San Toy is the daughter of the Mandarin, Yen How. The fame of her beauty reaches the ears of the Emperor, who summons her to court. There, the ladies of the court, envious of her beauty and personal appeal, contrive to destroy her. San Toy's complications mount when Fo Hop, a student, tries to win her love. But the Emperor finally intercedes for her and extricates her from her various entanglements; and then he gives his royal blessing to her marriage to the man she really loves, Bobby Preston, son of the British consul.

San Toy's songs, and one of her duets with Bobby, are among the score's leading musical attractions: the songs are "The Petals of the Plum Tree" and "The One in the World"; the duet, "The Little China

Maid." Two other musical numbers are of interest, both of them delivered by Bobby: "Love Has Come from Lotus Land" and "The Butter-
fly."

(Der) Schauspieldirektor [*The Impresario* or *The Music Master*] by
Wolfgang Amadeus Mozart.

> Comic opera in one act with text by Gottlieb Stephanie. First perform-
> ances: Orangerie, Schoenbrunn, Austria, February 7, 1786 (private);
> Kaernthnerthor Theater, Vienna, February 18, 1786 (public). First
> American performances: New York, November 9, 1870 (in German);
> New York, October 26, 1916 (in English).

After Mozart had settled permanently in Vienna, the Austrian Emperor,
Joseph II, commissioned him to write a little divertissement for an entertainment planned at the Schoenbrunn Palace for the Governor General of the Netherlands. As first seen at Schoenbrunn, and two weeks after
that in Vienna, the work was made up of two sections. The first was entirely dramatic—a topical play concerned with matters of direct interest
to the Austrian public of that day. The second part was a Singspiel, an
early Austrian form of musical comedy. In the latter, the plot concerned
the harassment of a theater manager by two prima donnas seeking the
principal role in a forthcoming opera.

Only the second part, the Singspiel, is now heard when *Der Schauspieldirektor* is given. The setting is the studio of Maestro Vogelsang, a
composer. (Mozart had himself in mind as the prototype of this character.) Two prima donnas—Mmes Herz and Ulich—are in a tussle over
who should be allowed to appear in the main role of *The Magic Flute*.
(Mme Herz was meant to represent Mme Hofer, Mozart's sister-in-law,
who actually created the role of the Queen of the Night in *The Magic
Flute*.) Of incidental interest in this story is a love affair between Mme
Ulich and a young man named Philip. The character of the Impresario,
named Buff, was intended to depict Schikaneder who had commissioned
Mozart to write *The Magic Flute* and had produced it in Vienna.

The music consists of an overture and four numbers. One is particularly amusing: a trio in which each of the prima donnas tries to outsing
the other to impress the composer, who is at wit's end to calm them.
Mme Herz's sentimental arietta, *"Da schlaegt die Abschiedsstunde,"*

Mme Ulich's gavotte-like air, and the gay finale in which all the problems are neatly solved are some of the other provocative episodes.

Schoen ist die Welt [*The World Is Beautiful*] by Franz Lehár.

> Operetta in three acts with text by Ludwig Herzer and Fritz Loehner.
> First performance: Vienna, December 21, 1931.

In 1914 there was produced in Vienna *Endlich allein*, a Lehár operetta
which was seen in New York in 1915 as *All Alone*. It was not successful in
either Europe or America. Seventeen years later, Lehár reworked his
score and, with a revised libretto, called the operetta *Schoen ist die Welt*.

Just before World War I the Austrian Emperor comes to the Tyrol,
to promote the marriage of his son, George, the crown prince, to Princess
Elisabeth of Lichtenberg. George deeply resents his father's interference
in his personal life; besides he has fallen in love with an enchanting
little girl whom he had met casually at the Alps Hotel. Both George and
the girl refuse to reveal their identities to each other, preferring to
designate themselves as a tourist and a mountain guide, respectively.
They decide to embark on a mountain-climbing trip. There, over a
portable radio, George hears that Princess Elisabeth is missing, last seen
with an irresponsible mountain guide. Only then does George discover
that the charming little girl at his side is the Princess which his father
had singled out for him. A sudden storm makes it impossible for George
and Elisabeth to return to their hotel until the following morning. At
that time, Elisabeth confides to her aunt she has fallen in love with a
mountain guide, and for this reason will not consider marrying the Crown
Prince. When informed that the Crown Prince and the mountain guide
are the same man, she is delighted. So are her aunt and the Emperor, for
their plan to unite the two families has been brought to a happy resolution.

The musical highlight is the principal waltz, one of Lehár's best: "*Sag,
armes Herzchen, sag.*" "*Liebste, glaub' an mich*" is George's principal
love song. Other outstanding musical numbers are the tango "*Rio de
Janeiro,*" the march "*Frei und jung dabei,*" and the sentimental song
"*Ich bin verliebt.*" The second-act Alpine storm provides Lehár with an
opportunity to produce some brilliant programmatic music for orchestra.

(Die) Schoene Galathea [*Beautiful Galatea*] by Franz von Suppé.

> Operetta in one act with text by Poly Henrion (Leopold K. Ditmar
> Kohl von Kohlenegg). First performance: Maysel's Theater, Berlin,
> June 30, 1865. First American performances: New York, September 6,
> 1867 (in German); New York, September 14, 1882 (in English).

Offenbach was the greatest single influence upon Suppé. And it is not
too difficult to uncover a close family relationship between Offenbach's
masterwork, *Orphée aux enfers,* and Suppé's *Die schoene Galathea.* Both
represent a burlesque of characters from Greek mythology, both boast
scores with decided satiric overtones.

Pygmalion has fallen in love with Galatea, a statue of a sea nymph he
has molded. He entreats Aphrodite to bring the statue to life, and his
prayer is answered. The woman Galatea, like most beautiful women, is
willful, capricious, domineering, coquettish, and vain. Willy-nilly, Pygmalion becomes her helpless slave. Midas, Pygmalion's friend, is a guest
at a dinner party given by Pygmalion. Midas has designs upon Galatea,
but in this he finds a formidable rival in Pygmalion's assistant, Ganymede,
with whom Galatea has been flirting outlandishly. Now Galatea exchanges kisses with Ganymede; now she is coquettish with Midas while
receiving drinks from him. After giving voice to a robust drinking song,
Pygmalion realizes that Galatea is not the ideal woman he had hoped
for. He warns her not to partake of too many drinks, an admonition that
sends her into a frenzy. Later on, when Pygmalion catches her in an
ardent embrace with Ganymede, he begs Aprhodite to make her again
into a statue. When his plea is answered, the disenchanted Pygmalion
sells the statue to Midas.

The overture opens in a stately fashion with a solemn thought for
horns and woodwinds followed by a religious melody for strings. A transition carries us to a broad, lyrical subject, followed by a dramatic episode
for full orchestra, then the main theme of the overture—a soaring waltz
first heard in the strings, with harmonies filled in by the woodwinds,
later reemerging triumphantly in full orchestra.

These are some of the more prominent vocal pages: Midas' arietta
with which he makes his first appearance, *"Meinem Vater Gordios"*;
Galatea's drinking song, *"Hell im Glas"*; the "kiss duet" of Galatea and
Ganymede, *"Ach mich zieht's zu dir"*; Galatea's lovely air, *"Ja, wenn die
Musik nicht waer"*; and the song of Ganymede, *"Wir Giechen."*

Since World War II, *Die schoene Galathea* has been seen in revised and updated versions on several different occasions. In 1952 it was revived in Vienna with an altered text by L. Bender and A. P. Waldenmaier. On July 12, 1951, it was presented at the Central City Opera House in Colorado in a new English adaptation by Phyllis Mead.

Schwarzwaldmaedel [*The Black Forest Maid*] by Leon Jessel.

Operetta in three acts with text by August Neidhart. First performance: Berlin, August 25, 1917.

The picturesque region of the Black Forest in southern Germany just before World War I is the setting of Jessel's most famous operetta, a work long in favor with German theater audiences.

Blasius Roemer, choirmaster and bandleader, has two hobbies—one is music and the other is collecting costumes for religious festivals. On the eve of the St. Cecilia Festival, he is visited by two strangers who identify themselves as wandering musicians: Hans, come from Berlin as a refugee from the unwelcome amatory advances of Malvina, and his friend, Richard. Malvina has followed Hans from Berlin and finds him at Roemer's house, where she insists he dance with her during the Festival. For the event she borrows a native costume from her host. During the festivities, Malvina tries to make Hans jealous by flirting with Richard, but Hans is completely oblivious to her strategy since he is attracted to Barbara, Roemer's young maid. When Barbara is insulted by a local bumpkin, Hans rises to her defense. A rowdy free-for-all ensues. The instigators of the brawl are brought to judgment in a court session hastily improvised in a room in a local tavern. Each one states his case and is exonerated. During the proceedings, Roemer discovers he is really in love with Barbara. But his revelation has come to him too late, since Barbara and Hans have by now become a loving pair; and so have Richard and Malvina.

Folk tunes and dances are the main assets of a lively score, beginning with a peasant polka which is the core of the overture. Also of particular interest are two infectious waltz duets ("*Muss den die Lieb' stets Tragoedie sein*" and "*Erklingen zum Tanze die Geigen*"); Richard's air, "*Malwine, ach Malwine*"; and the ensemble number, "*Maedel aus dem schwarzen Wald.*"

(The) **Secret Marriage** by Domenico Cimarosa. *See (Il) Matrimonio Segreto.*

(The) **Secret of Suzanne** [*Il Segreto di Susanna*] by Ermanno Wolf-Ferrari.

> Opera buffa in one act with text by Enrico Golisciani. First performance: Munich Opera, December 4, 1909 (in German, under the title *Susannens Geheimnis*). First American performance: New York City, by the visiting Philadelphia-Chicago Opera Company, March 14, 1911 (in Italian).

Although built on an incident considerably slighter and more trite than those to which opera buffas are generally partial, *The Secret of Suzanne* remains the composer's comedy masterwork—a never-ceasing delight because of its ebullient, effervescent score.

The opera boasts only three characters, one of whom (Santi, a servant) is mute. In Piedmont, at the turn of the present century, Count Gil suspects his recently wedded wife, Suzanne, of being unfaithful to him. The reason for this suspicion is the fact that whenever he comes home he detects an odor of cigarette smoke. The more evasive she becomes to his barrage of questions and accusations, the more convinced he is of her guilt. In a fit of anger he smashes some of the furniture, then announces he is off to his club. Outside the house he loiters to spy on his wife through the window. Thus he discovers his wife likes to partake of an occasional cigarette when he is away. He is so delighted to learn his wife is faithful to him that he rushes inside to join her in a smoke. The opera ends as the mute servant cleans up after them.

The gay mood prevailing throughout the little opera is forthwith established by the sprightly overture. A jolly tune is given by violins and woodwinds without preliminaries. After this idea has been elaborated upon, a second pleasing tune is offered by flute and clarinet accompanied by strings. Later on, the two themes are combined contrapuntally with delightful effect.

Equally fresh and spontaneous are a melodious intermezzo for orchestra and three vivacious vocal excerpts. Of the latter, two are by Suzanne ("*Gioia, la nubbe leggera,*" in which she sings the praises of cigarettes, and *"Vial così non mi lasciate"*). The third is a duet of Suzanne and her husband, *"Il dolce idillio."*

The reason why *The Secret of Suzanne* was first heard in German instead of Italian—and first presented in Germany and not Italy—was that the composer's publisher was German, Wolf-Ferrari having grown dissatisfied with the terms offered him by the powerful Italian firm of Ricordi. The first time *The Secret of Suzanne* was given in Italian was when the Metropolitan Opera offered it on December 13, 1912, with a cast headed by Geraldine Farrar and Antonio Scotti. "I never realized what was in my opera until I heard it today in Italian," said Wolf-Ferrari, who had come to New York to attend the performance.

(La) Serva padrona [*The Servant-Mistress*] by Giovanni Battista Pergolesi.

> "Intermezzo" in two parts with text by G. A. Federico. First performance: Teatro de S. Bartolomeo, Naples, August 28, 1733. First American performances: Baltimore, Maryland, June 12, 1790 (in Italian); New York, May 7, 1917 (in English).

If any single work can be said to have created the opera buffa form that one is Pergolesi's *La Serva padrona*. The opera buffa reacted against the clichés of serious Italian opera with its partiality for classical subjects and characters and its overcomplicated plots. Instead of large casts, elaborate stage effects, and plots of remote interest—to all of which serious eighteenth-century Italian opera was addicted—opera buffa favored farcical situations involving only a limited number of performers, and situations which were part of the everyday experiences of Italian audiences. In place of mythical characters, opera buffa recruited everyday people: scheming servants, cuckolds, deceived wives. Elaborately ornamented arias (with which Italian opera sought to exploit the great voices of the day) were replaced by simple, catchy little tunes.

Long before Pergolesi had crystallized the genre of opera buffa with *La Serva padrona*, comic characters had been utilized within the context of serious Italian operas. They were found in short comic scenes known as "intermezzi." An "intermezzo," in turn, was an outgrowth of the *commedia dell'arte*. Intermezzi proved so popular with Neapolitan audiences that, in 1709, an intimate theater was opened solely for the performance of these short musical farces. Veteran Neapolitan opera composers (including Alessandro Scarlatti and Nicola Logroscino) were commissioned to write intermezzi, as independent little comic operas for the new theater. And it was Logroscino who is believed to have invented the finale (a device favored by all later opera-buffa composers to close an act). As early as 1731, Pergolesi wrote an intermezzo, but as a part of a sacred drama. Other of Pergolesi's subsequent serious operas also had comic interludes.

But his first self-sufficient comic opera was *La Serva padrona,* which though still an "intermezzo" is in actuality an opera buffa, the first of its kind. So complete a realization of opera-buffa style and approaches was this early work that to this day it can still afford considerable pleasure to operagoers. This, most certainly, is no mere museum piece. Masters like Verdi and Puccini were unqualified in their admiration for it.

There are only three characters: Uberto, master of the household; Serpina, his maid; Vespone, a valet, who is mute. There is no chorus. The musical score is made up of an overture and, in each of the two parts of the one act, an aria for each of the two leading characters, and a duet.

In eighteenth-century Naples, Uberto laments that his servant, Serpina, is difficult to live with, that she neglects him woefully, that she is willful and capricious, sharp-tongued and domineering (*"Sempre in contrasti"*). In despair, Uberto asks Vespone to find him a bride—marriage apparently offering him the only solution to his domestic problem. When Serpina learns her master is thinking of marriage, she tries to make him jealous in the hope that his choice might fall upon her. She informs him she plans to marry a soldier, that she greatly regrets having to leave Uberto's employ, and that she hopes Uberto will never forget her (*"A Serpine penserte"*). Vespone falls in with Serpina's scheming and poses as her soldier-lover. The ruse works. Uberto is inflamed with jealousy (*"Son imbrogliato io già"*) to a point where he decides he wants to marry Serpina. Even after he discovers the trick that has been perpetrated upon him, Uberto remains pleased with himself, since he now realizes how much he loves Serpina (*"O gioia, gioia, gioia!"*).

The impact of *La Serva padrona* upon the music world of its day was powerful. It was responsible for the emergence of the opéra-comique in France. Pierre Monsigny, recognized as the parent of this art form, was so impressed by a hearing of *La Serva padrona* in 1754 that he decided to write French light operas in a similar vein. Grétry, another fine opéra-comique composer, insisted that "Pergolesi was the creator, and my own music is but a continuation of his." In Italy, *La Serva padrona* was the model imitated by Cimarosa for *Il Matrimonia segreto,* by Galuppi for

Il Filosofo di campagna, and by Paisiello for *The Barber of Seville.* Thus the techniques and rituals of opera buffa were permanently established. *La Serva padrona* can also be said to have been a predecessor of the German Singspiel, with which German comic opera comes into existence.

There were other ways in which *La Serva padrona* contributed a rich and eventful chapter to the history of opera performances. A traveling company brought the work to Paris on August 1, 1752, and scored such a triumph that a cult arose acclaiming this the true operatic art as opposed to the more stylized and cerebral writings of such serious French opera composers as Rameau; this group included such Encyclopedists as Diderot and Rousseau. Indeed, so affected was Rousseau by *La Serva padrona* that, in 1752, he wrote, and had produced, a little comic opera of his own—*Le Devin du village* (which see). In any event, a musical war erupted in Paris, later identified by history as the *"Guerre des Bouffons."* On the one side were those who upheld the Italian tradition as found in Pergolesi's comic opera, and on the other those who sided with Rameau. And, in the end, it was Rameau's operas, rather than those of the lighter Italian composers, which emerged triumphant.

(The) **Servant-Mistress** by Giovanni Battista Pergolesi. *See (La) Serva Padrona.*

(Il) **Signor Bruschino** or **Il Figlio per azzardo** [*Mister Bruschino* or *The Son by Accident*] by Gioacchino Rossini.

> Opera buffa in one act with text by Giuseppe Maria Foppa, based on a French comedy by Alissan de Chazet and E. T. M. Ourry. First performance: Teatro San Moïse, Venice, January 1813. First American performance (probable): Metropolitan Opera, New York, December 6, 1932.

Legends are not easily destroyed. Those surrounding *Il Signor Bruschino* have plagued the history of opera for years. This musical farce was one of two commissioned from Rossini by the San Moïse Theater in Venice late in 1812, after his phenomenal success at La Scala with *La Pietra del paragone* on September 26, 1812. The story goes (and it was long believed) that Rossini was infuriated at the manager of the San Moïse

Theater for giving him an impossible libretto. In reprisal, it was said, Rossini filled his score with all kinds of extravagances and absurdities: in the overture he had the violinists strike their bows on the music stands; he wrote low notes difficult, if not impossible, for a soprano to negotiate, and decorative passages equally formidable for basses; at the height of a comic scene he interpolated a funeral march, and so on.

One would have to stretch one's credulity well beyond normal limits to believe that, first, Rossini would perpetrate such a trick in writing a comic opera, and, second, that such a trick could possibly work. For one thing, the episode would presuppose that the manager of the San Moïse never went to rehearsals and thus was not aware of Rossini's prank before the première; or, even if he had failed to attend rehearsals, that nobody took the trouble to bring him the news of Rossini's strange behavior. We would also have to assume that the libretto of *Il Signor Bruschino* was worse than many others which Rossini set to music, which simply was not the case.

The truth of the matter is that Rossini allowed himself free rein for his pronounced comic bent. It is true that there *is* a funeral march in a comic scene, but that march is brief and only serves to emphasize the comedy; that violinists tap their music stands in the overture, but this also the product of a very inventive comic mind which is not afraid to try something new and original. However, it is simply not true that there is any writing for voices which cannot easily be sung; Rossini's vocal technique here, as elsewhere, is both sound and brilliant.

Il Signor Bruschino was a failure when first performed, and it had only two performances. Nor did it fare better when revived in Milan in 1844. But in 1857, with Rossini's consent, Jacques Offenbach revived it at the Bouffes-Parisiens in Paris, where it proved a pronounced success. When first heard in America in 1932, at the Metropolitan Opera, it was the curtain raiser for Richard Strauss's grim and realistic opera, *Elektra;* the cast for the Rossini opera included Ezio Pinza as Gaudenzio, Armand Tokatyan as Florville, and Giuseppe de Luca in the title role.

Florville is in love with Sofia, daughter of his political enemy, Gaudenzio. The latter refuses to consider Florville as a son-in-law; instead, he sends a letter to the son of a certain Signor Bruschino designating the son as the proper suitor for Sofia. Young Bruschino is sowing his wild oats at a local inn and gets heavily in debt. Posing as Bruschino's cousin, Florville comes to extricate the young man from his troubles—on condition he turn over to him Gaudenzio's letter. Florville then impersonates his rival, comes to, and is warmly welcomed in, Gaudenzio's household. Meanwhile, the older Signor Bruschino has come to visit Gaudenzio, and is in a state of uncontrollable fury over his son's dissolute ways. When Gaudenzio presents Florville to the elder Bruschino, the latter angrily protests that this man is not his son. Gaudenzio, however, believes that the older Bruschino is merely renouncing his son because he is in no forgiving mood. To thwart the old man, Gaudenzio arranges a marriage between the two young people without further delay. When this marriage is consummated, the real young Bruschino finally makes an appearance. Gaudenzio, with the best possible grace, must now accept Florville as his son-in-law.

Two basso-buffo airs demonstrate Rossini's uncommon skill in writing music with a comic bent, both of them presented by Gaudenzio: "*Nel teatro del gran mondo*" and "*Hola testa.*" Sofia's beautiful song, "*Ah voi condur volette alla disperazio,*" on the other hand, points to Rossini's equally formidable powers at expressive lyricism.

Si j'étais roi [*If I Were King*] by Adolphe Adam.

Opéra-comique in three acts with text by Adolphe Philippe d'Ennery and Jules Brésil. First performance: Théâtre Lyrique, Paris, September 4, 1852. First American performances: New Orleans, 1858 (in French); New York, December 14, 1882 (in English).

Story, characters, and settings of this comic opera might have been snatched out of *The Arabian Nights*. Zephoris, a humble fisherman in an old Arabian village, rescues from drowning the lovely Nemea, cousin of King Oman. But Zephoris is unaware of her identity, just as she is of his. Besieged by numerous admirers and suitors, Nemea insists she will marry only the man who has saved her life. One day, Zephoris espies her from a distance, recognizes her, and only then discovers she is of royal blood. The thought crosses his mind that if only he were king he would be in a position to woo her. He even scribbles such a wish in the sand, just before falling asleep. He and his message are seen by King Oman, who capriciously decides to fullfil the fisherman's wish for a day. Zephoris awakens in the king's palace to discover that he is really a king. He makes the most of his opportunity by ordering Nemea to marry him. But this goes beyond King Oman's calculations, and he sees to it that the fisherman forthwith is restored to his former humble status. Now fully cognizant of whom her beloved is, Nemea follows him to his hut and tells him she wants to be his wife. Such a state of affairs is reluctantly accepted by King Oman, who now appoints Zephoris commander of the troops. After emerging a hero in battle, Zephoris marries Nemea.

The overture begins dramatically, but before long a tune for violins lightens the atmosphere. Another delightful subject follows in the woodwinds. A crescendo leads to two more significant themes, one a powerful idea for the violins, and the second a whimsical thought for the woodwinds.

The oriental background and atmosphere of the text have been caught in the exotic melodies and in the harmonic and instrumental colors of the overture. The same oriental character prevails in some of the main vocal numbers, two of the most important being those of Nemea: *"De vos nobles aïeux"* and *"Des souverains du rivages."* Also noteworthy are a duet of Nemea and Zephoris (*"Vous m'aimez"*); three lyrical airs by Zephoris (*"J'ignore son nom," "Un regard des ses yeux,"* and *"Elle est princesse!"*); and a beautiful cavatina, *"Dans le sommeil."*

Sissy by Fritz Kreisler.

> Operetta in two acts with text by Ernest and Hubert Marischka, based on a comedy by Ernst Decsey and Gustav Holm. First performance: Vienna, December 23, 1932.

The world-famous violin virtuoso Fritz Kreisler wrote the music for two delightful operettas. The first, *Apple Blossoms*, was introduced on Broadway on October 7, 1918. The second was written for the Viennese stage, where it was an outstanding success. Fritz Kreisler himself conducted the première performance, and the cast included two outstanding Viennese performers, Paul Wessely and Hans Jaray; in addition Hedy Lamarr made her stage debut in a minor role, and Paul Henried was Jaray's understudy. Besides its long run in Vienna, *Sissy* was successfully performed in Amsterdam, Munich, Basel, Paris, and London, as well as in some of the smaller cities on the Continent. It was revived in Vienna in 1948, and from time to time has returned to major European capitals.

The sentimental story and the romantic settings are of pre-World War I vintage—a nostalgic throwback to the Austria of a happier day. The action takes place partly at the Possenhofen Castle on Lake Sternberg in Bavaria, and partly at Bad Ischl in Austria; the time is mid-nineteenth century. Duke Max of Bavaria has two daughters who are opposites. Nené is feminine, demure, attractive; Elizabeth, nicknamed Sissy, is a tomboy with no respect for court ceremonials or traditions. The mother aspires to have Nené marry the young Emperor of Austria, Francis Joseph, but Nené is in love with the dashing Prince of Thurn-Taxis. The mother is about to give her consent to their marriage when a message arrives inviting mother and daughter to a birthday celebration for the Emperor at Bad Ischl. Sissy and her father also come to this royal party, where Sissy joins her sister in trying to break up a possible match between Nené and the Emperor. At the party Sissy is arrested when she picks up roses intended for the Emperor. Brought before Francis Joseph, she lies about her identity, explaining she is a tailor's apprentice come to deliver a dress for Nené. With Francis Joseph it is a case of love at first sight. Thus Nené is free to marry her Prince, while Sissy soon is selected by the Emperor as his bride.

Kreisler's score is a fullsome reminder of a bygone era in Vienna, with two waltzes in the best tradition of Johann Strauss II: "*Ein stilles Glueck, ein bisserl Musik*" and "*Ich waer' so gern einmal verliebt.*" Not the least of the musical attractions are the vocal adaptations of some of Kreisler's most famous concert compositions for the violin, including *Liebesleid, Liebesfreud, Schoen Rosmarin,* and *Caprice Viennois.*

(The) Sorcerer or The Elixir of Love by Gilbert and Sullivan.

> Comic opera in two acts with text by W. S. Gilbert and music by Arthur Sullivan. First performance: Opéra Comique, London, November 17, 1877. First American performance: Broadway Theater, New York, February 21, 1879.

Hard on the heels of *Trial by Jury,* the first comic opera to establish the popularity of Gilbert and Sullivan in London, came *The Sorcerer* to introduce a few Gilbert and Sullivan traditions. It was the first of their comic operas to open at the Opéra Comique, a theater leased by D'Oyly Carte as a home for a new comic-opera company that never materialized; from then on, and until D'Oyly Carte built the Savoy Theater for Gilbert and Sullivan, their operas were produced there. *The Sorcerer* was the first Gilbert and Sullivan production to star George Grossmith and Rutland Barrington. Neither had had much stage experience when Gilbert chose them for the roles of John Wellington Wells and Dr. Daly, respectively. Each justified Gilbert's faith by becoming a star in *The Sorcerer* and later adding to his fame and stature in subsequent Gilbert and Sullivan operas.

Although many critics took *The Sorcerer* severely to task for allowing its plot to depend for its motivation upon an old chestnut (a love philtre), they also found a good deal to admire. "Strange as this play may be pronounced," said the *Musical World*, "so cleverly is it developed that—the impossible world through which the author conducts his spectators once admitted—it appears consistent enough." As for Sullivan's music, *The Examiner* said, "here is a work of entirely English growth, which bids fair to hold its own by the side of numberless foreign importations."

At a gay village fair, the townspeople are celebrating the betrothal of the guardsman Alexis and Aline ("Ring Forth Ye Bells"). During these festivities, the discovery is made that Constance Partlet is attracted to the vicar, Dr. Daly. But after reminiscing about his youth ("A Pale Young Curate"), Dr. Daly confesses he loves Aline. Overjoyed at her imminent marriage ("Happy Young Heart"), Aline awaits the arrival of her beloved Alexis. After they rush into each other's arms, Aline's mother betrays the fact that she has a weakness for Alexis' father, Sir Marmaduke. The Notary arrives with the marriage contract for Alexis and Aline, after which Alexis sings a hymn to the raptures of true love ("For Love Alone"). In an attempt to share his rapture with his fellow villagers, he decides to spread among them a love philtre. At this point, the sorcerer, John Wellington Wells, comes upon the scene. He first introduces himself ("Oh, My Name is John Wellington Wells"), then performs an incantation during which he prepares a love potion for the villagers. The philtre works its magic. When Constance appears, she falls in love with the Notary. Sir Marmaduke falls a victim to the charms of Constance's mother ("I Rejoice That It's Decided"). Aline's mother is drawn to Mr. Wells. Provoked by Alexis, Aline decides to drink the potion, too; then, hearing Dr. Daly in a poignant chant ("Time Was When Love and I Were Well Acquainted"), she proceeds to fall in love with him. By now, Alexis is convinced that the philtre has messed things up pretty badly. He is further upset to learn that the only way Wells can undo the havoc is by offering Alexis or his beloved Aline as a sacrifice. Yielding to outside pressure, Alexis accepts the role of victim. All comes right again, and the lovers return to their original partners. A convivial atmosphere is engendered with a rousing tea party.

(The) Spanish Hour by Maurice Ravel. *See (L')Heure espagnole.*

(Lo) Speziale by Joseph Haydn. *See (The) Apothecary.*

(Das) Spitzentuch der Koenigin by Johann Strauss II. *See (The) Queen's Handkerchief.*

(The) Spring Maid or **The Sweet Maid** [*Das suesse Maedel*] by Heinrich Reinhardt.

> Operetta in two acts with book by Wilhelm Willner. First performance: Vienna, October 25, 1901. First American performances: Irving Place Theater, New York, April 19, 1910 (in German); New York, December 26, 1910 (in English).

Reinhardt completed about a dozen operettas and two grand operas. *The Spring Maid* proved his most popular work on both sides of the Atlantic.

Although it has a contemporary setting, the text was based on an age-old legend which tells that the famous spa at Carlsbad, Bohemia, was once a wild forest, a favorite haunt of hunters. One day a huntsman, who has spared the life of a fawn, was led to a rock by a water sprite; when the rock was struck, the celebrated spring of Carlsbad gushed forth. Most of this operetta centers around the appearance at Carlsbad of Princess Bozen, a gay young lady, and her impoverished father. They attend a pageant in which the legend of Carlsbad is dramatized.

When *The Spring Maid* came to Broadway, the book was adapted by Harry B. Smith and the cast starred Christie MacDonald and William Burress. During the New York run, several musical numbers became extremely popular: the duet "Day Dreams" (with its lilting refrain, "Visions of Bliss"); the choral episode "Folk Songs"; and the rousing "Hungaria" with which the operetta ends.

(The) Sunshine Girl by Paul Rubens.

> Operetta in two acts with text by Paul Rubens and Cecil Raleigh. First performance, London, 1912. First American performance: Knickerbocker Theater, New York, February 3, 1913.

Under the terms of the will of his eccentric uncle, Vernon Blundell must work for five years in the Sunshine soap factory without getting married. There he falls in love with Dora Dare, who does not suspect whom he really is. When the day comes for him to cast aside his anonymity, he wants to assure himself that Dora loves him for himself alone. He induces a friend, Lord Bicester, to pretend that he is the real Blundell. Howard Schlump, a German cabbie, recognizes Bicester but is willing to stay silent if Lord Bicester accepts him in his social circle. Schlump enjoys his exalted status up to the moment that Blundell is ready to admit who he is and claim Dora as his bride.

The successful American production boasted an all-star cast that included Julia Sanderson in the title role, Vernon Castle, and Joseph Cawthorn. In America, as well as England, the following songs became popular: "Here's to Love," "You and I," "Ladies," and "Goodbye to Flirtation."

(Der) tapfere Soldat by Oscar Straus. *See (The) Chocolate Soldier.*

(The) Thieving Magpie by Gioacchino Rossini. *See (La) Gazza Ladra.*

(A) Thousand and One Nights [*1001 Nacht*] by Johann Strauss II.

> Operetta in two acts with prologue and epilogue, with text by Leo Stein and Carl Lindau. First performance: Vienna, June 1906.

This is a synthetic product, made up of the score of Johann Strauss's first operetta, *Indigo und die vierzig Raeuber* (introduced in Vienna on February 10, 1871), and a completely new text prepared in 1906, after

Strauss's death. Strauss's score for *Indigo und die vierzig Raeuber* had been a cornucopia of melodic riches, despite which it had been a failure in 1871, entirely the fault of Maximilian Steiner whose text had been so confused that it was impossible to follow the story line. And *A Thousand and One Nights*—music adapted by Ernest Reiterer—was still a storehouse of musical delights.

The story is built around an episode which might well have appeared in *The Arabian Nights*. In the prologue, the Caliph is in love with beautiful Leila, who refuses to marry him unless he gives up his harem. But the Caliph refuses to change the custom of his land; and yet he continues to pine away for the girl he loves. Leila's uncle brings her to the Caliph—disguised as Scheherazade and heavily veiled—as solace for the Caliph's unhappiness. As Scheherazade, Leila begins to spin for the Caliph a story abount a fisherman. As she relates this tale, the Caliph falls asleep. The heart of the operetta tells of his dream. . . . His kingdom is threatened by revolution. Leila has married Mossu, a fisherman who bears a striking resemblance to the Caliph. After the outbreak of the revolution, Leila is willing to sacrifice the life of her fisherman-husband (who is mistaken for the Caliph) in order to save the ruler, with whom she is very much in love. . . . In the epilogue the Caliph awakens and is ready to accede to any demand made upon him by Leila.

Two exultant melodies are among Strauss's finest. One is the Caliph's waltz song, *"Nun lachts du mir wieder,"* and the other is a hymn to country and home, *"Ja, so singt man in der Stadt wo ich geboren."* The latter brought down the house when *Indigo und die vierzig Raeuber* was first produced, and it again brought down the house in *A Thousand and One Nights*. Equally attractive is Leila's song to the Caliph, *"Niemals kann man die vergessen"* with its fervent declaration of love.

(The) Three-Penny Opera [*Die Dreigroschenoper*] by Kurt Weill.

Musical play in eight scenes and prologue, with text by Bertolt Brecht, based on *The Beggar's Opera*. First performance: Theater am Schiffbauerdamm, Berlin, August 31, 1928. First American performance: Empire Theater, New York, April 13, 1933.

The *Three-Penny Opera* is probably the most successful musical play produced in Germany between the two world wars. Certainly it was the most dynamic, the most exciting, and the most provocative example of

Zeitkunst ("Contemporary Art"), which was an artistic cult in Germany soon after World War I.

A revival of John Gay's ballad opera, *The Beggar's Opera*, in a German translation, led Brecht's secretary to suggest that he work on a modernized version of the same opera. The idea impressed Brecht, since, being of leftist political and social leanings, he saw in Gay's text an opportunity to point up the social and political corruption in Germany in the 1920's, at the same time infiltrating into the text some of his own thinking. Since Brecht knew that the old musical score by Pepusch could not serve his purpose, he asked Kurt Weill to collaborate with him. They had previously worked on a one-act song sequence, *Mahagonny,* which they later expanded into the exciting three-act opera, *The Rise and Fall of the City of Mahagonny* (which see).

After Brecht had completed a few scenes of *The Three-Penny Opera,* he showed them to the young German actor, Ernst-Joseph Aufricht. Aufricht was thinking of becoming a producer, and for this purpose had just rented the Schiffbauerdamm Theater. The samples Brecht showed him so excited Aufricht that he urged Brecht and Weill to complete their opera as soon as possible so that it might become his initial production. Librettist and composer went off to the French Riviera where they worked at a furious pace, day and night.

There was a feeling of disaster about *The Three-Penny Opera,* which mounted as the work was being prepared for the stage. Word got around that the play was a dud: a ludicrous mixture of opera, operetta, cabaret, and theater; a strange musical recipe combining a Bach chorale, on the one hand, and American jazz, on the other. As rehearsals progressed, the cast was filled with foreboding that they were getting themselves involved in a giant fiasco. This feeling—combined with numerous accidents—compelled a continual change of casting. The resultant confusion—what with new players continually stepping in to replace those who had already rehearsed—was further aggravated by bickerings and disagreements among the participants. Some members of the cast objected to singing "unsingable music," others to speaking "filthy lines."

The final dress rehearsal, a night before the première, lasted until five in the morning. Everybody was tense, combustible, and miserable. Aufricht was even tempted to call the whole thing off; only the impossible problem of finding another play with which to open his theater restrained him.

Many accounts exist of the fabulous opening night and its equally fabulous aftermath. That of Lotte Lenya may be regarded as definitive, since she was playing the role of Jenny at the première and later became Weill's wife. She has written: "Up to the stable scene the audience seemed cold and apathetic, as though convinced in advance that it had come to a certain flop. Then after the *Kanonen* song, an unbelievable uproar went up, and from that point on it was wonderfully, intoxicatingly clear that the public was with us. However, late the next morning we were waiting for the first reviews, there persisted a crassy unreality about what had happened; nobody quite dared believe in our success. Nor did the reviews confirm it for us—they were decidedly mixed. Hollander wrote that he had slept through the entire performance."

What followed was without precedent in the Berlin theater of the 1920's. The city—and after that the entire country—was "swept by a *Dreigroschenoper* fever," as Lotte Lenya went on to say. "In the streets no other tunes were whistled. A *Dreigroschenoper* bar was opened where no other music was played." In its first year, *The Three-Penny Opera* was given over four thousand times in more than one hundred German theaters; in five years it was seen ten thousand times in Central Europe, and had been translated into eighteen languages. G. W. Pabst, the distinguished German motion-picture producer, adapted it for the screen and achieved a cinematic triumph. (This screen classic was revived in 1960.)

When the Nazis came to power, *The Three-Penny Opera* was banned both because Weill was a Jew and because the work was regarded as decadent. Indeed, when the Nazis opened their Museum of Degenerate Art, *The Three-Penny Opera* was a major exhibit; in one of the rooms the score was played continuously. But after people continued to crowd the room to listen to the music—with obvious approbation rather than disapproval—the Nazis removed the opera from their museum. *The Three-Penny Opera*, however, continued to haunt the Nazis: the theme from the song, "Mack the Knife," was used as a signal for members in the German underground movement.

Strange to say, in view of its European triumph, *The Three-Penny Opera* was such a box-office disaster when it was first produced in New York—in 1933—that it lasted only thirteen performances. But if America rejected the opera in 1933, it was to make full amends in a later era. With a new modernized text by Marc Blitzstein (but with Weill's music unchanged), *The Three-Penny Opera* was revived off Broadway on March 10, 1954, at the Theater de Lys. It had to close after ninety-six performances to make room for another production previously scheduled in that intimate house. When it reopened on September 20, 1955, it continued for over six years and 2,500 performances to become the longest running musical production in the history of the American theater. In 1960, a national company was formed to tour the United States, and in 1961 a second national company, headed by Gypsy Rose Lee, was created.

Brecht's text follows that of John Gay (see *The Beggar's Opera*) with some significant modifications. In the prologue, a Soho street musician is singing the "Moritat," or "Mack the Knife," number, in which he recounts the history of Macheath, the highwayman. Since this musical number has achieved such unprecedented popularity throughout the world— and especially in the United States—its origin may be of particular interest.

Paulsen, who originated the role of Macheath, insisted that some song be introduced early in the opera to set the stage for his entrance. "Brecht made no comment but the next morning came in with the verses for the 'Moritat' of Mack the Knife, and gave them to Kurt to set to music," says Lotta Lenya. "This . . . tune, often called the most famous . . . written in Europe during the past half century, was modeled after the moritats ('mord' meaning murder, 'tat' meaning deed) sung by singers at street fairs, detailing the hideous crimes of notorious archfiends. Kurt not only produced the tune overnight, he knew the name of the hand-organ manufacturer—Zucco Maggio—who could supply the organ on which to grind out the tune for the prologue."

"Moritat" became one of the most important production numbers in the Pabst screen adaptation of the opera. After the epical off-Broadway success of *The Three-Penny Opera,* "Moritat," or "Mack the Knife," four times became a nation-wide hit song in the United States, was recorded in forty-eight versions, and sold over ten million discs. In 1955 the song was recorded over twenty different times and was often on the top of the Hit Parade; in 1959, revived by Bobby Darin, it sold over a million discs and was largely responsible for first establishing the success of this young singer.

In the first scene, Filch, a beggar, manages to get a license for his trade from Peachum, chief of the Beggar's Guild, in return for half his income. After this transaction, Peachum learns that his daughter, Polly, is having a rendezvous with her lover Macheath, a robber known as Mackie Messer, or Mack the Knife. The second scene represents the marriage of Polly and Macheath, attended not only by Macheath's confederates, but even by the chief of police, who is ever ready to alert the robber about an impending police raid in return for some of the stolen loot. In Peachum's shop, after that, Polly is severely reprimanded by her parents for marrying a thief; Polly's father even threatens to go to the police and inform on Macheath. In a Soho stable, Polly reveals her father's threat to her husband, who is aware that not even the police chief can help him now and that he must go into hiding. He finds refuge in a brothel where he reviews his past, together with his present dilemma, in a celebrated ballad (the *"Zuhaelter-ballade"*) and where he is finally apprehended. Imprisoned, Macheath meets another prisoner, Brown, to whose daughter, Lucy, Macheath had once made love. Polly and Lucy meet and quarrel, but both are overjoyed to learn that Macheath has managed to escape, and that he plans a disturbance among the beggars during a forthcoming coronation festivity. But Macheath is captured a second time and the gallows now await him. So much of an attraction is his imminent execution that even the coronation festivities begin to lose their appeal for the people. Just as the rope is about to be tied around Macheath's neck, word arrives that the Queen has given the thief a pardon; more than that, she has even bestowed on him a castle and a yearly pension. These tidings inspire the crowd to chant a mighty chorale of thanks: *"Verfolgt das Unrecht nicht zu sehr"* ("Injustice Is Not Inevitable").

Besides the individual popular tunes with which the Weill score is so generously studded, its music consists of an amazing marriage of popular and serious music. The popular element is found in blues, a shimmy, and Tin Pan Alley type ballads; the serious music appears within such classical forms as arias, canons, and chorales.

The title, *Die Dreigroschenoper*, was conceived by the distinguished German novelist, Lion Feuchtwanger, while the opera was in rehearsal.

Three Waltzes by Oscar Straus. *See Drei Walzer.*

Tom Jones by Edward German.

Comic opera in three acts with text by A. M. Thompson and Robert Courtneidge, based on the novel of the same name by Henry Fielding. Lyrics by Charles H. Taylor. First performance: Manchester, England, March 30, 1907. First American performance: Astor Theater, New York, November 11, 1907.

Out of the mid-nineteenth-century classic of realistic fiction by Henry Fielding, the librettists extracted the love interest involving the hero and Sophia Western. Sophia's father insists that she marry Bilfil. Rather than do so, she runs away from home. Domestic problems also send Tom Jones wandering, following bitter altercations with a ruthless guardian. During his travels he rescues Lady Bellaston from a highwayman's assault. For this, she is duly grateful and consents to accompany him to London. During her travels, Sophia meets them. Heartbroken to discover ·Tom Jones with another woman, she renounces him for good. But after Lady Bellaston grows cool to Tom, he and Sophia are reconciled, and, at the same time, Tom Jones, at long last, uncovers the identity of his real parents.

Much of the opera's sentiment and enchantment come from three of Sophia's songs: "I Wander," "Dream O'Day Jill," and "Beguile, Beguile With Sweet Music." Tom has an outstanding love song in "If Love's Content," and a rousing choral number is found in "West Country Lad."

The London première of *Tom Jones* took place at the Apollo Theater on April 17, 1907. Sadler's Wells gave the opera a highly successful revival in 1959–60.

Traveling Artisan by Edmund Eysler. *See Bruder Straubinger.*

Trial by Jury by Gilbert and Sullivan.

> Comic opera in one act with text by W. S. Gilbert and music by Arthur Sullivan. First performance: Royalty Theater, London, March 25, 1875. First American performance: Eagle Theater, New York, November 15, 1875.

Gilbert and Sullivan were introduced to each other in 1870 by the singer-composer, Fred Clay, a mutual friend. But it was John Hollingshead, founder and manager of the Gaiety Theater, who brought them together as collaborators: Hollingshead suggested to Gilbert that he write a libretto for Sullivan for a Gaiety Theater production. The result was an "operatic extravaganza" entitled *Thespis*, the first of the Gilbert and Sullivan comic operas, produced at the Gaiety Theater on December 23,

1871. This was a burlesque in which a group of actors, headed by Thespis, exchanged places with the Olympian gods. The actors take over on Mt. Olympus while the gods come down to earth in the form of actors, to try and learn why they had lost their influence with the people. "*Thespis*," said Isaac Goldberg, "is indeed highly original and grotesque. . . . It looks forward more often than it glances backward. It forecasts the characteristic methods, and now and then a character, of the later series. Its dialogue is comical."

Thespis was a failure, lasting only a month. The collaborators parted company, each to follow his own direction. It seemed hardly likely that they would ever again work together. Then, one day in 1875, D'Oyly Carte, manager of the Royalty Theater in Soho, met Gilbert in the street and suggested that he and Sullivan team up again for a new production for his house. D'Oyly Carte had a specific need to fill. He was planning to produce Offenbach's *La Périchole* and he needed a "trifle" to fill out the program. As it happened, Gilbert had just finished dramatizing a story he had previously published in *Fun*, for which Carl Rosa was supposed to write the music. But Rosa's sudden death left the play without a score. When D'Oyly Carte became convinced of the potentialities of this text, he made an appointment for Gilbert and Sullivan to meet and discuss the musical adaptation.

One blustery winter day Gilbert brought his play to Sullivan. "He read it through, as it seemed to me, in a perturbed sort of way," Sullivan later recalled, "with a gradual crescendo of indignation, in the manner of a man considerably disappointed with what he had written. As soon as he had come to the last words he closed up the manuscript violently, apparently unconscious of the fact that he had achieved his purpose so far as I was concerned, inasmuch as I was screaming with laughter the whole time. The words and music were written, and all the rehearsals completed within the space of three weeks time."

The new Gilbert and Sullivan comic opera was *Trial by Jury*, and it was the authors' first success; it stayed on the boards until the end of the year. (Although D'Oyly Carte originally planned to use the opera as a curtain-raiser, he actually placed it as an afterpiece to Offenbach's opéra-bouffe.) It differs from later Gilbert and Sullivan comic operas in that it contains no spoken dialogue whatever, but is made up entirely of lyrics set to song. But in other respects, it was a model for their later works. For the first time it created the world of paradox, absurdity, and topsy-turvydom over which Gilbert and Sullivan were henceforth to rule. It used the chorus as a basic element of the plot, rather than a decorative appendage, and often enlisted it to echo some of the basic lines of an important solo number. It had some of the principal characters carrying musical instruments. It boasts the first Gilbert and Sullivan travesty on grand opera—in this instance a parody on the ensemble number, *"D'un pensiero"* from Bellini's *La Sonnambula*. And it contained the first of those autobiographical songs without which, it seemed, no Gilbert and Sullivan opera could function: the judge's song, "When I, Good Friends, Was Called to the Bar."

Trial by Jury was a satire on the English courts and made a mockery of trials. Indeed, it was "calculated to bring the Bench to contempt," as some of Sullivan's legal friends said. The play begins without the preliminaries of an overture. Angelina has summoned Edwin to court for a breach of promise action. The Usher addresses the all-male jury ("Now Jurymen") and makes the charge ("Oh Listen to the Plaintiff's Case"). Edwin, the defendant, arrives with guitar in hand; he is followed by the Judge who introduces himself in his autobiographical number. At last, the plaintiff, Angelina, appears, followed by a train of bridesmaids all dressed up for a wedding. The Judge is completely taken with her ("Oh Never, Never") and the jury denounces Edwin. After Angelina's counsel makes his address, Edwin offers to marry today the girl with whom he is in love and to marry Angelina on the morrow ("O, Gentlemen Listen"). The judge is sympathetic to this arrangement, but the counsel dismisses it as so much "burglaree." Thus the whole proceedings become enmeshed in a seemingly insoluble dilemma. Angelina protests she is still in love with Edwin, but he rejects her. Finally the Judge comes up with a solution to the entire mess. He himself stands ready to marry the girl ("All Legal Furies Seize You"), a decision which meets with the full approval of the court ("Of Such as She, a Judge is Here, and a Good Judge, too!").

Trial by Jury was the first Gilbert and Sullivan opera to be produeed in the United States, its première preceding that of *H.M.S. Pinafore* by some three years.

(II) Turco in Italia [*The Turk in Italy*] by Gioacchino Rossini.

Opera buffa in two acts with text by Felice Romani. First performance: La Scala, Milan, August 14, 1814. First American performance: New York, March 14, 1826.

Having succeeded decisively with his opera buffa, *L'Italiana in Algeri* (which see) in 1813, Rossini was led a year later to woo success with an imitation. *Il Turco in Italia* (though by a different librettist) is *L'Italiana in Algeri* in changed costuming. In the latter opera, an Italian woman comes to Algiers and then escapes with her lover by boat; in *Il Turco in Italia*, a Turk comes to Italy and also goes off by boat with his beloved. But lightning rarely strikes twice in the same place. Presented as the opening attraction of the new La Scala season, *Il Turco in Italia* was a miserable failure; the audience started leaving the theater after the first act. Not until seven years later was the opera seen again, and once again it failed to make any sort of an impression. Only in much later revivals in Italy did *Il Turco in Italia* establish itself as one of Rossini's more pleasing comic operas.

Fiorilla, frivolous wife of wealthy Don Geronio, comes to a gypsy haunt where she explains she is looking for a love her husband cannot give her. A Turkish vessel comes to port. Its leader, the Sultan Selim, is smitten by Fiorilla's beauty. Fiorilla is also strongly attracted to the Sultan and, much to Geronio's chagrin, invites him to her home. The Sultan makes plans to elope with Fiorilla, but before this can happen she comes upon Zaide, the seductive gypsy, who reveals that she was once the Sultan's beloved. Zaide and Fiorilla engage in a bitter argument over which one of them will go off with the Sultan. Zaide proves no match for the wily, scheming Fiorilla. But at a masked ball, the Sultan mistakes Zaide for Fiorilla and is about to run off with her when he discovers his mistake. By now, Fiorilla has had a sudden change of heart. She decides to stay with her husband, Geronio, after all—a development which leaves the Sultan and Zaide free to sail back to Turkey together.

Two beautiful airs about love, and one about springtime—all sung by Fiorilla—stand out prominently: The first two are *"Perchè mai se son tradito"* and *"Chi servir non brama amor,"* the third, *"Quando di primavera."* The score is also rich in ensemble numbers, including a quartet, a quintet, and a duet between Fiorillo and Geronio which Francis Toye considers "one of the most plastic and varied essays of its kind ever written by the composer."

Two Hearts in Three-Quarter Time by Robert Stolz. *See Zwei Herzen in Dreivierteltakt.*

Undine by Albert Lortzing.

> Light fairy opera in four acts with text by the composer, based on a
> tale of the same name by Baron de la Motte Fouqué. First perform-
> ance: Magdeburg, Germany, April 21, 1845. First American perform-
> ance: New York, October 9, 1856.

In 1811, Baron de la Motte Fouqué published a German romance describing the legend of Undine, a water sprite, who acquires a soul after
marrying a mortal. When her husband falls in love with a female mortal, Undine returns to the sea. But on the young man's wedding night,
she rises from the deep to deliver him a fatal kiss. This story is the source
of Lortzing's *Undine,* a remarkable German light opera in which the
German romantic movement, previously established by Karl Maria von
Weber, is successfully continued.

The libretto is only freely based on the Fouqué romance. Hugo von
Ringstetten is a knight errant in legendary times. He meets and falls
in love with Undine, whom he believes to be a village girl. Undine finally
confesses she is a water sprite who can regain her soul only if she finds
a mortal husband who will remain ever true to her. Hugo promises to
become that husband. But soon after their marriage, he succumbs to the
seductive attractions of Berthalda, the Duke's daughter. Because she has
been betrayed, Undine must return to the sea. Though his conscience
is tormented, Hugo decides to marry Berthalda. On his wedding night,
Undine rises out of the sea. Seeing her, Hugo rushes to embrace her.
Undine drags him down to his death in her watery kingdom.

The composer who influenced Lortzing most decisively in this opera
was not Weber but Mendelssohn. Lortzing's romantic melodies have
Mendelssohnian sweetness and grace rather than the expressive and dramatic qualities of Weber. Such ear-caressing lyricism is one of the reasons why this opera has become a favorite. This lyricism can be found
in Undine's first act air, *"Ich scheide nun";* Hugo's second-act romance,
"Es wohnt am Seegestade," and his subsequent arias, *"Vater, Mutter,
Schwestern, Brueder"* and *"An des Rheines gruenen Ufer";* Undine's
third-act song, *"Nun ist's vollbracht";* and the fourth-act duet, *"Ich war
in meinen jungen Jahren,"* with its poignant refrain, *"In Wein ist Wahr-
heit."* But beyond such affecting lyricism, the score is distinguished for
the way in which comic episodes and sprightly choral pages are interpolated within the tragic framework of the play as a whole, giving the

work a lightness of mood and character it would not otherwise possess. In a similarly light manner is the graceful ballet music for orchestra in the second act.

(The) Unforeseen Meeting or **The Pilgrims to Mecca** by Christoph Willibald Gluck. *See* (*La*) *Rencontre imprévue.*

Utopia Limited or **The Flowers of Progress** by Gilbert and Sullivan.

Comic opera in two acts with text by W. S. Gilbert and music by Arthur Sullivan. First performance: Savoy Theater, London, October 7, 1893. First American performance: New York, March 26, 1894.

This is the last written Gilbert and Sullivan comic opera which is still given an occasional performance; in New York it received an off-Broadway revival on April 7, 1960. Only one more Gilbert and Sullivan opera came after *Utopia Limited: The Grand Duke,* which opened at the Savoy Theater on March 7, 1896, but today is rarely given. *The Grand Duke* had to wait until May 11, 1961, to receive its first professional performance in the United States; a non-professional première had taken place in 1937 and a non-professional revival in 1956.

Four years separated *Utopia Limited* from its distinguished predecessor, *The Gondoliers.* During the run of the latter comic opera, Gilbert and Sullivan had come to what then seemed a permanent separation, after a relationship which (however fruitful artistically) had been given to continual stormy outbursts of temper and fiery displays of temperament by poth parties. The immediate cause of the rupture was the price of new carpets for the Savoy Theater which D'Oyly Carte had charged to the expense account of *The Gondoliers.* Gilbert blew up insisting that he was no more required to pay for carpets for the theater than for other repairs. An effort to placate Gilbert was made at a meeting arranged in D'Oyly Carte's office. But Gilbert again lost his temper and became abusive. When he demanded from Sullivan where he stood on this issue, and discovered to his horror that the composer sided with D'Oyly Carte, he left in a huff. The next day he demanded an apology from Sullivan; more, he insisted that they break off all business relations with D'Oyly Carte. When Sullivan stoutly refused, Gilbert announced flatly he would never again work with Sullivan.

During the next few years, Sullivan pursued a career in grand opera which was nothing short of disastrous. Gilbert wrote some plays that were, at best, only moderately successful. D'Oyly Carte, who had produced Sullivan's operas at a terrible financial loss, began to seek some way of rehabilitating his fortunes and urged Sullivan to return to writing comic operas. At first D'Oyly Carte had in mind for Sullivan a collaborator other than Gilbert, his first choice being young James Barrie and his second, Bernard Shaw. Barrie's libretto, however, proved unacceptable to Sullivan, and Shaw was not interested in writing comic opera texts. It was only then that D'Oyly Carte realized that what was now called for was a resumption of the old Gilbert and Sullivan partnership. By the end of 1892 he had managed to convince both men to work together again—and the partnership was resumed with *Utopia Limited.*

Utopia Limited was a political satire in the vein of *Iolanthe* (which see). Almost as if in recapitulation, Gilbert poked his satirical barbs at most of the English institutions he had previously mocked in earlier operas: the Army, Navy, Parliament, British monarchy, English commerce, the courts, women's colleges. *Utopia Limited* is an island in the South Pacific ruled over by Paramount the First, a kindly, well-tempered, naïve, and humorous fellow who delights in writing in a private journal scandalous (and often apocryphal) pieces about his own escapades. His eldest daughter, Zara—who looks askance at these pieces without knowing that their author is none other than her father—is sent back to England for her education. During her absence, Lady Sophy, an English governess, is presenting the two other princesses as models of English behavior. After Zara comes back from England, accompanied by six British "flowers of progress" trained in the ways of English life and mores and embodying the essence of English virtue, she tries to remodel the island along English lines. A promoter goes about the business of organizing the island into a well-financed corporation, while its social life is radically revamped to conform to British standards, with laughable consequences. Zara's two sisters become caricatures of English propriety; a cabinet council is conducted along the lines of a minstrel show. When things go from bad to worse, Zara suddenly recalls that she has forgotten to introduce the most English of all reforms—government by party. It is immediately instituted: "Utopia will no longer be a Monarchy (Limited) but, what is a great deal better, a limited Monarchy." The king of Utopia salutes the king of England. The king's two aides who had been conspiring a revolt are banished. And Zara finds romantic fulfillment with Fitzbattle.

Utopia Limited is decidedly third-rate Gilbert and Sullivan. Isaac

Goldberg points out that Gilbert's humor was "repetitious and forced. . . . By the time he had come to the end of the piece, he had forgotten the beginning. . . . Topsy-turvy had gone to seed." Sullivan's music is not much better, for the most part "hasty and even careless. . . . His court music is uniformly bad. The entrance song of King Paramount in Act I reeks with musical platitudes." Goldberg sums up by saying that the score as a whole was little more than "skilled routine from a tired master. Sundown was near."

The collaboration of Gilbert and Sullivan did not progress smoothly during the writing of *Utopian Limited*. Sullivan had insisted that he no longer found a middle-aged woman in love a funny spectacle, and to please him Gilbert had to give his female character some "pathetic interest." Sullivan insisted that the second-act finale was weak and demanded radical revisions; in rebuttal, Gilbert told Sullivan to write his music first and he, Gilbert, would then try to fit words to music (the first time they ever attempted such an arrangement).

The opera did not do too well. It had been costly to mount and the receipts during its run of 245 performances were consistently poor. Thus the renewal of collaboration between Gilbert and Sullivan proved for the most part an unhappy event—even if, on opening night, it was a highly sentimental one. At that performance, after the final curtain, while Gilbert was taking his bow, Sullivan suddenly appeared from the wings to join him and to shake hands with him warmly. The audience, fully aware of the rift that had so long separated the pair, rose to its feet and shouted itself hoarse, happy to witness the reconciliation of the two collaborators. But that reconciliation proved short-lived. After one more sorry effort—*The Grand Duke*—the separation of Mr. Words and Mr. Music became complete and permanent.

(The) **Vagabonds** by Carl Ziehrer. *See (Die) Landstreicher.*

(Die) **Verkaufte Braut** by Bedřich Smetana. *See (The) Bartered Bride.*

(Das) **Verwunschene Schloss** [*The Haunted Castle*] by Karl Milloecker.

Operetta in five scenes with text by Alois Berla. First performance: Vienna, March 23, 1878.

This operetta, with which Milloecker gained his first success, preceded the same composer's masterwork, *The Beggar Student* (which see), by some four years.

In an eighteenth-century Tyrolean village, the castle of the banished Count von Geiersburg is regarded as haunted. Only Seppel, a cowherd, is skeptical, and this cynicism brings about his dismissal from his job. With his faithful friend, the shepherd Andreas, he leaves his lodgings and finds shelter within the castle. There, to their amazement, they are confronted by a beautiful and attractively gowned woman. Their terror is somewhat assuaged when they learn she is Coralie, a famous singer, one of several guests invited to a masquerade party given by the Count who has secretly returned to the village. Coralie playfully informs Seppel and Andreas that all the women in the castle are under the spell of enchantment, from which they can be released only by a kiss. Andreas proceeds to kiss all the charming girls. When the lights in the castle go out, Andreas faints with fright. He is carried off to an old woman's hut where he is led to believe that everything he had just witnessed in the castle had been a dream. Seppel, however, has been detained within the castle. Convinced that the earlier events never happened, Andreas heads a group of peasants to storm the haunted citadel and free Seppel. The Count then informs them that all is well. The castle is not haunted at all; all the goings-on are the consequence of his return home. Seppel, now reemployed as a cowherd, can woo and win Myrtle, a girl he has loved all the while.

Some impressive moments in the score arises from Milloecker's gift to portray realistically the ghostlike and macabre world of a hunted castle. But the most popular vocal exerpts are those in which he simulates the fresh, open charm of Austrian folk songs: in the duet of Seppel and Andreas, "*O du himmelblauer See,*" and in Myrtle's ballade of the haunted castle. Austrian, too, in their lusty vitality are the peasant dances.

Victoria und ihr Husar [*Victoria and Her Hussar*] by Paul Abraham.

> Operetta in three acts and prologue with text by Alfred Gruenwald and Fritz Loehner-Beda, based on a Hungarian play by Emmerich Foeldes. First performance: Vienna, December 23, 1930.

A wide geographical area is covered by the setting of an operetta which has enjoyed outstanding success in the Germanic countries and which in

1933 was made into a successful European motion picture: from a little village in Hungary to St. Petersburg, Siberia, and even the Orient, in the years just before 1918. Countess Victoria is in despair, having heard that her fiancé, Aladar Koltay, a Hungarian cavalry captain, has been killed in action during World War I. After a period of mourning, she marries John Cunlight, an American diplomat, with whom she travels to Tokyo where he has been appointed envoy. Meanwhile, in Siberia, Koltay is a prisoner-of-war awaiting death sentence. He manages to escape and makes his way to Tokyo where he seeks help at the American legation. Thus Victoria and her Hussar are brought face to face again. Victoria's husband, however, has no idea that this refugee is Victoria's one-time lover. When John gets a new appointment in St. Petersburg, he takes the Hussar with him under embassy protection. In St. Petersburg, Koltay begs in vain for Victoria to desert her husband and return to him. In time, John learns about Koltay—a discovery, however, which does not keep him from protecting the Hussar from the Russians. The Hussar, in a fit of wounded pride, gives himself up to the enemy. Crushed by this second loss of the man she really loves, Victoria returns to her native land, and her husband, John, once again in a spirit of generosity, effects Koltay's release from the Russians. Some time later, at a Hungarian harvest festival, three couples are to be honored. John Sunlight arrives, meets his long-absent wife, and together they are selected as the third couple for honors. When Koltay suddenly appears on the scene, both John and Victoria can no longer ignore the glaring truth that Victoria and the Hussar belong to each other. Magnanimously, John steps aside and allows his wife to go to the man she loves.

Paul Abraham, a serious composer before turning to operetta, was unusually skillful in creating music that evoked the rapidly shifting backgrounds. At turns, as demanded by the setting, his music acquires a delightful Russian or Hungarian or Japanese personality. But the score is also rich with fox trots and waltzes. In the fox-trot rhythm are *"Ja, so ein Maedel," "Meine Mama war aus Yokohama,"* and *"Mausi, suess warst du heute Nacht."* The best waltzes are *"Reich mir zum Abschied noch einmal die Haende"* and *"Pardon, Madame, ich bin verliebt."* Still another popular melody is found in Koltay's love song, *"Nur ein Maedel gibt es auf der Welt."*

(La) Vie parisienne [*Parisian Life*] by Jacques Offenbach.

> Opéra-bouffe in five acts with text by Henri Meilhac and Ludovic Halévy. First performance: Théâtre du Palais-Royal, Paris, October 31, 1866. First American performances: Booth Theater, New York, March 29, 1869 (in French); New York, November 15, 1869 (in German); New York, March 18, 1884 (in English).

This paean to the gaiety of Paris differs markedly from other and earlier Offenbach opéra-bouffes. In *La Belle Hélène* (which see) and *Orpheus in the Underworld* (which see), Offenbach satirized contemporary life by recreating the mythological or distant past within contemporary terms. In *La Vie parisienne*, it is the Paris of Offenbach's own time that comes in for mockery and laughter. In his earlier masterworks, Offenbach's characters were either ancient gods, mythological figures, or medieval heroes. In *La Vie parisienne*, the characters come from recognizable Parisian society, often the society of the lower classes. Indeed, it is in its sympathetic treatment of some of its humbler characters that *La Vie parisienne* strikes an altogether new democratic note for Offenbach. To S. S. Kracauer, this comic opera provides a picture of "the social turmoil produced by liberal capitalism. A cobbler and glovemaker are called upon to perform great deeds; domestic servants imitate the behavior and manners of their employers; a headwaiter is required to serve as diplomat and judge."

Baron von Gondermark and his wife have come to Paris for a holiday. At the railway station they are noticed by Baron von Gardefen who, attracted to the lovely female visitor, offers his services. He introduces himself as an employee of the Grand Hotel, but then he conducts them to his own home where he has Jean the shoemaker and Gabrielle the glovemaker, and their friends, disport themselves as the upper crust of French society. Eager to plunge into the whirling night life of Paris with the beautiful Baroness von Gondermark, Gardefen induces the Baron to go out on the town with Bobinet, a friend of Gardefen's who assumes the identity of the Baron. The two men-on-the-town have the time of their lives, surrounded by beautiful women, and at one place Baron von Gondermark even participates in the notorious can-can. Meanwhile, the real Baron von Gardefen makes love to Baroness von Gondermark until the latter is rescued by Bobinet's aunt, the Baroness von Quimper. Gardefen then makes a discreet withdrawal, Baron von Gondermark returns from his escapade, and all the members of the cast give vent to their happy spirits at a festive ball.

Those concerned with its production were sure that *La Vie parisienne* would be a failure, since they regarded contemporary characters a bore, the topical subjects dull, and the escapades of the two Barons thoroughly unconvincing. But Offenbach had faith in the play and was sure of the outcome; and he proved to be right. *La Vie parisienne* was a sensation. Its effect on the audience was, as Jules Claretie said at the time, as if "the whole house had been taking hashish." The whirling can-can music; the rapturous ballroom music of the concluding scene; the intoxicating airs of Baroness von Gondermark, "*Je suis veuve*" and "*On va courir*"; the no less appealing melodies of Baron von Gardefen, "*Avant toute chose*" and "*Dans cette ville*"—all proved irresistible. There was more than one critic to insist that here the composer had succeeded in creating one of his freshest and most exciting scores.

Vienna Life or **Vienna Blood** by Johann Strauss II. *See Wiener Blut.*

(The) Village Soothsayer by Jean-Jacques Rousseau. *See (Le) Devin du village.*

(Der) Vogelhaendler [*The Bird Dealer*] by Karl Zeller.

> Operetta in three acts with text by M. West and L. Held. First performance: Theater-an-der-Wien, Vienna, January 10, 1891. First American performances: New York, October 5, 1891 (in English under the title, *The Tyrolean*); New York, December 26, 1892 (in German).

Though certainly much less popular in America than either Suppé or Johann Strauss II, Zeller enjoyed a vogue in Vienna not far below these two masters of the operetta. Zeller's waltzes are of the same vintage as Strauss's: abundant in melodic sparkle and rich with the wine of good living. And it is his waltz writing that distinguishes his best operettas.

In the Rhine Palatinate, in or about 1700, Baron von Weps is a forest ranger and gamekeeper who has come to financial difficulties largely because of the extravagance of his nephew, Count Stanislaus. The latter comes for the first time to his uncle's village where, since he is unknown, he passes himself off as the Elector Palatinate. Another visitor to the village is the wandering bird merchant, Adam, come to see Christel, his fianceé. Before he can contact her he meets and flirts with the "peasant girl," Marie, in the local tavern; actually she is not a peasant girl at all, but the wife of the real Elector Palatinate, who plans to spy on her husband whom she suspects of carrying on an affair with Baroness Adelaide. When Adam finally gets to see Christel, he is disturbed to learn from her that she has no intention of marrying him unless he gets a permanent job. In fact, Christel has gone so far as to visit the palace of the Elector to entreat him to find a job for Adam. Stanislaus, playing the part of the Elector, grants her wish. This infuriates Adam who is certain Christel has compromised herself to get him this opportunity. Later on, Adam does get a job with the Elector, but through the efforts of the Elector's wife. Meanwhile, the Elector learns how Stanislaus has been masquerading, and at a party at the Elector's palace the young impostor is seized and faced with punishment. He must choose between a career in the army or mariage to Christel. The latter alternative proving the more attractive, preparations are hastily made for the wedding. But Christel has no intention in the world of marrying Stanislaus, having by this time become reconciled with Adam. Christel and Adam finally get married and leave for a Tyrolean honeymoon. Stanislaus is now willing and happy to accept Baroness Adelaide as his bride.

Two of the most attractive tunes are the waltzes "*Schau mir nur recht ins Gesicht*" and "*Froelich Pfalz, Gott, erhalt's.*" These are also attractive numbers: the sprightly march melody, *Kaempfe nie mit Frau'n*"; two songs of Adam, "*Schenkt man sich Rosen in Tirol*" and "*Wie mein Ahn'l zwanzig Jahr,*" the latter sometimes identified as the "nightingale song"; and Christel's joyful tune, "*Ich bin die Christel von der Post.*"

(Der) Waffenschmied [*The Armorer*] by Albert Lortzing.

Comic opera in three acts with text by the composer, based on *Liebhaber und Nebenbuhler in einer Person*, a comedy by F. W. Ziegler. First performance: Theater-an-der-Wien, Vienna, May 31, 1846. First American performance: New York, February 4, 1867.

Albert Lortzing's comic operas—of which *Undine* and *Der Wildschuetz* are represented in this volume—assume a place of acknowledged historic importance in the German musical theater. They combine the old traditions of the Singspiel with some of the aesthetics and approaches of the Romantic opera as crystallized by Weber. From the Singspiel, Lortzing derived gay entertainment, slight musical forms, light popular style, and pleasing little tunes. In *Der Waffenschmied,* also one of his masterworks, these lilting tunes are most often found in those characterizing Marie, whose portrayal was one of the freshest and most ingratiating creations of the German musical stage up to that time. His light touch is further evident in many of his comic scenes. From German romantic opera, Lortzing inherited an expansive manner in writing both for the orchestra and for chorus (as in the choral hymn to Spring in the second act, the chorus of the journeymen with which the opera opens, and the second-act finale). Thus, in a manner of speaking, *Der Waffenschmied* is a work that helped bring a comic style to folk opera.

Der Waffenschmied, which followed *Der Wildschuetz* by three and a half years, is probably the composer's most celebrated comic opera. It was first performed in Theater-an-der-Wien in Vienna soon after Lortzing had come there to assume the post of conductor, and it was an immediate favorite.

The action takes place in the city of Worms in the sixteenth century. Count von Liebenau is in love with Marie, daughter of the armorer, Stadinger. In order to win her, the Count goes to work for the armorer, disguised as a humble apprentice, Conrad. He woos her first as a Count, then as a smithy. Marie is more attracted to Conrad, but only because she thinks a man of the Count's social station is out of her reach. The Count assumes an air of wounded pride and jealousy in being beaten out by a smithy. To resolve this complicated situation, the Count attacks the house of the armorer and demands that Marie be turned over to him. Everybody is greatly pleased by this dramatic turn of events when they learn that the Count and Conrad are the same person.

One of the most brilliant, unforgettable vocal excerpts in this score is Marie's poignant description of Conrad during the first-act finale, *"Reichtum allein, tuts nicht auf Erden."* More vigorous in style is Stadinger's famous first-act "Armorer's Song." To Stadinger are assigned several more robust and effective pages: in the second act, *"Du laesst mich kalt von hinnen scheiden,"* and his third-act reminiscences, *"Auch ich war ein Juengling."* Also worthy of special note are the first-act aria of Marie's governess, *"Welt du kannst mir nicht gefallen"* and Conrad's second-act air, *"War einst ein junger Springinsfeld."*

(A) **Waltz Dream** by Oscar Straus. *See (Ein) Walzertraum.*

(Ein) **Walzertraum** [*A Waltz Dream*] by Oscar Straus.

> Operetta in three acts with book by Felix Doermann and Leopold Jacobson, based on *Buch der Abenteuer*, a story by Hans Muellers. First performance: Karlstheater, Vienna, March 2, 1907. First American performance: Broadway Theater, New York, January 27, 1908 (in English); Weber's Theater, New York, December 25, 1911 (in German).

Oscar Straus, then already the composer of several successful operettas, used to visit *Eisvogel,* a restaurant in Vienna's Prater. One of its attractions was an all-girl orchestra, "The Prater Swallows," led by an attractive young blond violinist. One evening, this young musician stopped at Straus's table and asked him why he didn't write a waltz for her orchestra. The next day Straus came to the restaurant with the waltz. The leader of the orchestra hummed the melody as she scanned the manuscript, Straus went over to the piano to support her with the accompaniment, and soon members of the orchestra started to join in the performance. This episode provided Straus with an infectious idea: A scene such as this could provide a wonderful climax for an operetta, and a wonderful frame in which to place a soaring waltz melody. The more he thought about it, the more he liked the idea. Why not, indeed, an operetta about an all-girl orchestra, with a heroine like its attractive violinist?

He discussed these ideas with Leopold Jacobson, another of the habitués of the restaurant. Jacobson was a Viennese writer who harbored the ambition to write an operetta libretto. As it happened, Jacobson had just devised a plot about a Viennese officer commandeered into a foreign country to marry a princess. He told Straus that a subject like this could be made to fit in nicely with Straus's suggestions. The lieutenant could be made to fall in love with the orchestra leader, and she might then renounce him for the sake of the State.

Felix Doermann, a man nimble in the writing of song lyrics, was called in by Jacobson and Straus as a third collaborator. The three men went off to Baden, the resort near Vienna, and went to work with such enthusiasm and industry that they completed their operetta in about two weeks.

The hero is Lieutenant Niki, who is ordered by the Austrian Emperor to marry Helen, princess of a neighboring state. The heroine in Franzi, leader of a Viennese girl orchestra. As the operetta begins, the wedding of Niki and Helen is being celebrated in a foreign kingdom. But Niki does not love Helen, and besides he is homesick for his beloved Vienna. His nostalgia for home is intensified when he suddenly hears a Viennese all-girl orchestra play the soft strains of a rapturous Viennese waltz. He meets its leader, Franzi, and falls in love with her. She returns that love, but Franzi has no idea who the dashing lieutenant is. When she discovers he is the Prince Consort, she decides to return to Vienna and forget all about the man she loves, leaving him free to marry the princess.

A Waltz Dream is one of the most successful operettas ever written— one of those magic Viennese productions which helped to establish for all time the formulas and ritual of operetta entertainment. It has had over ten thousand performances in all parts of the civilized world, a thousand performances in Vienna alone. It has been a triumph in Berlin, Paris, Milan, St. Petersburg, Sydney, Tokyo, Johannesburg, London, and New York. (Strange to say, initially it was a failure in London when first given at Hicks Theater on March 7, 1908. But when revived by George Edwardes in a lavish production—and with Lily Elsie playing Franzi— it finally conquered English theatergoers decisively.) In New York, in 1908, it rivaled only Lehár's *The Merry Widow* in the hearts of Broadwayites. In this production, Edward Johnson (later a famous opera tenor, and after that general manager of the Metropolitan Opera) was starred as Niki. In 1931, *A Waltz Dream* became one of Maurice Chevalier's early Hollywood triumphs. Renamed *The Smiling Lieutenant,* it co-starred Claudette Colbert and was directed by Ernst Lubitsch. *A Waltz Dream* helped to make Straus one of the most celebrated and wealthiest composers in Vienna, second only to Lehár himself. It also helped to make a fortune for the Karlstheater where it was introduced and which had been on the verge of bankruptcy before the operetta opened.

The world-famous waltz, *"Da draussen im duftigen Garten"*—with its soaring refrain, *"Leise, ganz leise, klingt's durch den Raum"*—is the pivot on which the entire operetta spins so gaily; it is introduced by Niki and his companion, Lieutenant Montschi, in the first act. This waltz must be included in the dozen or so of the greatest Viennese waltzes ever written. No less inviting in their gracious style and infectious mood are the second-act love duet of Niki and Franzi, *"O du lieber"*; Helen's beautiful air in a folk-song style, *"Ich hab' einen Mann"*; the arresting little march with which the second act opens and closes; the amusing "Dynasty Trio" which dared to poke fun at the pretentious attitudes of the Hapsburgs; the piquant little duet, *"Piccolo, piccolo, tsin, tsin, tsin,"* with its amusing interpolations by solo violin, solo piccolo, solo flute, and strings.

During the Nazi regime in Germany and Austria, *A Waltz Dream* was banned, since its authors were Jews. But in 1951 the operetta was revived in Munich with phenomenal success. On this occasion, the book was modernized by Robinson and Rogati. Straus happened to be passing through Munich when his operetta was being played, and he came to the performance midway in the first act. He was soon recognized. The audience rose to its feet to give the eighty-two-year-old composer a rousing ovation. After the second-act curtain, Straus was dragged to the conductor's stand to lead the orchestra in the instrumental interlude preceding the third act. Once again the applause and cheers were prolonged and deafening. "Ladies and gentlemen," Straus said simply, "thank you very much, indeed. But please remember—there's still a third act." Only then did the storm subside and the performance continue.

(The) White Lady by François Boieldieu. See (La) Dame blanche.

(The) White Horse Inn [Im Weissen Roessl] by Ralph Benatzky.

Operetta in three acts with text by Erik Charell and Hans Mueller, freely adapted from one by Blumenthal and Kadelburg. First performance: Berlin, November 8, 1930. First American performance: Center Theater, New York, October 1, 1936.

By the late 1920's, the conventional German and Austrian operetta was becoming a dying form of musical theater. But at the dusk of a long and rich career it was still capable of occasionally sending forth a wondrous burst of light. *The White Horse Inn* was one of the last of these German operettas to circle the globe, the last of a royal breed that had produced *Die Fledermaus, The Merry Widow,* and *The Chocolate Soldier* (all which see). It was given well over a thousand performances throughout Europe, enjoyed a moderately successful run in New York, and has become a stage classic, continually revived in the German-speaking world.

The White Horse Inn directs a nostalgic and sentimental glance back to Hapsburg Austria; indeed, Emperor Francis Joseph himself is one of the characters. Just before World War I, Frau Josepha, owner of a lovely inn fronting Wolfgangsee in Austria, is pursued by two men. One is her head waiter, Leopold. The other is Erich Siedler, a lawyer and perennial guest at the hotel. Leopold, aroused by jealousy, gets embroiled in an ugly quarrel with Frau Josepha. Impatient with his surly moods she fires him, ordering him to leave the inn as soon as possible. But she quickly changes her mind and humbly asks Leopold to stay on, when she receives the awesome news that the Emperor himself is due to visit her place for a few days. When the Emperor arrives, Leopold welcomes him with a carefully prepared speech. But seeing Josepha at the side of Siedler makes him lose his presence of mind and he suddenly denounces the proprietress vehemently. This leads Josepha to pour out her heart to the Emperor, to confess that she loves the lawyer. But the Emperor tries to convince her that Siedler is not the man for her, that she would be wise to consider Leopold who is so deeply in love with her. When Leopold comes to bid Josepha farewell, she coyly tells him that he is no longer her head waiter. But she adds hastily she is giving him a new job—as her husband. Siedler is by no means upset by this arrangement, for he has fallen in love with young, vivacious Ottilie.

The popularity of this wonderful operetta brings hordes of visitors each year to the White Horse Inn at Wolfgangsee, in St. Wolfgang, Austria. Busload after busload comes to this picturesque little Austrian town to disgorge tourists at the setting of Benatzky's operetta—the visitors enjoying the wonderful vista while sipping coffee with whipped cream. A portrait of the composer hangs prominently on the wall of the terrace, as do several other pictures on which are inscribed quotations from the two main songs of the operetta. Ash trays, in which similar quotations are reproduced, are favorite souvenirs.

The two main melodies which are quoted on the walls and ashtrays are, *"Es muss ein wunderbares sein"* (the principal love song), and the waltz, *"Im weissen Roessl am Wolfgangsee."* In the score can also be found a fox-trot (*"Was kann der Sigismund dafuer"*), a tango (*"Und als der Herrgott Mai gemacht"*), an intoxicating song in a "Heuriger" (*"Erst wann's aus sein wird mit aner Musi"*), and a haunting tune (*"Zuschau'n kann ich nicht"*).

When *The White Horse Inn* came to Broadway in 1936, the book was adapted by David Freedman and lyrics were written by Irving Caesar.

The cast (which included a troupe of *Schu'plattl* dancers from Austria) was headed by William Gaxton and Kitty Carlisle.

(The) White Lady, by François Boieldieu. *See* (*La*) *Dame Blanche.*

Wiener Blut [*Vienna Blood* or *Vienna Life*] by Johann Strauss II.

> Operetta in three acts with text by Victor Léon and Leo Stein with Johann Strauss's music adapted by Adolf Mueller, Jr. First performance: Vienna, October 26, 1899. First American performance: Broadway Theater, January 23, 1901.

Johann Strauss did not write a score specifically for the text of *Wiener Blut*. This is a synthetic operetta for which Strauss's music was borrowed and adapted. (This stage work is not to be confused with Strauss' famous waltz of the same name.) The operetta was written and produced a few months after Strauss's death.

The period is that of the Congress of Vienna. Count Zedlau, a delegate from a small Thuringian province, becomes a playboy in the Austrian capital. He is carrying on an affair at a Doebling villa with Franzi, a Viennese dancer. When the Count's superior, Prince Ypsheim, comes to visit him, he mistakes Franzi for the Count's wife, and the Count's wife, Gabriele, for his mistress. To avoid scandal, the Count prevails on the Prince to pass Franzi off as his own wife. But at the embassy ball—to which both Franzi and Gabriele are invited—the Count's extra-marital activities are complicated by the fact that he is suddenly attracted to Pepi, with whom he is plotting a rendezvous in Hietzing. Both Franzi and Gabriele get wind of this and follow the Count to the Hietzing Casino, where they surprise him with Pepi in a secluded arbor. Franzi now washes her hands of the Count, and even becomes a willing ally in effecting the reconciliation of the Count and his wife.

The theme song of the operetta is the waltz sung in the second act by the Count and Countess: "*Wiener Blut, eig'ner Saft, voller Kraft, voller Glut!*" The score boasts three more ravishing waltzes in "*Du, suesses Zuckertaeuberl mein,*" "*Gruess dich Gott, du liebes Nesterl,*" and "*Stoss an, stoss an, du Liebchen mein.*"

When given on Broadway in 1901 as *Vienna Life,* book and lyrics were adapted by Glen MacDonough, and the cast was headed by Raymond Hitchcock and Ethel Jackson.

(Der) Wildschuetz or **Die Stimme der Natur** [*The Poacher* or *The Voice of Nature*] by Albert Lortzing.

> Comic opera in three acts with text by the composer, based on *Der Rehbock*, a comedy by A. von Kotzebue. First performance: Leipzig, Germany, December 31, 1842. First American performances: New York, March 25, 1859 (in German); Brooklyn, New York, November 9, 1931 (in English).

This was the composer's first successful comic opera, the first in which he skillfully combined basic elements of the Singspiel (early German musical comedy) with nineteenth-century German romantic traditions. *Der Wildschuetz* preceded Lortzing's masterwork, *Der Waffenschmied* (which see), by three and a half years. We can detect in the earlier work the composer's special gift for writing for the popular stage. Here he reveals a fine sense for humorous characterizations (as in his witty music portraying the bumpkin Baculus and the vivacious Baroness in her disguise as Gretchen); extraordinary skill in writing for ensembles and chorus (as in the contrapuntal "billiard quintet" and the children's chorus in the finale); and his gift for parody (as in the travesty on Mendelssohn's *Antigone* in the scene where the Countess compels her servant to listen to a reading of Sophocles).

Der Wildschuetz has been described as "a bustling comedy of intrigue and disguise." In the early nineteenth century, in a small German village, Baculus, the schoolmaster, is celebrating his marriage to Gretchen. His joy, however, is dampened by the news that he has just lost his job for having shot a deer. He wants to send Gretchen to plead his case with Count of Eberbach, but is hesitant to do so, knowing full well the Count's weakness for young, lovely ladies. To help out Baculus, the Count's sister, Baroness Freimann, goes to her brother disguised as Gretchen. The Count invites her to a party he is giving in his castle, where he entreats her to desert the schoolmaster and come to live with him. In fact, the Count offers Baculus a bonus of five thousand dollars to relinquish all his rights in Gretchen, which the schoolmaster accepts eagerly. When Baculus arrives to complete the bargain with the Count, he brings with him the real Gretchen, but the Count refuses to accept her since he recognizes she is not the girl he had bargained for. Only then does the false Gretchen appear to reveal herself as the Count's sister. Baculus gets back his job as schoolmaster, and Gretchen appears willing to let bygones be bygones—to forget the humiliating fact that Baculus had been willing to sell her to the Count for a price.

One of the most celebrated basso arias in the entire German comic-opera literature can be found in this work: It is Baculus' second-act song of delight when he discovers he can sell Gretchen for five thousand dollars (*"Fuenftausend Thaler"*). The first act is distinguished for the duet of Baculus and Gretchen as they celebrate their marriage ("A.B.C.D., *der Junggesellenstand tut weh*") and the Baroness' entrance song (*"Auf des Lebens raschen Wogen"*). Outstanding in the third act are the robust song with chorus of the Count of Erebach as he disports himself with village girls, *"Heiterkeit und Froehlichkeit,"* and the quartet, *"Kann es im Erdenleben."*

Women Are Like That by Wolfgang Amadeus Mozart. *See Così fan tutte.*

(The) World of the Moon by Joseph Haydn. *See (Il) Mondo della luna.*

(The) World Is Beautiful by Franz Lehár. *See Schoen ist die Welt.*

(The) Yeomen of the Guard or **The Merryman and His Maid** by Gilbert and Sullivan.

> Comic opera in two acts with text by W. S. Gilbert and music by Arthur Sullivan. First performance: Savoy Theater, London, October 3, 1888. First American performance: Casino Theater, New York, October 17, 1888.

Both in text and music, *The Yeomen of the Guard* is one of the most ambitious of the Savoyard operas; indeed, it is the one that comes closest to being an opera. Gilbert had become impatient with the kind of trivialities and nonsense he had thus far been dispensing, and wanted this time to write a libretto with some depth, emotional impact, and effective characterization. Sullivan also aspired to new horizons and deeper values. Each thought he had succeeded; each considered *The Yeomen of the Guard* his best comic opera; each saw in it a fulfillment (or at least a partial one) of his aim to reach for higher artistic levels.

In writing his text, Gilbert was more than subconsciously influenced by the libretto prepared by Edward Fitzball for the romantic English opera of William Vincent Wallace, *Maritana* (which see). Both the *London Times* and *Punch* commented on the similarity between the two texts— the *Times* graciously, *Punch* with a dash of vitriol. Perhaps it was this strong leaning on the work of another man that made *The Yeomen of the Guard* one of the least characteristic of the Savoyard operas.

It is the only Gilbert and Sullivan comic opera that does not open with a chorus. When the curtain rises, Phoebe, daughter of Sergeant Meryll (yeoman of the guard) points out the tribulations of a girl in love ("When a Maiden Loves"). Wilfred Shadbolt, head jailer and assistant tormenter, loves her, and in vain does he try to win her interest. Now the yeomen make their appearance ("Tower Warders, Under Orders"), followed by Dame Carruthers, housekeeper to the Tower, who pledges her loyalty to it ("When Our Gallant Norman Foes"). Meanwhile, Phoebe is disconcerted to learn that Colonel Fairfax is about to be executed. Leonard, son of Sergeant Meryll, brings an additional piece of news, namely, that no reprieve is forthcoming for Fairfax. After making his entry, Fairfax speaks about his fortitude ("Is Life a Boon?"). At this point two strolling players appear, Jack Point and Elsie Maynard ("I Have a Song to Sing, O"). Though Elsie is in love with Jack, she is willing, for a price, to marry a man about to be beheaded; for Fairfax made this offer in order to keep a hated relative from inheriting his fortune. Jack becomes autobiographical and speaks about his career as a jester ("I've Wisdom from the East and from the West") just before Elsie carries the news that her marriage to the condemned man has been consummated ("'Tis Done! I am a Bride!"). Phoebe meanwhile has managed to cajole Wilfred Shadbolt into giving her the keys to Fairfax's cell ("Were I Thy Bride"). Thus Fairfax manages to escape, disguised as Leonard. Confusion runs riot. The jailer is arrested for neglect of duty, and Elsie laments the strange turn of events.

In the second act, Point describes all the trials of a jester's life ("Oh, a Private Buffoon is a Light-Hearted Loon"), after Dame Carruthers has taken the yeomen to task for having let their prisoner escape. Point and Shadbolt make a pact. Point will teach the jailer the niceties of his profession if, in return, the jailer swears to shoot Fairfax. Fairfax now contemplates his newly won freedom ("Free From His Fetters Grim"), while also pondering the question as to whom he had married, since Elsie had been masked and her identity kept a secret. But Dame Carruthers tells him his wife is Elsie. Still in disguise as Leonard, Fairfax tests Elsie by proposing marriage to her and is turned down, even though she is somewhat attracted to him ("When a Wooer Goes a-Wooing"). And now it is Point's turn to woo Elsie and be rejected. Matters get increasingly involved until the real Leonard comes forth with Fairfax's reprieve. Fairfax is now free to reveal his true identity to Elsie, who is overjoyed to discover she is married to the man she really loves. And Dame Carruthers and Meryll learn that Fate had intended them for each other.

The *London Times* described Sullivan's music as "most imaginative, and most unpredictable." Undoubtedly what had inspired such an appraisal had been Sullivan's contrapuntal skill in writing the choral passages and the new dramatic impact in some of his tunes. If any doubt at all existed in Sullivan's seriousness of purpose, it was dispelled by the overture. Here was no mere potpourri of main melodies assembled and orchestrated by a hack, but an overture written by Sullivan himself in which the thematic material from the opera is developed into an integrated tone poem full of character and personality, rich in atmosphere, and skillful in architectonic construction. Sullivan once said—with an enthusiasm that was probably excessive—that this overture was good enough to be played at symphony concerts.

Zampa or **La Fiancée de marbre** [*Zampa* or *The Marble Betrothed*] by Louis Ferdinand Hérold.

Opéra-comique in three acts with text by Anna Honoré Joseph Mélesville. First performance: Opéra-Comique, Paris, May 3, 1831. First American performances: Park Theater, New York, August 12, 1833 (in French); New York, March 29, 1841 (in English); New York, May 21, 1862 (in German); New York, December 17, 1866 (in Italian).

The legend about the marble statue which comes to life to destroy its enemy is most famous in opera through Mozart's immortal *Don Giovanni*. Hérold's *Zampa*, like the Mozart opera, emphasized the dramatic element in the legend, has a somewhat somber cast, and comes to a tragic ending.

This is much sterner stuff than we generally encounter in opéra-comique. Nevertheless, *Zampa* belongs with light opera because of its tuneful score. "There is the song," said B. Jouvain of this music, "beautifully attired; the musician takes it by the hand and places it in a setting of instrumentation which has languor, grace, buoyancy, and color."

The central character, Zampa, is the leader of a pirate band. He comes to the castle of Count Lugano on the Mediterranean where the marriage of Camilla and Alfonso is being celebrated. On the threat of killing both her father and her bridegroom if she prove unreasonable, Camilla is forced to desert Alfonso and go off with Zampa. Zampa celebrates his forthcoming marriage to Camilla in the castle. While inebriated, he impudently places a wedding ring on the forefinger of a statue of Alice, a girl who had died of a broken heart after Zampa had deserted her. Suddenly the statue crooks the finger and does not permit the ring to come off. Camilla comes to Zampa to beg him to free her. When Zampa refuses, Alfonso attacks him, and Camilla flees. Zampa orders his men to kill Alfonso at sight, while he himself goes in pursuit of Camilla. But the statue of Alice has come to life, to drag Zampa to his death in the sea. Camilla and Alfonso are now free to marry, and the statue of Alice emerges from the sea to return to its pedestal.

The overture has been a particular favorite of salon and semiclassical orchestras. It begins with the strong melody of the first-act pirate chorus. After a brief pause, rolls of the timpani and loud chords in the winds preface a beautiful song for the wind instruments. The religious atmosphere thus invoked is soon shattered by a dramatized section in which we hear a lovely melody for clarinet against plucked strings and a second lyrical thought for the violins.

One of the most poignant vocal excerpts comes in the third act—a song of heart-rending pathos in the form of a barcarolle, the duet "*Pourquoi trembler.*" Other distinguished vocal episodes include the first-act chorus of the pirates, the so-called "Recognition Duet," and the finale of the second act.

Zar und Zimmerman or **Die Zwei Peter** [*Czar and Carpenter* or *The Two Peters*] by Albert Lortzing.

Comic opera in three acts with libretto by the composer, based on *Le Bourgemestre de Sardam,* a play by Anna Honoré Joseph Mélesville,

J. T. Merle, and E. C. de Boirie. First performance: Municipal Theater, Leipzig, December 22, 1837. First American performances: Broadway Theater, New York, January 13, 1857 (in German); New York, February 8, 1882 (in English).

Lortzing described this, his masterwork, as "a sentimental comedy of contrasts." It is a folk comic opera based on an actual event in history: when Peter the Great of Russia worked as a carpenter in Holland. In the comic opera, Czar Peter of Russia is in Saardam, employed as a ship's carpenter under the assumed name of Peter Michaelov. His companion is Peter Ivanov, a Russian renegade, who is in love with Marie, daughter of the Burgomaster, Van Bett. She is a notorious coquette who takes delight in arousing her lover's jealousy by flirting with the French Ambassador, Chateauneuf. When the word circulates around Saardam that the Russian Czar is in town incognito, Peter Ivanov is suspected of being the ruler in question by the bungling and stupid Burgomaster. With the same gift for confusion, Van Bett also suspects the real Czar of being a criminal. Peter Michaelov allows his friend to pose as the Czar until he can decide when the time is ripe for his return to Russia. Van Bett, meanwhile, has written and rehearsed an elaborate cantata to honor Peter Ivanov. When the Burgomaster comes to sing in his cantata, he discovers to his horror that the real Czar has just sailed for his homeland. But before departing from Saardam, the Czar had pardoned Ivanov and had him appointed Imperial Superintendent, in which office Ivanov can woo and win Marie.

The best characterization in the text is that of Van Bett, around whom most of the comical episodes revolve. Perhaps the most amusing scene occurs in the third act when Van Bett comes to sing in his cantata for the supposed Czar. His first-act entrance song has long been a favorite with German comic bassos: "*O Sancta justitia,*" with its catchy refrain, "*O, ich bin klug und weise.*"

In the first act, besides the Burgomaster's buffo aria, the best vocal episodes include the opening chorus of the carpenters ("*Auf Gesellen, greift zur Axt*") and Marie's lament about the evils of jealousy ("*Die Eifersucht ist eine Plage*"). In the second act, special musical interest is centered upon the opening wedding chorus; Chateauneuf's beautiful air, "*Lebe wohl, mein flandrisch' Maedchen*"; and Marie's bridal song. The third act includes the Burgomaster's song with chorus, "*Heil sei dem Tag*"; the most celebrated romantic song in the entire opera, Peter's "*Sonst spielt' ich mit Zepter*"; the duet of Marie and Ivanov, "*Darf eine niedre Magd es wagen";* the Clog Dance (*Holzschutanz*); and the closing chorus in which Handel is parodied.

(Der) Zarewitsch [*The Crown Prince*] by Franz Lehár.

> Operetta in three acts with text by Béla Jenbach and Heinz Reichert, freely adapted from a play of the same name by Gabriella Zapolska-Scharlitt. First performance: Berlin, February 21, 1927.

Because its main setting is Russia, *Der Zarewitsch* finds Lehár occasionally introducing a Slavic personality into his musical writing. The hero —son of the Czar—is a young ascetic who has no use for physical or sensual pleasures. In order to stimulate his interest in women, the Prime Minister smuggles into his chambers Sonia, a delectable dancer. At first the young prince rejects her. When she finally succeeds in winning his interest, the Prince agrees to allow her to visit him each evening, but only on condition that their relationship remain platonic. Inevitably, a love interest grows between them, a development complicated by the fact that the girl finally selected as the Crown Prince's bride has just come to court. The Grand Duke now conspires with Sonia to have the Prince lose interest in her by having her hint darkly she has a whole legion of lovers. But on seeing how deeply she has hurt him with this confession, Sonia breaks down and confesses she was lying. They now vow that nothing must come between them. Escaping to Naples, they spend several idyllic weeks in a secluded villa. Their happiness is shattered when the Grand Duke arrives to remind the Prince of his royal duties. He must break with Sonia once and for all and return to Russia to marry the woman designated for him. The Crown Prince hesitates until a dispatch reaches him with the news that his father is dead and that he is now the Czar of all the Russias. He bids Sonia a tender farewell and goes home.

The song most strongly touched with Russian melancholy and languor is the touching Volga ballad of the Crown Prince, *"Es steht ein Soldat am Wolgastrand,"* with its touching refrain, *"Hast du dort droben vergessen auf mich?"* Two other melodies are in Lehár's more recognizable Austrian style: Sonia's song, *"Einer wird kommen,"* and that of the Crown Prince, *"Hab' nur dich allein."* The score also includes an infectious tango in *"Willst du?"* and a one-step in *"Heute abend komm' ich zu dir."*

(Der) **Zigeunerbaron** by Johann Strauss II. *See (The) Gypsy Baron.*

Zigeunerliebe by Franz Lehár. *See Gypsy Love.*

(Die) **Zirkusprinzessin** by Emmerich Kálmán. *See (The) Circus Princess.*

Zwei Herzen im Dreivierteltakt [*Two Hearts in Three-Quarter Time*] by Robert Stolz.

> Operetta in three acts with text by Paul Knepler and J. M. Welleminsky, based on the German motion picture of the same name with scenario by W. Reisch and F. Schulz. First performance: Zurich, Switzerland, September 30, 1933.

This operetta is most unusual in that it was adapted from a motion picture released three years earlier. The film had starred Oscar Karlweiss, Willy Forst, and Gertl Theimer and had enjoyed world-wide success. In fact, it was one of the earliest German art motion pictures imported from Europe to receive a wide and profitable distribution throughout the United States. And its main waltz—title the same as that of the picture—proved a hit on both sides of the Atlantic; it is not only Stolz's greatest song success, but also one of the most popular Austrian waltzes ever written.

The stage play, like the motion picture from which it came, told the story of an operetta being put into production in Vienna. The main characters involved in this undertaking are Nicki and Vicki Mahler, two librettists who are preparing a text for the composer, Anton Hofer. By the time their operetta reaches rehearsal, the producer demands a new waltz. The librettists are tempted to believe that the only way Hofer can be inspired to write such a waltz is to fall in love, and they contrive to have a young and charming actress, Mizzi, visit him. Mizzi's younger sister, Hedi—recently come home from boarding school—overhears the plan, waylays her sister, and goes in her stead to meet the composer. Hofer is so enchanted by her that he becomes inspired with a most wonderful melody. As he develops it at the piano, Hedi disappears. Later the same evening, Hofer discovers he has completely forgotten what his inspired melody sounds like. He is certain it will come back to him when Hedi does, but nobody seems to know who this Hedi is. During one of the rehearsals, Hofer is at the piano trying to recall his idea, when from the wings of the stage he hears a girl singing his waltz. She is, of course, Hedi. The opera has now found its main melody—and Hofer, the woman he loves.

The waltz that plays such a prominent part in this story, and recurs throughout the operetta, is *"Zwei Herzen im Dreivierteltakt"* ("Two Hearts in Three-Quarter Time")—now a Viennese classic. But there are other delightful tunes in the score: the waltz, *"Heute besuch ich mein Glueck"*; a torch song in a "blues" style, *"Du bist mein schoenste Traeumerei"*; the pert march tune, *"Wenn man zweimal leben koennte"*; the slow fox trot, *"Das ist der Schmerz beim ersten Kuss"*; and a secondary fox trot, *"Meine kleine Schwester heisst Hedi."*

APPENDIXES

Appendix One:

A Chronology of the European Musical Theater

1728 *The Beggar's Opera* (Pepusch)
1733 *La Serva padrona* (Pergolesi)
1752 *Le Devin du village* (Rousseau)
1754 *Il Filosofo di campagna* (Galuppi)
1760 *La Buona figliuola,* or *La Cecchina* (Piccinni)
1761 *Le Cadi dupé* (Gluck)
1764 *La Rencontre imprévue* (Gluck)
1768 *The Apothecary* (Haydn)
      Bastien and Bastienne (Mozart)
1769 *La Finta semplice* (Mozart)
1775 *La Finta giardiniera* (Mozart)
1777 *Il Mondo della luna* (Haydn)
1782 *The Abduction from the Seraglio* (Mozart)
      The Barber of Seville (Paisiello)
1786 *The Doctor and the Apothecary* (Dittersdorf)
      Der Schauspieldirektor (Mozart)
      The Marriage of Figaro (Mozart)
1790 *Così fan tutte* (Mozart)
1791 *The Magic Flute* (Mozart)
1792 *Il Matrimonio segreto* (Cimarosa)
1800 *The Caliph of Bagdad* (Boieldieu)
1810 *La Cambiale di matrimonio* (Rossini)
1811 *Abu Hassan* (Weber)
1813 *L'Italiana in Algeri* (Rossini)
      Il Signor Bruschino (Rossini)

1814   *Il Turco in Italia* (Rossini)
1816   *The Barber of Seville* (Rossini)
1817   *La Cenerentola* (Rossini)
        La Gazza ladra (Rossini)
1825   *La Dame blanche* (Boieldieu)
1828   *Le Comte Ory* (Rossini)
        La Muette de Portici (Auber)
1830   *Fra Diavolo* (Auber)
1831   *Zampa* (Hérold)
1832   *L'Elisir d'amore* (Donizetti)
        Le Pré aux clercs (Hérold)
1835   *L'Éclair* (Halévy)
1836   *Il Campanello di notte* (Donizetti)
        Le Postillon de Longjumeau (Adam)
1837   *Zar und Zimmermann* (Lortzing)
        Le Domino noir (Auber)
1840   *The Daughter of the Regiment* (Donizetti)
1841   *Les Diamants de la couronne* (Auber)
1842   *Der Wildschuetz* (Lortzing)
1843   *Don Pasquale* (Donizetti)
        The Bohemian Girl (Balfe)
1845   *Maritana* (Wallace)
        Undine (Lortzing)
1846   *Der Waffenschmied* (Lortzing)
1847   *Martha* (Flotow)
1849   *The Merry Wives of Windsor* (Nicolai)
1850   *Crispino e la comare* (Ricci)
1852   *La Poupée de Nuremberg* (Adam)
        Si j'étais roi (Adam)
1853   *Les Noces de Jeannette* (Massé)
1858   *The Barber of Bagdad* (Cornelius)
        Orphée aux enfers (Offenbach)
        Le Médecin malgré lui (Gounod)
1862   *Beatrice and Benedick* (Berlioz)
        The Lily of Killarney (Benedict)
1864   *La Belle Hélène* (Offenbach)
1865   *Die schoene Galathea* (Suppé)
1866   *Barbe-bleue* (Offenbach)
        The Bartered Bride (Smetana)
        La Vie parisienne (Offenbach)

1867 *The Grand Duchess of Gerolstein* (Offenbach)
1868 *La Périchole* (Offenbach)
1872 *La Fille de Madame Angot* (Lecocq)
1873 *Le Roi l'a dit* (Delibes)
1874 *Die Fledermaus* (Strauss)
      Giroflé-Girofla (Lecocq)
1875 *Cagliostro in Wien* (Strauss)
      Trial by Jury (Gilbert and Sullivan)
1876 *Fatinitza* (Suppé)
1877 *The Chimes of Normandy* (Planquette)
      The Sorcerer (Gilbert and Sullivan)
1878 *H.M.S. Pinafore* (Gilbert and Sullivan)
1879 *Boccaccio* (Suppé)
      The Du Barry (Milloecker)
      Olivette (Audran)
      Pirates of Penzance (Gilbert and Sullivan)
1880 *Donna Juanita* (Suppé)
      La Mascotte (Audran)
      The Queen's Handkerchief (Strauss)
1881 *Patience* (Gilbert and Sullivan)
1882 *The Beggar Student* (Milloecker)
      Iolanthe (Gilbert and Sullivan)
1883 *One Night in Venice* (Strauss)
      Mam'zelle Nitouche (Hervé)
1884 *Princess Ida* (Gilbert and Sullivan)
1885 *Erminie* (Jakobowski)
      The Gypsy Baron (Strauss)
      The Mikado (Gilbert and Sullivan)
1887 *Le Roi malgré lui* (Chabrier)
      Ruddigore (Gilbert and Sullivan)
1888 *The Yeomen of the Guard* (Gilbert and Sullivan)
1889 *The Gondoliers* (Gilbert and Sullivan)
1891 *The Nautch Girl* (Solomon)
      Der Vogelhaendler (Zeller)
1893 *Hansel and Gretel* (Humperdinck)
      Utopia Limited (Gilbert and Sullivan)
1894 *Donna Diana* (Rezniček)
      Der Obersteiger (Zeller)
1896 *The Geisha* (Jones)
1898 *Der Opernball* (Heuberger)

1898   *The Runaway Girl* (Monckton and Caryll)
1899   *A Chinese Honeymoon* (Talbot)
       Florodora (Stuart)
       Frau Luna (Lincke)
       Die Landestreicher (Ziehrer)
       San Toy (Jones)
       Wiener Blut (Strauss)
1901   *The Spring Maid* (Reinhardt)
1902   *Merrie England* (German)
1903   *Bruder Straubinger* (Eysler)
       Le Donne curiose (Wolf-Ferrari)
1905   *Lady Madcap* (Rubens)
       The Merry Widow (Lehár)
1906   *I Quattro rusteghi* (Wolf-Ferrari)
       A Thousand and One Nights (Strauss)
1907   *The Dollar Princess* (Fall)
       Tom Jones (German)
       Ein Walzertraum (Straus)
1908   *The Chocolate Soldier* (Straus)
1909   *The Arcadians* (Monckton and Talbot)
       The Count of Luxembourg (Lehár)
       The Secret of Suzanne (Wolf-Ferrari)
1910   *The Quaker Girl* (Monckton)
1911   *L'Heure espagnole* (Ravel)
1912   *Alt Wien* (Lanner)
       Der Liebe Augustin (Fall)
       The Sunshine Girl (Rubens)
1913   *L'Amore medico* (Wolf-Ferrari)
       Polish Blood (Nedbal)
1914   *Mârouf* (Rabaud)
1915   *Die Czardasfuerstin* (Kálmán)
1916   *Das Dreimaederl haus* (Berté)
1917   *L'Arlecchino* (Busoni)
       Schwarzwaldmaedel (Jessel)
1918   *Gianni Schicchi* (Puccini)
1920   *The Last Waltz* (Straus)
1922   *Frasquita* (Lehár)
       Mavra (Stravinsky)
       Renard (Stravinsky)
1923   *Madame Pompadour* (Fall)

1924   *Countess Maritza* (Kálmán)
1925   *Paganini* (Lehár)
1927   *Der Zarewitsch* (Lehár)
1928   *Friederike* (Lehár)
       The Three-Penny Opera (Weill)
1929   *Bitter Sweet* (Coward)
       The Land of Smiles (Lehár)
1930   *Meine Schwester und Ich* (Benatzky)
       The Rise and Fall of the City of Mahagonny (Weill)
       Victoria und ihr Hussar (Abraham)
       The White Horse Inn (Benatzky)
1931   *Schoen ist die Welt* (Lehár)
1932   *Sissy* (Kreisler)
1933   *Zwei Herzen im Dreivierteltakt* (Stolz)
1934   *Conversation Piece* (Coward)
1935   *Drei Walzer* (Straus)
1939   *The Dancing Years* (Novello)
1945   *Perchance to Dream* (Novello)
1949   *King's Rhapsody* (Novello)

Appendix Two:

Listing by Composers

ABRAHAM, PAUL (born Apatin, Hungary, 1892; died Hamburg, Germany, 1960). *See: Victoria und ihr Hussar.*

ADAM, ADOLPHE[-CHARLES] (born Paris, 1803; died there, 1856). *See: (Le) Postillon de Longjumeau; (La) Poupée de Nuremberg; Si j'étais roi.*

AUBER, DANIEL FRANÇOIS ESPRIT (born Paris, 1782; died there, 1871). *See: (Les) Diamants de la couronne; Fra Diavolo; (Le) Domino noir; (La) Muette de Portici.*

AUDRAN, EDMOND (born Lyons, France, 1840; died Tierceville, France, 1901). *See: Olivette; (La) Mascotte.*

BALFE, MICHAEL [WILLIAM] (born Dublin, 1808; died Rowney Abbey, Hertfordshire, England, 1870). *See: (The) Bohemian Girl.*

BENEDICT, SIR JULIUS (born Stuttgart, 1804; died London, 1885). *See: (The) Lily of Killarney.*

BENATZKY, RALPH (born Moraskvské-Budejovice, Bohemia, 1884; died Zurich, Switzerland, 1957). *See: Meine Schwester und Ich; (The) White Horse Inn.*

BERLIOZ, HECTOR[-LOUIS] (born Côte-Saint-André, Isère, France, 1803; died Paris, 1869). *See: Beatrice and Benedick.*

BERTÉ, HEINRICH (born Galgócz, Hungary, 1858; died Vienna, 1924). *See: (Das) Dreimaederlhaus.*

BOIELDIEU, FRANÇOIS[-ADRIEN] (born Rouen, France, 1775; died Jarcy, France, 1834). *See: (The) Caliph of Bagdad; (La) Dame blanche.*

BUSONI, FERRUCCIO [BENVENUTO] (born Empoli, near Florence, Italy, 1866; died Berlin, 1924). *See: Arlecchino.*

CARYLL, IVAN [really Felix Tilkin] (born Liège, Belgium, 1861; died New York, 1921). *See: (The) Runaway Girl.*

CHABRIER, [ALEXIS-] EMMANUEL (born Ambert, Puy de Dôme, France, 1841; died Paris, 1894). *See: (Le) Roi malgré lui.*

CIMAROSA, DOMENICO (born Aversa, near Naples, Italy, 1749; died Venice, 1801). *See: (Il) Matrimonio segreto.*

CORNELIUS, PETER (born Mainz, Germany, 1824; died there, 1874). *See: (The) Barber of Bagdad.*

COWARD, NOËL (born Teddington, Middlesex, England, 1899). *See: Bitter Sweet; Conversation Piece.*

DELIBES, LÉO (born St. Germain-du-Val, Sarthe, France, 1836; died Paris, 1891). *See: Le Roi l'a dit.*

DITTERSDORF, KARL DITTERS VON (born Vienna, 1739; died Castle Rothlhotta, near Neuhaus, Bohemia, 1799). *See: (The) Doctor and the Apothecary.*

DONIZETTI, GAETANO (born Bergamo, Italy, 1797; died there, 1848). *See: (Il) Campanello di notte; (The) Daughter of the Regiment; Don Pasquale; (L') Elisir d'amore.*

EYSLER, EDMUND (born Vienna, 1874; died there, 1949). *See: Bruder Straubinger.*

FALL, LEO (born Olmuetz, Hungary, 1873; died Vienna, 1925). *See: (The) Dollar Princess; (Der) Liebe Augustin; Madame Pompadour.*

FLOTOW, FRIEDRICH VON (born Teutendorf, Germany, 1812; died Darmstadt, Germany, 1883). *See: Martha.*

GALUPPI, BALDASSARE (born Burano, Italy, 1706; died Venice, 1785). *See: (Il) Filosofo di campagna.*

GERMAN, SIR EDWARD [real name Edward German Jones] (born Witchurch, England, 1862; died London, 1936). *See: Merrie England; Tom Jones.*

GLUCK, CHRISTOPH WILLIBALD (born Erasbach, Upper Palatinate, 1714; died Vienna, 1787). *See: (Le) Cadi dupé; (La) Rencontre imprévue.*

GOUNOD, CHARLES (born Paris, 1818; died there, 1893). *See: (Le) Médecin malgre lui.*

HALÉVY, JACQUES (born Paris, 1799; died Nice, France, 1862). *See: (L') Éclair.*

HAYDN, [FRANZ] JOSEPH (born Rohrau-on-the-Leitha, Austria, 1732; died, Vienna, 1809. *See: (The) Apothecary; (Il) Mondo della luna.*

HÉROLD, LOUIS [JOSEPH-FERDINAND] (born Paris, 1791; died Thernes, France, 1833). *See: (Le) Pré aux clercs; Zampa.*

HERVÉ, [FLORIMOND RONGER] (born Houdain, France, 1825; died Paris, 1892). *See: Mam'zelle Nitouche.*

HEUBERGER, RICHARD [FRANZ JOSEPH] (born Graz, 1850; died there, 1914). *See: (Der) Opernball.*

HUMPERDINCK, ENGELBERT (born Siegburg, near Bonn, Germany, 1854; died Neustrelitz, Germany, 1921). *See: Hansel and Gretel.*

JAKOBOWSKI, EDWARD (born London, 1858; died   ). *See: Erminie.*

JESSEL, LEON (born Stettin, Germany, 1871; died Berlin, 1941. *See: Schwarzwaldmaedel.*

JONES, SIDNEY (born London, 1861; died there, 1946). *See: (The) Geisha; San Toy.*

KÁLMÁN, EMMERICH [IMRE] (born Siófok, Hungary, 1882; died Paris, 1953). *See: (The) Circus Princess; Countess Maritza; (Die) Czardasfuerstin.*

KREISLER, FRITZ (born Vienna, 1875; died New York City, 1962). *See: Sissy.*

LANNER, JOSEPH [FRANZKARL] (born Vienna, 1801; died Oberdoebling, near Vienna, 1843). *See: Alt Wein.*

LECOCQ, ALEXANDER-CHARLES (born Paris, 1832; died there, 1918). *See: (La) Fille de Madame Angot; Giroflé-Girofla.*

LEHÁR, FRANZ (born Komorn, Hungary, 1870; died Bad Ischl, Austria, 1948). *See: (The) Count of Luxembourg; Frasquita; Friederike; Gypsy Love; (The) Land of Smiles; (The) Merry Widow; Paganini; Schoen ist die Welt; (Der) Zarewitsch.*

LINCKE, PAUL (born Berlin, 1866; died Klausthal-Zellernfeld, Germany, 1946). *See: Frau Luna.*

LORTZING, ALBERT (born Berlin, 1801; died there 1851). *See: Undine; (Der) Waffenschmied; (Der) Wildschuetz; Zar und Zimmermann.*

MASSÉ, FELIX MARIE [VICTOR] (born Lorient, Morbihan, France, 1822; died Paris, 1884). *See: (Les) Noces de Jeannette.*

MILLOECKER, KARL (born Vienna, 1842; died Baden, near Vienna, 1899). *See: (The) Beggar Student; (The) Du Barry; (Das) verwunschene Schloss.*

MONCKTON, LIONEL (born London, 1861; died there, 1924). *See: (The) Arcadians; (The) Quaker Girl; (The) Runaway Girl.*

MOZART, WOLFGANG AMADEUS (born Salzburg, Austria, 1756; died Vienna, 1791). *See: (The) Abduction from the Seraglio; Bastien and Bastienne; Così fan tutte; (La) Finta giardiniera; (La) Finta semplice;* (*The*) *Magic Flute;* (*The*) *Marriage of Figaro;* (*Der*) *Schauspieldirektor.*

NEDBAL, OSKAR (born Tábor, Bohemia, 1874; died Zagreb, Jugoslavia, 1930). *See: Polish Blood.*

NICOLAI, OTTO (born Koenigsberg, Germany, 1810; died Berlin, 1849). *See:* (*The*) *Merry Wives of Windsor.*

NOVELLO, IVOR (born Cardiff, England, 1893; died London, 1951). *See:* (*The*) *Dancing Years; King's Rhapsody; Perchance to Dream.*

OFFENBACH, JACQUES (born Cologne, Germany, 1819; died Paris, 1880). *See: Barbe-bleue;* (*La*) *Belle Hélène;* (*The*) *Grand Duchess of Gerolstein; Orphée aux enfers;* (*La*) *Périchole;* (*La*) *Vie parisienne.*

PAISIELLO, GIOVANNI (born Taranto, Italy, 1740; died Naples, 1816). *See:* (*The*) *Barber of Seville.*

PEPUSCH, JOHN CHRISTOPHER (born Berlin, Germany, 1667; died London, 1752). *See:* (*The*) *Beggar's Opera.*

PERGOLESI, GIOVANNI BATTISTA (born Jesi, Italy, 1710; died Pozzuoli, Italy, 1736). *See:* (*La*) *Serva padrona.*

PICCINNI, NICCOLò (born Bari, Italy, 1728; died Paris, 1800). *See:* (*La*) *Buona figliuola.*

PLANQUETTE, JEAN-ROBERT (born Paris, 1848; died there, 1903). *See:* (*The*) *Chimes of Normandy.*

PUCCINI, GIACOMO (born Lucca, Italy, 1858; died Brussels, 1924). *See: Gianni Schicchi.*

RABAUD, HENRI (born Paris, 1873; died there, 1949). *See: Mârouf, Savetier du Caire.*

RAVEL, MAURICE [JOSEPH] (born Ciboure, Basses-Pryénées, France, 1875; died Paris, 1937). *See:* (*L'*) *Heure espagnole.*

REINHARDT, HEINRICH (born Pressburg, Germany, 1865; died Vienna, 1922). *See:* (*The*) *Spring Maid.*

REZNIČEK, EMIL NIKOLAUS VON (born Vienna, 1860; died Berlin, 1945). *See: Donna Diana.*

RICCI, FEDERICO (born Naples, 1809; died Conegliano, Italy, 1877). *See: Crispino e la comare.*

RICCI, LUIGI (born Naples, 1805; died Prague, 1859). *See: Crispino e la comare.*

ROSSINI, GIOACCHINO (born Pesaro, Italy, 1792; died Paris, 1868). *See:* (*The*) *Barber of Seville;* (*La*) *Cambiale di Matrimonio;* (*La*) *Cenerentola;* (*Le*) *Comte Ory;* (*La*) *Gazza ladra;* (*L'*) *Italiana in algeri;* (*Il*) *Signor Bruschino;* (*Il*) *Turco in Italia.*

Rousseau, Jean-Jacques (born Geneva, 1712; died Ermenon-ville, near Paris, France, 1778). *See: (Le) Devin du village.*

Rubens, Paul Alfred (born London, 1875; died Falmouth, England, 1917). *See: Lady Madcap; (The) Sunshine Girl.*

Smetana, Bedřich [Friedrich] (born Leitomischl, Bohemia, 1824; died Prague, 1884). *See: (The) Bartered Bride.*

Solomon, Edward (born 1853; died London, 1895). *See: (The) Nautch Girl.*

Stolz, Robert (born Graz, Austria, 1882). *See: Zwei Herzen im Dreivierteltakt.*

Straus, Oscar (born Vienna, 1870; died Bad Ischl, Austria, 1954). *See: (The) Chocolate Soldier; Drei Walzer; (The) Last Waltz; (Ein) Walzertraum.*

Strauss, Johann II (born Vienna, 1825; died there 1899). *See: Cagliostro im Wien; (Die) Fledermaus; (The) Gypsy Baron; One Night in Venice; (The) Queen's Handkerchief; (A) Thousand and One Nights; Wiener Blut.*

Stravinsky, Igor (born Oranienbaum, near St. Petersburg, Russia, 1882). *See: Mavra; Renard.*

Stuart, Leslie [real name Thomas A. Barrett] (born Southport, England, 1866; died Richmond, Surrey, England, 1928). *See: Florodora.*

Sullivan, [Sir] Arthur Seymour (born London, 1842; died there, 1900). *See: (The) Gondoliers; H.M.S. Pinafore; Iolanthe; (The) Mikado; Patience; (The) Pirates of Penzance; Princess Ida; Ruddigore; (The) Sorcerer; Trial By Jury; Utopia Limited; (The) Yeomen of the Guard.*

Suppé, Franz Von (born Spalato, Dalmatia, 1819; died Vienna, 1895). *See: Boccaccio; Donna Juanita; Fatinitza; (Die) schoene Galathea.*

Talbot, Howard [real name Munkittrick] (born Yonkers, New York, 1865; died London, 1928). *See: (The) Arcadians; (A) Chinese Honeymoon.*

Wallace, William Vincent (born Waterford, England, 1812; died Château de Bagen, France, 1865). *See: Maritana.*

Weber, Karl Maria Von (born Eutin, Oldenburg, Germany, 1786; died London, 1826). *See: Abu Hassan.*

Weill, Kurt (born Dessau, Germany, 1900; died New York, 1950). *See: (The) Rise and Fall of the City of Mahagonny; (The) Three-Penny Opera.*

WOLF-FERRARI, ERMANNO (born Venice, 1876; died there, 1948).
  See: (*L'*) *Amore medico;* (*Le*) *Donne curiose;* (*I*) *Quattro rusteghi;*
  (*The*) *Secret of Suzanne.*

ZELLER, CARL (born St. Peter-in-der-Au, Austria, 1842; died Baden,
  near Vienna, 1898). *See:* (*Der*) *Obersteiger;* (*Der*) *Vogelhaendler.*

ZIEHRER, KARL MICHAEL (born Vienna, 1843; died there, 1922).
  See: (*Die*) *Landstreicher.*

Appendix Three:

Selected Recordings *

The Abduction from the Seraglio [Mozart]. Complete recording. London A-4301.

Abu Hassan [Weber]. Overture. London. T-5223.

The Apothecary [Haydn]. Complete recording. Epic LC-3739.

The Barber of Seville [Paisiello]. Complete recording. Mercury 2-110.

The Barber of Seville [Rossini]. Complete recording. Victor LM-6143.

Bastien and Bastienne [Mozart]. Complete recording. Cetra 1263.

Beatrice and Benedick [Berlioz]. Overture. Columbia DX-1145.

The Beggar Student [Milloecker]. Complete recording. Vanguard 474-5.

La Belle Hélène [Offenbach]. Highlights. Renaissance X-51.

Bitter Sweet [Coward]. Complete recording. Angel 35814.

Boccaccio [Suppé]. Overture. Westminster 18922.

The Bohemian Girl [Balfe]. Overture. Decca F-7946. "Then You'll Remember Me." Victor 10-1276.

Le Cadi dupé [Mozart]. Complete recording. Epic LC-3645.

Cagliostro im Wien [Strauss]. Cagliostro Waltz. Victor LM-2548.

The Caliph of Bagdad [Boieldieu]. Overture. Epic LC-3079.

La Cambiale di matrimonio [Rossini]. Complete recording. Mercury OL-2-109.

Il Campanello di notte [Donizetti]. Complete recording. Cetra 50027.

La Cenerentola [Rossini]. Complete recording. Cetra 1208.

The Chocolate Soldier [Straus]. Highlights. Victor LOP-6004.

---

* Only recordings available in the United States have been listed. All listings are for monophonic recordings; local dealers should be consulted for availability of stereophonic recordings.

Le Comte Ory [Rossini]. Complete recording. Angel 3565.

Così fan tutte [Mozart]. Complete recording. Angel 3522.

The Count of Luxembourg [Lehár]. Complete recording. London 5352.

Countess Maritza [Kálmán]. Complete recording. London 5351.

Die Czardasfuerstin [Kálmán]. Highlights. Vox VX-21500.

La Dame blanche [Boieldieu]. Overture. Epic. LC-3079.

The Daughter of the Regiment [Donizetti]. Complete recording. Cetra 1213.

Les Diamants de la couronne [Auber]. Complete recording. London A-4127.

Le Domino noir [Auber]. Overture. London CM-9274.

Donna Diana [Rezniček]. Overture. Westminster 18732.

Don Pasquale [Donizetti]. Complete recording. Cetra 1242.

Das Dreimaederlhaus [Berté]. Complete recording. Vox PL-20800. Also complete recording under English title of *Lilac Time*. Angel 53817.

The Du Barry [Milloecker]. Complete recording. Epic LC-3758.

L'Élisir d'amore [Donizetti]. Complete recording. Angel 3594.

Fatinitza [Suppé]. Overture. Victor LM-2470.

La Fille de Madame Angot [Lecocq]. Ballet Suite. Victor LM-2285.

La Finta giardiniera [Mozart]. Complete recording. Epic LC-3543.

La Finta semplice [Mozart]. Complete recording. Epic SC-6021.

Die Fledermaus [Strauss]. Complete recording. Angel 3539.

Fra Diavolo [Auber]. Complete recording. Urania 204.

Frasquita [Lehár]. Highlights. Victor 26775.

Friederike [Lehár]. Highlights. Elect 60035.

La Gazza ladra [Rossini]. Overture. Mercury 50139.

Gianni Schicchi [Puccini]. Complete recording. Cetra 50028.

The Gondoliers [Gilbert and Sullivan]. Complete recording. London. A-4204.

The Grand Duchess of Gerolstein [Offenbach]. Complete recording. Urania 115-2.

The Gypsy Baron [Strauss]. Complete recording. Angel 3566.

Gypsy Love [Strauss]. Complete recording. Urania 205.

H.M.S. Pinafore [Gilbert and Sullivan]. Complete recording. London A-4234.

Hansel and Gretel [Humperdinck]. Complete recording. Angel 3506.

L'Heure espagnole [Falla]. Complete recording. London A-4102.

Iolanthe [Gilbert and Sullivan]. Complete recording. London A-4242.

L'Italiana in Algeri [Rossini]. Complete recording. Angel 3529.

The Land of Smiles [Lehár]. Complete recording. Angel 3507.

The Last Waltz [Straus]. Complete recording. Period 1904.

The Magic Flute [Mozart]. Complete recording. Decca 9932.

The Marriage of Figaro [Mozart]. Complete recording. Angel 35326.

Martha [Flotow]. Complete recording. Cetra 1254.

Il Matrimonio segreto [Cimarosa]. Complete recording. Cetra 1214.

The Merry Widow [Lehár]. Complete recording. Angel 3501.

The Merry Wives of Windsor [Nicolai]. Complete recording. Oceanic 303.

The Mikado [Gilbert and Sullivan]. Complete recording. London A-4231.

La Muette de Portici [Auber]. Overture. London CM-9274.

One Night in Venice [Strauss]. Complete recording. Angel 3530.

Orphée aux enfers [Offenbach]. Complete recording. Renaissance SX-204.

Paganini [Lehár]. Highlights. Epic LC-3130.

Patience [Gilbert and Sullivan]. Complete recording. London A-4211.

La Périchole [Offenbach]. Complete recording. Victor LOC-1029.

The Pirates of Penzance [Gilbert and Sullivan]. Complete recording.
London A-4230.

Princess Ida [Gilbert and Sullivan]. Complete recording. London A-4218.

I Quattro rusteghi [Wolf-Ferrari]. Complete recording. Cetra 1239.

Renard [Stravinsky]. Complete recording. London CM-9152.

The Rise and Fall of the City of Mahagonny [Weill]. Complete recording. Columbia KL-2L-243.

Ruddigore [Gilbert and Sullivan]. Complete recording. London A-4206.

Der Schauspieldirektor [Mozart]. Complete recording. Period 532.

Schoen ist die Welt [Lehár]. Highlights. Epic LC-3758.

Die schoene Galathea [Suppé]. Complete recording. Urania 7167.

The Secret of Suzanne [Wolf-Ferrari]. Complete recording. Cetra 1249.

La Serva padrona [Pergolesi]. Complete recording. Cetra 50240.

Il Signor Bruschino [Rossini]. Complete recording. Vox PL-8460.

Si j'étais roi [Adam]. Highlights. Electrola 80590.

The Sorcerer [Gilbert and Sullivan]. Complete recording. London A-4215.

A Thousand and One Nights [Strauss]. Complete recording. Urania 203.

The Three-Penny Opera [Weill]. Complete recording. Columbia. O2L-
257.

Trial by Jury [Gilbert and Sullivan]. Complete recording. London A-4101.

Il Turco in Italia [Rossini]. Complete recording. Angel 3535-5S.

Undine [Lortzing]. Ballet Music. Epic LC-3102.

Victoria und ihr Hussar [Abraham]. Complete recording. Westminster.
WST-14146.

La Vie parisienne [Offenbach]. Highlights. Epic LC-3344.

Der Vogelhaendler [Zeller]. Highlights. Telefunken 8029.

Ein Walzertraum [Straus]. Complete recording. Victor LM-2407.

The White Horse Inn [Benatzky]. Complete recording. Angel 35815.

Wiener Blut [Strauss]. Complete recording. Angel 35191.

The Yeomen of the Guard [Gilbert and Sullivan]. Complete recording. London A-4205.

Zampa [Hérold]. Overture. Columbia CM-9274.

Zar und Zimmermann [Lortzing]. Complete recording. Decca DX-129.

Der Zarewitsch [Lehár]. Complete recording. Telefunken 8030.

INDEX